Also by Brian A. Catlos

Muslims of Medieval Latin Christendom, c. 1050–1614

The Rough Guide to Languedoc and Roussillon

*The Victors and the Vanquished: Christians and Muslims
of Catalonia and Aragon, 1050–1300*

AS EDITOR
Worlds of History and Economics: Essays in Honour of Andrew M. Watson

INFIDEL KINGS AND UNHOLY WARRIORS

INFIDEL KINGS

AND

UNHOLY WARRIORS

FAITH,

POWER, AND

VIOLENCE

IN THE AGE

OF CRUSADE

AND JIHAD

BRIAN A. CATLOS

FARRAR, STRAUS AND GIROUX / NEW YORK

Farrar, Straus and Giroux
18 West 18th Street, New York 10011

Owing to limitations of space, illustration credits can be found on pages 389–390.

Library of Congress Cataloging-in-Publication Data
Catlos, Brian A.
    Infidel kings and unholy warriors : faith, power, and violence in the age of
crusade and jihad / Brian A. Catlos. — First Edition.
        pages   cm
    Includes bibliographical references and index.
    ISBN 978-0-8090-5837-2 (hardback) — ISBN 978-0-374-71205-1 (ebook)
    1. Mediterranean Region—History—476–1517.   2. Crusades.
3. Crusades—Influence.   I. Title.

DE94.C37 2014
909.07—dc23

                                                          2013043160

Designed by Abby Kagan

Farrar, Straus and Giroux books may be purchased for educational, business, or
promotional use. For information on bulk purchases, please contact the Macmillan
Corporate and Premium Sales Department at 1-800-221-7945, extension 5442, or
write to specialmarkets@macmillan.com.

www.fsgbooks.com
www.twitter.com/fsgbooks • www.facebook.com/fsgbooks

1   3   5   7   9   10   8   6   4   2

For my own little infidels, Alexandra and Raymond

Contents

Map: The Mediterranean World, c. 1050   ix
A Note on Sources   xiii
A Note on Names   xv

Introduction: The Mediterranean World   3

PART I: THE (JEWISH) MAN WHO WOULD BE KING

1. An Ornament, Tarnished   15
2. The Rules of the Game   44

PART II: A CHRISTIAN SULTAN IN THE AGE OF "THE RECONQUEST"

3. The Cid Rides Again   69
4. Rodrigo Díaz, Taifa King of Valencia   98

PART III: KINGS OF SICILY, KINGS OF AFRICA

5. A Norman Conquest   127
6. Don't Ask, Don't Tell   156

PART IV: INFIDEL RULERS OF A HERETICAL CALIPHATE

7. After the Messiah   183
8. Traitors and Spies   213

PART V: AMBITION, OPPORTUNISM, AND THE END OF AN ERA

9. A Heavenly Kingdom?   241
10. Jerusalem Restored   275

Epilogue: The Decline and Fall of the Roman Empire   307
Afterword: Holy War, a User's Manual   317

Dynasty Trees   325
Glossary   329
Sources, Background, and Further Reading   335
Notes   345
Works Cited   353
Acknowledgments   367
Index   369

Map: The Mediterranean World, c. 1050

Atlantic Ocean

FRANCE

HOLY ROMAN EMPIRE

Oviedo

Santiago de
Compostela
LEÓN
Porto
CASTILE
NAVARRE
AQUITAINE
LANGUEDOC
PROVENCE
Marseille
Genoa
Venice
Pisa
CROATIA
PAPAL
STATES

Toledo
Zaragoza
ARAGON
CATALONIA
Barcelona
Rome
Salerno
Normans
APULIA

Lisbon

TAIFA KINGDOMS
Valencia
MALLORCA

Córdoba
Sevilla
Granada
Almería
Mediterranean Sea
Palermo
SICILY
Kalbids

Fez
Zanata
Bougie
Hammadids
Bône
Mahdia

Marrakesh
Zirids

MAGHRIB
IFRIQIYA

Almoravids
Banu Hilal
Tripoli

0 Miles   200   400

0 Kilometers   400

© 2014 Jeffrey L. Ward

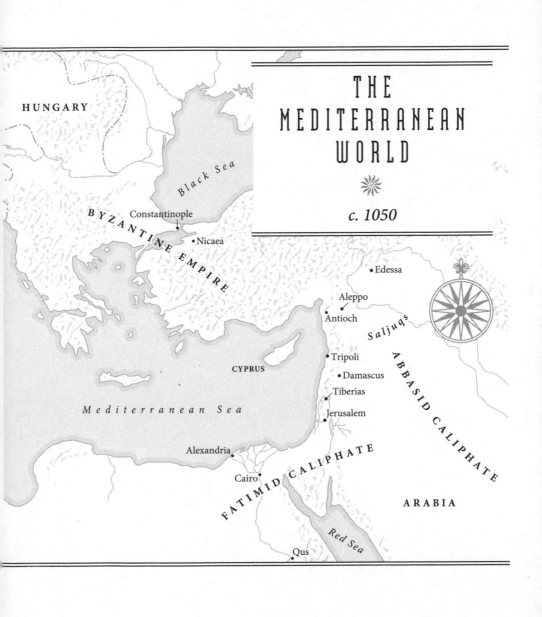

THE
MEDITERRANEAN
WORLD

c. 1050

HUNGARY

Black Sea

BYZANTINE EMPIRE

Constantinople
• Nicaea

• Edessa

• Aleppo
• Antioch

Saljuqs

CYPRUS

• Tripoli
• Damascus
• Tiberias
• Jerusalem

ABBASID CALIPHATE

Mediterranean Sea

• Alexandria

FATIMID CALIPHATE

Cairo •

ARABIA

Red Sea

Qus •

A Note on Sources

Every historical narrative is the product of a series of deliberate choices and interpretations on the part of the historian, irrevocably imbued with his or her own subjectivity and biases. But this is not to say that history is fiction, or that a historian should arbitrarily choose evidence that suits an intellectual, personal, or political agenda. Historians are bound to seek out, read, and analyze all the material relevant to the subject they are studying, and to make their interpretations in good faith, based on accepted principles of weighing and analyzing evidence, and to guard against the intrusion of their own prejudices. In a book intended for a narrow scholarly readership, all of this would be laid bare in an interminable series of footnotes and technical digressions. Conflicting evidence would be discussed, substantial interpretative decisions would be explained, and the full range of source material for each significant event would be cited. What makes for good science, however, does not necessarily make for good reading, just as seeing how sausage is made does not necessarily make one hungry. With that in mind, I have not cited the long list of works and sources that I consulted for each of the chapters. Instead, I have included references only for those passages taken directly from contemporary sources. I also provide, in the back of the book, a short overview of the relevant historical literature, for those who would like to explore the Mediterranean world of 1050–1200 in more detail.

A Note on Names

Our custom of using a first name followed by a surname is a relatively new development, and one that until recently was particular to the cultures of Western Europe. In the Middle Ages, names functioned somewhat differently. First names tended to be scriptural in origin, but nonbiblical names were popular, especially among Christians, who drew on Latin and Greek (Philip, Andronikos) and Persian (Vahram) culture, or Germanic roots—William, Richard, Alfonso, Bohemond, and so on. Muslims and Jews sometimes also used nonreligious names, whether Berber (Tashufin), Persian, Turkic, classical (al-Iskander, or "Alexander"), or Aramaic (Hasdai or Hasday).

A common way of forming a "last name" was to use a patronymic. Who your father was was perhaps the most important piece of information about you: it indicated your social class, power, and wealth. The Arabic *ibn* (abbreviated as *b.*) and Hebrew *ben* mean "son of" (or *bint*, "daughter of," for women). Yusuf b. Tashufin was "Yusuf, son of Tashufin," and might be known simply as Ibn Tashufin. In Latin lands, the genitive construction (the suffix *-is*, which means "of") was prevalent. Thus, Sisnando Davídez meant "Sisnando, [son] of David." Some Berbers, alternatively, traced their ancestry through the female line. By stringing together a series of patronymics, Muslims and Jews created names that acted as genealogies. The Christians of the borderlands often imitated these naming conventions: the brother and antecessor of Alfonso the Battler, King Pedro I of Aragon, for example, signed his name in Arabic as *Bitr ıbn Shanju* (Peter, son of Sancho), using shaky Arabic script.

Last names were also sometimes taken from places. Robert Guiscard and Roger of Sicily and their descendants were known as d'Hauteville in reference to their ancestral home. The Cid was Rodrigo Díaz del Vivar because his hometown was Vivar. The Islamic system used by both Muslims and Jews resulted in similar names. "Al-Qurtubi" refers to someone from Córdoba, "al-Siqilli" to someone from Sicily, "al-Mahdiyya" to someone from Mahdia, and "al-Misri" to someone from Cairo. Because tribal and clan affiliation remained important in much of the Islamic world, these were also used in naming; any member of the Zirid clan, for example, might be referred to as "al-Ziri." Non-Muslims often used names that referred to their ethnic origin or religious community: al-Nasrani ("the Nazarene," or Christian), al-Yahudi ("the Jew"), or al-Armani ("the Armenian"). The name of an early or famous ancestor could also come to serve as a family name. Any of Salah al-Din's descendants could take the name al-Ayyubi, after Salah al-Din's father, Ayyub.

Prominent individuals often took honorific names based on an illustrious deed or a physical attribute, or as an ideological advertisement. Roger of Sicily's oldest brother was known as William "Iron Arm," while Nur al-Din's father, Zengi, took the title 'Imad al-Din, "Pillar of the Faith," to reinforce his political-religious image. People of humbler origins often identified by the trade they or their families practiced; the name Ferrer means "blacksmith," al-Najjar is "carpenter."

One naming element was unique to the Islamic world and was used by both Jews and Muslims: the filionymic. *Abu* means "father," and men could be referred to as Abu so-and-so, either in reference to their first-born or a famous son, or the son they were expected to have. A firstborn son was usually named after the paternal grandfather, so a young boy named Hisham whose father was named 'Abd Allah could be called simply Abu 'Abd Allah. The Jewish *wazir* of Granada, Isma'il ibn Naghrilla, was referred to as "Abu Ibrahim" by his Muslim supporters, out of respect.

Since every other name an individual was given or acquired served as an adjective, in Christian, Muslim, and Jewish cultures, what mattered most was the first name. The caliph 'Abd al-Rahman III could use his name to show his descent from the first Umayyad amir of al-Andalus: 'Abd al-Rahman b. Muhammad b. 'Abd Allah b. Muhammad b. 'Abd al-Rahman b. Hakam b. Hisham b. 'Abd Allah al-Dhakil. Or he could go as "'Abd al-Rahman," or as "Ibn Muhammad," or as "Abu Hisham" (after his son), or by his honorific al-Nasir li-Din Allah ("the Victorious by God in God's Faith")—but never as "'Abd" or as "Rahman," which are only parts of his first name.

INFIDEL KINGS AND UNHOLY WARRIORS

Introduction: The Mediterranean World

> . . . without Mohammed, Charlemagne would indeed have been in-
> conceivable.
>
> —EDWARD GIBBON, *The Decline and Fall of the Roman Empire*

To Henri Pirenne, an early-twentieth-century Belgian historian, it was clear that the destinies of the Islamic and Christian worlds were deeply intertwined, although, like the great majority of European scholars until recently, he imagined the relationship as primarily one of aggression and opposition. According to the "Pirenne Thesis," the Arab invasions of the seventh century had provoked the final collapse of the Greco-Roman world, which Pirenne and others of his day imagined as the summit of civilization. For such scholars, "the East," as wealthy and sophisticated as it might have been, was characterized by despotism, decadence, and effeminate passivity and duplicity.

A century and a half earlier, in his monumental *Decline and Fall of the Roman Empire*, the English historian and politician Edward Gibbon had famously heaved a retroactive sigh of relief that the Arab armies, hell-bent on conquering Europe, had been stopped in 742 C.E. at Poitiers by the Frankish leader Charles Martel. Had that horde of "circumcised peoples" not been stopped, Gibbon warned, "Perhaps the interpretation of the Koran would be taught in the schools of Oxford, and her pulpits might demonstrate to a circumcised people the sanctity and truth of the revelation of Muhammed." Oxford, of course, would not be founded for another four hundred years, and the Arabs of the eighth century, in reality, had little interest in journeying to the cold north to conquer Saxon Lundenwic (as London was called), a ragged collection of hovels in a poor and primitive land. And as for Jews, the members of the third major religious community in the region, they were also seen as "Orientals," and viewed with even more suspicion and disdain than Muslims, who were seen to possess, if little else, the capacity to establish and rule over their own empires. Indeed, the idea of a "Judeo-Christian civilization" did not come into vogue until after the Second World War, and it was coined originally as an expression of contempt.

Gibbon, Pirenne, and the other European historians of the "long" nineteenth century saw the Middle Ages as an interruption in the march of historical progress initiated by Athens and Rome. But to them it was an important interruption, in that it paved the way for the emergence of the nation-states: Britain, France, Germany, Spain, and eventually Greece and Italy, which arose out of the chaos of feudal Europe once Greco-Roman culture was rediscovered during the Renaissance, and once classically inspired rational humanism demolished the hypocrisy and superstition of the medieval Catholic Church. For these thinkers, modernity was a European phenomenon, and, more specifically, a northwestern European phenomenon, to which Jews had made no substantial contribution since the birth of Christ and for which Muslims served only as a foil and a provocation. The Crusades were defensive wars, rational responses to irrational and unrestrained Muslim aggression, rather than symptoms of European violence and expansionism. The Mediterranean had always been how it appeared to them then: a region of dark-skinned, indolent, inferior, and superstitious peoples. In the circular rationalizations of Pirenne and like-minded scholars, the Romans and Greeks had actually been Northerners.

To a remarkable extent the Middle Ages still invites preconceptions, particularly when it comes to the Crusades and *jihad*. Today, many people, following in Pirenne's tradition, imagine the time as one when an intractable struggle between Christianity, Islam, and Judaism crystalized—when three fundamentally incompatible "civilizations" collided in a series of violent pogroms, massacres, and wars that continues, in different forms, to this day. In this view, Muslims and Christians of the Middle Ages are seen as either predatory aggressors or righteous champions, while Jews are portrayed as passive and powerless, living under the permanent threat of oppression and violence. Others, in contrast, see the era as one of enlight-enment and *convivencia*, in which Christians, Muslims, and Jews strove to construct a rational world of peace and harmony, only to be frustrated by religious ideologues and a coldly calculating Church, puritanical "Islamic fundamentalists," or both.

Each of these perspectives is at bottom nostalgic, and each romanti-cizes the Middle Ages. The assumptions underlying them are that in the Middle Ages one's identity as a Christian, Muslim, or Jew was concrete and immutable; that it shaped one's actions and experience in the world to the exclusion of almost all other traits; and that it circumscribed one's social, economic, and political community. And behind these assump-tions lies yet another: that it is only in the modern world, and more spe-cifically the modern "West," that more sophisticated and flexible notions of religious belief, communal affiliation, and individual identity have emerged.

This book presents a rather different account of the age of Crusade and *jihad*. It does not take as a starting point the supposed incompatibil-ity of Christianity, Judaism, and Islam, nor an allegedly "timeless" strug-gle between East and West. It is not a tale of a protocolonial Europe, nor of a reactionary and introverted Islamic Middle East. It does not set out to trace the antecedents of a marginalized and afflicted Jewish commu-nity, nor indict its oppressors. Nor does it presume that religious belief was hollow and Machiavellian, or superstitious and ignorant. It does not begin with European Crusaders setting off to foreign lands to conquer Muslims, nor with Islam striking—or striking back—at Christian Europe. Rather, I open about a half century earlier, when the distinctive relation-ships among Christians, Muslims, and Jews that would characterize the era of the Crusades had already begun to coalesce, and when the Latin, Byzantine, and Muslim worlds had already begun to clash and merge. And unlike other modern historians of the Crusades, I do not focus either on Christian Europe or on the Islamic Middle East, but rather on the Mediterranean region.

By the mid-eleventh century, the Mediterranean Sea and the lands sur-rounding it—populous, diverse, and dynamic—had long constituted, in almost every sense, the center of the Western world. The region was the meeting point of Europe, Africa, and Western Asia. For millennia it had been a site of trade, and had become progressively more integrated until it was formally unified under the Romans. The Mediterranean served as the cradle of the Abrahamic religions and cultures, of Persian and Hellenistic philosophy and science, of Roman institutions, and of beliefs, social mores, and customs common to members of all three religions. Indeed, despite their religious and ethnic differences, the peoples of the Mediterranean shared many traditions and habits, including folk and magical beliefs, ideas regarding honor and gender, myths and tales, and the veneration of holy men and women.

While the third through fifth centuries of the Common Era witnessed the advent of Judaism and Christianity as formally elaborated religions, it also saw the breakdown of Roman order and unity. "Barbarians"— pagans and heretical Christians, for the most part—were drawn into the resulting vacuum from northeastern Europe, northwestern Africa, and later from Arabia. This final group, believers in a new iteration of the Abrahamic tradition they called Islam, irrupted into the Mediterranean region in the late seventh century, sweeping across Syria, Palestine, North Africa, and into "Hispania" and what is now southern France. The Mediterranean became a "Muslim lake," while the Roman Empire, by this point culturally Greek and based in Constantinople, was reduced to a rump state spanning little more than modern Turkey and southeastern Europe. What remained of the empire's Latin territory fractured into insular and backward kingdoms and counties, whose infrastructure consisted of the crumbling roads and bridges the Romans had constructed nearly a thousand years earlier. Isolated and overwhelmingly illiterate, former Roman subjects spoke a Latin that soon degenerated into local, incomprehensible dialects, which, by the time of the Crusades, had become new languages: Spanish, French, Catalan, Occitan, Italian, Romanian, and others.

The Muslim Mediterranean, in contrast, was part of a larger Islamic world that by the 800s stretched as far east as the Indus, had clashed with the Chinese, and had established outposts along the East African and Indian coasts. The *dar al-Islam* (Abode of Islam) was fast becoming a cosmopolitan commercial imperium, bound not by the power of a single ruler or a large bureaucracy but by tremendous linguistic, cultural, and religious unity based on Arabic and Islam. This consensus allowed for the development of a dynamic and open urban society that confidently drew on the institutional and cultural models of Persia, Greece, and Rome, and welcomed outsiders and non-Muslims as nearly full citizens. As more and more non-Arabs converted to Islam, they transformed its culture with their own ideas, practices, and customs—and even those in the *dar al-Islam* who did not convert spoke Arabic and imitated Arabo-Islamic customs. Arabic-speakers, Muslim or not, could with relative ease and safety travel from the Atlantic coast to the foothills of the Himalayas and to most points in between. The Islamic world was a tremendous free-trade zone, both a center of production and an immense market, its booming economy growing hand in hand with a vibrant scientific, technological, and intellectual culture driving innovation and exchange.

The Christian lands of the Mediterranean were gradually drawn into the Islamic world's orbit. Byzantium, rich but beset by political crises, alternated between a hot peace and a cold war with its Muslim neighbors, while the Latin lands, rustic and underdeveloped, began to provide key commodities to Islamic markets: timber, salt, and slaves. By the year 1000 the backward fringes of the Islamic world—Latin Europe, Saharan Africa, and the steppes north and east of the Black Sea—were gravitating toward the Greek and Islamic Mediterranean, setting the stage for the encounters that would at times express themselves as contests between religions.

At many other times, these encounters would be peaceful and fruitful ones. To be sure, the populations of the Mediterranean were intensely invested in religious culture and identity, religious rhetoric was common, and Christianity, Islam, and Judaism were in theory opposed to one another. Nevertheless, members of competing ethno-religious groups often found themselves to be natural collaborators, engaging in relationships of mutual benefit and support with those they qualified as "infidels," even when doing so explicitly contradicted their religious doctrines. Just as often, they found themselves clashing violently with coreligionists and pursuing agendas that ran contrary to the broader goals of their religious ideologies.

Even the Crusades and the corresponding Islamic "Counter-Crusade"—long seen as marking the beginning of an era of intractable holy war—fit within this frame. Indeed, the Crusades were not a reaction on the part of the Christian West to Muslim attacks, but rather the consequence of transformations and tensions within Christian society. Likewise, the development of *jihad* in this period, which is often portrayed as the Muslim response to the Crusades, also had as much or more to do with changes within Islamic society than with the arrival of the Franks, and had preceded the latter.

In fact, the greatest tensions and the worst violence tended to take place among people of the same faith. This was true on both a political and an ideological level. Surprising as it may sound, Muslim princes frequently allied with Christian kingdoms, and Christian kings with Muslim powers, against common enemies, whether Christian or Muslim. And holy war was waged among members of the two religions as often as between them: Latin (Catholic) Christians crusaded against Greek (Orthodox) Christians, while Sunni Muslim rulers proclaimed *jihad* against Shi'a Muslim rulers. Nor were Jews merely hapless bystanders in these conflicts. On the contrary, Jewish communities from Spain to Egypt were powerful and politically engaged; and Jews acted as governors, generals, warriors, and administrators in Christian and Muslim kingdoms. Like Christian and Islamic society, the Jewish world was one riven by brutal internal power struggles. All of this flies in the face of popularly established notions of the age of Crusade, and of the history of encounters among Christianity, Islam, and Judaism.

If not religion alone, then what drove the politics in the Mediterranean? To a great extent, power, lust, greed, and fear did. People's capacity and will to live together and to collaborate in spite of their differences were the consequences not of notions of tolerance but of a common sense of humanity, and of necessity. As much as rulers may have sought power at almost any cost, many were aware of the need to share it. In order to rule effectively, they and their advisers—whether defined by ethnicity, by religion, or both—realized that they had to grant significant liberties and privileges to the minorities among their subjects.

Because religious doctrine was regarded by all as the foundation of law, it followed that each community would need to be subject to its own legal codes. And since each of the Abrahamic religions values free will, forced conversion was viewed as immoral. Religious minorities in Mediterranean societies thus lived according to both their own religious tenets and social customs. They enjoyed liberty of worship, and their communities remained cohesive and autonomous. In return they had to recognize formally that the dominant group's religious culture and law were superior; if there was any contradiction between the law of the rulers and that of the minorities, the law of the majority would take precedence. In Islamic lands it was considered illegal for Christians and Jews to insult Islam, to preach to or to convert Muslims, or to otherwise publicly offend Islamic sensibilities or Islamic law. Church bells were frequently prohibited from ringing, and the public observation of non-Muslim religious rites and festivals was often viewed as dangerously provocative. Corresponding laws applied to Muslims and Jews in Christian lands, where efforts were made to silence muezzins and to outlaw pilgrimage, and where Muslims and Jews were ordered to wear distinct clothing or hairstyles, and to hide or prostrate themselves when Christian religious processions passed. All of this meant that, for instance, the Christian minority in Fatimid Egypt in the twelfth century and the Muslim minority in Christian Spain in the twelfth and the thirteenth enjoyed similar privileges and faced analogous limitations. Indeed, for most of the Middle Ages, minorities under Christian rule seemed to do about as well (or as badly) as minorities living under Islamic rule.

But rulers did not necessarily see it as their duty to respect religious laws; at bottom, their ultimate goal was the continuation of their own regimes. In the complex world of the Mediterranean this could not be accomplished by brute force alone; they needed to win the confidence and gain the willing cooperation of their "unbelieving" subjects. Members of these minorities tended to dominate key sectors in government and the economy, and served as indispensable liaisons with the infidel kingdoms that rulers needed to cultivate as trading partners and allies. But there were other advantages to empowering minority subjects. By doing so, rulers undermined powerful factions within their own groups that might seek to overthrow them. As vulnerable second-class citizens, minority subjects were in no position to do this; moreover, they could be put forward as scapegoats when rulers decided to implement unpopular policies that ran counter to the religious ideology they espoused.

The pragmatism of rulers across the Mediterranean arose out of a fear of the volatility built into their societies. Warfare and catastrophic paroxysms of popular violence were commonplace. When members of minority groups became too visibly powerful or began to compete economically or politically with members of the majority population, or when it seemed that either the Devil or infidel enemies were at the gates, the accommodations of daily life were cast aside. Suddenly, those who were just previously seen as partners, comrades, and fellow countrymen could be seen as strangers, interlopers, or traitors; bloodshed could erupt almost without warning, and driven by ideology, greed, or panic, friend turned against friend and neighbor against neighbor.

Infidel Kings and Unholy Warriors moves from west to east across the Mediterranean in the era of the Crusades (1050–1200), from Spain, North Africa, and southern Italy to Egypt, the Crusader States, and Byzantium. It recounts the lives and deaths of a series of individuals who exercised great power in these religiously and ethnically diverse societies, and who therefore shed light on the complex nature of religious identity and interaction in the Christian and Muslim Mediterranean of the Middle Ages.

In Islamic Spain, or al-Andalus, we encounter a short-lived dynasty of Jews, the Banu Naghrilla of Granada, a Muslim kingdom ruled by Berber warlords. Famed as rabbis and esteemed as men of learning, Samuel ibn Naghrilla and his son, Yusuf, wielded the true power behind the throne, until palace intrigues threatened Yusuf's position and he made a fateful play to take the throne for himself.

A few decades later and to the north, Rodrigo Díaz de Vivar, a knight outlawed by his king and exiled from Christendom, found glory and fame as a mercenary in the service of the Muslim king of Zaragoza. Hungry for power, he battled both Christians and North African *mujahidin* to stake out a kingdom of his own, and ruled for five brief years as the sultan of Islamic Valencia. His unmatched bravery and success made him a living legend, and he was transformed unwittingly by posterity into the Cid—the holy warrior credited with leading the Christian "Reconquest" of Spain.

As Rodrigo was marauding across the Iberian Peninsula, uncultured soldiers of fortune from the north of France were attacking Byzantines and Muslims in a bid to carve out lands for themselves in southern Italy and Sicily. The result was Norman Sicily, a rich and populous kingdom that boasted the most culturally diverse and sophisticated Christian royal court of the time. As the Crusades in the Holy Land raged, the Kingdom of Sicily allied with the Fatimid Caliphate of Egypt and conquered Muslim North Africa—a transformation managed by a clique of palace eunuchs who continued to secretly practice their native faith, Islam—and was presided over by Roger II, an Arabophile prince who styled himself "King of Africa."

Fatimid Egypt, the greatest power in the contemporary Mediterranean, was a land populated by dozens of distinct Muslim, Christian, and Jewish sects, all jockeying for privilege, influence, and survival. Their rulers—a dynasty of messianic Shi'a caliphs considered heretical by orthodox Muslims—survived by playing the various groups against one another, by favoring their Jewish and Christian minorities, and by recruiting Central African and Armenian mercenaries for their armies.* Yet these foreigners would ultimately plot to take control of the state, with disastrous consequences.

It is symptomatic of the profound entanglement of the Christian and Muslim Mediterranean that the collapse of the Fatimids heralded the demise of the Frankish principalities established in the wake of the First Crusade. The Crusade movement that led to the Latin conquest of the Holy Land at the turn of the twelfth century was not the singular, unified phenomenon it is often portrayed as, but rather represented the momentary alignment of the interests of competing Christian groups. The divergence of these interests would transform the Crusade movement and the history of the Near East, precipitating a series of outcomes no one would have expected.

Many of the figures we will meet, such as the Cid and Salah al-Din, are famous. Others, including Samuel ibn Naghrilla, Roger II, Ibn Hazm, Andronikos Komnenos, and Reynaud de Châtillon, are somewhat less so, while a few, like Philip of Mahdia, Bahram Pahlavuni, and Ibn Dukhan, are quite obscure. If some of their stories have not been told up to now, or have not been told in quite this way, it is not because historians have not had access to them. The sources I have drawn on are readily available; all have been published, and many have been translated into English. Rather, it is because the construction of history is largely a matter of perspective. The questions we ask, the position we start from, the presumptions we make—all of these determine our approach and how we interpret the evidence at hand. This is particularly true for those who study the Middle Ages, because we have so little material to work with. Moreover, extant sources are often untrustworthy; their inaccuracies

* The term "caliph" is a borrowing of the Arabic *khalifa*, which means "successor," and refers to the successor of the Prophet Muhammad. As such, there could only be one caliph at any time, who served in theory as the leader and highest authority over all Muslims everywhere.

must be weeded out and their agendas must be understood and accounted for. There is sometimes no way to be certain which one of a group of medieval chroniclers (if any) was telling the truth.

Which brings us back to Pirenne. Their biases nothwithstanding, Pirenne and his ilk may have been correct that the emergence of Islam in the Mediterranean accounts for the emergence, in turn, of Europe. But they undertook their investigations with their conclusions already in mind, and saw what they wanted to see: conflict, rupture, and fragmentation. A more critical, self-aware, and open-minded approach reveals that it was, rather, Christian Europe's engagement with the diverse, complex, and contested Mediterranean region that set the stage for European and Middle Eastern modernity. Just as the Islamic world of the time could not have come into being without the precedents of Persian, Latin, and Greek cultures, most of the great advances in European thought, technology, science, philosophy, literature, and art can be traced back to Latin Christians' encounters with medieval Islam, as well as with Byzantium and Judaism. As the stories that follow will show, it was the collaboration and integration of the Muslim, Jewish, and Christian peoples of the Mediterranean that laid the foundation for the modern world. And through these stories we can better understand the conflicts that we find ourselves embroiled in today.

PART I

The (Jewish) Man Who Would Be King

1

An Ornament, Tarnished

It was the evening of December 30, 1066—the ninth of Teveth, 4827, by the Hebrew calendar, and the year 459 of the *Hijra*, on the tenth day of Safar, a month characterized in Arabic folklore by calamity. It would have been a quiet Saturday night in Granada, a city of mazelike alleys huddled against the northern face of the Sierra Nevada. Perhaps a few white flakes blew down from the mountains. The only sounds to be heard, aside from the barking of stray dogs, would have been the voices of the city's muezzins, calling out in near unison from their minarets, "*Allahu akbar!* God is most great! *Allahu akbar!* God is most great!" and sending the most faithful grimly shuffling through the dusky, unlit streets to *salat al-'isha*, the evening prayer. The Sabbath would be drawing to a close, and the city's Jewish inhabitants would be preparing for the start of the new week. Light from the waxing crescent moon may have reflected off the snow-covered peaks above, and between the mountains and the city, Granada's residents would have seen the flickering yellow of oil lamps outlined by the shutters along the walls of *al-Hamra'*.*

* Yusuf ibn Naghrilla's *al-Hamra'* was later built over and transformed into the present Alhambra, the palace-fortress of the Muslim kings of Granada.

This, the "Red Palace," named after the hillside on which it stood and separated from the main part of the city by the creeklike River Darro, was the home of a Jew, Yusuf ("Yehosef" or "Joseph") ibn Naghrilla, who had recently been deposed as *wazir*, or prime minister, of the Muslim Kingdom of Granada. On this evening, inside his palace, Yusuf and a band of his most trusted confederates were feasting in celebration of what they were sure would be the ex-*wazir*'s imminent coronation as king. As the guests ate and drank, listened to music, and recited poetry, an army led by Ibn Sumadih, the king of Almería, was on the march. In exchange for a declaration of submission, he would place Yusuf on the throne of Granada. As the story goes, a combination of overabundant wine and overconfidence led Yusuf to boast to his *'abid*, his African-born slaves, of the estates and honors that he would grant them once he was king. One of these slaves demanded to know whether the current king, Badis al-Muzaffar, had been killed. When he was rudely silenced, he burst out of the palace in a fit of panic and outrage, shouting, "The Jew has betrayed al-Muzaffar; Ibn Sumadih is about to enter the city!" Hearing his cries, the city's Muslims poured out of their homes and rushed to *al-Hamra'*, where they stormed the banquet hall and pillaged the palace. Even the appearance of Badis, still very much alive, could not calm them, and Yusuf, attempting to flee the city in a blackened cloak, was cornered and killed. Next the mob turned on the Jewish inhabitants of the capital, putting them to the sword and plundering their homes.

As dawn rose on the city the king was safe and the armies of Almería had turned back. At least this is the tale as it has been told. It seems both incredible and predictable: a Jew very nearly became king of a Muslim kingdom in medieval Spain, and a community of innocents was massacred. And it has long appeared to represent a turning point in Jewish-Muslim relations in Islamic Spain and beyond. But was it? To understand the events of that December night in 1066 we must go back to the turn of the millennium, to the collapse of the Caliphate of Córdoba and the founding of the Kingdom of Granada.

THE CALIPHATE IN THE WEST

In the tenth century, Islamic Spain—al-Andalus—developed into the greatest economic and cultural power in the West. In the early 900s under the amir 'Abd al-Rahman III, a long period of upheaval, civil war, and foreign attacks came to end. 'Abd al-Rahman subdued the ever-rebellious Arab elite of al-Andalus—the descendants of the warriors who conquered Visigothic Hispania in the early eighth century—forced the small Christian principalities that dotted the mountainous north of Spain to submit to his authority, and undertook the conquest of northwest Africa. With that campaign Córdoba gained access to gold that originated on the far side of the Sahara, in the Niger Delta and the Akan Forest farther beyond. Intrepid Muslim merchants began to take cloth and salt across the vast desert and trade them pound for pound for high-quality gold, as well as ivory, pelts, and slaves. Much of this gold found its way into the royal treasury, funding a navy with which the amir controlled the Western Mediterranean, and a new army that soon had no serious adversary on the Iberian Peninsula. Up to this time, the Arab tribal elite of al-Andalus had dominated the army of a relatively united Umayyad Spain, and 'Abd al-Rahman's predecessors could not rule without their consent. But now, with a new army made up largely of Berber mercenaries recruited from Tunisia and Morocco and paid for with African gold, 'Abd al-Rahman cowed both the tribal elite and his Christian tributaries, some of whom were his own kin. The submission of these tributaries to Córdoba was so complete that the Muslim court became a center of Christian diplomacy and intrigue, and its harem a destination for their daughters.*

The African gold also inaugurated a time of unprecedented prosperity in al-Andalus, and a cultural and scientific renaissance. Córdoba became the center of both trade and culture. The city's population swelled to nearly half a million, making it, alongside Constantinople and Cairo, the largest metropolis west of Baghdad. The streets were paved, and unlike the filth, squalor, and danger of the stunted and primitive cities of Northern Europe, the capital had a working sewage system, a police force, and street lighting. On those streets peoples from across the Mediterranean and beyond rubbed shoulders: most of the city's inhabitants were Muslims, but there were also many Christian Mozarabs and Jews, who

---

* Many of the amirs took Christian women as wives and concubines; some were captured as slaves, some were of royal or noble blood. 'Abd al-Rahman was the son of a Christian concubine and the grandson of Oneca Fortúnez, a princess of the Kingdom of Pamplona (later Navarre). Hence he was a direct blood relative of the rulers of Navarre and a relative by marriage to those of León and Castile.

were all but indistinguishable in language, dress, and habits from one another and from their Muslim neighbors. The strange accents and languages of foreign visitors could also be heard: merchants and scholars from the expanse of the Islamic world, and not a few Latin foreigners, as well as slaves imported from the "land of the Blacks" and pagan Eastern Europe or captured in raids on Christian lands, and even the occasional Byzantine Greek. These peoples were joined by an increasing number of new arrivals from North Africa, Berber warriors and their families who were looked down on by the native Andalusis for being dark-skinned, and—as they saw it—rude and uncultured.* The city was a tumult of workers and craftsmen, traders and merchants, stern royal officials, veiled courtesans, haughty slaves, beggars, soldiers, scholars, and holy men. The aromas of Africa and India wafted from the covered market northeast of the royal fortress, where cloth merchants hawked silks and linens and where gold- and silversmiths' hammers added to the din caused by the braying of donkeys, the bellowing of camels, and the chatter of townsfolk, visitors, officials, and charlatans of all kinds.

Next door to the market sprawled the majestic Great Mosque, which 'Abd al-Rahman renovated, doubling its size to accommodate the city's burgeoning population. Outside of the magnificent structure, scribes-for-hire wrote petitions, contracts, and letters for all and sundry. Within the stone walls, a broad patio, shaded by orange trees and cooled by sprinkling water fountains, served as a public park and gathering space. Near the doors to the prayer hall, the *qadi*, or magistrate, held court and passed sentence on cases both mundane and sensational. Inside, among the marble columns taken from Roman ruins in the Western Mediterranean and beneath the red-and-white-banded arches that crowned them, people read, meditated, or dozed. Here, on Fridays at noon, the amir himself joined his Muslim subjects, prostrate on the carpeted floor. They faced the ivory-inlaid *mihrab*, the amir separated from the masses only by the wooden honeycomb of a *mashrabiyya* screen.

Buoyed by his successes, in 929 'Abd al-Rahman took a monumental step and declared himself to be the caliph (*khalifa*) and Córdoba to be the center of power in the Islamic world. This was not only a blow to the prestige of the 'Abbasid caliph in Baghdad, who had been universally recognized

---

* "Andalusis" refers to the native Muslim inhabitants of al-Andalus, the descendants of native peoples, Arabs and Berbers, but who identified culturally as Arabs.

The Great Hall, Madinat al-Zahara, Córdoba, tenth century

as legitimate by Sunni Muslims, but a challenge to 'Abd al-Rahman's enemies, the Shi'a Fatimids of Tunisia, who had declared their own independent caliphate twenty years before. More than anything it marked a shift in
the practice of leadership in Islamic Spain. To that point, the amirs had been
"men of the people" in the style of the tribal Arab warlords of old: earthy,
practical, and simple. In a stroke 'Abd al-Rahman transformed himself into
a near-divine autocrat, in the mold of Persian and Byzantine emperors. His
act had profound consequences. Most immediately it meant that he would
withdraw from public life. Protected and served by an ever more efficient
and elaborate civil service, his direct intervention in the daily affairs of
his realm was no longer practical or necessary. And in 939 a rare defeat at
the hands of the forces of Christian León persuaded 'Abd al-Rahman to
end his military career—the life of the caliph could not be risked.

Three years earlier 'Abd al-Rahman had begun construction on
Madinat al-Zahara a few miles west of Córdoba, imagining it as a self-
contained palace-city. For forty years, ten thousand workers and slaves
were said to have labored on the immense complex, which included residences, a huge mosque, barracks, storerooms, and baths. To its luxurious
and extensive gardens were brought exotic plants and trees gathered

from as far away as India. The poet Ibn Zaydun would recall "the meandering waterway . . . its silvery waters . . . like a necklace unclasped and thrown aside," and the "fragrant breaths from the pome of the water lilies." Once finished, Madinat al-Zahara was staffed by thousands of slaves, officials, and soldiers. It became the official seat of government in 947; there would be no reason for the caliph to venture beyond its walls. The center of the palace was the great reception hall, its ceiling decorated with gilt and multicolored panels of translucent marble, interspersed with gold and silver panels and sheltering an ornate fountain sent from Constantinople by Emperor Constantine VII. On sunny days, the light streaming into the great hall was said to be sublime, and when the caliph wanted to awe visitors, his slaves would knock a mercury basin, and its ripples would send shimmers of reflected sunlight through the chamber. It was here that envoys from Africa, the Holy Roman Empire, and Constantinople would come to offer their respects, and the rulers of Christian Spain would come to bear homage.

A contemporary Muslim observer recorded one such visit. In 962 Ordoño IV, King of León, journeyed to Córdoba for an audience with al-Hakam II, the caliph's son and successor. After stopping to pray at the tomb of 'Abd al-Rahman III, the Christian king proceeded under escort to Madinat al-Zahara. The caliphal bodyguard had been deployed in parade regalia and the notables of the court had assembled. As Ordoño made his way through the resplendently decorated palace toward the inner sanctum, he was gradually deprived of his own entourage, until he was surrounded only by his closest advisers. Before reaching the reception hall he was forced to dismount his horse. Entering the dazzling room, the king must have been awestruck by the gilded and marbled walls, which were intended to give a sense of Heaven on Earth. At the center, surrounded by well-coiffed and perfumed officials, slaves, and eunuchs, and flanked by soldiers—blond-haired and bearded "Slavs" and Africans whose black skin had been oiled to a glistening sheen—sat the caliph, garbed in exquisite, brightly dyed silk robes. As he drew near al-Hakam's throne Ordoño bowed, rose, took a few steps, and bowed again, repeating this performance until he reached the caliph, who held out a hand. After Ordoño retreated respectfully, his grandees each rose to kiss al-Hakam's hand, and then the king exclaimed, "I am a slave of the Commander of the Faithful, my lord and my master; and I am come to implore his favor and to witness his majesty, and to place myself and my people under his protection." The desired effect—to overwhelm the visiting Christian king, to render him speechless—had clearly been achieved.

Though the caliph's move to the palace increased his isolation and resulted in new powers for the palace bureaucrats, notably the *wazir*, the top administrator, and the *hajib*, or chamberlain, who controlled access to the sovereign, 'Abd al-Rahman remained involved in the affairs of his kingdom. He was astute enough to realize that the loyalty of his various officials, generals, and wives was tenuous at best—any of them might plot to depose or assassinate him and place a kinsman on the throne. And so he relied for his own protection on bodyguards recruited or captured from the Christian lands in the north, men called "the Silent Ones" for their inability to speak Arabic, who, having no natural allies in al-Andalus, would be unlikely to betray him.

In the same spirit, one of the keys to maintaining the political equilibrium in the caliphate was his cultivation of *dhimmis*, the Jews and Christians who were the "protected" subject peoples of the Islamic regime. Both communities were granted broad liberties, and both were integrated into Muslim society. A century earlier, after a brief flurry of resistance, the local Christian Church had effectively become a branch of the Andalusi civil service.* Thus, for example, the Christian aristocrat and courtier Reccemund, who went by the name Rabi' ibn Zaid in Muslim circles, was rewarded for his faithful service to the regime when he was appointed bishop of Elvira by the caliph. Jews found themselves with similar opportunities. The Jewish physician and rabbi Hasdai ibn Shaprut became the caliph's close friend and adviser, and even led the caliph's most delicate diplomatic missions. As a consequence of his influence in Córdoba (not to mention his extraordinary devotion and learning), Hasdai was recognized as *Nasi*, "prince," and became an advocate for Jews across the caliphate and beyond.†

Non-Muslims, slaves, and Berbers were useful to 'Abd al-Rahman because they were in their own ways outsiders, and would be unable to

---

* In the mid-800s, a number of Christian reactionaries, including at least one high-ranking official, publicly insulted Islam and the Prophet and demanded that they be executed in accordance with Islamic law. They were, and in death became known as "Voluntary Martyrs of Córdoba."
† In the last years of his life, Hasdai sent his own diplomatic mission east in an effort to make contact with the legendary Jewish kingdom of the Khazars in Central Asia, but his efforts were sabotaged by the Byzantine emperor Constantine VII.

harness popular support in a coup. As a consequence, each group served the caliph as counterweights to potentially subversive Muslim and Arab factions within the kingdom. In essence, the administration oversaw a dynamic meritocracy in which neither class nor ethnic background nor religion posed insurmountable obstacles to success. This is not to say that Córdoba's political culture was based on a principle of tolerance, but rather that the Umayyad rulers were interested only in power. But the regime's pragmatic self-interest fostered a situation in which Christians, Muslims, and Jews found themselves working together to build a caliphate in the West, each group secure and confident, and each speaking Arabic and moving within an Islamic social, cultural, and intellectual milieu. Muslims felt no threat from the *dhimmis* among them, and Christians and Jews were accommodated and integrated to such a degree that only the most stalwartly reactionary would harbor any resentment against the still superior status of Muslims.

By 961, when 'Abd al-Rahman's son, al-Hakam II, came to the throne, the caliphate was practically running itself, leaving the heir free to pursue his scholarly and intellectual interests. This suited al-Hakam, who had little interest in affairs of state. A bookish type, he patronized scholars, poets, and scientists. During his reign the royal library possessed, if the sources are to be trusted, close to a half million volumes. (This at a time when the Abbey Library of St. Gall in Switzerland, one of the great centers of learning in the Latin West, boasted just over one hundred.) The caliph and other grandees funded translations of literary and scientific works, and scholarship and research progressed apace. But for all his learning, al-Hakam did not foresee the perils of entrusting bureaucrats and administrators with the day-to-day running of his wealthy and complex kingdom.

AN ANDALUSI CAESAR

One of these administrators was an ambitious young man who claimed Arab descent, named Muhammad ibn Abi Amir, who had come to Córdoba from the provinces, hoping to work as a scribe. Through good fortune and persistence he managed to find employment not only in the palace but in the caliph's harem. He became the personal administrator to Subh, a former Christian, who as the mother of al-Hakam's sole son and heir, Hisham, was herself a powerful figure. Coaxing al-Hakam to produce an heir had been no easy feat; the caliph's predilection for men was said to be so strong that he kept a male harem. Subh, it was claimed, had managed to succeed in seducing the unwitting caliph by cropping her hair and disguising herself as a boy. Whatever the truth, Ibn Abi Amir rose quickly in her service; and there were rumors of an affair between the two. However he won Subh's affection and trust, though, the young scribe was evidently after power, not sex.

Marriage was a separate matter. Ibn Abi Amir married Asma, the daughter of Ghalib al-Nasiri, a leading "Arab" aristocrat and general, with whose support he secured valuable experience and then popular acclaim as a military commander.* In 976 al-Hakam died and ten-year-old Hisham ascended to the caliph's throne. After heading off a coup by the palace eunuchs, Ibn Abi Amir, Ghalib, and Subh made a pact to keep young Hisham a virtual prisoner while they ran the caliphate. Over the subsequent decades Ibn Abi Amir gradually consolidated his power, disposing of rivals and having himself appointed both *wazir* and *hajib*. At the same time, he imported increasing numbers of North African troops and launched spectacular expeditions against the Christian lands to the north. These, along with his conspicuous acts of public piety—copying his own Qur'an by hand and purging the caliphal library of "subversive" works— earned him broad support among the religious elite and the Muslim public over which they held sway. Then Ibn Abi Amir turned on his allies with Stalinesque thoroughness: Subh, Ghalib, and any others who might threaten him were eliminated. Ibn Abi Amir had become the uncontested ruler of al-Andalus.†

Hisham, the caliph in name only, was forced to formally cede political authority to the *hajib* in 997. By then Muhammad ibn Abi Amir had become known as al-Mansur—"the Victorious by God"—a name that

---

* Ghalib identified as an Arab, but he was, in fact, a former slave, probably a Christian, whom 'Abd al-Rahman had freed and, in accordance with custom, had allowed to appropriate his genealogy. Ghalib the slave thus became Ghalib ibn 'Abd al-Rahman ("the son of 'Abd al-Rahman").

† Subh was sent to a rural estate, where she lived out her remaining years in isolation. Ghalib was not so lucky. By 981 he had realized the scope of his son-in-law's ambitions and had raised an army against him. After Ibn Abi Amir defeated him in battle, he had the general's head placed in a decorated box and sent as a present to his wife and Ghalib's daughter, Asma.

swiftly became synonymous with terror in the Latin world. Called "Al-manzor" by his Christian enemies, Ibn Abi Amir sacked the major towns of Christian Spain, including Barcelona, León, and Pamplona. In 997 his armies marched to Santiago de Compostela, the legendary resting place of the Apostle Saint James in the far northwest of the peninsula, and carried the bells from his church back to Córdoba as trophies to be hung in the Great Mosque. For al-Mansur these campaigns served three purposes: to keep the Christian kingdoms weak and on the defensive; to provide an outlet for the energies of his army; and to cement his popular reputation as a *mujahid*, or a warrior of Islam. At home, he placated the old Arab elite—Hisham's immense extended family, the Umayyad clan—by ensuring that they had access to powerful and lucrative positions in the administration and by not challenging their social and cultural prestige.

To all appearances the caliphate was at the height of its power under al-Mansur. But beneath the surface tensions were building. Despite his efforts, the Umayyad clan chafed at having been shunted aside by an upstart scribe. Provincial governors and palace slaves plotted uprisings. The *'ulama'*, or clerics, pressured al-Mansur to pursue a repressive domestic policy designed to protect the status of the native Muslim elite and maintain religious rigor. In order to placate them, he burned the books they considered offensive, including a large part of al-Hakam's immense library. And Andalusis of all classes and backgrounds came to loathe and fear the increasingly powerful Berber element. In the previous decades North African domination of the army had translated into broader political power for Berbers, many of whom had been appointed to administrative posts. The notion that these illiterate, dark-skinned non-Arabs were taking over galvanized the alarmed native populace.

In 1002, returning from his fifty-second biannual invasion of Christian territories, Muhammad ibn Abi Amir took ill. His army stopped in Medinaceli, a wind-swept plateau not far from the northern frontier of the caliphate, and where an arch built by the Roman emperor Domitian nine hundred years earlier still stands today. Here al-Mansur died. His army mournfully carried his body four hundred miles south, back to Córdoba. The *hajib* was first succeeded by his favorite son, 'Abd al-Malik, who carefully kept up the facade of the caliphate, but who died unexpectedly in 1008. He was succeeded in turn by his younger brother, 'Abd al-Rahman, known popularly as Sanjul, or "little Sancho," for his resemblance to his maternal grandfather, King Sancho II of Pamplona. Sanjul shared none of his father's or brother's discretion or restraint. Not content to hold power in practice, Sanjul wanted also to hold it in name, and a year after his appointment, he forced the aging and childless Hisham II to designate him the official heir to the title of caliph. This was simultaneously an act of betrayal to the Umayyad clan, an affront to the 'ulama', who upheld the religious legitimacy of the caliphate, and an outrage to the Muslim populace of al-Andalus. Then, further stoking the growing opposition, he ordered state dignitaries to abandon their traditional multicolored headdresses—the symbol of their aristocratic status—in favor of the Berber-style turban. To the people of Córdoba it seemed as though the Berbers were taking over.

Recognizing that he had gone too far, Sanjul attempted to regain popular support among the Arab-identifying Andalusis, but this served only to alienate him from his North African military. In 1009 he was seized by his own troops and put to death, and the people of Córdoba rose up against the Berber clans, who had settled on the outskirts of the city. The period that followed would come to be called the *fitna*, or "disorder." A generation-long civil war, it would witness the destruction of Madinat al-Zahara, the sacking of Córdoba, and the collapse of the caliphate. It would herald the beginning of the end of Muslim dominance of the peninsula. Islamic Spain tilted into anarchy: the cities became unsafe, bandits and mercenaries roamed the countryside, and local governors declared themselves independent rulers. A few decades before, the German poetess and nun Hrosvitha of Gandersheim had described it as "the brilliant ornament of the world [that] shone in the west"; now Córdoba was reduced to a shell of its former self. The scholars, merchants, and soldiers of fortune who had lived there scattered as refugees in the aftermath of the uprising. Among these were a Jew, Shmuel Ha-Levi, and a Berber, Zawi ibn Ziri. Although they would never meet, their destinies were deeply intertwined. Between them, they would found the Kingdom of Granada and make it prosper, and Shmuel's son, Yusuf ibn Naghrilla, would one day aspire to seize its throne.

A SOLDIER OF MISFORTUNE

Zawi ibn Ziri would not have referred to himself as a "Berber," a label invented by condescending Arab geographers for the diverse indigenous peoples of the Maghrib (Arabic for "the West"; what is now northwestern Africa, from Libya to Morocco). The term derived from the Arabic *barbara*, "to babble nonsensically."* Arab-identifying Spanish Muslims viewed Berbers as illiterate, brutish, and uncouth; the prejudice originated during the age of Islamic conquest, and has been perpetuated unthinkingly by writers and historians to this day. In fact, the tribal hill and desert dwellers of the region—farmers, herders, and warriors—spoke a number of languages, including Tamazight, Taqbaylit, and Tarifit, and had used an alphabet developed by the Phoenician colonists at ancient Carthage. Their generic word for themselves, *Imazaghen*, meant "the nobles."

When the Arabs arrived in northwestern Africa in the late seventh century, the Berbers (with the exception of some tribes who may have identified as Christians or Jews) were pagan, and so were not considered eligible to live within the *dar al-Islam*. They were given the choice of converting to Islam or fighting to the death. Some resisted but most acquiesced, and gradually the various tribes of the Mediterranean's African coastland became Muslim (at least in name), and subjects and allies of the Arab warlords. They relinquished their alphabet as they were gradually Arabized. It was Berber troops who were largely responsible for the Islamic conquest of Spain in the early 700s. Those who stayed in the peninsula after the campaigns were absorbed into the new Hispano-Arabic society of al-Andalus, and by the time of 'Abd al-Rahman III their origins had been forgotten. This was not the case, however, with the North Africans who had been recruited during the years of the caliphate. Brought over as clans, complete with their women and children, these warriors maintained their distinct customs, language, and identity. Although they took their Islam very seriously, many did not even speak Arabic. Along with the disdain the Andalusis felt for them, this fact made integration impossible. Moreover, the recently arrived Berbers maintained their ties with family members and tribes back home across the Straits of Gibraltar, and saw themselves not so much as immigrants but as temporary mercenaries in the service of the caliphate, or as the vanguard of a new conquest.

Two of the largest nomadic tribal groups of the Maghrib were the Zanata in the west and the Sanhaja in the east. They were traditional

---

* The Arabs adopted the word from the Greek *barbaros*. To Greeks the languages of foreigners appeared to be unintelligible grunting, "bar-bar-bar," symptomatic of their uncivilized nature.

enemies. When, under 'Abd al-Rahman III, Islamic Spain began to conquer and colonize North Africa, it engaged with the Zanata first, as by turns an antagonist and an ally. As a consequence, most of the mercenaries who swelled the ranks of the caliphal army were from Zanata tribes. The Sanhaja, on the other hand, were dependents of the Fatimids, the Umayyads' archenemies, who had established their own caliphate in Ifriqiya (Tunisia, or the former Roman province of "Africa") in the early 900s. In 969, after their conquest of Egypt, the Fatimids founded a new capital at Cairo, leaving the Sanhaja to govern Ifriqiya in their place.

The Sanhaja were ruled by a clan called the Banu Ziri, whose men were famous for their fierce prowess in war.* But the Zirids, as they were also called, were riven by internal power struggles, and in 999 a civil war erupted that pitted Zawi ibn Ziri and his brothers against their nephew, Badis ibn Mansur, who had been appointed official governor of Ifriqiya by the Fatimid caliph. Despite their skill on the battlefield, the rebels were defeated, and with his brothers dead, Zawi was left as head of his clan. Seeing no future for his people in Ifriqiya, with great reluctance he turned to his old enemies, the Umayyads, for a way out. Al-Mansur reacted to the overture with cautious interest. Although the Zirids had been his implacable enemies, Zawi was renowned as a warrior from Cairo to Córdoba, and al-Mansur saw how he could prove useful. Though bringing Zawi and his clan to al-Andalus might unsettle the ranks of the caliphal forces, which were drawn from tribes hostile to the Sanhaja, it would also help temper the growing influence of the Zanata, who, in the preceding decade, had come to dominate the army and had taken over key positions in the civil and palace administration.

After prolonged negotiations, Zawi ibn Ziri and the members of his clan, including their families and households, arrived in al-Andalus sometime after 1002. Al-Mansur had died, but Zawi had reached an agreement with his son and successor 'Abd al-Malik. The future seemed to promise a respite from years of danger and insecurity. But it was not to be; in 1009 the caliphate descended into civil war. After Hisham II's

---

* *Banu* is the plural of *ibn*, or "son." While it can be used literally to mean "the sons of," it is also a way of designating common descent, normally in reference to the most recent illustrious ancestor of a family. In other words, it is a way of referring to tribes, clans, or familial subgroups. For example, were they Arabs, the Kennedys of the twentieth century might be known collectively as the Banu Yusuf (the descendants of Joseph).

death, two of 'Abd al-Rahman III's descendants made claims to the throne. The first, al-Musta'in, had the support of the Berber armies, whereas his rival, al-Mahdi, was backed by the Arab elite and the people of Córdoba. In 1013 al-Musta'in triumphed, and his victorious Berber forces swept through the capital, taking bloody vengeance against the city. But his victory did not make for peace, and many North Africans fled the peninsula in the aftermath. To restore stability and placate the people of Córdoba, the new caliph stationed the bulk of his remaining Berber forces in the provinces.

The Zirids were assigned to Elvira, a prosperous and fertile region south of Córdoba with a vibrant economy based on abundant orchards and the production of some of the finest silks in al-Andalus. Elvira was also distinguished by its substantial Jewish population.* The region had suffered Berber attacks since the time of Sanjul's death, and Zawi feared that his family might become targets for retribution. The Elvirans, however, saw in the fearsome Zirids their best hope for survival. They petitioned Zawi to be their protector, offering safety for his kin and generous payment for his troops. Zawi accepted, and not a moment too soon. In 1018 al-Musta'in was assassinated in his bath and two new rivals rose to contest the title of caliph. The Zirids had lost their protector and were now vulnerable to enemies who would seek to destroy them. Moreover, wealthy Elvira become an irresistible target for raiders. An attack was all but inevitable.

Set on open terrain and minimally fortified, the city was vulnerable. Zawi determined that the only hope in the event of an invasion was to retreat to higher ground. Summoning all his eloquence and tenacity, he persuaded the people of Elvira to evacuate their homes and relocate to a town just to the south called Granada, which, because of its proximity to the Sierra Nevada range, would be relatively easy to fortify. Together, the Elvirans and the Zirids settled in Granada and rebuilt and extended its defenses. In the meantime, forces representing al-Murtada, one of the two claimants to the caliphal throne, assembled to subdue or destroy

---

* That Elvira should be a city known for its Jewish population is not without irony. It was here, in the early 300s, before Christianity became permissible in the Roman Empire, that a Church council ruled, among other things, that Christians should not marry Jews or heretics, nor should priests dine with them.

the Zirids. A huge host composed of Muslim troops and Christian mercenaries began to plunder the countryside and to encircle the city. Seeing no other option but to strike, the greatly outnumbered Sanhaja warriors sallied forth from Granada's gates on horseback. They overran the invaders' camp and scattered al-Murtada's ill-prepared forces. Against all odds, Granada had been saved, which made Zawi ibn Ziri's next move all the more surprising.

In the wake of the great victory, Zawi mustered his troops and announced his intention to immediately return to Ifriqiya, and his hope that his warriors and their families would follow. Sixteen years in al-Andalus had left him disillusioned, and convinced that there was no future there for the Sanhaja, who were hated despite their loyal service to the caliphate. The Andalusis and the Zanata, he claimed, would always plot to wipe them out. "If we kill one of them, a thousand will replace him [and] as their power grows ours will weaken, for we can never replace our dead." While the allure of his homeland was powerful, Zawi may have had other motives. News from Ifriqiya had led him to believe he might be able to reestablish himself and his clan in the region. His old enemy and kinsman Badis ibn Mansur had died, and Zawi had received permission from Badis's son and heir, al-Mu'izz, to return from exile. Whatever the case, Zawi's appeal to his kinsmen in Granada fell on deaf ears. The younger generation had little memory of North Africa, and flush with victory, they were confident that they had achieved security and prosperity in al-Andalus. They refused to follow Zawi home.

By 1020 Zawi was gone, having sailed with his immediate household to settle in the Zirid capital of Qayrawan. His return, however, was not a happy one. Soon after his arrival, he received word that his nephew, an equally audacious warrior named Habbus ibn Maksan, had seized power in Granada from Zawi's sons, whom he had left in charge of the city. And in Ifriqiya itself, he was allotted a large palace as his home, but far from being invited to share power, he was blocked from any access to Maghribi politics. Of Zawi's ultimate fate we cannot be certain. One account claims he was poisoned not long after his arrival in his homeland, another that he succumbed to illness after some years, isolated and forgotten. In any event, this proud and principled old warrior died without realizing that quite by accident he had founded what would become one of the most powerful kingdoms in al-Andalus.

ONE KINGDOM AMONG MANY

By the time of Zawi's departure from Spain, it was clear that the caliphate was nothing more than a convenient fiction. Although assorted Umayyad family members would be trotted out as legitimate successors of Hisham II until the 1030s, no informed observers saw these men and boys as anything but puppets of the various factions battling for supremacy in al-Andalus. None of these candidates captured wide popular support and each met with a nasty end. Still, even though what had once been the most powerful and centralized European state since the time of the Romans had splintered into a multitude of petty principalities that would become known as the *taifa* or "sectarian" kingdoms, the concept of a single caliphate loomed large in the Andalusi imagination (just as Rome did for Northern Europeans). Wary of offending popular opinion or Islamic unity, the rulers of these independent states avoided openly referring to themselves as "kings." Rather, in emulation of the great al-Mansur, they took the title of *hajib*, and presented themselves as mere representatives of a temporarily absent caliph. But kings they were in virtually every sense of the word, and virtually everyone else referred to them as such—they were independent rulers who pursued earthly political agendas, the final aim of which was nothing more or less than the perpetuation of their own power and that of their families.

With the sudden collapse of the power centered in Córdoba following the death of Sanjul in 1009, a frantic free-for-all had begun. Provincial governors, military leaders, and local administrators all rushed to seize power over the city or region in which they were stationed. At the outset no less than thirty separate principalities emerged out of the ruins of the caliphate. Some were ruled by members of the Umayyad clan or other powerful Arab families, some by palace eunuchs, and some by Berber warriors and mercenaries breaking free from their Andalusi overlords. Many of these new statelets were not viable. In some cases the new leaders failed to attract the support of the local populace and were either expelled or put to death. "Slav" *taifa* rulers—who originated as Eastern European slaves or captured Christians—were particularly vulnerable in this respect, not because they were slaves or former slaves, but because as foreigners they had no wider community or families of their own to draw on for support. Berber clans also found themselves in a delicate position; given the hatred and mistrust the local people directed at them, they could only cling to power if they managed to negotiate a compromise with their subjects. The most secure rulers were the governors of the frontier provinces, like the *Thaghr al-'Aqsa*, "the Farthest Frontier," of Zaragoza, whose families had been ruling their regions as de facto independent kingdoms for generations, and on whom the end of the caliphate had little immediate impact.

Thus, by the 1030s, the less tenable *taifa* kingdoms had disappeared, with the smaller principalities being absorbed by their more powerful neighbors until only a handful of major players remained. In the south of Spain, there were four. Córdoba, the former capital, had become a small and traditional Arab-style republic, ruled by the local Banu Djahwar family with the consent of a popular council composed of its leading citizens. On the Mediterranean, the important seaport and silk production center of Almería was ruled initially by slaves, until it was seized in 1041–42 by al-Mansur's surviving son, 'Abd al-'Aziz, who then established his seat in Valencia and appointed the Banu Sumadih clan as his governors. By 1060 they would reign as independent kings. To the west there was Seville, the most powerful *taifa* kingdom in the south. Here, a *qadi* of Arab origin, Abu 'l-Qasim Muhammad ibn 'Abbad, came to power and set about subduing his neighbors. Both Abu 'l-Qasim and his son, al-Mu'tamid, proclaimed Seville as the champion of Andalusi Arabs against the foreign Berbers, attracting great popular support, particularly among those Muslims loyal to the memory of the Umayyad caliphs. Naturally, their archenemies were the Banu Ziri, Zawi ibn Ziri's clan, of the now formidable Kingdom of Granada—the greatest obstacle to Seville's domination of the rich southern provinces of the former caliphate.

The political atmosphere in the *taifa* period was brutal and volatile; there were few alliances, except of the most temporary and Machiavellian sort, and each *taifa* ruler dreamed of destroying his rivals and being the one to reestablish the unity of al-Andalus. For an Islamic society this was a shocking state of affairs, not so much because inter-Muslim warfare had not existed previously—in fact, Islamic history to this point had been rife with internecine conflict—but because the Umayyad Caliphate had seemed so stable and permanent only a generation before, and because disunity ran counter to the political and religious ideology of Islam. Unlike Christianity and Judaism, Islam was at once a religious and a political system. Muhammad had not only been the Prophet of God and the religious leader of the *'umma*—the community of believers—but its political leader as well. A theory of just warfare, *jihad*, was elaborated in the time of Muhammad, and became enshrined in Scripture. Judaism had its own religiously ordained military policy, as expressed in Deuteronomy and Kings, but with the collapse of the Kingdom of Judah and the "Babylonian captivity" this became irrelevant. By the time the Hebrew Scriptures finally took the form we know today, Judaism in the Mediterranean was a religion of kingdomless exiles. Christianity, by contrast, first appeared not just without a state but threatened by one (Rome), and its Scripture was formally pacifist and apolitical. However, no sooner had Constantine I, in 325 C.E., made Christianity an official religion of the Roman Empire than theologians such as Saint Augustine began to frame principles of just and holy warfare.

On a conceptual level, there could be no easy division between "secular" and "religious" spheres in Islam when the goal of the faith was individual salvation as well as the creation of a world governed by God's law. Muslims aspired to create a world defined by religious unanimity and one ultimate political authority. Hence, the earliest conflicts in Islam were not separatist movements that proposed alternative Islams (as happened in Christianity during the time of the early Church and with later Protestant movements), but struggles over who should wield this authority over all Muslims. And so, although Islamic unity had clearly ceased to be a political and religious reality by the early eighth century, all Muslims, both Sunni and Shi'a, continued to support the ideal of a single caliph, at least outwardly.* The experience of the Umayyad family, the first caliphal dynasty, reflects this conviction. Ruling from Damascus starting in 660 C.E., they were overthrown in a coup in 750, and supplanted by the 'Abbasids, who were based in Iraq. In the uprising that swept them from power, almost the entire Umayyad family was massacred by the rebels, with the exception of a young prince named 'Abd al-Rahman, who escaped from Syria and arrived in al-Andalus in 756. However, even after 'Abd al-Rahman had established himself as an independent prince in al-Andalus, far from the reach of the 'Abbasids, he did not claim his grandfather Hisham's title of caliph. Instead, he styled himself as *amir*, or "prince," formally acknowledging the authority of the legitimate caliph in Baghdad, despite the circumstances of the latter's rise to power.

* An exception was the Kharijites, members of a splinter group that denied the authority of the caliphs. For the Kharijites, see chapter 7, "After the Messiah," p. 187.

Nonetheless, in certain ways the division between secular and religious was far clearer in Islamic societies than in Christian ones. The notion that the caliph wielded religious or doctrinal authority over the Muslim 'umma had come to an end in 656 with the death of 'Uthman, the third successor to Muhammad, who had overseen the creation of a standard version of the Qur'an. Unlike medieval Christianity and traditional Judaism, in which access to God is mediated by a priestly hierarchy who interprets the divine will, Islam was from the start strongly rooted in the notions of the fundamental and absolute equality of all believers before God, and of freedom of conscience. There was no priesthood and no magical element to the liturgy. The caliphs were not popes. The holy writings of Islam were in Arabic, the common spoken language, and therefore accessible to all believers. Muslim ritual was generally practical (such as the pre-prayer washing) and participatory (such as the Ramadan fast and the hajj pilgrimage to Mecca). Doctrine was so straightforward that it could be expressed in a mere eight words: the Arabic for "There is no god but God, and Muhammad is His Messenger." Moreover, there were few counterintuitive paradoxes such as the idea of God having an incarnate son, or God being simultaneously three and one. Religious authority was informal and based on one's understanding and interpretation of the sacred texts of Islam: the Qur'an, the revealed Word of God, and the *Sunna* or "tradition," accounts of the customs of Muhammad and other early Muslims. Unlike in the Roman tradition, where the emperor and the state were the sources of law, in Islamic lands the law was derived not from the will of a ruler, but from Scripture. Similar to Deuteronomy but nothing like the Gospels, the Qur'an was in part an explicit—if far from complete and not entirely consistent—guide to what rules should govern a just society.

The individuals who were believed to have the ability and capacity to interpret Scripture—the *'ulama'* ("those who have knowledge")—decided to a large extent the laws in Islamic societies and how to apply them. Scripture was the basis of criminal law and punishment; family law, including matters such as inheritance, divorce, and custody; commercial law; and even fiscal policy, in that the Qur'an set forth the kinds of taxes that could be levied on members of a Muslim community. All of this meant not only that the judiciary in Islamic lands was functionally independent from the political rulers, but that its power extended into areas we would today consider the prerogative of the state. As a consequence, within the first century and a half of Islam, the authority of political leaders was limited for the most part to military matters. They enforced the laws but did not create them. A symbiotic relationship predominated: the religious elite confirmed the legitimacy of the political and military elite in exchange for protection and security. In reality, no one was under any illusions about who held the real power, but when the political elite failed to hold up their end of the compromise, the *'ulama'* could declare them illegitimate and mobilize the popular forces to resist or overthrow them.

The *'ulama'* owed their power to their interpretative skills but also to their ability to represent the people. They were themselves politicans, in some respects. Unlike Latin Christian society, which was explicitly divided into peasant and noble classes, and in which the most influential and powerful positions in the clergy were all but reserved for the aristocracy, widespread literacy, the lack of formal class barriers, and the great socioeconomic mobility of the Arabo-Islamic world made it possible for people from all walks of life to become influential *'ulama'*. Many influential *faqihs* (legal experts) and *muftis* (interpreters of law) came from humble backgrounds, starting out as tradesmen, workers, or even slaves. Further, they cultivated their popular reputation by rejecting the potentially corrupting patronage, favor, and government appointments offered by rulers. Because the power of the *'ulama'* was independent and real, they could not be ignored. Hence the *taifa* kings' cautious respect for the ideal of the caliphate was critical to their ability to govern.

Because it was in the hands of scholars who were not constrained by the traditions or dictates of the states in which they lived, Islamic law functioned more or less consistently throughout the *dar al-Islam*, as scholars and judges traveled from Córdoba to Cairo and Baghdad, practicing their profession without regard to the borders of kingdoms and caliphates. As unusual as it may sound, the collapse of the Caliphate of Córdoba represented a minor disruption in the lives of most common people in al-Andalus in terms of the laws that they lived under. *Taifa* kingdoms would come and go as superficial disturbances that hardly affected the currents shaping Islamic society. The wars of the *taifa* kings were not wars among enemy states or competing societies or ideologies; they were clashes between rival elites within a single system. All the factions respected Islamic law as it was interpreted by the *'ulama'*, and few citizens felt any special loyalty to or affinity for their rulers.

Because the laws remained basically intact after Sanjul's death in 1009, the Andalusi economy was hardly affected, either—if anything, it may have improved, despite the bandit raids that plagued some areas. The flow of African gold continued, and after the first period of civil war commercial networks were revived. The countryside had been nearly untouched by the war, and the cities, with the exception of Córdoba, escaped damage. In fact, the destruction of Córdoba had the effect of stimulating provincial economies, which could now keep the taxes they collected instead of sending them to the capital. Former provincial backwaters became little capital cities and thriving markets in their own right. Culturally, too, the *taifa* period was a time of progress. While the holdings of the famous caliphal libraries may have been scattered—first by al-Mansur to placate the religious right, and subsequently in the sacking of Córdoba—new centers of patronage and learning sprang up across the peninsula. As with modern nations, the *taifa* kings tried to outdo one another in funding culture and education. In its four centuries of existence, as a consequence of its melding of Arab, Hebrew, Greek, and Persian traditions, Arabo-Islamic culture had fostered an etiquette of sophistication and courtly behavior, known as *adhab*. Muslim rulers, even warriors who threw most of their energy into campaigning, revered (or saw the political use in showing reverence for) the arts and sciences. Several *taifa* kings were even accomplished poets, authors, or scientists in their own right.

A LAND OF OPPORTUNITY

Zawi ibn Ziri had been only one of many people, prominent and otherwise, eager to put the destructive unrest in Córdoba behind him. Also among the refugees of all backgrounds and creeds who fled for the provinces after the fall of the caliphate in 1013 was a young Jew named Shmuel (Samuel) Ha-Levi ben Yusuf ibn Naghrilla.

Abu Ibrahim Isma'il, as he would be better known, was born in 993 into a wealthy family originally from Merida that had moved south to Córdoba after the establishment of the caliphate. He distinguished himself at a young age, becoming a disciple and protégé of Rabbi Hanok, the head of the Rabbinical community in the caliphate and the successor of the legendary Hasdai ibn Shaprut. Isma'il's parents were evidently raising him for a career in the administration of the caliphate and the leadership of its Jewish community. He was given a comprehensive grounding in Hebrew and in theology, appropriate for any affluent member of the Jewish elite, as well as a superb education in Arabic science and letters. This was not surprising. Arabic had become the preferred spoken and written language of Jews in the Islamic world, from the Indus to the Atlantic. When in 993 Rabbi Saadia Gaon produced his *Book of the Articles of Faith and Doctrines of Dogma*, the first analytical treatment of Jewish theology, not only did he model it on the work of contemporary Muslim rational philosophers, but he wrote it in Arabic. Hebrew, which had been for some time a fossilized liturgical language, was only beginning to be revived, as Jewish philologists and literati started to adapt the systematizing work of Arabic grammarians to the language of the Old Testament. Most telling was that young Isma'il was also sent to learn Latin from a priest, and evidently learned one of the Berber languages as well. His uncommonly wide-ranging education would allow him to thrive in the multicultural world of al-Andalus. As a young man, he moved with ease among the elite of the capital, in his element among Jews, Muslims, and Christians alike. In 1013, however, at the age of twenty, his education may have seemed to be a waste; the caliphate had all but collapsed, apparently taking his prospects with it.

If we are to believe Isma'il's own account, though, the setback did not discourage him; he would later recall how as a young man he had been visited by the Archangels Gabriel and Michael, who promised to protect him from danger. But little is known of the years that followed the fateful events of 1013. Our best source for Isma'il's life, the Jewish chronicler Ibn Daud's *Book of Tradition*, idolizes him as a near-messianic figure and is, because of this, far from dependable. It seems that after leaving Córdoba, the young would-be courtier eventually settled in Málaga, a teeming city of about twenty thousand (twice the size of contemporary London), its native Muslim and Christian population swelled by Arabs and Berbers of various tribes, as well as Jews. Málaga was a major producer of fruits and other high-value crops, an important center of cloth production, a fishing port, and an entrepôt for North Africa and the Eastern Mediterranean. In the 1030s it would, as an independent *taifa* kingdom, ally with Granada against Seville. Here, Isma'il established himself in some sort of commercial capacity—according to Ibn Daud, as a spice merchant or grocer—and undoubtedly rose to a leadership role in the local Jewish community.

As early as 1020, Isma'il left Málaga for Granada, where he became the secretary to 'Abu 'l-'Abbas ibn al-'Arif. While Ibn al-'Arif held the official post of chief secretary (*katib*) to Habbus, King of Granada, it was, in fact, Isma'il who composed royal letters and documents and whose counsel and advice was heard by the king. Ibn Daud fancifully recounts how Ibn al-'Arif and Isma'il were neighbors in Málaga, and how the former recruited the latter after discovering by chance Isma'il's talent for love letters. But this is clearly an invention. Ibn al-'Arif had probably heard of Isma'il because they moved in the same aristocratic circles, and Isma'il was already known for his savoir faire and his command of Arabic. Composing formal diplomatic correspondence in the language was no small feat; one had to be able to draw on the styles and traditions of a rich and varied Arabo-Persian literature, and to be able to leaven one's compositions with references, both direct and oblique, to Islamic sacred texts. The skill escaped the Sanhaja nobility, most of whom could not read Arabic. But so clearly had Isma'il mastered the form that on his deathbed, 'Abu 'l-'Abbas ibn al-'Arif confessed to King Habbus that the Jewish merchant had been the one guiding the kingdom in his name. Habbus reacted by naming Isma'il his new *katib*. Soon Isma'il would serve him also as *wazir*, although for the moment the deceased *katib*'s son, Abu 'l-Qasim ibn al-'Arif, was given the official title, while Isma'il did all the work and quietly attempted to discredit the younger Ibn al-'Arif before the king.

It may seem incredible that a Muslim king would appoint a Jew as *wazir*, but the Berber rulers of Granada were nothing if not practical, and they were warriors before they were politicians, administrators, or believers. Forty years earlier, when al-Mansur's son, 'Abd al-Malik, had offered Zawi ibn Ziri a position as his *wazir*, Ibn Ziri is said to have answered, "Warfare is our line of work, not administration; our lances are our pens, and fallen bodies are the pages on which we write." But there were other reasons for Isma'il's appointment, even aside from his campaign against Ibn al-'Arif. Then as now the key to a state's success was its capacity to generate revenue, and Isma'il demonstrated a ruthless efficiency in collecting taxes for Habbus. His success was largely the result of his extraordinary administrative and organizational capacities, but he was helped by the fact that a considerable proportion of the kingdom's subjects—particularly in the countryside—were Jews. The overwhelming majority of the people in the capital, by contrast, would have been

Arab-identifying Andalusi Muslims. The rest of the twenty thousand or more inhabitants of the city—it was similar in size to Málaga—were a few hundred Sanhaja warriors and their extended families, a small Christian community, and probably about one thousand Jews. This last number was notably large; Arab geographers referred to the city as "Granada of the Jews." Unlike contemporary Christian Europe, where Jews lived in tiny, marginalized, urban communities and were forbidden from owning land and entering many professions, Jews in the Islamic world were a diverse group, profoundly integrated and spanning the social and vocational spectrums. This worked to Isma'il's advantage; he had the knowledge and skills to wring every penny in taxes he could out of his coreligionists, many of whom were wealthy themselves.

Given the importance of Jews in the kingdom, Isma'il's appointment as *wazir* can also be seen as Habbus's means of satisfying a portion of his population, but it would also have had a more far-reaching purpose. Years later, 'Abd Allah ibn Buluqqin, the deposed and exiled king of Granada, explained his grandfather's motives as follows:

> The Jew [Isma'il] possessed the kind of astuteness and diplomacy that were consonant with the times in which they lived and the people intriguing against them. Badis therefore employed Abu Ibrahim because of his lack of confidence in anyone else and the hostility of his kinsmen. Moreover, Abu Ibrahim was a Jewish *dhimmi* who would not lust after power. Nor was he an Andalusi against whom he needed to be on his guard lest he scheme with non-Berber princes. Badis also needed money with which to placate his kinsmen and maintain his royal position . . .

Habbus understood that to rule Granada, a city with a number of distinct ethnic and religious factions, he needed to play these factions against one another to prevent any from growing too strong. The biggest threat was the enmity between Arabs and Berbers. Despite the stability and prosperity that Zirid rule had produced, many Arabs chafed at being governed by a people they viewed as near-barbarians. Not a few looked longingly to the Zirids' enemies, the 'Abbadids of Seville, who called for the restoration of the old Arab-dominated Umayyad order. The Berbers, for their part, were internally divided and distrustful of the other groups. Indeed, the Zirids ruled the kingdom not as "Berbers" but as one clan among many, and their relations with the other Sanhaja families were

A lute player entertaining women, from *The Story of Bayad and Riyad*,
thirteenth century

complex, especially in the 1020s, after Zawi's departure, the murder of
his sons, and the recriminations that followed. There were also non-
Sanhaja Berbers in Granada, who had a history of bad blood with the
Zirids and whose support of the regime was even more fickle and self-
interested.

Extended family was central to the workings of both Arab and Berber
societies. Unlike the model of primogeniture that would come to dominate in Christian lands, in which power and position was passed down
from father to eldest son, in the so-called Oriental model, authority typically devolved to the senior or eldest member of a broad family group
dominated by a clique of uncles. In the Christian lands, it was politically
advantageous to marry outside of one's family to establish alliances and
thereby increase one's power—a practice the Church supported by passing laws forbidding cousins to marry (though these were often ignored).
In the *dar al-Islam*, the aim was to secure the property of one's family by

marrying within it; marrying one's women to outsiders entailed a loss of property and prestige.* The ideal was for a man to marry his first cousin on his father's side. In cases where a title or position was passed down from father to son, the father was not required to designate his eldest as his heir. He could choose from among his sons, or even skip a generation and select a grandson. But the leader of a clan understood that the decision was not his alone; the opinions of the elders, or sheikhs, would have to be taken into account if the heir was going to enjoy the necessary support.

While this flexibility meant that the most able candidate was often chosen, it also fostered competition among sons. Among Muslims, the practice of polygamy was a further complication. A powerful leader might have up to four wives and many concubines, each of whom could bear him sons eligible to succeed him. The wives and concubines who produced sons, moreover, were rewarded with property and estates, and wielded considerable power, which they used to maneuver a favored son into the position of heir. Conflicts among potential heirs to the throne, and among their mothers, slaves, and dependents—not to mention various allies among the Berber, Andalusi, Christian, and Jewish communities—provided opportunities for collaboration between members of the different communities, but at the same time gave Zirid Granada an instability that not even Habbus's best efforts could put an end to.

"SOAR, DON'T SETTLE . . ."

This was the environment Isma'il ibn Naghrilla stepped into when he moved to Granada sometime before 1020. He soon showed that, in addition to possessing a sharp intellect and impressive linguistic skills, he was a man of natural political instincts. He made himself indispensable to Ibn al-'Arif, as an adviser and secretary of correspondence, as a liaison to the Jewish community, and—most importantly—as an unmatched tax collector. But he stayed in the background, a smart move with the future of the kingdom in doubt. The lingering bitterness Zawi ibn Ziri's

---

* In the European Christian tradition fathers had to offer dowries to prospective husbands in order to marry off their daughters, who were seen as a liability, whereas in the Islamic tradition daughters were seen as a valuable commodity, and could only be obtained by outsiders through the payment of a bride-price.

clan harbored after Habbus's coup was only partially defused by the latter's successes defending Granada on the battlefield. But the real threat was posed by those among Habbus's clan who would stir up trouble, most notably his favorite nephew, Yiddir (or Yaddayr). Habbus had two sons, Badis and Buluqqin. Badis was the heir apparent but Buluqqin was favored by the Sanhaja, and al-Yiddir recruited a party of conspirators, including a number of leading Jews and Isma'il's employer, Ibn al-'Arif, to back the younger prince. Yiddir at one point even counseled Buluqqin to have his brother killed.

In the meantime, Isma'il consolidated his position. He had risen in the estimation of both King Habbus and the Jewish community in Granada and beyond. In 1027 he had been acclaimed as *ha-Nagid*, "the Prince," and in theory held authority over Jews in all of Spain and parts of North Africa; in reality, though, the title involved no formal authority outside of Granada. Whether the title, the first of its kind in Spain, had been granted by the Jewish exilarch in Baghdad—the "official" head of Judaism—or invented by Isma'il himself, he was regarded, and comported himself, as the leader of Andalusi Jewry. He came from a wealthy family from Merida, the Jewish community that claimed to have descended from the Judean nobles the emperor Titus settled in the city in the first century C.E. He was a Levite, a member of the priestly tribe. His educational pedigree, going back to the great Hasdai ibn Shaprut, was unimpeachable. He had all the attributes, in other words, of the small and self-perpetuating Judeo-Arabic elite of al-Andalus: birth, learning, family connections, and money. Owing to his background and talents he had acquired a reputation that reached as far as the 'Abbasid court, and political connections to match. And he did much on behalf of the Jews of the Mediterranean. As Ibn Daud recalled, Isma'il "achieved great good for Israel in Spain, the Maghrib, Ifriqiya, Egypt, Sicily, indeed as far as the academy in Babylonia and the Holy City." He purchased and sent copies of the Torah, the Mishnah, and the Talmud to congregations across the Mediterranean and funded scholarships for young students. The lamps of the synagogues of Jerusalem burned with oil sent from his home in Granada.

Muslim recognition came with his appointment as *wazir* by Habbus in 1037. As the fourteenth-century Muslim historian Ibn 'Idhari would write, "the king raised him above every other rank and dignity." It was unheard of for a Jew to hold such an exalted official position in a Muslim principality. The Qur'an was explicit on this point: *dhimmis* were not to serve in positions of authority over the faithful:

> O you who believe! do not take the Jews and the Christians for
>   friends; they are friends of each other;
> and whoever amongst you takes them for a friend, then surely he is
>   one of them; for surely God does not guide the unjust people.

And yet, the next year Isma'il would have an even greater opportunity in Zirid Granada. When Habbus died in 1038 after sixteen years of effective governance, he was succeeded by Badis, a warrior like his father, but also a dedicated drunkard. Whatever misgivings the new king may have had over confirming a Jew as his prime minister were quickly put to rest. Soon after Badis took the throne, Yiddir's faction, which included several leading Jews, confided to Isma'il their plans to overthrow the new king, in the hope that he would support them. Feigning sympathy, Isma'il invited them to hold their meetings in his palace, but arranged for Badis himself to spy on the conspirators from behind a curtain. Having witnessed the treachery, the enraged king swore he would execute the plotters. Yiddir and others fled to enemy Seville upon learning of their peril. But Isma'il interceded and successfully lobbied for clemency for those who had remained, and in doing so positioned himself as the king's loyal confidant. He also earned the gratitude of the rebels—including his Jewish rivals—for saving their lives.

Isma'il would repeat this tactic on other occasions. In 1053, for instance, as a deliberate affront to Badis, al-Mu'tadid of Seville killed three Berber chieftains under a flag of truce by bricking them up alive within a bathhouse. In retaliation, the Granadan king resolved to massacre the Arabs of his city, who often sympathized with the 'Abbadid cause. Badis's plan was to put them to death as they arrived for Friday prayers at Granada's main mosque. But at noon, the time of prayer, on the appointed day, the mosque was empty; Isma'il had warned the sheikhs to stay away. Badis was furious, but soon realized that his *wazir*'s discretion had saved him from causing great harm to his own kingdom. Badis's esteem for Isma'il grew, and even the pro-Umayyad Arabs of the city felt gratitude toward and had confidence in Isma'il.

Isma'il was a master of dissembling and self-control, of charming his superiors and winning the respect of his enemies. He was praised even

by those who were in principle opposed to his position in a Muslim kingdom. Decades later, as 'Abd Allah ibn Buluqqin composed his apologetic
history of the Zirid kings of Granada, he may have referred to Isma'il on
occasion as "the Jew," but when he referred to him directly, it was as "Abu
Ibrahim," a respectful honorific usually reserved for elders and sheikhs.
Isma'il, for his part, saw his role as nothing short of kingly and prophetic.
A true polymath, he was also the greatest Hebrew poet of his age, and his
favorite subject was himself. His verse reveals both his self-assurance
and his ambition:

> Soar, don't settle for earth
> and sky—soar to Orion;
> and be strong, but not like an ox or mule
> that's driven—strong like a lion.

2

The Rules of the Game

As it turned out, Isma'il both needed and possessed the strength of a lion. Moving from the shadows to the forefront of Granadan administration, he began, in 1038, to accompany Badis and his troops into battle. From 1040 he seems to have risen to the role of field commander, and eventually commander in chief—a Jewish general leading a Muslim army into battle against its Muslim foes. And in the chaotic world of the *taifa* warlords, there was no shortage of enemies. With no universally recognized political authority in al-Andalus, the constantly shifting alliances and rivalries of the petty kingdoms were shaped by self-interest and opportunity. More powerful kings courted weaker ones as allies and clients, until the opportunity to eliminate them and seize their cities presented itself. The same gold that fueled the economy and culture of al-Andalus paid for the loyalty of Berber warriors and the support of the Christian mercenaries and adventurers, who found easy employment among the many warring factions. Although warfare was largely restricted to the ruling classes and cliques and seldom affected ordinary citizens, the regular fighting contributed to a general atmosphere of insecurity and uncertainty in the region, generating anxiety and driving many to doubt the fundamental character of Andalusi society.

The two most serious foreign threats to Isma'il and Badis were Seville and Almería, the kingdom's neighbors to the west and east, and, along with Granada, the strongest of the *taifa* kingdoms of the south. The nature of politics and warfare in this era dictated that the relationship between the king and his *wazir* and their enemies was one of intimate and enduring hatred. Fortunately, Granada was well positioned both to guard its frontiers and to maintain peace and security within them. Isma'il's talent for wringing every last bit of tax revenue out of the populace ensured that the kingdom's treasury was always full, and the fact that the Sanhaja clans had remained united and loyal meant that there was a cohesive and reliable standing army at Badis's disposal.

No sooner had Badis come to power than war broke out with Almería. Known as "the Gateway to the East," the city had been founded in 955 by 'Abd al-Rahman III and had swiftly become one of the major trading centers of the Andalusi coast. After the collapse of the caliphate, palace slaves had established it as a separate kingdom. Zuhayr, a eunuch who had ruled the city since 1028, had been an ally of Badis's father, Habbus, and the two had gone into battle together against their common enemy, Seville. But because Badis was weak and vulnerable at the outset of his reign, and because Zuhayr's Arab *wazir* Ibn 'Abbas hated the idea that either Berbers or Jews would wield power in al-Andalus, the alliance came to an end. Ibn 'Abbas was particularly incensed at the rise of Isma'il, which he viewed as an intolerable aberration. As Isma'il put it in one of his poems,

> his . . . *wazir* observed
> my status with my king, [and] realized
> that all state councils and affairs were in my hands . . .
> they felt resentment over my high rank,
> resolved to see me overthrown at once;
> for how (they said) can aliens like these
> be privileged over Muslim folk . . . ?

Under the influence of Ibn 'Abbas, Zuhayr began to stir up trouble among Granada's allies, and courted Seville. Finally, Almería went on the offensive in 1038 with a large army made up of Berbers, Andalusi forces, and Sudanese slaves.

Badis attempted to make peace, but Ibn 'Abbas was supremely confident, and he and Zuhayr marched their troops across the border. But the

Almerían forces almost immediately found themselves in a treacherous and confusing terrain of scrubby ravines. At Alpuente, Badis's forces struck. Although many fewer in number, they knew the territory and had prepared an ambush. The surprise Granadan onslaught threw the enemy forces into disarray. Zuhayr's own bodyguard of African slaves abandoned him. The retreating Almeríans soon found that a crucial bridge had been destroyed, and that they were trapped. The Granadans, showing none of Isma'il's vaunted, calculating mercy, annihilated them. As he recalled in a celebratory poem,

> We left them lying in the fields to feed
> the jackals, leopards, hyenas, and the boar.

Zuhayr was never seen again, and Ibn 'Abbas was led in chains back to Granada, where to the delight of Isma'il, Badis personally put the defeated *wazir* to death.

Isma'il was certainly present at the fateful battle, although his role in it is not clear. In his poem to commemorate the victory, which he wrote in Hebrew, the entire campaign is framed as an attack by Almería on him and, by extension, on the Jewish people as a whole. He presents himself as the commander of the Granadan forces. But it is unlikely that the newly crowned Badis, a renowned warrior, would have put the campaign in Isma'il's hands. And his contention that the Almeríans' plan was to "wipe out all the Jews" reflects both scriptural convention and Isma'il's own epic sense of self-importance rather than reality. Important as he may have been, Isma'il was not supported by all the Jews of Granada, and there was also a vibrant Jewish community in Almería at the time. Indeed, not long after, Almería apparently also had a Jewish *wazir*. But the poem does reveal two key facts: many Muslims were not comfortable with the idea of a Jew controlling a Muslim kingdom, and this discomfort could be used as a political weapon against Granada.

Whatever his role at Alpuente, there is no doubt that Isma'il became Granada's most important military commander in the years that followed. His life became a constant succession of campaigns against an increasingly aggressive Seville. After Alpuente, Badis attacked Seville and killed the *qadi*-king Abu 'l-Qasim in battle. For the dead king's son and successor, al-Mu'tadid, war against Badis and Isma'il would be a personal affair. When Seville attacked Granada's ally, the tiny Kingdom of Carmona, and the forces that Badis sent in support were defeated, the poet Abu Bakr ibn 'Ammar praised al-Mu'tadid for defeating "those Berber-Jews," the Zirids. Meanwhile, the exiled Granadan prince al-Yiddir and his Muslim and Jewish sympathizers—among them three of Granada's leading rabbis—had taken refuge with al-Mu'tadid. When, in 1041, Isma'il defeated al-Yiddir at the Battle of Arjona, he evoked the scene as follows:

> You [Badis] walk, and your foot treads on back and skull
>   And to your ears the soul of the wounded cries out.
> Here, the guard and the avenger and another loaded with loot.
>   There, another one groaning from his gushing wounds.

Al-Yiddir escaped the battlefield and sought refuge in Córdoba, but the local *taifa* ruler handed him over to Badis as a gesture of goodwill. He spent the rest of his days imprisoned in the castle of Almuñecar, beneath the walls of which he would have heard, if not seen, the gentle lapping of the Mediterranean on the rocks below.

Contemporary Muslim historians recorded few of Isma'il's military exploits, but they figure prominently in his own *diwan*—his collected poetic works—particularly in the volume *Ben Tehellim* ("After the Psalms"). Here, he recalls with relish the defeat and death of Abu 'l-Qasim of Seville and his victories against al-Mu'tadid's forces.

> Tell me, has the body of Ibn Abi Musa [Abu 'l-Qasim] been stabbed?
> And his corpse—is it dragged through the streets and cast away?

And just as his enemies portrayed their struggle in Jewish-Muslim terms, Isma'il styled himself a divinely ordained protector of the Jewish people. Of a battle against Seville he recalled:

> As my foes approached to consume me,
>   I rose and they fell in grief
> And my heart hurt—but the Lord
>   Sent ministering angels to heal me.

And of his defeat of Yiddir:

> . . . by God's sword my troops were successful
> While his followers were cut down by the sword.

Though he did not grow up, like Badis, in a warrior culture, and though he came to generalship later in life, Isma'il rode with his men into battle and on more than one occasion faced capture and near-death. Because his campaigning took a toll on his own physical state and forced him to spend time away from his beloved son, Yusuf, his triumphant, gore-filled verses are balanced by visions of the desolation and loss associated with battle. For Isma'il war was transformed from a beautiful and seductive young girl "with whom everyone wants to flirt" to "a repulsive old whore."

Even as he dealt mercilessly with Granada's foes, Isma'il fought less bloody but still consequential battles at home. As always, the various individuals and factions within the Zirid clan were constantly vying for position. After the mysterious death of Badis's brother Buluqqin, a rivalry between the king's two sons, Buluqqin and Maksan, became prominent; each attracted supporters within the palace and the Sanhaja clans and among the general populace. There were also direct threats to Isma'il's authority from rival officials seeking to rise in Badis's court. The king, however much he trusted Isma'il, had the power of life and death over his officials, including his *wazir*. In his poetry, Isma'il reflected on the nature of political service in the *taifa* era, especially under a personality such as the alcoholic Badis:

> The king's fickleness
>   resembles the drunk's;
> what should anger him pleases—
>   what should please, he debunks.

Isma'il also faced off against Jewish foes, not merely rivals for wealth and influence or those who begrudged his success but those he considered heretics or incompetents. In one poem Isma'il recalls passing a building in Granada and being distracted by what he assumes are the "braying of an ass and the shrieks of oxen." But on entering, he finds it is a synagogue—"a teacher and his students, their heads swaying like palms in the desert." Isma'il was a champion of Rabbinical Judaism, the term for the scholarly interpretation of Scripture and the oral tradition that developed in the centuries following the destruction of the Second Temple by the Romans in 70 C.E. Unlike today, when Rabbinical Judaism is overwhelmingly dominant, in the Middle Ages it did not have a monopoly on Jewish religious thought. It faced serious competition from Qaraism, a tradition that rejected Rabbinical interpretations and focused on the literal observation of Hebrew Scripture, and which the rabbis viewed as heretical. Since both groups, along with the smaller Samaritan sect, were recognized as legitimate by Islamic authorities—both were, in fact, influenced by Islamic thought and philosophy—the proponents of each were left to fight for the hearts and minds of the Jewish faithful. There had likely been Qaraites in al-Andalus for two hundred years by Isma'il's time. The *Nagid* was a fierce partisan in the battle against them, recalling with pride how "Our ancestors had flogged some of them" to death. But in the eleventh century the sect was resurgent, and common enough to be familiar to the contemporary Muslim literary figure and pioneering scholar of comparative religion, Ibn Hazm.

A major doctrinal question in Judaism revolved around the arrival of the Messiah, who was long overdue. Qaraites had rendered the Messiah a nonissue. As far as they were concerned, He may have already come. For Rabbinical Jews, however, the coming of the Messiah would profoundly transform the world, heralding a new age of justice and redress, and making clear Jews' status as the Chosen People. Critics of Jewish messianism of the time, including Christians and Muslims, pointed out that all worldly evidence seemed to indicate that the Jews were unloved by God. While Qaraites and Rabbinical Jews blamed each other for undermining the fate of the Jewish people, anxiety grew in the Rabbinical camp over when the Messiah would appear. During Isma'il's lifetime at least one major Spanish rabbi defected to the Qaraites. But there were reasons for hope. The Christian (Roman) Empire had long ago disappeared, and now the fall of the Umayyad Caliphate of Córdoba and the decline of the 'Abbasid Caliphate in Baghdad seemed to be signs that Edom—the biblical enemy of Israel—would be destroyed and the messianic age would soon begin.

In the Mediterranean world of the mid-eleventh century, if there was anyone who seemed to be a possible Messiah of the Jews, it was Isma'il ibn Naghrilla. A theological authority, scholar, poet, general, and a king in all but name, he was at once a prophet, a warrior, and a singer of songs. With all the modesty of a king, Isma'il declared, "I am the David of my day," and in other poems he inhabited the roles of Samuel the Prophet, Levi the priest, Assaf the writer of psalms, and Mordecai the astute statesman. His battle poems are rife with biblical imagery; he portrays himself not as an infidel official in one of a number of petty Islamic kingdoms, leading a motley Berber cavalry against their Andalusi Muslim rivals in the name of power and profit, but as marshaling Israel against the Amalekites and Philistines in the name of God. Isma'il's conviction that he had a divine purpose on Earth had apparently first appeared in his youth. If Ibn Hazm is to be believed, when he was still living in Córdoba the teenage Isma'il had disclosed to him that he, Isma'il, was nothing less than the Redeemer foretold in the Book of Genesis.

TOLERANCE AND TENSION

Abu Muhammad 'Ali ibn Ahmad ibn Sa'id ibn Hazm, to whom Isma'il confessed this rather important news, was only a few months younger than Isma'il ibn Naghrilla. He, too, had been born into the highest circles of the Córdoban elite and educated in religion, literature, language, and philosophy. Like Isma'il he demonstrated an undeniable and precocious genius, and was seemingly destined for a life among the powerful. The only major differences were that he was a Muslim, a full member of Andalusi society, and had been raised within the confines of al-Mansur's palace, Madinat al-Zahara.

For Ibn Hazm the destruction of the caliphate and the emergence of the *taifa* kingdoms did not represent hope or opportunity, only loss, the shattering of an order that had ensured justice in the world around him. During the *taifa* period he would become an outcast, admired for his learning but constantly running afoul of the political authorities, whom he considered illegitimate by nature. He became a fervent champion of the revival of the Umayyad Caliphate—a cause that landed him in prison on more than one occasion—and an advocate for the restoration of a true Islamic society, one in which, following the dictates of Scripture, Jews and Christians would be secondary, subject peoples.

But Ibn Hazm was no reactionary crank. If, as contemporaries contended, Isma'il emerged as the greatest Hebrew poet of his time, Ibn

Hazm was the greatest Arabic poet of the same period. His major work on love and passion, *The Dove's Necklace*, is perhaps the single most important work of Hispano-Arabic literature. In addition, he wrote some four hundred treatises on Islamic law, philosophy, and history, and produced what has been heralded as the first study of comparative religion in history. Although as an outspoken dissident he was forbidden by the authorities from taking on students, his fame as a writer and thinker rose to proverbial heights across Islamic Spain during his lifetime. And he was nothing if not cosmopolitan. He grew up alongside the wealthy and influential *dhimmis* of the caliphal court in Córdoba. He knew the Gospels and the Torah, and had spent a lifetime conversing with Jews and Christians. Yet late in his life he would write a major critique aimed at Isma'il in particular and Jews in general.

The two met at least once, though if Ibn Hazm's account of Isma'il's confession of his prophetic mission is true, the two had some sort of rapport that bespeaks a deeper relationship. This would not be surprising, as both were immersed in Arabo-Islamic culture, which embodied all that was modern and sophisticated in the eleventh-century Mediterranean world. It was the culture of the elite, and even those who were in principle excluded from participating fully because of their religious identity were drawn toward it and welcomed into it. Unlike in Islamic society, where the religious, political, and cultural elites were diverse, in Jewish society a handful of ancient families dominated all aspects of life. That Isma'il and his peers and elders considered themselves a class above their fellow Jews allowed them to live simultaneously as Muslim courtiers and Jewish rabbis, despite the incredible self-contradictions that this involved.

Ibn Hazm and Isma'il would have each enjoyed the lifestyle of the Islamic elite. The upper classes across the Arabo-Islamic world at the time cultivated ideals of sumptuous spending and sensual abandon. Quranic prohibitions and pious sensibilities notwithstanding, well-to-do Muslims wore dazzling outfits and drank wine by the pitcher. Islamic prescriptions of chastity and restraint meant little, undermined as they were by the easy availability of inexpensive slave girls and a Helleno-Persian eroticization with young men. Fine foods from around the world arrived in the local markets, and raiding and trade ensured a bottomless supply of slaves and concubines. Music was becoming more complex at the time, but poetry was the premier art form. For the privileged few, it embodied Heaven on Earth. Emblematic of the upper reaches of Arabo-Islamic culture was the "wine party," an occasion when a group of men would while the night away in a garden or on a riverbank as they were served food and drink by young male servants and cavorted with slave girls and adolescent boys. As one contemporary poet described such an event:

> In the morning dark
>   feelings of desire
> whirled round us, spheres
>   of dalliance and pleasure . . .
> Red wine, then mounds of myrtle
>   for our pillows.
> We looked like kings
>   on our green thrones . . .
> Love was stringing beads
>   for our merrymaking.
> We were the pearls,
>   endearing words the strands.

The guests would pass the night in pleasant delirium, talking, reciting poetry, and extemporizing their own compositions, satirical or serious.

Isma'il and his Jewish peers often hosted such gatherings, held in both Hebrew and Arabic. Isma'il himself devoted verse to these nights of passion and transcendence:

> The eyes of the young lad who has served me have ravished
>   my heart,
>   His master has been captured without a net.
> Though waters can quench the fires of love,
>   My desire for you is yet like a flame within me.

And

> When he said: "Bring me down honey from your swarm of bees,"
>   I replied: "Kiss me with your sweet tongue."
> Whereupon he became angry and with ill-temper spoke: "Shall
>   we sin
>   Before the living God!" I replied: "Your sin be upon me, my lord!"

Coin (front and back) minted under the rule of Badis ibn Habbus, 1038–73

The homoeroticism (or rather, ephebophilism—eroticism centered specifically on adolescent boys) in the poetry composed by Isma'il and other Jewish poets illustrates the degree to which they had adopted the values and
aspirations of the Arabo-Islamic elite, however much these seem to clash
with their self-proclaimed status as guardians of Jewish faith and morality.*

Far from being considered effeminate or effete, poetic talent was seen
as a masculine virtue, and control of language and intellectual dexterity
were held to be indispensable characteristics in leaders. Isma'il and his
Jewish peers did not see themselves as Jews who occasionally acted as
Muslims in order to fulfill their functions at court, but as members of an
Arabic-speaking courtier class that transcended their religious identity.
Indeed, this membership reinforced rather than contradicted their role
as leaders of their own communities, and powerful Jewish officials and
intellectuals had colleagues, dependents, and admirers among their
Muslim counterparts, for whom Jewishness was often hardly an issue. Of
Isma'il, the poet Ibn al-Fara wrote,

* Our modern notions of heterosexuality and homosexuality are cultural constructs;
through much of the world (including, until recently, in Europe), the erotic attraction of
men to adolescent boys is not necessarily considered "homosexual"—rather, being "on
top" is what marks masculinity. Ephebophilia was either openly celebrated or uncom-
fortably condoned in the premodern Mediterranean and Western Asian worlds. Indeed,
in 2009 Archbishop Silvano Tomasi, the Vatican's envoy to the United Nations, noted
that clerical sexual abuse was a manifestation not of pedophilia but ephebophilia (whatever little comfort that might give the victims).

Seek his welfare and find hope and success
See in his chamber the loveliness of the sun in Aries [the god of war]
Never has a friend found in him fault . . .

Another poet, al-Munfatil, identified Isma'il's Jewishness as the only minor flaw in an otherwise unblemished character:

You exceed in generosity the people of East and West as pure gold exceeds the value of bronze. If people could distinguish error from truth, they'd kiss naught but your ten fingertips! They'd embrace your hands like the [Ka'aba's] Black Cornerstone . . .

Despite the lack of religious prejudice among the elite, everyone involved in Andalusi politics was in a delicate position; the danger of betrayal was constant, temperamental kings could execute subordinates at will, and a misstep could mean not only death but the destruction of one's family. Politics was a cutthroat profession in the most literal sense. There were many kings, officials, poets, and theologians of all religions whose careers ended in death, sometimes for the most arbitrary reasons. In case the message was lost on anyone, al-Mu'tadid, Badis's enemy in Seville, kept a garden in which the skulls of his enemies were arranged as planters, each labeled by name and sprouting flowers. Moderation and discretion were necessary for survival. An overly successful official could provoke the envy and suspicion of a king, or might tempt a ruler to destroy him so as to seize his fortune. No one was to be trusted. Isma'il knew this better than most, and his proverbs and poems abound with advice to the would-be courtier:

Respect and discretion
    will lead to wealth
and bring the way on
    to power . . .

And

The foolish enemy's face tells all—
    but the clever's deceives and offers you smiles
and talks as though his heart was with yours,
    and acts like your friend or your child.

By exercising public authority in a Muslim kingdom, Jews and Christians were defying the spirit if not the word of the Qur'an. Hence Isma'il's and Badis's enemies focused on the *wazir*'s Jewishness as a means of discrediting the Zirid dynasty as a whole. The 'Abbadid court of Seville became a hotbed of anti-Granadan poetry, much of it centered on the fact that Isma'il was Jewish and that Badis, because he had elevated him to *wazir*, was a traitor to Islam. To more thoroughly discredit Isma'il, Jews in general were vilified in this literature. But they were not particularly hated in Seville and elsewhere in al-Andalus. The 'Abbadid kings welcomed the rebellious rabbis who fled Badis, and Seville's Jewish community was significantly larger than that of Granada. And then there was the case of the Jewish *wazir* of Almería, who was appointed after the death of Zuhayr. To be fair, this individual was murdered in a public bath by a pious Muslim—though not because of his status as an official, but because he had been seen dallying with a young Muslim slave boy. In many other cases, attacks both literary and physical were expressed in sectarian terms when, in fact, their motives were purely personal. For example, the Islamic magistrate Abu Ishaq of Lorca wrote a venomous poetical tract against Isma'il's son, Yusuf. Behind this was not religious conviction or a long-standing hatred of Jews. Abu Ishaq had been a political rival of Yusuf's, and under Yusuf's influence, Badis had ordered the *qadi* into exile. In response, the poet shamed the Granadan king for employing a Jew and inverting God's order, turning a deep personal hatred into a religious and political platform.

> Go, tell all the Sanhaja . . .
> Your chief has made a mistake . . .
> He has chosen an infidel as his secretary
>   when he could, had he wished, have chosen a Believer.
> Through him, the Jews have become great and proud
>   and arrogant—they, who were among the most abject . . .
> Their chief ape has marbled his house
>   and led the finest spring water to it.
> Our affairs are now in his hands
>   and we stand at his door.
> He laughs at us and at our religion
>   and we return to our God.
> If I said that his wealth is as great
>   as yours, I would speak the truth.

Hasten to slaughter him as an offering,
   sacrifice him, for he is a fat ram
And do not spare his people
   for they have amassed every precious thing.

At some point, it came to Ibn Hazm's attention that Isma'il had had the temerity to write a polemical tract attacking Islam. To Ibn Hazm this must have seemed beyond the pale. A Jew, a member of the subject peoples who prospered thanks only to the largesse of Islam, and who was as wealthy and powerful as a king and proudly lorded over Muslims, had insulted and undermined the True Faith. In Ibn Hazm's eyes, Isma'il's tract was nothing short of an attack by Judaism on Islam.

Ibn Hazm responded in an essay portraying Judaism as inherently inconsistent and the Rabbinical elite as deceivers. Focusing on the Torah and the Talmud, he enumerated a series of contradictions and aberrations. These included the illicit sexual relationships that so many of the Prophets were either said to have engaged in or been the offspring of, including Moses (born to his own aunt), Abraham (who married his sister, Sarah), and Solomon (born out of David's adultery); the idolatry practiced by Solomon; and passages in the Torah in which God has a human form. Once he established the incoherence and duplicity of Judaism, Ibn Hazm turned explicitly against Isma'il: "A man who was filled with hatred towards the Apostle [Muhammad]—a man who is, in secret, a materialist, a freethinker, a Jew—of that most contemptible of religions, the most vile of faiths . . ."

But we cannot be certain that Isma'il even wrote an anti-Muslim tract in the first place. Ibn Hazm admitted that he had not seen the text in question, but rather had been given an essay written by a Muslim that had refuted it, and in the process described Isma'il's arguments in detail. In fact, it is unlikely that someone as circumspect as Isma'il, his immense pride and power notwithstanding, would be so rash as to publish an anti-Muslim pamphlet. It may have been written by someone else in Isma'il's name, or it may have been an invention of the anonymous polemicist who had inspired Ibn Hazm.

In the attempt to understand Ibn Hazm's response to Isma'il's perceived attack, it is important to note that there was a deeply ingrained tradition of religious polemic common to the three major faiths in the Mediterranean. Muslims, Christians, and Jews had to defend their religious beliefs against one another and against those whom they perceived as heretics within their own communities. Religious authorities became quite adept at attacking the scriptures of other faiths, and in the most aggressive and incisive terms—they knew one another's faiths intimately, and like bickering siblings, they knew precisely how to push one another's buttons. Within the Islamic world, it was both illegal and dangerous for Jews to directly attack Islam (although they were free to attack Christianity). Jews were expected by Muslims to be humble and submissive, and Jewish thinkers chafed at their humiliation as often as Muslim thinkers enjoyed reminding them of it. In the polemical literature, this was idealized as submission and humility, although this was not normally expected in daily social interaction. Yet during times of crisis or tension Islamic demagogues could harness popular indignation by appealing to the notion that all Jews were beneath even the lowest of Muslims, and that the entire Jewish community needed to be reminded of their base status.

The fulminations of the courtiers of Seville, of Abu Ishaq, and of Ibn Hazm against Isma'il were nonetheless exceptions to the rule. They were not symptomatic of a widespread hatred of Jews on the part of Muslims, but rather of these individuals' personal hatred of Isma'il, and more concretely their conflicting political aims. Jew though he may have been, Isma'il was considered a great man by many Muslims. The contemporary Ibn Hayyan, regarded as the greatest historian of Islamic Spain, described the *wazir* as follows: "This accursed Jew was in himself one of the most perfect men." After enumerating Isma'il's many skills and his knowledge of Islam and Arabic, Ibn Hayyan concluded, "And he was wise; he spoke little . . . although he thought much."

THE IMPOSSIBLE DREAM

Isma'il died in 1056, shortly after returning from yet another military campaign. He would have been sixty-four, exhausted after a life of warfare, politics, and scholarship. As his end approached, both he and his admirers would have transferred any hopes for the dawn of a messianic age from himself to his son and protégé. Yusuf had been born on September 15, 1035, and his father endeavored to raise him in his own mold. He was educated in Hebrew and Arabic, and in the Jewish and Islamic traditions. Isma'il's palace in Granada doubled as a salon and an academy, where the *wazir* gathered Jewish thinkers and writers from al-

The Fountain of the Lions, a possible remnant of Yusuf ibn Naghrilla's
al-Hamra' Palace

Andalus and beyond. As the Exilarchy of Baghdad fell apart, it was to
Isma'il's home in Granada that the two sons of Rabbi Hezekial, the last
exilarch, fled. His palace became a hothouse of theological dispute,
scientific speculation, and literary innovation. Its library of Jewish works
was regarded as without equal. Just about every major Jewish poet of the
following generation enjoyed Isma'il's patronage; as Ibn Daud put it, if
"in the age of Rabbi Hasdai the *Nasi* the bards began to twitter, in the
days of Rabbi Samuel the Nagid they burst into song." Yusuf was his father's son: in the years after the latter's death, the salon of the Naghrillas
remained the cultural center of Jewish al-Andalus. While Yusuf did not
inherit his father's poetic talent, he edited his father's work and wrote
short introductions (in Arabic) to each of the poems, when he was not
patronizing scholars and enlarging the great library's holdings.

Yusuf was dear to his father, whose poetry records the grief of separa-
tion resulting from the demands of Isma'il's military career. When he
was on campaign in 1044 and Yusuf, age eight, fell ill with boils, Isma'il's

subordinates kept the news secret so as not to distract him from his duties. When he was finally told, the *Nagid* dispatched a poem to his son:

I'm sick with the service of kings
    who are ready only for war,
and live for a letter from your right hand,
    with news of your cure.

It was customary at the time for very young princes to accompany their fathers to war. The goal was to inure boys to the traumas and dangers of battle and prepare them for command. Once his son had recovered from his illness, Isma'il did take Yusuf with him on campaign, but the boy grew homesick and was sent back to Granada, never to repeat the experience. Yusuf's only surviving poem was written on the occasion of his return: "I was taken with him when he went on a mission to fight . . . but my soul longed for home and my loved ones and I wrote these four verses . . . and he helped me with them." It was an early sign that Yusuf might not live up to his father's legacy. According to Ibn Daud, "Of all the fine qualities which his father possessed he lacked but one. Having been raised in wealth and never having had to bear a burden of responsibility in his youth, he lacked his father's humility. Indeed, he grew haughty—to his destruction."

When Isma'il died, Yusuf was appointed his successor as *Nagid*, and was the natural candidate to succeed him as *wazir*. Badis had his misgivings, however; Yusuf was only twenty-one, and untested. So Badis and Yusuf together pressured a former *wazir*, 'Ali ibn al-Qarawi, himself a convert from Judaism, to pose as a "front" for Yusuf. At first the collaboration worked, but soon Yusuf began to see al-Qarawi as an impediment to his own promotion. At Yusuf's prompting, Badis was persuaded to depose 'Ali and confiscate his fortune; Yusuf then set out to destroy his family. The Sanhaja were incensed, as they had supported al-Qarawi, and saw Yusuf's actions as an attack on their status and position. Unlike his father, who had delicately cultivated the trust of the various Muslim factions in the kingdom, Yusuf focused his energies solely on Badis and his heir Buluqqin, heedless of his father's advice about the trustworthiness of kings, and confident that his ability to squeeze tax revenues out of the kingdom's Jewish subjects would make him indispensable.

But resentment within the Zirid harem, stoked by the al-Qarawi family, turned Buluqqin against Yusuf, and in response the new *wazir* subtly began to discredit the heir apparent before his father, and to appeal to the younger brother, Maksan, as a patron. When Buluqqin suddenly died in December 1064, Yusuf was widely regarded as responsible; it was rumored that the prince had been passed a poisoned cup by Yusuf at a drinking party hosted by the *wazir*. Whatever the truth, the fact that Yusuf was publicly blamed shows the degree to which opinion within the court and among the populace had turned against him.

The death of his elder son plunged Badis further into drunkenness; this, coupled with Yusuf's reluctance to lead the army, emboldened Granada's long-standing enemy Seville to attack. In Granada, the power vacuum in the military allowed a former African slave named al-Naya, who had defected from al-Mu'tamid of Seville, to challenge Yusuf's position at court. In addition, with his own army losing its cohesion and effectiveness, Badis began to admit Zanata Berber refugees into the kingdom, upsetting the delicate balance the Sanhaja and the Arab Andalusis had achieved. Al-Naya inveigled himself into Badis's trust, and during one drinking session persuaded the inebriated king to order the *wazir*'s execution. Yusuf was able to escape death when the spies he had among the king's slaves alerted him to the plot, but he still lost his official status as *wazir*.

Yusuf's new hope for a patron was an unlikely one: Maksan, who blamed him for killing his brother. To make matters worse, Maksan's mother began to plot with Yusuf's own father-in-law against Badis. When the conspiracy was uncovered, at Yusuf's prompting Badis had Maksan's mother—one of his own wives—put to death. (It was left to the ex-*wazir* to punish the Jewish conspirators.) The king already disliked his second son, and as was his prerogative, he disqualified Maksan as a successor, designating instead his grandson, Tamim, the son of Buluqqin, as heir to the throne. Yusuf encouraged rumors that Maksan was planning to overthrow his father, and as a result the prince was condemned to be executed, a fate he avoided by fleeing the kingdom. At this point, Yusuf hoped that when Tamim eventually succeeded Badis, he would restore him to power in gratitude for his role in the removal of Maksan.

Yusuf turned to the elders of the Jewish community for advice. They counseled him to prepare quietly for exile by sending his wealth abroad. But what king would defy the powerful Zirids and shelter him? It would have never occurred to Yusuf to move north to a Christian kingdom. For Yusuf, flight was not an option. Not only would it be risky, but his aban-

donment of Granada would signal a colossal personal failure and an end
to his father's dreams and ambitions for him. These must have weighed
heavily on Yusuf, who knew the poem Isma'il had written to him when
he was no more than seven:

Yehosef, all that I carry and endure
And all for the sake of which I expose myself is for your sake,
Were it not for you I would go through the world
And live like many others in your time.

Yusuf decided on a daring plan. He secretly made overtures to Ibn Sumadih al-Mu'tasim, the *taifa* king of Almería, an ally of Badis. The proposal
was simple: if Ibn Sumadih would march his army against Granada,
Yusuf would see to it that the city would be left undefended and that its
gates would be open. As Yusuf envisioned it, the Almerían would
occupy the capital and he would rule in their name as king—a new
Solomon. Having set this sequence in motion, Yusuf then committed his
final betrayal.

Owing to their memory of his father and resentment of the interlop-
ing al-Naya, the most powerful Sanhaja warriors still supported Yusuf.
In the lead-up to the Almerían incursion, he convinced Badis that the
kingdom's frontier defenses had become weak, and advised the king to
appoint his allies as wardens of the border castles. The king assented,
and, grateful to Yusuf for what they believed were important assign-
ments, the key Sanhaja military leaders left the capital for the countryside. Meanwhile, Ibn Sumadih's forces began their march from Almería.
But as they entered Granadan territory, they were reminded of their
stunning defeat at Alpuente. When the army stopped at the Castle of
Cabrera, less than a day's march from Granada, Ibn Sumadih sent his
scouts to reconnoiter the city. Returning, they described towering walls
and stalwart gates, and the king of Almería lost his nerve—he would
advance no farther. Yusuf sent messages urging him forward, and retreated with his family to the safety of his fortified residence on the Red
Hill. Refusing to believe that the battle had been lost, he gathered his
faithful slaves and clients for a celebration, drunkenly regaling them
with visions of the fortunes that would soon be theirs. Soon enough, the
fury of the Muslim populace would be unleashed on Yusuf and the Jews
of Granada on a Saturday night in December 1066.

WHAT IF THERE WAS A POGROM AND NOBODY CAME?

In the 1960s, the historian Eliyahu Ashtor famously described the massacre in Granada as follows:

> All the resentment and hatred of the masses were vented that Sabbath morning . . . the mob of Andalusians who assembled the next morning were dissolutes thirsting for blood and loot . . . They crossed the Darro and with terrifying shrieks, broke into Jewish quarters. A group of young men tried to block the path at the entrances to the Jewish sector, but their desperate opposition intensified the passion of the Moslems . . . They smashed wooden doors with their axes and people were dragged, frightened and shivering, to be beheaded by a sword blow. The mob watched with enjoyment . . . Here an old man was stabbed, there a woman was hung from a beam; here a rapist violated a woman while his companion ravished her daughter, and when they were sated, they slaughtered both; the beheaded corpses of infants were everywhere. The bodies of men lay with bellies split asunder and weltered in their own blood; close by small girls lay dying, quivering in final, convulsive jerks . . . The rioters came and went for hours, having donkeys with them on which to load the valuables, and not ceasing until they divested the houses of every worthwhile thing . . . On that Black Sabbath hundreds of Jews of Granada were murdered.

Ashtor's account, sensational and moving, was almost wholly the product of his own imagination. Nevertheless, it was widely accepted in its time as reflecting historical reality, and the pogrom against Granada's Jews was seen as an anti-Jewish uprising and a major turning point in Muslim-Jewish relations in al-Andalus and more generally. But in fact we do not know how many people, aside from Yusuf, were killed that night, or who they were. In later life 'Abd Allah ibn Buluqqin, our only eyewitness to the event, who was thirteen years old at the time, laconically wrote, "The Jew turned and fled for his life inside the palace pursued by the populace, who finally ran him down and did him to death. They then turned their swords on every Jew in the city and seized vast quantities of their goods and chattels." 'Abd Allah, who had reigned as the last Zirid king of Granada, wrote this while a prisoner of the Almoravids, and would have had good reason to exaggerate the massacre.

Moreover, he hated Yusuf, whom he referred to as "the pig" throughout his memoir—not because he had been a Jew, but because 'Abd Allah believed he had poisoned his father, Buluqqin. Ibn Daud is also vague on the particulars of the supposed massacre: "The Berber princes became so jealous of [Yusuf] that he was killed on the Sabbath day, the ninth of Tebet 4827, along with the community of Granada and all of those who had come from distant lands to see his learning and power." Ibn 'Idhari, a Moroccan historian writing two hundred years after the events in question, devoted four lines of his monumental history of the Islamic West to the incident, putting the death toll at "more than three thousand." But like all the figures given by medieval chroniclers, this is without question a significant exaggeration.

There can be little doubt that many innocents died that night, some for no other reason than that they happened to be Jews. But Granada's Jewish community, which may have numbered less than a thousand, was not annihilated. There were several high-profile survivors, including Yusuf's wife, his son Azariah, the sons of Hezekial the exilarch, and a noted rabbi, Isaac ben Baruk. Of the fate of the common Jews, we know almost nothing—the elites who wrote chronicles cared little for common people and provided no details—except that there were evidently many refugees in the aftermath of the riots. There is evidence, moreover, that the community was revived: Rabbi Isaac returned to the city when he retired from public life, dying peacefully there in 1094, and Moses ibn Ezra, the great philosopher and linguist, was born in Granada only a few years after Yusuf's death. Although Azariah and his mother may have fled, they did not leave the kingdom but took refuge in the city of Lucena, just to the west; when the young heir to the Naghrilla name died shortly thereafter, it was from natural causes. Most of the refugees, it seems, fled to the Granadan countryside, or farther afield, to Seville, Almería, and Zaragoza, all of which had vibrant Jewish communities. Interestingly, although Córdoba was home for Rabbi Isaac, immediately following the riots he moved to Seville, where he entered the service of the Zirids' enemy al-Mu'tamid. For all the anti-Jewish propaganda produced by the court of Seville, in reality the 'Abbadid kings welcomed Jews and supported the local Jewish community. Those Jews who stayed in the Zirid kingdom did not live in fear of further violence; through the 1070s and 1080s they remained confident, even threatening rebellion when they felt that the burden of taxation fell unfairly on them.

In short, the riots were not seen at the time as cataclysmic for Jews, nor as signifying a new arrangement between Jews and Muslims in al-Andalus. It was a local political event and a terrible tragedy, but one that was understandable to contemporaries: Yusuf was a powerful official who had betrayed his king and his city. In any event, tensions had likely been building for some time. His living arrangements, for instance, pushed beyond the boundaries of what Islamic society thought acceptable for a Jew. Yusuf's luxurious *al-Hamra'* Palace, with its gardens and streams, its marble facing, and its energetic court of scholars and ambassadors, had overshadowed the fortress residence of the Berber kings both in size and in culture. When Isma'il had been there to manage the kingdom's financial administration, direct the military, and keep the ethnic, religious, and political parties of Granada in equilibrium, such an apparent affront to the ruling clique was tolerable. But Yusuf was not his father.

Nor was the riot a symptom of pervasive anti-Jewish sentiment. As non-Muslims, Jews were by definition a subordinate group, but they were not widely despised. The attacks on Judaism by Abu Ishaq, Ibn Hazm, and the 'Abbadid court poets were rooted in mundane motives, not in an ideology of anti-Judaism. There is no indication that the Jews of Granada and al-Andalus took the event as the start of a general shift in Muslim opinion or policy toward them—there was no exodus of refugees from al-Andalus to Christian lands, for instance.

In reality, the events of 1066 were little more than politics as usual in the world of the *taifas*. That the Naghrillas were Jewish was largely incidental; many Muslim officials suffered the same fate. Nor was it uncommon for innocents to die in such upheavals; in Córdoba after the death of Sanjul in 1009, the Berber soldiers' wives and children bore the brunt of the Andalusis' rage. Moreover, the Naghrillas' claims to be the protectors and patrons of the Jews of Granada had the unfortunate consequence of implicating their community, however unfairly, in their transgressions. And Yusuf's sin was a cardinal one. It was worse than high treason or attempted regicide; had the armies of Ibn Sumadih entered the city, much of the Muslim population (and most likely a good number of Jews) would have seen their homes sacked and their wives and children killed or carried off as slaves. The rage at Yusuf's betrayal would have been overwhelming. At the same time, those Muslims who believed that Jews were untrustworthy and inferior, who envied the success of the Naghrillas, or who merely saw an excuse to plunder the homes of their wealthy Jewish neighbors, might have been eager to exploit the opportunity Yusuf's misstep had provided. Notably, though, Jews were not alone in suffering in the reprisals against Yusuf; the *wazir*'s Muslim and Christian allies and dependents were also forced to flee the city or face execution.

Yusuf's nemesis and successor as *wazir*, the Muslim al-Naya, did not fare much better than he. In the aftermath of the riots, the kingdom lurched toward disaster. Guadix, the Kingdom of Granada's most important town in the east, had been seized by Ibn Sumadih. Málaga, on the coast, and Jaen, to the north, were each on the verge of rebellion, and Seville was poised to exploit any weakness. Al-Naya at first was a source of stability. He managed to recuperate Guadix, repress the rebellions, and launch a series of successful raids against the neighboring *taifa* kingdoms. However, he made enemies among the Sanhaja, not the least because of his recruitment of Zanata soldiers for the kingdom's army.

Soon it was rumored that he was planning to overthrow the aging and alcoholic Badis. Now it was al-Naya who was suspected of betraying his city, and a group of grandees, including members of his own inner circle, resolved to assassinate him. Wasil of Guadix, a Mozarab Christian aristocrat who was a trusted protégé, lured the *wazir* to his palace. The two friends sat down for an evening of drinking, and al-Naya felt so at ease that he dismissed his bodyguards. When the *wazir* succumbed to the effects of the wine, Wasil brutally thrust a lance through him. The next day al-Naya's severed head was paraded through the city—a fate little different from Yusuf's.

The rise of the Naghrillas, only one of many Jewish minidynasties that briefly flourished and declined in *taifa*-era al-Andalus, tells us much about the openness, optimism, and confidence of the Islamic society of the medieval Mediterranean in the twelfth century, in which Jews and Muslims, at least at the level of the elite, became profoundly interlinked and interdependent. The riots of Granada, meanwhile, remind us of the contingencies of these relations and how they were shaped by the distinct political situation of a given kingdom.

Above all, Isma'il's ascent and the sequence of events that led to his son's death demonstrate that al-Andalus cannot be understood merely on Jewish-Muslim terms. The Muslim and Jewish societies of al-Andalus were complex and divided, and the tumultuous political environment of the time encouraged Muslims and Jews to reach out across the confessional aisle in search of allies to help defeat rivals within their own communities. It was ultimately common bigotry, pride, envy, greed, and fear that brought about the fall of Yusuf and the suffering of the Granadan Jews, not an intolerant culture or society.

The lust for power that did define al-Andalus at the time would bring about the decline and fall of Zirid Granada and the rest of the *taifa* kingdoms only twenty-four years after Yusuf's death. Their destruction would come not at the hands of Christian enemies or Jewish subversives, but as a result of the *jihad* of the North African Almoravids, fearsome Sanhaja warriors on a mission to depose the decadent, squabbling rulers of al-Andalus. In the meantime, in twelfth-century Islamic Spain, a Jew could indeed dream of becoming a king, but in striving to realize this dream he would gamble the fate of his family and his community. Such were the rules of the game.

PART II

A Christian Sultan in the Age of "the Reconquest"

3

The Cid Rides Again

The year is 1102. An immense train of horses, carts, and donkeys, heavily laden with bundles of clothes and bedding, household items, candelabras, statues of saints, and even furniture, trailed by a long line of men, women, and children, snakes its way slowly up a winding pass toward the crest of a great escarpment. Near the head of the procession, just behind a detachment of chain-mailed and helmeted horsemen, rides a richly garbed group. Red pennants flutter on the long lances as the knights of the vanguard struggle to keep upright as their steeds clamber up the rocky trail. Behind them rides an old but rigid man bearing the embroidered ensign of an emperor on his gleaming mail. At his side is a woman, the Lady Ximena. Perhaps she is on horseback, or perhaps, burdened by her age and grief, and as a sign of her station, she is being carried on a palanquin. Regardless, following her is a heavy casket bearing the desiccated, three-year-dead corpse of her husband, pitching and heaving against the sides of a cart.

Reaching the top of the ridge, they would have paused, and the lady must have turned to cast one long and regretful look at what until that very morning had been her city. Most likely it was one of those intense sunny days of late spring in Spain. If so, with the sun behind her, she would have had a clear view over a broad expanse of lush plain, fields of undulating wheat punctuated by the iridescent white of almond bloom, orange blossoms and date palms clustered around the waterwheels that churned and groaned as they had for centuries. Far beyond lay the shimmering blue of the Mediterranean, and just before land became sea, the formidable walls, towers, and minarets of a city now consumed by bright flames and billowing black smoke. According to a poet, a decade earlier and accompanied by her two daughters the lady had descended the same path, younger and happier, to take up residence in this city, Valencia.

Somewhere in the distance, one can picture another group of riders. Perched on compact barb horses, wrapped in black cloaks, with veils drawn across their geometrically tattooed, blue-dye-smudged faces, they would have gazed impassively at the column of Christian refugees disappearing over the ridge, and then turned toward the burning city and the streams of Muslim common folk issuing from its gates. Would they have cursed in their melodic Zanaga—the tongue of the nomads of the southwestern fringes of the Sahara—the Christian lady who had ordered the city to be burned? Or would they have spat contempt for those weak-willed and degenerate "Arabs," who for five years had consented to be ruled by an infidel, and who were now suffering for their lack of faith and resolve? A week or so later, on May 5, 1102, the commander, Mazdali ibn Tilankan, an Almoravid prince and general, would ride into Valencia and make it his own. He had at last vanquished in death the enemy he could not defeat in life: Rodrigo.

Such details may be conjecture, but beneath them lies a kernel of truth. For five years, a knight and soldier of fortune, born of the lower nobility in a then poor and backward Castile, had ruled Islamic Valencia as sultan. Rodrigo Díaz de Vivar had been the most feared and respected warrior south of the Pyrenees. But few called him by that name; he was better known as *Sayyidi*, "my lord" in Arabic, which the Christians parroted as "Cid," and *Campi doctor*, or "the master of the battlefield" in Latin, which the Muslims garbled as "al-Kanbitur" and the Castilians as "Campeador." Undoubtedly the single most famous figure of medieval Spain, he has long been the stuff of legend. In life, he was hailed as both a valiant savior and a barbarous traitor by Muslims and Christians alike. Within a century of his death, the epic *Song of My Cid*, together with many other tales, would be sung in noble courts and around campfires across the peninsula, glorifying and distorting his exploits. The *Song* presented the Cid as a proud paladin, a hero of Christendom, and a fierce defender of his daughters' besmirched honor. But this, too, was fiction. To understand how this enigmatic figure emerged as the first and only Christian *taifa* king of al-Andalus requires disentangling the man from his legend.

LEGEND AND HISTORY

In his most recent incarnation, in Anthony Mann's 1961 film *El Cid*, Rodrigo Díaz de Vivar is a progressive Hollywood patriot in anachronistic fourteenth-century armor played by Charlton Heston. He is a figure propelled by his honor into reluctant violence. Professing to be weary of war with his Muslim neighbors and hankering, like Cold War America, only for détente, he is a secular pragmatist who respects Arabo-Islamic culture and treats his Muslim allies as near-equals. A man of honor, not superstition, and a proud individualist, Heston and Mann's Cid would sooner fight an unscrupulous or cowardly Christian to the death than betray a brave and righteous Muslim. This portrayal of the Cid and of his world is rooted in the work of the Spanish historian Ramón Menéndez Pidal, who coined the term *convivencia* (and who advised on the film). Later, the historian Américo Castro popularized the word, giving rise to a nostalgia-tinged notion of "living together," the idea that modern Spanish identity emerged out of a largely peaceful engagement among Muslims, Jews, and Christians in medieval Spain.

At the time that Mann was shooting his epic, Spain's dictator, Francisco Franco, the ruler of a brutal and corrupt Catholic-fascist regime, imagined *himself* as a modern Cid—a paladin engaged in a Holy Crusade not against Islam but against "Reds" at home and Communism and democracy abroad. In this he drew on another tradition, one that imagined Rodrigo as a proto-Crusader, a fervent Christian warrior whose destiny was to serve in the *Reconquista*, the "Spanish Reconquest" that had begun in the 720s with the objectives of expelling the foreign, Muslim "Moors" from the peninsula and restoring the Visigothic monarchy that they had destroyed. This version of history, espoused by Castro's contemporary and rival Claudio Sánchez-Albornoz, is, like Castro's, tied to the notion that there is a discernible, unique, and essentially Christian "Spanish" character that can be traced back at least to Roman times, if not before. But where Castro saw coexistence, Sánchez-Albornoz saw conflict, describing this character as "the eternal Spaniard"—one forged in the crucible of war with the Jews and Muslims of the Middle Ages.*

Although both Mann's and Franco's Cids were based in medieval traditions, each was an anachronistic fantasy, and neither bore much resemblance to the eleventh-century warrior who, over the course of four decades, by blade and spear and by cunning and brutality, carved out for himself a place alongside the greatest lords of the Iberian Peninsula. Franco's Cid was a variation on a nineteenth-century nationalist fiction, while Mann's script was based on a seventeenth-century play, *The Youthful Adventures of Rodrigo*, itself based on a cycle of legends first set down no earlier than two centuries after the Cid's death.

But even *The Song of My Cid*, the famous Old Castilian poem, nearly four thousand lines in length and composed perhaps only a century or so after Rodrigo's death, is a work of literature rather than history. In it, the Cid is driven by honor into exile, after a life spent rising from humble roots to the highest circles of royal power. Glossing over the Cid's service as a warrior for Muslim kings, *The Song of My Cid* tells a wholly fictional story: the dishonor his cowardly aristocratic Christian rivals subjected him to, their defilement of his daughters, and his vengeance and rehabilitation. It is a tale of masculine honor, vindication, and revenge. And yet, as a result of the movingly evocative work of Menéndez Pidal, Spain's great nationalist historian, the Cid of the *Song* has been popularly accepted as the Cid of history.

As we get closer to Rodrigo's times, the tales are sparer and more believable. *The Deeds of Rodrigo the Master of the Field* (known now as the *Historia Roderici*), a short Latin prose history, was composed shortly after his death (likely prior to 1125) by a Christian cleric in the Rioja region. *The Song of the Master of the Field* (*Carmen Campidoctoris*), a 128-stanza Latin poem, was apparently the work of a Catalan monk that may have appeared during the Cid's lifetime, and probably echoed the first songs about his adventures. Each has its own biases, agendas, and imperfections, and each was meant for a distinct audience with distinct

---

* Despite his nationalist loyalties, Sánchez-Albornoz, like his rival Castro, was exiled in the wake of Franco's victory in the Spanish Civil War. In the 1950s and '60s these titans of Spanish medieval studies battled each other from Argentina and California, respectively.

expectations. They do share certain characteristics, though. In both, he is lionized, but not beyond reproach; he is a man of some faith and ideals, but no saint. Questions of veracity aside, it is remarkable that a nobleman of relatively humble birth was the subject of such popular and literary attention in an age when the lives of most kings often went all but unrecorded.

While we know the Cid mostly through these untrustworthy accounts, Rodrigo was no literary creation. He was a man of flesh and blood, who figures notably in the Muslim and Christian chronicles of his time as both hero and villain, and in administrative documents generated by the primitive bureaucracy of the "Empire" of León. He was a unique historical figure, but in some ways he was far from exceptional. Rodrigo Díaz de Vivar was one of scores of knights-errant, dispossessed lords, landless nobles, and mercenaries, Muslim and Christian, who ranged across an Iberian Peninsula electrified by the rhetoric of passion and faith and crackling with opportunity, as the gilded edifice of Islamic Spain crumbled and the primitive, fledgling Christian principalities on its peripheries competed to claim its rich prizes.

Getting as close as possible to the historical Cid involves stripping away the layers of literary varnish that have been applied to his portrait since the day he died. We are left with frustratingly little, and much of it tentative. Rodrigo was born in the early 1040s to a second- or third-tier noble family from near Burgos, in Castile. By the late 1060s he was serving as a warrior under King Sancho II of Castile, and evidently distinguished himself in action against the forces of Christian Navarre, Aragon, and León. On one occasion the chroniclers report he held off fifteen Leónese soldiers single-handedly; on another, that he killed a Navarrese champion in single combat, the incident that led to his being acclaimed as *Campi doctor* and earned him the personal support of the king. With Rodrigo at his side, Sancho II conquered the kingdoms of his brothers: Galicia in 1071 and León in 1072. García and Alfonso, the defeated kings, sought refuge in Muslim Seville and Toledo, respectively. But as Rodrigo rose in Sancho's esteem he quarreled with other noblemen of better pedigree, notably García Ordóñez, lord of the Rioja. Moreover, Sancho's death—he was assassinated during the Siege of Zamora, his sister's town, in 1072—weakened Rodrigo's position, particularly since it was Sancho's brother, Alfonso (whom Rodrigo had helped force into exile) who now returned as king of León and Castile.

Respected but not trusted in the new royal court, Rodrigo served Alfonso under arms and in the mid-1070s he married Ximena Díaz, likely a woman of middling noble rank. As an envoy to León's Muslim tributaries in the south, the 'Abbadids of Seville, Rodrigo led Muslim and Christian troops in 1079 as they repulsed an attack by the *taifa* kingdom's traditional enemy, Granada. It was in the aftermath of this battle that Rodrigo's Muslim troops hailed him as *sayyidi*. But by no later than 1082 the Cid had fallen out with Alfonso and been sent into exile. Lordless, he put himself in the service first of al-Muqtadir, the ruler of Zaragoza, and then his successor, al-Musta'in II. Serving the latter, he gained the gratitude of the Muslim kings and their people by defending them against the attacks of the king of Aragon and the count of Barcelona. In 1085 Alfonso VI captured Toledo, the former Visigothic capital of Spain, and appeared to be on course to conquer the rest of al-Andalus. But the following year he very nearly lost his life and his kingdom when he was defeated at the Battle of Zallaqa by the North African Almoravids, who had come ostensibly to rescue, but ultimately to conquer the *taifa* kingdoms. The vulnerable Alfonso soon reconciled with the Cid, apparently rewarding him with lordships of a clutch of wealthy towns and castles.

But it was not to last; by 1089 Rodrigo was an exile once more, declared a traitor after having failed to join Alfonso's forces in their relief of the castle at Aledo from an Almoravid siege. Kingless again, and finding himself at odds not only with the count of Barcelona and the king of Aragon but also increasingly with his old patron, al-Musta'in, the Cid set out to forge his own principality in eastern al-Andalus. In his efforts to take control of Muslim Valencia, Rodrigo worked first under the cover of Alfonso's vassal, al-Qadir, the former king of Toledo, whom he used as a front for his own ambitions. But when al-Qadir was assassinated in 1092 during a popular uprising led by a local Muslim cleric, Rodrigo decided to take the city by force. It fell to him on June 15, 1094, even as Almoravid hosts surrounded the city before silently and mysteriously withdrawing on the eve of what Rodrigo assumed would have been their assault.

The Cid, now a Christian *taifa* king, would rule Valencia for the next five years, until his death from natural causes in his mid-fifties. The royal chronicles of Castile presented his rule as tolerant and enlightened, and his reputed regard for the sensibilities of his Muslim subjects became the stuff of legend. Muslim accounts, however, underscore the Cid's violence and avarice. Rodrigo was certainly not a secular ruler; whether as a reflection of his personal faith or in recognition of the inseparability of religion and politics at the time, he set out to Christianize Valencia. He had the city's main mosque repurposed as a cathedral and tried to attract Latin colonists to the town. By the time of his death, there was a popular perception among Spaniards and Christians abroad that the Cid was a hero of Christendom and a foe of its "pagan" enemies. The Christian Mediterranean was at the time in need of such heroes, though they would soon find others: as Rodrigo was drawing his last breaths the armies of the First Crusade were surrounding Muslim Jerusalem, intent on restoring the Holy City to the Mother Church.

Grudgingly recognized as one of the most powerful rulers in the peninsula, the Cid made pacts with his former rivals. Meanwhile, the Almoravids circled, probing the Cid's realm for weaknesses and plotting to retake Valencia. But they would not dare strike; Rodrigo's reputation for invincibility endured even after he suffered his first reverses. His successes were undeniable, though, and it is their scale, not their nature, that reveals Rodrigo as an exceptional figure. Indeed, he was not a timeless hero but rather a product of the era in which he lived—as was his liege lord, Alfonso VI, King of Castile and Emperor of León.

THE EMPEROR OF THREE RELIGIONS

Prince, exile, conqueror, king, and emperor—Alfonso VI was all of these. It was his reign, not Rodrigo's, that came to be perceived as a turning point for the peninsula. It coincided with the creation of the modern notion of Spain, a drama in which the Cid played a substantial supporting role. Alfonso was the son of Fernando I, who was himself the son of Sancho the Great of Navarre. In the late tenth century, when the Caliphate of Córdoba was at its peak, Navarre, in the peninsula's mountainous far north, was the most powerful Christian kingdom in Spain. Its preeminent position was due both to geography—its distance from Córdoba and the difficult terrain invading armies would have had to march over—and to the fact that it was an ally and tributary of the caliphate. Navarre dispatched concubines and noblewomen to the royal harems as part of its tribute, and in this way the Umayyads and the dynasty of Pamplona intermarried, deepening their interdependence and ensuring Navarre the political and military support that enabled it to exercise its will over the other Christian kingdoms.

When Sancho died in 1035 he observed the ancient Germanic custom (a vestige of the Spanish aristocracy's Visigothic origins) of dividing his realms among his sons. Fernando, his youngest, had been given the title Count of Castile and was betrothed to the sister of Sancho's distant vassal, King Bermudo III of León. Two years later, a border dispute between the two brothers-in-law was settled at the Battle of Tamarón, when an un-horsed Bermudo was killed, Richard III–style, by the forces of Fernando and his brother García, who had inherited the Kingdom of Navarre. Soon after, Fernando took the title King of León, basing his claim on his wife, who as Bermudo's sister was the surviving descendant of that royal house. Nineteen years later, Fernando would turn against García, killing him at the Battle of Atapuerca in 1054. But Fernando did not seize the throne of Navarre; for him, it was clear that the greater prize lay to the south, in Muslim al-Andalus, where the rich but weak *taifa* kingdoms were locked in a contest for domination over the remnants of the Caliphate of Córdoba.

By 1060 Fernando had embarked on a series of campaigns against the major Muslim kingdoms—Badajoz, Toledo, Zaragoza, and Seville—not to conquer them but rather to force them into submission. The kingdoms were still wealthy, in part as a result of the continuing influx of African gold and silver, and Fernando obliged the *taifa* rulers to pay *parias*, a form of tribute exchanged in return for "protection." As long as the kings continued to pay, Fernando would provide them with troops and defend them from any Muslim or Christian princes. It was a brilliant strategy. Without having to conquer and occupy these kingdoms, and without hav-ing to subdue or displace their populations, Fernando simultaneously filled his coffers and prevented competing Christian powers from gain-ing footholds of their own in al-Andalus. It was a consequence of this pol-icy that (if the *Historia Roderici* is to be believed) in 1063 Sancho II, then a mere prince, found himself, together with his liege man, Rodrigo Díaz de Vivar, assisting the forces of Muslim Zaragoza at the Battle of Graus, where they killed Fernando's other brother, King Ramiro of Aragon. In 1065 Fernando attacked Valencia, but was too ill to make the ensuing victory a decisive one. Instead, he returned home, and died later that same year.

In imitation of his father, Fernando had divided his realms among his three sons: Sancho received Castile, Alfonso was given León, and a kingdom of Galicia was created in the west for García. In 1071 Sancho and Alfonso seized García's kingdom, and then Sancho conquered Alfonso's lands, only to be assassinated as he was attacking the town of Zamora, held by his sister, Urraca (who was later rumored to have had an incestuous affection for Alfonso). In 1072 Alfonso returned from exile in Muslim Toledo and claimed Castile, León, and Galicia as his own; and the Cid, the loyal knight of Sancho II of Castile, found himself in the service of his onetime enemy. As these events played out in the north, the situation in al-Andalus had deteriorated. The king of Toledo, al-Ma'mun, had seized Valencia, and the wars among Seville, Granada, and Almería dragged on. Increasingly desperate for military support, the *taifa* kings were obliged and prepared to pay ever greater sums of *parias* to Alfonso. Christian allies and soldiers of fortune became indispensable in the defensive strategies of the decadent Muslim kings. As a contemporary poet wrote satirically,

> They give themselves grandiose names, like "The Powerful" and
> "The Invincible," but these are empty titles.
> They are like little pussy cats, who puffing themselves up, imagine
> they can roar like lions . . .

Seville, the most powerful Muslim realm in the south, was now a vassal kingdom of Alfonso VI. As a consequence, its king, al-Mu'tamid, was obliged to hand over Alfonso's exiled brother, García, who was immediately packed off to a monastery. But in return Seville would have Alfonso's knights at its disposal in the ongoing war against Granada. It fell to Rodrigo, Alfonso's fixer, to command these forces. In the wake of his victory over Granada in 1079, Rodrigo earned his Arabic epithet, "the Cid," and the Zirid kingdom also became a tributary of the king of Castile and León. Years later, in his memoirs, the same 'Abd Allah ibn Buluqqin who reigned as king of Granada from 1073 to 1090 and wrote about the death of Yusuf ibn Naghrilla, recalled the visit of one of Alfonso's envoys to collect the tribute he owed. 'Abd Allah was only too aware of Alfonso's long-term designs, which the Castilian agent confirmed, explaining with surprising candor:

> Al-Andalus originally belonged to the Christians. They were defeated by
> the Arabs and driven to the most inhospitable region, Galicia. Now that
> they are strong and capable, the Christians desire to recover what they

have lost by force. This can only be achieved by weakness and encroach-ment. In the long run, when it has neither men, nor money, we'll be able to recover it without any difficulty.

The agent that 'Abd Allah spoke with was Count Sisnando Davídez, a Mozarab Christian. "Mozarab," a corruption of the Arabic *must'arab*, means "wanna-be Arab," and refers to the indigenous Christians of al-Andalus, the descendants of the great majority of Spanish Christians who, when faced with the Islamic invasion of 711, chose to stay in their native lands as subjects of a Muslim prince rather than decamp to the north. Over the centuries most of these people converted to Islam, but even those who remained Christian could not resist the allure of Arabo-Islamic culture. By the ninth century they were dressing like Muslims, behaving like Muslims, and speaking Arabic. As a minority in the open and inclusive society of al-Andalus, they did more than survive; many Mozarabs rose to influential positions in the civil service and as diplo-mats. Sisnando was one of them. As a youth he had been in the service of the *taifa* king of Badajoz, who ruled his hometown of Coimbra. He later moved to the court of al-Mu'tamid, the king of Seville (and archenemy of Isma'il ibn Naghrilla). In 1064 Sisnando was lured by Fernando from the court of Seville to his own with the promise that he would be the next count of Coimbra—Sisnando had just conquered the city. Sisnando's de-parture was regarded as a tragedy for the kingdom and a betrayal of his Muslim lord, so admired was he by Seville's Muslim elite and commoners alike.

As the balance of power in the peninsula shifted during the *taifa* period, new opportunities arose for Mozarabs, as their community was one the Christian princes were eager to cultivate. Some moved north to Latin lands, taking with them their knowledge of Arabic letters, num-bers, and science, as well as their Arabo-Islamic sensibilities. But there were also political reasons why kings like Fernando and Alfonso would back Mozarabs—above all, they believed that individuals such as Sisnando would be crucial intermediaries in what would come to be known as the Spanish Reconquest—which was not, in actuality, what we usually think of when we think of a conquest.

The Christian kingdoms of the north may have been poorer and more primitive than the Muslim south, but their predatory, warrior culture gave them an advantage over urbane al-Andalus. Leaders and rulers among the Christians, whether they were knights, lords, or bishops, were trained from youth in the art of hand-to-hand and horse-to-horse combat. One's skill at killing enemies on the battlefield was what determined one's wealth, power, and prestige. This was long before the emergence of the elaborate codes of chivalry, of the gleaming armor and the courteous ceremony that we tend to associate with medieval knighthood. In the Christian north it was violence that ruled. The number of Christian kings who met their deaths in battle at the hands of their own brothers is perhaps the best evidence of the thoroughgoing brutality of their society.

Yet the Christian kings of the north did not see force as the best means to conquer al-Andalus—at least not at that moment. The wealth and prosperity of Islamic Spain was a consequence not of its resources but of its people, who ran an urbanized society with a sophisticated economy connected by trade to Africa and the Islamic Mediterranean. So when kings like Fernando or Alfonso imagined conquering al-Andalus and restoring Christianity, what they had in mind was restoring the preeminent position of Christianity and casting out the region's Muslim rulers. They did not plan to expel the Muslim population as a whole, as its presence was critical to the continuing welfare of al-Andalus. In fact, they made every effort to reassure their Muslim clients and subjects that they would preserve their society as long as they were loyal. Arabized Jews of al-Andalus fulfilled a similar role as the Mozarabs, particularly for their mastery of the knowledge and skills that the Christian kings needed in order to run the complex societies and economies they now ruled. Like Mozarab Christians and unlike many Muslims, Jews would have no moral qualms about putting such knowledge in the service of Christian kings.

The success of Alfonso's military and diplomatic campaigns against the Muslim south only strengthened the bond between Christian lord and infidel subject. And the more he relied on his policy of *parias*, the more dependent Alfonso was on its perpetuation. It became apparent to Alfonso that if he aspired to rule the entire peninsula—as "Emperor of All of the Spains" (meaning the Christian and Islamic kingdoms)—he would need to present himself as the legitimate ruler of all its inhabitants, "the Emperor of the Three Religions." His ambitions in this regard reached their zenith in 1085 with the conquest of Toledo, a significant event not only because it was the first major Muslim city in al-Andalus to fall under Christian rule, but because it had been the capital of the Christian

Alfonso VI, King of Castile and Emperor of León, being asked to adopt
the Roman rite, from a thirteenth-century manuscript of the
Chronicle of the Kings of León

Visigothic kings who had ruled Spain at the time of the Muslim conquest,
and from whom Alfonso claimed a dubious descent.

THE ROOTS OF THE *RECONQUISTA*

Toledo, where the young Alfonso spent his year of exile after his brother
Sancho had seized his kingdom, was a bustling provincial Muslim city
with a substantial population of Mozarabs and Jews. After the disintegration of the caliphate it had come under the control of a Berber warrior
clan, the Banu dhi'l-Nun, who ruled over the city and its hinterland with
the assent of the local Muslim bourgeoisie. During Alfonso's exile, the
king, Yahya al-Ma'mun, had become an ally and then a tributary of
Castile; but when he died in 1075 he was succeeded by his weak grandson, Yahya al-Qadir (incongruously, "the Powerful"). Al-Qadir had Alfonso's support, but not his subjects', and immediately after coming to
power he faced a series of popular revolts. In his first year as king the
people rose up and deposed him, inviting a rival Berber warlord, al-
Mutawakkil, the king of Badajoz, into the city. In response, Alfonso

reinstated al-Qadir by force, demanding increased tribute from him for doing so, and launched a series of punitive raids on the countryside. Al-Qadir, for his part, viciously persecuted his subjects upon his return to power. Although many of his opponents fled, it was clear that the days of the Dhi'l-Nun dynasty in Toledo were numbered.

Alfonso thrived on this sort of disorder. He soon struck a deal with a desperate al-Qadir that would see the Muslim king hand the city over to him in exchange for being installed by Alfonso's forces as king of Valencia, a city al-Qadir had inherited in 1075, but that had broken free of his rule. The Castilian king's troops ringed Toledo, and a six-month siege reduced the populace to desperation. They opened their gates to Alfonso's forces, a surrender document was signed, and Alfonso made his ceremonial entrance into the city on May 25, 1086. Legend has it that the Cid rode through Toledo's northern gate at Alfonso's side, and as they passed a tiny mosque (now the Church of Cristo de la Luz), the hoof of Rodrigo's mare, Babieca, stuck to the ground and could not be moved. The king and the Cid dismounted and, entering the mosque (which the fable describes as a former church), they found a statue of the Virgin Mary that had been secretly plastered into the walls at the time of the Muslim conquest. Thus the Virgin, along with Christian Toledo, had been rescued. Today, a single white cobblestone marks the spot where the hoof of Rodrigo's horse is said to have stopped. But the story, unsurprisingly, is a fabrication; dozens of nearly identical legends recounting the miraculous recovery of statues of the Virgin and Child secreted away from the infidel invaders are associated with towns and cities across the peninsula. The Cid was not at the king's side on that day, but off to the east in the Muslim Kingdom of Zaragoza, and Alfonso's conquest of Toledo represented only a first step in the re-Christianization of the city.

The person who was actually riding alongside the victorious king was Sisnando Davídez, who, as an individual respected by the Muslim population for his perfect command of Arabic and his philo-Islamic affinities, had been charged with negotiating the city's surrender. The terms were generous; Alfonso distributed a large cash subsidy to the populace and evidently guaranteed that they would be free to practice their religion and would be ruled by their own Islamic authorities. He even promised that the Muslims would continue to have use of the city's congregational mosque (built on what had been, three centuries earlier, the royal Visigothic cathedral). As the contemporary historian Ibn Bassam remarked,

Sisnando "endeavored to lighten the suffering of the Toledans and make bearable the base condition at which they had arrived, demanding little and comporting himself justly, thereby reconciling them to Alfonso's presence . . ." The Castilian king whom Sisnando put his "blazing intellect" in service of comes off somewhat worse in the account: Ibn Bassam's Alfonso is a filthy brute who insults the Toledans and sputters commands as he scratches his privates in their presence. But, in reality, it was Alfonso who was behind the conciliatory policies. He understood that for Toledo to remain a functioning, revenue-producing city, he needed to leave the Muslim residents in place and undisturbed. And so, in the first year of Alfonso's rule, life for the city's Muslims, Jews, and Mozarab Christian communities slowly returned to normal.

But another, less sympathetic group had arrived in the city with Alfonso: the "Franks," foreign Christians from the cold North beyond the Pyrenees. They, too, spoke their own language and had their own customs and laws. They also practiced a Christian liturgy distinct from that of the Mozarabs, who had been all but cut off from developments in Latin Europe during the centuries of Muslim rule in Spain. Many of the Franks were Burgundians, inhabitants of a prosperous, dynamic region in what is now northeastern France that was at the time becoming known not only for its wine but for its knights and clergymen.

Alfonso needed both, and had courted the Burgundian elite, hoping to incorporate them into his imperial strategy. In 1079 he had married Constance, the daughter of the Duke of Burgundy (she would be the second of his five wives), and soon after betrothed his young daughters, Theresa and Urraca, to two of her kinsmen, the knights Henry and Raymond of Burgundy. With the Burgundians came their retinues; Alfonso gained valuable soldiers as well as many other allies and dependents who had no stake in the incestuous intrigues, deeply rooted local loyalties, and bitter family rivalries that characterized the fractious native nobility. Unlike the Spanish kings, the northern French had broken with their barbarian past and adopted primogeniture, the custom by which a nobleman or king would bequeath his estates to a single son, usually the eldest, instead of dividing them up equally among his children. The practice produced large, centralized, and powerful princedoms, but also many landless warriors, all seeking their fortunes. Many of these second, third, and fourth sons, dazzled by the civilization of al-Andalus and the easy wealth that its decline promised, made their way to Christian Spain.

The Christians of Northern Europe had been vaguely aware of the sophistication and affluence of Islamic Spain for some time, from the reports of traders and diplomats. In the tenth century, curious clergymen began to visit the monasteries of the Christian Pyrenees, having heard of impressive libraries with advanced Arabo-Islamic scientific and philosophical works that Mozarab clerics and pilgrims had brought out of the caliphate. A few intrepid Frankish scholars were said to have journeyed to Córdoba itself, where they encountered knowledge that was so beyond theirs that they could only describe it as "magic." One such individual was Gerbert of Aurillac, a monk of modest origins from the mountainous Auvergne of central France. Inclined toward mathematics and astrology, he studied under Muslim masters both in the caliphal capital and in Seville, at least according to legend. Reputed to have learned "sorcery" and made a pact with the Devil, he returned to Northern Europe and in 999 was elected pope, as Sylvester II.

Many Franks who came to Spain, however, came in search of salvation rather than knowledge. Around the time of Gerbert's stay in al-Andalus, a tiny settlement in the far northwest of Spain had started to develop as a major destination for Frankish pilgrims. At some point in the early 800s, inspired by a vision of celestial fireworks, a local monk began to dig at the site of an ancient burial ground (a *compostuela*, or "little cemetery") near the former Roman cathedral town of Iria Flavia. Soon after, in a vision, the bones he discovered there were revealed to him to be those of Jesus's disciple, Saint James the Greater. In Christian lore, James had evangelized Spain prior to his martyrdom in 44 C.E., after which his body had been miraculously borne by boat to the farthest reaches of Roman Hispania, where he was buried. To the eighth century mind, it all made perfect sense.

The monk's find caused a sensation in the tiny Kingdom of Asturias, which at that point comprised the last bastion of the defeated Visigothic nobility, holding out against the conquering Muslims. Taken as a sign of divine favor, it bolstered the tenuous legitimacy of its rulers and the morale of its beleaguered Christian population. The discovery also made the kingdom the only place in Latin Christendom, aside from Rome, where the remains of an Apostle could be visited and venerated. Thanks to the support of the kings of Asturias, over the following two centuries the site had become so well known and well endowed that in 997, when al-Mansur raided the area, he ordered his forces to respect the sanctity of the cathedral, even if he made a point of carrying off the bells to be hung in the Great Mosque of Córdoba as trophies. As the eleventh century progressed, the fame of the site only grew, and more and more pilgrims, including clergy, noblemen, and commoners, made the trek from Frankish lands to Santiago (Saint James) de Compostela. On the return leg they carried with them the scallop shells they picked off the Atlantic shore as a token of their pilgrimage, as well as exciting tales of the splendor of Islamic Spain and the conviction that a grand conflict was playing out on the peninsula between Christianity and Islam.

This notion found a receptive audience among the Frankish clergy. Their faith had coalesced in the context of the unforgiving frontier of the pagan north and the chaos and violence of "Dark Age" Europe. After the brief and shaky order that Charlemagne had imposed on the Latin West in the early ninth century, when he declared himself "Roman Emperor," Northern Europe had slid into anarchy, riven by warfare between its nobles and the target of invasions by barbarian Norsemen and Magyars. The Church—divided, weak, and corrupt—had followed; monasteries had become refuges for the indolent younger sons of the nobility, and their effectiveness as centers of education, administration, and piety declined as a result. Yet out of this crisis there emerged in the 900s a new order of monks, who possessed the discipline and dedication that would revive the Church and the society its mission was to minister to. Before the rise of this order, the monks of Europe, whose prayers, purchased with donations, the nobility depended on to ensure their sinful souls and those of their kin would be pardoned by the Lord, had grown insincere in their religion, not to mention libidinous and dissolute.

The center of the reform was the Burgundian Abbey of Cluny, which welcomed novices of any social class or standing, educated them, and promoted them on the basis of ability and nothing else—a true meritocracy in an age of rigid class distinctions. The local nobility took notice, and, eager to have truly pious monks interceding for them before God in Heaven, began to donate money and lands to the Cluniac Order. The monks proved to be sharp administrators, politicians, and businessmen, much-needed talents at a time when even upper-class laymen were usually illiterate. The order quickly expanded, founding scores of daughter abbeys, all of which were obedient to the abbot of Cluny; every monk was required to train for a year at the "home office." As the power of Cluny grew, it attracted the best and brightest Christian minds—young men intent on transforming and modernizing the Church, and on reinventing the weak and corrupt papacy.

The leaders of the Church, which as an institution was drifting into obsolescence and decline, embraced the order with enthusiasm. Gregory VII, the greatest reforming pope in history, was influenced by Cluny, and Urban II, who would call the First Crusade in 1095, was a member of the order. It was the Cluny-inspired Gregorian Reform of the eleventh century that wrested the Church out of the so-called Dark Ages by seeking to clean up the papacy, eliminate clerical corruption, turn the Church into a force for peace, and formalize Christian worship through the use of a standard set of sacraments.

Most of Cluny's "soldiers of Christ," as monks were referred to at the time, had no direct experience with Muslims but, confrontational to the core, with few exceptions considered them irredeemable infidels or agents of the Devil. Yet even if the order saw Islam as a threat to the sovereignty of the Church and the salvation of the faithful, it had been in contact with the Muslim world since the late 900s and had warily begun to study its language and culture.

For Alfonso, Cluny and the Burgundians would prove to be tremendously effective agents of conquest and colonization. For the Muslims of Toledo, they would prove to be agents of disaster. After no more than a year as governor of the city, Sisnando Davídez was summoned by Alfonso to other duties and Toledo came under the control of Queen Constance. When she had arrived in Toledo shortly after Alfonso took it, she had brought Bernard de Sedirac, a Cluniac monk whom Alfonso appointed archbishop and who served as her confessor and spiritual adviser. Constance and Bernard quickly dismantled Sisnando's regime of tolerance. Ignoring the treaties that had been signed, they seized the city's main mosque and reconsecrated it as the Cathedral of Santa María. This spurred the exodus of the city's Muslims, which had begun even before the conquest; some had opted to settle farther north in Alfonso's lands, but most fled south to al-Andalus. In the vivid but unreliable imagination of the thirteenth-century archbishop of Toledo, Rodrigo Jiménez de Rada, Alfonso swore to burn Constance and Bernard alive in revenge for having broken his treaty, but demurred when the local Muslims begged him to show the queen and archbishop mercy lest they be blamed for their deaths.

For his efforts on behalf of the faith, Bernard was rewarded by Urban II with a privilege that named him the supreme Church authority in the peninsula. As Europe emerged from the eleventh century, royal and clerical power became codependent and mutually reinforcing (when they were not in competition). Urban's concession was an early example of this new paradigm, and an effective one at that. Bernard and Alfonso, bishop and king, embarked on a campaign to impose the power of the papacy and to destroy the autonomy and undermine the authority of the native Church. To Bernard, the Mozarab Church represented a dangerous aberration, and as such a threat to the Roman Church and the salvation of Christian souls. To Alfonso, it was a source of strength for his troublesome and undependable nobility, whose families filled its ranks. Bernard began to replace native clergymen with foreign appointees loyal to the papacy, and to replace the native Mozarabic liturgy with the new Latin liturgy approved by Rome.

The local clergy resisted the changes, especially the move away from the traditional liturgy, which they saw as a symbol of the independence and antiquity of the native Spanish Church. The matter had been put to the test in 1079 at Burgos, the capital of Castile, in the quintessential means of medieval justice: trial by battle. According to the *Crónica najarense*, a monastic chronicle likely compiled just after the writing of the *Historia Roderici*, an assembly was held outside the cathedral in the presence of Alfonso VI. On one side stood the black-robed monks of Cluny and their cousins, the neatly kempt Burgundian knights and noblemen; on the other, the colorfully robed Mozarab clergy, surrounded by their bearded and rough kinsmen from among the native nobility. Champions were chosen, and two knights, one representing the Roman liturgy and the other the Mozarabic, began a duel. Both sides believed that God would show His will by ensuring victory to the virtuous party. One can imagine the hush that would have fallen over the supremely confident Frankish contingent as their champion was defeated by the Mozarab. Immediately a retrial was ordered, this time by "ordeal." A large bonfire was lit and the two books of service were cast onto it. All eyes gazed expectantly at the flames, until suddenly and miraculously the Mozarab liturgy leaped out of the fire and landed unsinged at Alfonso's feet. Every inch a king, Alfonso promptly kicked the book back into the flames and said, "Let the horns of Law bend to the will of kings." The Latin rite would prevail.

The story is a parable, part of a typical medieval chronicle, but nonetheless reflects a broad historical truth: Alfonso VI and Cluny had formed a close relationship even before he had come to the throne and, once in power, Alfonso aided Cluny, the papacy, and the Frankish clergy at the expense of the native Church. Whatever his spiritual motivations, Alfonso's allegiance was essentially a political one. In return for his backing, over the following century Frankish monks, through the medium of the chronicles they wrote and the documents they forged (or, as they understood it, "reconstructed"), manufactured a legend and an ideology that not only justified the claims of the kings of León-Castile to sovereignty over the entire peninsula, but presented this manifest destiny as God's will. The Christian *Reconquista* of Spain, and the defeat of the supposedly foreign "Ishmaelites," became divinely sanctioned aims, and the Castilians became the new "Israelites," God's Chosen People, reclaiming their Promised Land.

An oral and written tradition that can be traced back to the ninth-century Kingdom of Asturias recounts how in 722 (or 718) one Pelagius, a member of the Visigothic nobility, miraculously won a decisive battle over a large army of invading Muslims. This battle took place in the mountainous northwest near the cave of Covadonga, a site sacred to the Virgin Mary, and initiated, according to Christian writers, the long struggle to expel the infidel invaders in a "Reconquest" of what was a Christian land.

Deemed by the Frankish chroniclers to be the descendants of Pelagius, the family of Alfonso VI were held to be the heirs of the Visigothic king, León, the successor to the Asturian kingdom, and ultimately to pre-Islamic Hispania. To this genealogy the Frankish clergy tied the story of Santiago. In the 1100s they invented a legend in which the Asturian king, Ramiro I, rebelled in 844 against the amir of Córdoba's demand for an annual tribute of one hundred Christian maidens. A punitive army was dispatched by the amir, and Ramiro confronted it at Clavijo (near modern Logroño). As the story goes, he would have been crushed had Saint James not appeared in the heat of battle, descending from the clouds on a white horse and leading the Christians in a massacre of the infidel army. Saint James the Apostle was transformed into Santiago Matamoros, "the Muslim-Killer," patron saint of Spain and of the kings of the House of León-Castile, whose divine destiny was to rule over the entire peninsula.

In short, in the minds of some Christians and some Muslims, events in Spain in the 1080s were part of nothing less than a grand struggle between Islam and Christianity. But many other Christians and Muslims saw only struggles between Christian and Muslim warlords who had little regard for the religious identity of their enemies or allies, and who pursued political, personal, and often short-term goals. The Cid was one of these warlords.

A MUSLIM HERO, A CHRISTIAN VILLAIN

When Toledo fell to Alfonso VI, Rodrigo Díaz was officially an outlaw in Castile, having been exiled by the king in 1081. The precise cause is lost to history, but it may have originated with the Cid's victory over Granada in 1079, after which Sevilleans had hailed Rodrigo as their hero and lord. Among the troops on the Granadan side was none other than García Ordóñez, lord of the Rioja, who had been sent by Alfonso to collect tribute from that kingdom. In the course of the battle, García had been captured by his old rival, the Cid—a public humiliation for a warrior, and one that was compounded by the fact that he would have been obliged to pay Rodrigo a significant ransom. In noble warfare of the period, high-ranking enemies were worth more alive than dead; the object was to avoid killing them, if possible, and instead to capture them for ransom or exchange. These rules were understood and respected by Christian and Muslim alike. There was nothing remarkable, for instance, in a seized nobleman being set free with the expectation that he return to his own lands and raise a ransom he had pledged to his captor. To fail to do so, or to renege, would bring one infamy as a man without honor, and would likely preclude similar treatment again.

Noblemen held grudges, and the Ordóñez family headed a powerful and well-connected clan at Alfonso's court. Their chance for revenge came in 1081. That year a raiding party from Muslim Toledo made an incursion into Castile and attacked lands belonging to Rodrigo's wife, Ximena. The Cid quickly mounted a retaliatory assault against Toledo, which he executed with his customary skill but without the permission of his king. At the time, Alfonso's control of the kingdom was rather uncertain, and he was attempting to cultivate the trust of its populace and of his client, al-Qadir. Consequently, he viewed the Cid's act as a betrayal, and was likely encouraged in this belief by the Ordóñez clan. Later that year he confiscated Rodrigo's estates and ordered him to depart the kingdom. Fortunately for Rodrigo there were plenty of opportunities for a lordless and unemployed warrior, and he set off for the kingdom he knew most needed his services, and would pay him more than any other: Muslim Zaragoza.*

Zaragoza, or *Saraqusta* in Arabic, was known as the White City to Islamic geographers. Its stout stone walls framed a rectangular grid of Roman-built streets; the emperor Augustus had founded Zaragoza nearly a millennium before, as the colony Caesaraugusta, for his retired legionnaires. Set on the broad, lush Ebro River and girded by barren red cliffs, its appearance would have brought Egypt and the Nile to the minds of the Arab conquerors who arrived in the early 700s. Indeed, it came to occupy a special place in their imagination, as it already did for the natives. In the Visigothic era Zaragoza had been an important ecclesiastical center; Christians believed the Virgin had appeared on its riverbank to the evangelizing Saint James in 39 C.E. For Muslims it would become known for the tombs of two men who had each been a friend and disciple of a Companion of the Prophet, and who had settled in the city after the Arab conquest.†

Under the Umayyads Zaragoza became the capital of the *Thaghr al-'Aqsa*, "the Farthest Frontier," one of the large, semiautonomous military provinces that girded the emirate. Ruled at first by the Banu Qasi, or "the Cassius family"—local post-Roman aristocrats who had converted to Islam—it was perennially rebellious. When Charlemagne came to the city in 778 with his army, in the episode inaccurately immortalized in *The Song of Roland*, he arrived not as a conqueror but to ally with the local Muslim ruler against the Umayyad amir in Córdoba. It was not malevolent Muslim armies who ambushed the Frankish rear guard and killed the hero of the tale at the Battle of Roncesvalles, as the *Song* would have us believe, but the nominally Christian Basques of Pamplona.

Through the 800s the aristocracy of the *Thaghr* continued to intermarry with the families of the Christian warlords of the Pyrenees, and

---

* The tradition that Rodrigo went to Zaragoza only after appealing to and being rejected by the twin counts of Barcelona, Ramon Berenguer II and Berenguer Ramon II, is in all likelihood a later invention, intended to demonstrate the Cid's preference for serving Christian lords.

† The "Companions of the Prophet" are individuals who were the friends and supporters of Muhammad during his lifetime. They are somewhat analogous to the disciples of Jesus in Christianity. Despite the fact that orthodox Muslim doctrine does not recognize saintly power, the tombs and relics of holy men and women are believed by many Muslims to embody *baraka*, or "blessed power," much as Christians believe in respect to their saints.

relations between Christians and Muslims remained cordial into the eleventh century. In the *taifa* period, Zaragoza easily transitioned into a quiescent independence punctuated only by a coup in 1039 that brought the Arab Banu Hud family to power under Sulayman ibn Hud al-Musta'in b'illah. Sulayman ruled briefly, and in a parallel to events in the Christian north, on his death in 1046 he divided his realm among his five sons, fracturing what had been the largest *taifa* kingdom and prompting a series of fraternal wars. The vulnerability of these small states forced them to cast about for allies, protectors, and warriors, and soon saw them drawn into Alfonso's system of *parias*.

Under Sulayman's son, Ahmad al-Muqtadir, Zaragoza itself entered a golden age. Al-Muqtadir was the epitome of the successful *taifa* king: cultured, epicurean, and Machiavellian, he was described by the poet Ibn Sa'id as constantly "plying the wine-cups and plucking off heads." Styling himself *hajib* to the now extinct caliphate—as heir to the great al-Mansur and sovereign of all of Spain—he set out to subdue his brothers one by one. Lleida, to the east, resisted longest, but gave up the fight by 1067; Ahmad added the valuable ports of Tortosa and Denia to his kingdom in 1076. Then he cast his eye toward Valencia, which he besieged just as the populace of the city was rebelling against the rule of al-Qadir, King of Toledo, Alfonso VI's incompetent client.

Al-Muqtadir achieved these successes by cleverly courting Christian allies, whom he then played against one another. A diplomatic exchange preserved from 1069 reveals Sancho IV of Navarre making a treaty with "his friend, Almuktadir Bille, may God exalt him," against anyone who dared attack them, Christian or Muslim. Ahmad responded, "to his friend King Sancho, God save him . . ." Even so, al-Muqtadir wanted to be known as a protector of the faith. When Norman adventurers besieged his town of Barbastro in 1064 and massacred the populace, he called on the *taifa* kings to unite, raised an army under the banner of Islam, and retook the town, repaying its conquerors in kind. Nor did he shrink from taking on his Christian neighbors. One source claims that it was one of al-Muqtadir's soldiers who, passing as a Christian knight, closed in on and killed King Ramiro of Aragon at the Battle of Graus— one of the Cid's first combat actions, in which he and his king, Sancho, fought alongside al-Muqtadir.

As his power grew, al-Muqtadir turned Zaragoza into a capital worthy of a king; and though the luxurious, domed Palace of Joys he built

Aljafería Palace, Zaragoza

vanished long ago, the imposing fortress residence he constructed, the Aljafería, survives to this day. Under his rule, the city became a cosmopolitan center for the arts, literature, religion, medicine, and science; a place where Muslim, Christian, and Jewish scholars found patrons, a massive reference library, and a spirit of open acceptance. Pilgrims and scholars traveled back and forth between Zaragoza, the Islamic East, and North Africa, and as conditions elsewhere in the peninsula worsened, the city became a haven for intellectuals and literati. The upheavals in Córdoba in 1031 sent elite Muslims and Jews to Zaragoza, as did the violence in Granada following Yusuf ibn Naghrilla's failed coup in 1066.

Among the Jewish refugees from Córdoba was Yusuf, the son of the *Nasi*, Hasdai ibn Shaprut, and a friend and correspondent of Isma'il ibn Naghrilla. His son Abu Fadl distinguished himself as a poet and rose in the service of al-Muqtadir, eventually to the office of *wazir*. It was Abu Fadl's skill as a diplomat that charmed Zaragoza's Christian allies, but ultimately, as the story goes, the charms of the king's half sister won over Abu Fadl, who married her, converted to Islam, and was appointed chief *qadi* of the capital. He was only one of scores of learned Jews in Zaragoza who produced scientific and philosophical works in Arabic even as they

Aljafería Palace, Zaragoza

wrote poetry and scriptural exegeses in Hebrew. The great poet and philosopher Solomon ibn Gabirol (who served for a time as tutor to Yusuf ibn Naghrilla) was perhaps the most famous Jew in the city. His Neoplatonic theological essay *The Fountain of Life*, written in Arabic, would later become tremendously influential among Latin philosophers.* There were Christians in the city, too, notably the Mozarab bishops who served the *taifa* kings as envoys and functionaries when they were not tending to their substantial flocks.

---

* *The Fountain of Life* had been translated into Latin as early as 1150, and was found to be so compelling by Latin thinkers that they assumed it must have been written by a Christian. A poor Hebrew translation was not produced until a century later, and it was only in the mid-nineteenth century that Ibn Gabirol was recognized as the author of the now-lost Arabic original.

Many Muslim intellectuals were drawn to al-Muqtadir's court as well. The most famous of these was Abu 'l-Walid Sulayman al-Baji ("Avempace" in the Latin tradition), a philosopher, theologian, and a religious and political activist who once debated Ibn Hazm in person. Al-Baji traveled the peninsula exhorting the Muslim kings to unite against the growing threat posed by the Christian kingdoms, but found his greatest patron and supporter in al-Muqtadir. The king understood that philosophy was another weapon in his political and ideological arsenal and depended on al-Baji at crucial moments.

The latter, for instance, composed the cordial yet firm replies to letters from a mysterious "monk of France" that reached al-Muqtadir in 1071 and 1079. The letters, which may have been written by (Saint) Hugh the Great—Abbot of Cluny, spiritual tutor to the future Urban II, and architect of the Roman Church's expansion in Spain—were intended to persuade al-Muqtadir to convert to Christianity. They represented a growing engagement with the Muslim world on the part of the papacy and Cluny, and a new approach to the problem of Islam as they perceived it. Innocent and earnest believers in the self-evident truth of the Gospels, Christian theologians wanted to bring about the mass conversion of the Islamic world by appealing to its princes in the hope that if they converted, their subjects would soon follow. The letters to al-Muqtadir flattered the king's "insights into explaining the changing conditions of the world" (an allusion perhaps to al-Muqtadir's affinity for astrology), after which the author, this "humblest of monks," invited the king to put "the everlasting Kingdom" of Christ before his and convert.

Al-Baji's refutation is a masterpiece of polemical rhetoric, balancing contempt and courtesy and displaying a remarkable understanding of Christian doctrine. "Now we have knowledge of your law and the disagreement of your doctors in regards to your religion," he wrote, before launching into a series of rational critiques of the doctrines of the Trinity and the Incarnation of the "Son of God." Christianity was, for al-Baji, Ibn Hazm, and fellow Muslim theologians, a tangle of inconsistencies and paradoxes. But even the force of reason would not have won the Cluny order what it sought. The Christian missionary endeavor in al-Andalus was based on a profound misunderstanding of Islamic society. The sultans of the Islamic world were not the barbarian kings of pagan Europe, who had converted to Christianity and then mandated that their illiterate populace do the same. Rather, as al-Qadir of Toledo had come to appreciate, the power in the *dar al-Islam* rested with its common people, not its kings. A ruler who was an open apostate would certainly be deposed. That said, for al-Muqtadir conversion might conceivably have held appeal, given the way the political balance in the peninsula was shifting, but this confident ruler had little cause to believe that within about a half century powerful Zaragoza would be under Christian rule. In spite of the political and religious tensions that were building to the north, he saw his kingdom as a stable one, its future secure in the person of his son al-Mu'taman, a patron of culture and an accomplished mathematician in his own right—although not, by temperament or ability, a warrior.

This is where Rodrigo came in. Exiled from Castile in 1081, he joined what was likely a sizable cohort of Christian soldiers of fortune employed by Zaragoza. Al-Muqtadir needed soldiers; not only were his Christian neighbors—Navarre, Aragon, Urgell, and Barcelona—launching raids across his borders, but the Franks and Normans were beginning to attack his territory with the blessing of Saint Hugh and the reforming papacy, and with promises of heavenly reward should they succeed. Still, having failed to learn the lessons of his father, al-Muqtadir planned to divide his realms between his two sons. Al-Mu'taman, the older, was heir to Zaragoza, and the younger, Mundhir, would become governor of Denia, Tortosa, and Lleida. Soon enough, Mundhir began to conspire with Berenguer Ramon II "the Fratricide," Count of Barcelona, and King Sancho Ramírez of Aragon and Navarre.* After al-Muqtadir died in 1081 or 1082, Mundhir made his move: as he turned on his brother, the Cid saw his first major action for Zaragoza, and scored his first victory of note.

As Mundhir and his Christian allies prepared to attack the northwest frontier of the Kingdom of Zaragoza, the Cid parried a lunge by Sancho Ramírez at the town of Monzón. He then attempted to buy off his enemies' more powerful army with an offer of tribute. This was refused, and Rodrigo, in a stroke of tactical brilliance or luck, swept down on and captured his enemies' baggage train. During this era of personal warfare and primitive logistics, armies had to carry everything they

---

* In 1076 al-Muqtadir's ally Sancho IV of Navarre had been killed. Invited on a hunting trip by his brothers, Sancho was pushed off a cliff by one of them, Ramon. Afterward, Navarre was invaded and partitioned by his cousins, Alfonso VI and Sancho Ramírez of Aragon. For Berenguer Ramon's nickname, see p. 107.

needed with them, including the cash to fund the campaign. And since military authority was based on personal prestige, kings and magnates who took to the field brought their households with them (except for their women, who were usually left at home to run their estates). They carried all their regalia, which they arrayed in richly appointed campaign tents. Thus to lose one's baggage train was not merely to lose one's supplies together with a tremendous fortune, it was to lose the very accoutrements of power. But that day the Cid seized an even greater prize, for he also personally captured Berenguer Ramon II. The count was led in humiliation to al-Mu'taman, who released him in exchange for a promise of ransom. Rodrigo, for his part, was showered with riches and glory, becoming a hero for the Muslims of Zaragoza and a favorite of their king.

In the aftermath of the victory, Rodrigo led the *taifa* kingdom's forces in a series of raids into the Kingdom of Aragon and the lands of Mundhir, terrorizing the countryside, carrying off livestock, and taking prisoners. In fall 1084 Mundhir and Sancho finally struck back at Rodrigo, and with all their might. The result was a debacle. The Cid's troops overran their forces, and in the rout captured a score of the highest-ranking noblemen of Aragon and Navarre. The Cid returned to Zaragoza in triumph, to the ecstatic ululating of the Muslim populace and the pride and pleasure of his king, al-Mu'taman. When in 1085 the king died, his son Ahmad took the throne. He was not an intellectual like his father, but a fighter. He took the name of his bellicose great-grandfather, al-Musta'in, and continued to employ the Cid.

Alfonso VI warily observed these events in the east. He may have been satisfied at the defeats Rodrigo was dealing to Castile's Christian rivals, but he was anxious to take Zaragoza for himself. An opportunity seemed to appear in 1083 when the rebellious Muslim castellan of Rueda, near the frontier with Castile, offered to change sides and give up his castle in exchange for a place in the Castilian court. Alfonso sent a detachment of knights to take the fort, but the garrison overthrew their disloyal commander and rained death (in the form of large rocks) on the king's men. Rodrigo, in nearby Tudela, could have intervened and saved his countrymen, but it was in his best interests to remain a loyal servant of Zaragoza. Despite this episode, which the Cid's rivals painted as a betrayal, there seems to have been a fleeting and shallow reconciliation between Alfonso and Rodrigo in 1084. But by the time Alfonso arrived with his forces before Ahmad al-Musta'in's capital and prepared to lay siege in summer 1086, they had once more become estranged. As the enemy armies made camp, the Cid may have stood on the walls of the Aljafería beside his sultan, contemplating how best to turn back the invasion, and capture and kill those who were once his own people.

A BOLT FROM THE BLUE

But Rodrigo would not have to face his old liege lord in battle. Before Alfonso could turn the screw on the city, he unexpectedly broke camp and marched speedily toward the west. There, on the banks of the Guerrero River, a few miles northeast of Badajoz, at a place called Sagrajas by the Castilians and al-Zallaqa by the Andalusis, he assembled his forces. Beside him was his former rival, Sancho Ramírez, King of Aragon. Alfonso was indignant; he had set aside his dream of conquering Zaragoza to teach a lesson to his Muslim tributaries who had stopping paying *parias*. Suddenly, with the cheers and shouts of "Santiago," the Christian cavalry charged in serried ranks, their spears fixed straight ahead, rising forward eagerly in their saddles, feet braced against their stirrups, their hauberk cloaks slapping against their thighs.

Waiting for them were the troops of the *taifa* kings, a large and colorful army: banners fluttering, long, thin lances pointed toward the sky, and horses stamping nervously. 'Umar ibn Muhammad al-Mutawakkil of Badajoz and 'Abd Allah ibn Buluqqin, King of Granada, sat on their mounts alongside their archenemy, Abu 'l-Qasim Muhammad ibn 'Abbad al-Mu'tamid, King of Seville, who on that day held the privilege of command. As the Christians approached, one wonders what passed through the three kings' minds. Did 'Abd Allah savor the reminiscence of a wine party in the fragrant gardens of the Alhambra? Did al-Mu'tamid, the poet, extemporize a verse on the beauty of Seville or of a certain young boy? Did al-Mutawakkil replay the sequence of events that ended with him, despite his every effort, sitting here, trapped between the walls of his capital and the lances of the Christians? It was October 23, 1086—a Friday, the day of worship, and the *taifa* kings would have done well to pray.

Even before Alfonso's cavalry hit, the uneven Andalusi line would have begun to waver; and while some bravely stood their ground and fought, others turned and retreated pell-mell across the open fields, to the gates of Badajoz. Alfonso and his knights did not let up, with his motley peasant infantrymen close on their heels. As he pressed on, intoxicated by a sense of certain victory, he would not have noticed the growing plume reaching skyward behind him.

The smoke came from his baggage train, which had been plundered and set alight. Just as his men were galloping over the fleeing Andalusi forces, his own rear guard was being overrun. The booming of drums would have drowned out the war cries and shouting of the host of lightly armored, blue-veiled horsemen riding down on the Christians from behind, unhorsing Alfonso's knights with deft precision and leaving them to be dispatched by the unmounted Sudanese contingents accompanying them. What could the rank-and-file Castilians have made of these otherworldly warriors, men with skin blacker than they had ever seen, and riding strange, gangly, humped beasts, like something between a horse and a dog? What other horrors did they confront? Great gray bellowing beasts, the size of ships, in whose thick hide arrows would hang dense as fur? They had never envisioned a camel or an elephant; nor had they imagined a defeat like this.

When Alfonso VI, King of Castile and Emperor of León, left the field, it was not as a proud victor but as a lucky survivor of a massacre. He had narrowly escaped death, unlike a thousand of his men. He rode north for the safety of Toledo. On that day, it seemed, al-Andalus, and perhaps León and Castile, had been lost.

4

Rodrigo Díaz, Taifa King of Valencia

At the head of the Muslim charge that ripped through Alfonso's ranks was a figure robed in black, leaning hard against the neck of his steed, shouting *Allahu akbar!* as he rode down the panicked troops of the Castilian king. This was Yusuf ibn Tashufin, "the Prince of the Muslims," a true son of the desert and the would-be savior of Islamic al-Andalus. But Abu Yaqub, as he was also known, was no *taifa* king. A dark-skinned Sanhaja Berber from the southern reaches of the Sahara, he was unschooled—his Arabic was rough at best—but rigorously pious, charismatic, and physically impressive. And while he may have appeared uncouth, he was a natural political genius. Those who underestimated him did so at their own peril.

As is typical, the accounts of the Battle of Zallaqa differ in most of their details. But they agree in a few crucial ones. Apparently, there had been a parley, as was customary before enemies clashed. Ibn Tashufin is said to have been shocked by the size of Alfonso's forces. "I didn't realize this pig—may God curse him—had grown to such a size," one chronicler has him remark to al-Mu'tamid. Nevertheless, he sent a letter to the Christian king, enjoining him to convert to Islam and recognize Yusuf as his lord—an invitation that would have only stoked Alfonso's rage. If the tales of Arabic chronicles are true, the king had his doubts when he arrived on the field. Before leaving Toledo he is said to have dreamed of riding atop an elephant and banging a drum. The priests and rabbis he consulted had assured him that this vision presaged victory and his taming of Islam; but a venerable old Muslim scholar of Toledo revealed another meaning: the drum was the signal of the judgment of God, and Alfonso, the infidel, was going to his doom.

Thus forewarned, Alfonso would take no chances. It seems the two forces had assembled on Tuesday, October 20, near Badajoz, but as the Muslims braced for attack, the Castilians hesitated. On Thursday Alfonso sent an envoy, who proposed to the Muslim generals that, since Friday was the Muslim day of prayer, Saturday the Jewish, and Sunday the Christian, they should set the battle for Monday. Yusuf, who had a considerable number of Christian mercenaries in his own ranks, consented. But the proposal was a ruse, and on Friday Alfonso struck, hoping to take the Muslims by surprise.

Some accounts say al-Mu'tamid had expected treachery and warned Ibn Tashufin, who had lain in wait as Alfonso's cavalry charged with abandon; others that the trick had worked, and the Muslims were caught praying. Whatever the case, there is no doubt about the outcome of the battle. The petrified *taifa* kings had been ordered by Yusuf to hold the line; given that the battle was a consequence of their impotence, Ibn Tashufin would make sure they took the brunt of Alfonso's attack. And they did, enabling Yusuf, together with Berber warriors from Morocco, slave soldiers from the "land of the Blacks," and mercenaries, to take the glory—though if some of the *taifa* soldiers broke before Alfonso's charge, others fought bravely.* Indeed, some sources have al-Mu'tamid himself fighting with distinction, sustaining several wounds and nearly perishing. All the sources say that the battle raged for the entire Muslim day of prayer, and some report that it did not conclude until after nightfall.

While Castilian sources are reticent on the subject of what must have been a humiliating defeat, the Battle of Zallaqa almost immediately took

* The Arabs called the lands along the southern edge of the Sahara *Bilad al-Sudan*, or "the land of the Blacks." It was a source of gold, slaves, and rare exotica such as ivory, skins, and spices. Beginning in the eleventh century, Muslim traders brought Islam, which, combined with traditional African beliefs and practices, gained a foothold in urban centers and among the ruling elite. In the thirteenth century substantial indigenous Islamic kingdoms would arise in the region.

on epic proportions in the Andalusi imagination. With the customary hyperbole of all medieval chroniclers, Muslim historians claimed that Alfonso's forces had numbered in the tens of thousands of knights, and that the king had escaped with only a tiny group of survivors. Some of these historians wrote about how, the morning after the battle, the severed heads of the thousands of Christian dead were heaped into piles, loaded into carts, and taken on a grisly victory tour through the cities and towns of al-Andalus. This was meant as a warning—but not to Christians. Rather, it was a message to the Muslims of al-Andalus that the new "Prince of the Muslims," Yusuf ibn Tashufin, unlike the *taifa* kings, had the power to punish "the tyrant Alfonso" and restore the dignity of Islam, and that no one, Christian or Muslim, should dare defy him. As for Alfonso, for the moment he was safe. Just as suddenly as the mysterious Yusuf ibn Tashufin had arrived in al-Andalus, he disappeared, withdrawing to Morocco and leaving the *taifa* kings once more as masters in their palaces.

A STORM FROM THE SOUTH

Yusuf ibn Tashufin was the ruler of the Almoravid federation, whose territory stretched from the Pillars of Hercules in the north to the steppes of the Sahel in the south. Its origins went back to the days of the Caliphate of Córdoba. Yusuf, though a Sanhaja Berber, was not from one of the urbane tribes of Ifriqiya, which had struggled against and then submitted to and served the Umayyad and Fatimid caliphates. His people were the pagans and nominal Muslim nomads from the far south, from the ragged edge of the great sand sea that separated the Mediterranean coastal lands from lush Central Africa. They had been drawn into the Islamic world by the trade in salt, gold, and slaves that crossed the desert; variously raiding and working as escorts for traders' caravans, they were exposed to the beliefs of the Muslim merchants, and to the rich possibilities of the Islamic world.

In the 1030s the chieftain of the southern Sanhaja tribes, Yahya ibn Ibrahim, journeyed to Qayrawan in Tunisia, the center of Sunni Islamic jurisprudence in the West. He returned with the simple and clear vision of a new convert to any religion. Yahya and his religious adviser, 'Abd

Allah ibn Yasin, adopted a righteous puritanism that resonated with the stark and unforgiving environment of the warrior-nomad, a binary world of oasis and desert, life and death, and right and wrong. Their followers took the name "al-Murabitun"—from the Arabic *rabata* (to bind), and corrupted by Europeans as "Almoravid"—a reference to their adherence to the faith. The term also resonated with the Sanhaja men's tradition of "binding" their faces with a veil (*litham*), and evoked the frontier fortress monasteries (*ribats*) that served as their bases along the pagan frontier, and from which these "veiled ones" launched raids deep into gold-rich Ghana.* As a result of Yahya ibn Ibrahim and Ibn Yasin's charisma, the various tribes of the Sanhaja quickly rallied to the Almoravid cause, and the *litham* soon became the emblem of authority in the lands south of the Atlas Mountains.

The disintegration of the Caliphate of Córdoba in the early eleventh century had not only thrown al-Andalus into chaos but also the Maghrib, unleashing tensions among the various Berber nations in the region. In the power struggle that followed, the Zanata tribes gained the upper hand in Morocco, taking over the great caravan terminus Sijilmasa and other important towns in the north. But the Sanhaja Almoravids went on the offensive in the 1050s, and under Abu Bakr ibn ʿUmar, who had succeeded Ibn Yasin as amir, they conquered Sijilmasa. Abu Bakr left it in the hands of his cousin, Yusuf ibn Tashufin, who continued the war against the Zanata and took Fez, the greatest city in the western Maghrib, in 1070. But true to their faith-based rejection of all things worldly, the Almoravids had instead selected Aghmat as their capital, a town high in the Atlas Mountains that had become a refuge for Muslim religious scholars fleeing the violence and disorder of postcaliphal North Africa. Most prominent among these new arrivals were the orthodox ʿulamaʾ of Qayrawan in Zirid Ifriqiya, whose city had been repeatedly sacked in the preceding decades. In Aghmat, the Almoravids, with the help of these scholars and men of religion, refined their ideology, forging a sophisticated elite culture out of what had been a society of unlettered nomadic tribesmen. Aghmat became to the Maghrib what Cluny had been to the Latin West.

In 1071, shedding their humility, Abu Bakr and Yusuf decided to build a grand new capital to match their ambitions, and the city of Marrakesh

---

* Sanhaja women did not typically wear the veil.

began to rise out of the broad plain below the western slopes of the Atlas. From this base, the Almoravids would expand their holdings, despite rebellion and resistance, over the next fifteen years, until by 1087 Yusuf ibn Tashufin had become the sole ruler over all of Morocco and Mauritania. The Saharan trade that had propelled the Umayyads to prominence in al-Andalus was now under Yusuf's control, and the high-grade gold coins that he minted, and that bore his titles, Imam and "Prince of the Muslims," soon became the standard currency throughout the Western Mediterranean. These were the coveted "Maravedis" that the Castilian kings would eventually produce their own poor imitations of. With his gold, Yusuf paid for the loyalty of allies, the services of mercenaries, and the building of his new capital. He also generously patronized the religious scholars who became instrumental to both the administration of his empire and the legitimacy of his dynasty.

Just as the Frankish warrior clans of Burgundy were harnessing the movement of monastic reform in the service of their own agenda, the Almoravids were marrying high religious ideology to tribal political power by cultivating the Islamic religious elite, and by publicly deferring to its authority. They supported the North African 'ulama', whose rigorous interpretation of Maliki jurisprudence resonated with the Almoravids' own sense of the law, and who provided a judicial and legal foundation for their empire.* The 'ulama' would be crucial when the Almoravids eventually expanded into al-Andalus. But crossing the Straits of Gibraltar was not a mission to be undertaken lightly; and anyway, Yusuf understood there was no need for him to challenge either Alfonso or the taifa kings. Better to turn them against one another first. He would risk his own men only when the taifa kings were weakened and exhausted.

He did not have to wait long. Even before Alfonso VI had taken Toledo the taifa kings had been chafing at the ever increasing parias he had been demanding. The gold and silver had to come from somewhere, and the taifa kings' dedication to opulence precluded any economizing on their part. Instead, they passed the burden onto their subjects, in the

---

* Of the four recognized Sunni Muslim "schools of law" (or interpretations of Scripture), the Maliki school, which was dominant in the Maghrib and al-Andalus, was the most strictly rational in approach.

form of higher taxes. Hence the importance in the *taifa* period of expert tax collectors, individuals such as Isma'il ibn Naghrilla.

While this burden may have fallen harder on the *taifa* kings' non-Muslim subjects, it also fell on the Muslim Andalusis, for whom "foreign" Berber kings like al-Mutawakkil, al-Qadir, and 'Abd Allah ibn Buluqqin felt little affinity. The middle class in particular grew restless. Here was one of the differences between the Islamic world and the Latin West: in the *dar al-Islam* there was an urban, moneyed, professionalized population whose prosperity derived from commerce. The Muslim middle class was not only wealthy, but educated and cultured. And it aspired to political action. Many members of the *'ulama'* were merchants, or came from merchant families, and had considerable popular support.

The wine drinking, worldly poetry, and sexual cavorting of the *taifa* kings offended the Islamic sensibilities of the middle class—as did the increase in taxes. Taxation is a religious matter in Islam. According to the immutable Revelation of the Qur'an, a ruler cannot demand anything beyond the *'ushr* ("the tenth") and the *sadaq* (the alms tax) from fellow Muslims. To make the situation even worse in the eyes of the Andalusi middle class, the illicit taxes demanded by the *taifa* rulers were being used to pay infidel kings intent on the conquest of Islamic Spain. As the middle class and commoners watched in dismay, their *taifa* kings ignored their religious obligation to unite against the Christian powers and warred against one another. They were agents of *fitna*, or "disorder," of the same immoral forces that had brought down the caliphate.

Nevertheless, the situation would hold as long as the illusion of security was maintained and commerce continued largely unimpeded. But when Alfonso conquered Toledo in 1085 and then launched a series of devastating raids deep into the south, it suddenly became apparent to both the middle class and the *taifa* rulers that al-Andalus was in mortal danger. There was only one faction they could turn to. Members of the local *'ulama'* had been making overtures to the Almoravids, who appeared to them as the antidote to *taifa* misrule, and now began to strengthen those bonds. It was said of Yusuf ibn Tashufin, "He never drank wine, listened to a singing-girl, did not amuse himself in hunting or with other pastimes . . . and he acquired a reputation for rectitude and respect for everything prescribed by the Law." Powerful, spartan, and pious, the Almoravids were exemplars of the Islamic moral integrity that was so lacking among the *taifa* kings, and that so appealed to the orthodox *'ulama'*.

After the fall of Toledo the *taifa* kings themselves begged Yusuf ibn Tashufin to come to Spain and overthrow Alfonso. They would have been all too aware of the risks involved; they understood that the Almoravids saw them as little better than the infidels to the north. But the king of Seville had little choice—Alfonso had targeted him. In 1082 the Castilian king had sent his Jewish ambassador, Ibn Shalib, to demand an increase in tribute from al-Mu'tamid, who, in a fit of rage, had ordered the envoy to be crucified. This was an act of open defiance that Alfonso could not allow to go unanswered. Al-Mu'tamid had no choice but to reach out to Yusuf ibn Tashufin. When his advisers warned him that it was likely Yusuf himself who would end up conquering Seville, al-Mu'tamid is said to have remarked with resignation, "Better [to be] a camel-driver [for the Almoravids] than a swineherd [for Alfonso]."

With a great show of reluctance, Yusuf rallied his African forces and marched with the Andalusis to Zallaqa, where they dealt the decisive blow to the king of Castile. Then Yusuf departed, leaving the *taifa* kings to their own devices once again. But Ibn Tashufin was far from finished with them. No sooner had they been saved than they descended into their customary bickering. Meanwhile, Yusuf set about consolidating his position in the Maghrib, and started to seek spiritual and political legitimization for the conquest of al-Andalus. Because he had staked the legitimacy of his rule on his piety and deference to the authority of the *'ulama'*, Yusuf could not commit so base and impious an act as to attack a Muslim land in search of conquest. He needed to appear (and perhaps to genuinely feel) that he was contributing to the stability of Islam, not the *fitna* that was its antithesis.

The permission Yusuf desired came soon enough, in the form of a *fatwa* delivered by a collective of Granadan religious scholars in 1088, who condemned 'Abd Allah ibn Buluqqin and the other *taifa* kings, and authorized Yusuf, in the name of Islam, to depose them and bring order to al-Andalus. Yusuf had the document sent to the great centers of Islamic learning, Cairo and the 'Abbasid East, where two of the greatest living authorities, Abu Bakr al-Turtushi (an Andalusi by origin) and Abu Hamid Muhammad al-Ghazali, ratified it. To what extent Yusuf was driven by genuine piety rather than ambition cannot be said. Whatever his motives were, they would now be seen as unimpeachable.

RODRIGO GOES ROGUE

In the meantime, Rodrigo Díaz remained in Zaragoza in the service of the new king, Ahmad al-Musta'in. But Alfonso's defeat at Zallaqa and the intervention of the Almoravids transformed Rodrigo's position. The desperate Castilian king soon reached out to the vassal he had outlawed and whose lances and cunning he now needed. Near-contemporary charters—which, in this era of institutionalized forgery, cannot be fully trusted—reveal the price of this reconciliation: Alfonso granted Rodrigo a lavish series of lordships, including the massive caliphal fortress of Gormaz, which loomed over the Duero River and controlled a rich swath of territory. His bond with his true king reestablished, Rodrigo departed Zaragoza.

In 1087 Alfonso sent the Cid to deal with the emboldened *taifa* kings. The Cid's mission required him to negotiate a treaty of mutual protection with Hisham al-Dawla, ruler of the tiny and vulnerable Kingdom of al-Sahla (present-day Albarracín), before heading southward to Valencia. There, the hapless al-Qadir, former king of Toledo, was facing rebellion from powerful elements within the city and the towns of its hinterland, *Sharq al-Andalus* (eastern Andalus). Al-Qadir's situation was of particular concern to Alfonso, not so much because of the Almoravid threat, but rather because Count Berenguer Ramon II of Barcelona was closing in. Berenguer Ramon had allied with Mundhir al-Hajib, King of Denia and Lleida (the uncle and rival of Ahmad al-Musta'in), in order to conquer Valencia and the *Sharq*—an outcome neither Alfonso VI nor al-Musta'in could permit.

At the same time, Alfonso VI was pressuring the *taifa* kings of the south to continue to pay their *parias* to him. He had taken the strategically important castle of Aledo, perched atop a hill southwest of Murcia, and made it into a forward operating base from which his troops would harass the *taifa* kingdoms. A desperate al-Mu'tamid of Seville soon took the initiative once again, and personally traveled to Morocco to implore Yusuf ibn Tashufin to intervene a second time. In 1090 Yusuf returned, now with the imprimatur of Muslim religious authorities, and again pressed al-Mu'tamid, 'Abd Allah of Granada, and Mu'izz al-Dawla of Almería (the dead Yusuf ibn Naghrilla's would-be ally) to raise armies, join his *jihad*, and attack Alfonso's stronghold.

As the Muslim army assembled around Aledo, Alfonso sent word to

Rodrigo to bring his knights to the castle's relief. It was not to be—whether it was a failure of logistics, miscommunication, or, as the Cid's enemies would present it, a deliberate betrayal, Rodrigo did not arrive at the appointed rallying point. Although the Almoravids lifted the siege and withdrew as Alfonso's army approached, and although Rodrigo offered reasonable explanations for his failure to appear, the king was livid. Once more the Cid was outlawed and stripped of his titles and property, and this time he suffered an additional humiliation when Alfonso imprisoned his wife and daughters.

The Cid was now alone—without rank, without a sovereign, and without an income—at the head of an army of knights who may have admired him, but for whom glory alone was not enough. They would not remain faithful to him without the gold and silver they saw as their just recompense for their loyalty. Many deserted Rodrigo, leaving him ever weaker and more vulnerable. But rather than throw himself on the mercy of his fickle king, Rodrigo, with the seasoned fighters who remained by his side, launched a campaign of terror across the lands of Denia and Valencia, in defiance not only of Berenguer Ramon but of Alfonso VI. He and his men attacked with impunity, rustling livestock, sacking towns, harassing civilians, and extorting gold from local authorities through torture. By 1090 Mundhir al-Hajib and al-Qadir were paying tribute to the Cid instead of Alfonso. From Alfonso's point of view, the incorrigible Cid would endanger the entire system of *parias* unless he, a powerful king, could show that he had the ability to rein him in.

And so the count of Barcelona and the king of Castile set aside their rivalries and joined forces, lobbying Denia, Zaragoza, and Aragon and Navarre to join them in a grand coalition the sole purpose of which was to eliminate the Cid. But, inevitably, divisions and doubts afflicted the alliance from the start. Sancho Ramírez, King of Aragon and Navarre, seeing that the Cid's defeat would only empower his Christian rivals, backed out. Al-Musta'in of Zaragoza preferred a weak Castile and Barcelona, and was himself eyeing *Sharq al-Andalus*. He, too, abandoned the coalition, and may have even begun to pass information to the Cid. Not long after, Alfonso VI was forced to withdraw after learning that the Almoravids were planning another campaign against him.

It was left to Berenguer Ramon II of Barcelona to defeat Rodrigo. He gathered his noblemen and knights and marched south. Outnumbered, Rodrigo withdrew to the Ports de Beseit, a rocky massif that rises dramatically along the coast between Valencia and the County of Barcelona. It is a rugged and remote region, even today; during the Umayyad period, its thick forests had provided the timber for the shipyards at Tortosa, where the caliphal fleet had been built. According to *The Song of My Cid*, Rodrigo made his camp in a mountainside pinewood named Tévar. Berenguer Ramon's army arrived in the vicinity and also made camp.

Each party was determined to gain the tactical advantage by choosing the field and terms of battle, and each commander attempted to provoke the other's rage with affronts to his honor, bravery, and prestige. The *Historia Roderici* has the count accuse the Cid of being a braggart, a thief, a false Christian, and a sorceror—the last a reference to Rodrigo's alleged practice of ornithomancy, or divining the future by observing the flight patterns and calls of birds. For his part, the Cid mocked the Catalans' "womanly courage," reminded the count of his humiliating capture, threatened to reveal him to be a coward before "all the nobility both Christian and Muslim," and scorned him as a fratricide. The final insult would have deeply stung. Berenguer Ramon had inherited the County of Barcelona together with his twin brother, Ramon Berenguer, in 1076; when Ramon was killed in a hunting accident in 1082, Berenguer was roundly accused of murdering him and became known as "the Fratricide."

During this back-and-forth, the count ordered a detachment of knights to move stealthily to a point higher on the mountainside from which they could outflank Rodrigo. Once they were in place, the battle started. The superior Catalan force swept into the Cid's encampment simultaneously from above and below, nearly overwhelming his men. In the melee Rodrigo himself was wounded and unhorsed, but fought on on foot. Soon, the battle turned, until it was Rodrigo's men who were charging through the count's camp. The result was a total victory. Once again Berenguer Ramon and his baggage train fell captive to the Cid. While his men divided the spoils, the "Master of the Battlefield" negotiated with his prisoners and, after they had set their ransoms, turned them loose, before riding north to Muslim Daroca to recover from his wounds. At about this time, the aging Mundhir al-Hajib, the Cid's last remaining rival and Berenguer Ramon's local ally, passed away.

These events made Rodrigo the uncontested master of *Sharq al-Andalus*, and the single most powerful individual in the peninsula. An exile and outlaw nobleman of obscure birth, he had nevertheless earned the deference and respect of Muslim and Christian rulers across Spain.

Indeed, in the aftermath of Tévar, Berenguer Ramon had no choice but to sue Rodrigo for peace, and he went to the royal palace of Zaragoza, where al-Musta'in II brokered the reconciliation. The count agreed to relinquish all claims to Valencia and Denia, and to recognize the Cid as lord over any lands he might conquer in the region. Both parties proclaimed a seal of "peace and friendship." The negotiations were conducted by letter—Rodrigo was too shrewd to leave the safety of Daroca for al-Musta'in's palace in Zaragoza. Once there, the *taifa* king might not have let him leave.

After he recovered from his wounds, Rodrigo rode south and camped not far from Valencia, probably to receive the tribute payments he was due from al-Qadir, who was now his de facto client and dependent. The Cid passed most of these riches directly to his troops. In the Christian world of the time, power was accrued not by amassing wealth but by distributing it. There was no true ownership: each property holder, from peasant to king, held his property in trust from the authority immediately above him. God was the only true owner. With few functioning institutions, power was personal; Christian monarchs and lords could sometimes coerce their subjects, but they more often needed their collaboration. Power lay in the ability to command loyalty. Failing to do so, one might face a claim of illegitimacy from a challenger or the Church. Largesse was key to effective governance. It was also, along with bravery and loyalty, one of the virtues of the chivalric ethos that was slowly taking shape in the Latin Christian West.

Rodrigo Díaz de Vivar embodied all three. Rather than piety or Spanish national spirit, it was his ruthless pursuit of plunder and his steady distribution of the spoils of war that made him a popular Christian hero in his own time. He was also a hero in the eyes of the Muslims of Zaragoza, for saving them from their Christian enemies. But for the Muslims of Valencia and the *Sharq*, he was nothing more than a godless and violent opportunist.

THE WILD, WILD WEST

Of the countless soldiers of fortune, Muslim and Christian, who exploited the anarchy of the Iberian Peninsula in the eleventh and twelfth centuries, Rodrigo was merely the most successful. Although even during his own life he was beginning to be portrayed as a dedicated holy warrior, he was, in fact, an indirect champion of Christianity, and probably no different from his peers in this respect. Everyone at the time spoke of political struggles using the language of religious confrontation: the Almoravids and the *taifa* kings called for *jihad* against both infidels and one another, while the Christian kings were grasping toward their own notions of holy war, drawing on a reservoir of cosmic righteousness and historical entitlement. Just as the Almoravids ostentatiously relied on the approval of the *'ulama'*, Alfonso VI and the other Christian sovereigns of the peninsula styled themselves as paladins in the service of God and the papacy. But the true lingua franca of Mediterranean politics was power, the single-minded pursuit of which could lead those same Christian and Muslim holy warriors to embrace each other shamelessly as comrades and equals, not only before man but before God.

Among other well-known mercenaries was the Ordóñez clan, Rodrigo's rivals in the Castilian court, who unlike him managed to stay in their king's unpredictable good graces. Another was Álvar Fáñez (or Háñez) Minaya, described variously as Rodrigo's cousin or nephew, who in the 1070s and 1080s rode alongside his exiled kinsman. He, too, served Alfonso VI as both warrior and envoy, managing to maintain his reputation for loyalty. A redoubtable general in his own right, he acquired no less of a reputation for ruthless cruelty than the Cid himself, and was blamed by Muslim chroniclers for ravaging villages, carrying off children, cutting off women's breasts, and castrating men, all to sow terror in his quest for gold. Opportunity abounded for anyone who was willing to set aside principle in the name of gain. Many of the Castilians captured by Yusuf ibn Tashufin or who came to his court as mercenaries rose to positions of authority in Almoravid North Africa, acquiring estates and honors. Under the amir's son and successor, 'Ali ibn Yusuf, a Catalan nobleman known as "Reverter" commanded the Almoravid praetorian guard, which was made up of Christian captives and soldiers for hire. He became a pillar of the Almoravid regime in North Africa, in whose service he was—so it was said—never defeated.

For many among the warrior elites of the Middle Ages, religion was for Sundays (or Fridays or Saturdays, depending on one's faith), at most. Their actions were rooted in an ethos of honor, a hunger for power and wealth, a sense of entitlement, and an appreciation of prestige, all of which often took precedence over religious differences. They were professional

Warriors, from the tenth-century *Urgell Beatus*

killers. A Christian knight and Muslim warrior facing each other in the field knew that the next day they might well be brothers-in-arms, and this understanding created a sense of mutual respect that easily transcended the dictates of faith. Muslim warriors and Christian knights swore oaths to each other, exchanged weapons, falcons, and tack, sang each other's praises, and bore each other gifts. They competed in tournaments, hunted together, feasted with each other, attended religious services together, and gave each other the "kiss of peace"—knowing full well that on another day they might be fighting each other to the death.

This vocational solidarity saw Muslim and Christian monarchs and warriors take refuge in each other's kingdoms (as the young Alfonso VI did in al-Qadir's Toledo) and recognize each other's nobility or command. It allowed Muslim Zaragoza to emerge as a cultural, political, and social hub for the Christian elite of northern Spain—the site of Sancha of Castile's marriage, Berenguer Ramon's accord with the Cid, and surely many other celebrations, negotiations, and exchanges. Jews figured in these moments of exchange and coexistence, rarely as warriors (as in the case of Isma'il ibn Naghrilla), but frequently as statesmen. Many Jews served

Muslim kings. In 1085 one in a series of Jewish *wazirs* of Zaragoza, the poet Abu Fadl Hasday ibn Hasday al-Isra'ili, was charged with arranging the wedding of a nephew of al-Mutaman to a daughter of al-Qadir's rival for the throne of Valencia, Abu Bakr al-Mansur, a ceremony at which the Cid and the king's other warriors were likely in attendance.

The Cid was not only the most successful soldier of fortune in pre-Crusade Spain, he was one of the first, which perhaps helps to explain why he captured the imagination of the inhabitants of the peninsula and beyond in the 1100s. Indeed, by the second decade of the eleventh century, foreigners were increasingly drawn as hired lances or privateers to the contested frontier between Muslim al-Andalus and Christian Hispania. Normans and Franks soon began to arrive in the peninsula, individuals like Robert Burdet, who seized control of the ancient archepiscopal city of Tarragona with the collusion of the archbishop in 1129, and established a principality that would last until the Catalans expelled the Normans in 1177. At the same time, fleets from the rising Italian mercantile city-states, Genoa and Pisa, began to attack Muslim port towns, with or without the assistance of local Christian kings. To the west, in Portugal, Geraldo Sem Pavor ("the Fearless") would lead his private army to capture key Andalusi towns in the 1160s, threatening the prerogatives of León and driving its king, Fernando II, to form an alliance with the Almohads—Masmuda Berbers who by this point had overthrown the Sanhaja Almoravids.

The peninsula's Muslim rulers and factions remained no less aggressive. The *taifa* kings had been at one another's throats since the fall of the Caliphate of Córdoba, and for all their posturing, the Almoravids and their commanders proved no less self-interested and corrupt. In the 1100s the last remnants of the *taifa* dynasties would join forces with Christian powers in a last-ditch attempt to turn back the blue-veiled tide. Disenfranchised members of the local elite, like Sayf al-Dawla, heir to the deposed Hudid dynasty of Zaragoza, and Muhammad ibn Mardanish of Murcia ("King Wolf" to the Christians), became Castilian vassals and fought the Almoravids and Almohads as self-styled defenders of the Spanish Muslims against these foreign foes. In no small irony, when Almoravid power, undermined by the Almohad insurgency, began to decline in the second half of the twelfth century, the Almoravids would present themselves as the defenders of the indigenous Andalusis and seek the protection of Christian kings.

But to many observers in the 1080s, the end of al-Andalus and the

Christian conquest did not seem probable, let alone imminent. The *taifa* kings had survived, owing to the intervention of the Almoravids, and with the latter now departed, normalcy, or what passed for it, resumed. But the accusations of the *'ulama'* against the *taifa* kings were becoming ever more shrill. Popular revolt was a real possibility. By 1090 provincial towns were refusing to send tribute to their kings, highly placed officials were defecting, *muftis* were thundering righteously, and petitioners were crossing the straits in droves to beseech Yusuf to intervene once again. The *taifa* kings countered with repression, denial, and mutual recrimination. Disobedient local governors were deposed and dissident clerics imprisoned, and the common folk grew ever more embittered.

Finally, in 1090, Yusuf crossed over for the second time, determined now to take al-Andalus for himself. The first *taifa* king to fall was 'Abd Allah ibn Buluqqin, who was summoned to Ibn Tashufin's camp under the assumption that he would be marching off to war alongside Yusuf, only to be arrested and sent off in chains to Aghmat. 'Abd Allah's brother, Tamim, ruler of Málaga, soon met the same fate. In this way the era of the Banu Ziri came to an end. Almería, which had become a center of learning and culture to rival Zaragoza, fell in 1091, its king, al-Mu'tasim b'illah (one of the few popular *taifa* rulers), having died a few months prior. With the far south secure, the Almoravids marched on Seville, the most powerful of the *taifa* kingdoms.

With the Sanhaja forces and their Andalusi allies on the move, al-Mu'tamid of Seville went humbly to Alfonso, who grew alarmed at the prospect of losing his last and most lucrative Muslim tributary. In a flurry of diplomatic correspondence with the *taifa* rulers, the Castilian king attempted to counter the rhetoric of the Almoravids by presenting himself as the legitimate sovereign of a Spain in which both Christians and Muslims were his natural subjects. He was, as he provocatively claimed in a letter to Yusuf ibn Tashufin, *Imbaratur dhu'l-millatayn*—"Emperor of the Two Religions"—a title not a few Andalusi Muslims were now prepared to entertain, given that the alternative was the Almoravids' uncompromising fundamentalism. But the Muslims who backed Alfonso did not include al-Mu'tamid, who, when ordered by Alfonso to hand the government of his kingdom over to Álvar Fáñez in exchange for protection, cursed the Castilian king's vanity and vowed to fight on his own.

For all their valor and determination, neither the king nor his sons could resist the force arrayed against them. Al-Mu'tamid's son, Fath al-Ma'mun, the governor of Córdoba, died in battle against the invaders and those among his own populace who wanted to open the city to the Almoravids. Al-Mu'tamid, now seeing the folly of his rejection of Alfonso, attempted to seal an alliance with the king by offering him his beautiful daughter-in-law, Sayyida, Fath al-Ma'mun's widow. Alfonso accepted the gift. But he could not save Seville.

The Almoravids marched on the *taifa* capital. Their general, Abu 'Abd Allah ibn al-Hajj, led the column; Yusuf had returned to Aghmat with his captive *taifa* kings.* The army was intercepted at Almodovar del Rio, just west of Seville, by a large detachment of troops under Álvar Fáñez; but they repulsed the Castilian-led force and continued on. Arriving at Seville, they encircled the city and hunkered down for a protracted siege. Inside the walls al-Mu'tamid and his remaining sons vowed to fight or outlast the siege. The latter was not an unrealistic hope, as the Almoravids were desert warriors whose tactics and temperament were not well suited to attacking stone fortifications, or to the boredom of the siege. But al-Mu'tamid also had to quell the restive elements within his walls, who yearned for Almoravid rule and were eager to hand over the city to them. During the summer months there were skirmishes, breaches, and attempted betrayals, until the assault came on a day in September. As the Almoravid forces converged on one of the city gates, the king himself rode out with his cavalry and fended off the attackers. But the Almoravids regrouped and breached the city's fortifications. After several days of house-to-house fighting in the narrow, twisting lanes of Seville, al-Mu'tamid sued for peace. Ibn al-Hajj demanded an unconditional surrender. If al-Mu'tamid's sons and castellans did not all hand over their fortresses, the king and his entire family would be slaughtered.

And so the 'Abbadid dynasty, traditional rival to the Zirids of Granada and standard-bearers of the native Andalusi elite, came to end. Their Kingdom of Seville was absorbed into the sprawling Almoravid imperium. For many Muslims in Córdoba, Seville, and elsewhere in the south,

---

* In Aghmat, 'Abd Allah ibn Buluqqin passed his days writing his memoir, *al-Tibyan* (Apology), an account of his family's rule over the Kingdom of Granada. Al-Mu'tamid's wives and daughters were reduced to spinning to earn their keep, while the former king wrote sycophantic poems for Yusuf ibn Tashufin in the vain hope he would rise in the amir's graces, and plaintive, melancholy verse in remembrance of his vanished al-Andalus.

Almoravid rule and the imposition of their brand of orthodox Islamic law would have come as a relief after so many years of tyranny and decadence, of insecurity and political violence, and of humiliating and costly subjugation to a Christian regime. They would soon be disabused of their optimism. From the Almoravid perspective, it was not the *taifa* kings alone who were to blame for the decline of al-Andalus. To the conquerors, the common people were accountable for their religious laxity and for colluding in the corruption of their kings.

After the fall of Seville, three major *taifa* kingdoms remained: Badajoz, Valencia, and Zaragoza. Al-Mutawakkil of Badajoz sensed quite correctly that the Almoravids would test him first, and so he threw his lot in with Alfonso VI, promising to hand over the towns of Lisbon, Sintra, and Santarem in exchange for his protection. Valencia remained ostensibly under the rule of al-Qadir, but in reality only the threat of violence from the Cid stood between al-Qadir and anarchy. As for Rodrigo, following a final estrangement from Alfonso, he went back to Zaragoza, where according to the *Historia Roderici*, "the citizens both great and small . . . besought him with many prayers to have love and peace and friendship with their king." He negotiated a peace between al-Musta'in and the aging Sancho Ramírez of Aragon, providing a respite for the king of Zaragoza and allowing him to turn once more toward Valencia. That same year, Alfonso, starved of the tribute he had depended on from the now defunct *taifa* kingdoms, laid siege to Valencia, supported by a naval blockade by Genoa and Pisa.

The object was to regain the *parias* Alfonso had lost from Albarracín, Denia, Valencia, and the other towns of the prosperous *Sharq al-Andalus*, if not to seize Valencia outright. But the king would lift the siege almost as soon as it had begun, seeing that he had underestimated the forces of the Cid and his allies. In the west, the Almoravid commander Syr ibn Abi Bakr (Yusuf's nephew), eager to take advantage of any weakness in Castile, massed his troops for an attack on Toledo, just as, in the east, Rodrigo led his Christian and Muslim troops on a diversionary raid deep into the Rioja, the power base of the Ordóñez clan. The Cid sacked Nájera and Calahorra and put Logroño, the major town in the region, to the torch. This episode became a source of discomfort for historians, both in the Middle Ages and more recently, who have striven to paint Rodrigo as an idealist and a Christian hero. Thanks to the Cid, Muslim Valencia was saved and the Christian Rioja was ravaged.

KING OF VALENCIA

There are a multitude of extant sources, in Arabic and Latin, that recount what happened next in Valencia, each of them with an agenda, many of them compiled after the fact, and several obviously borrowing from another. Though it is difficult to draw from them a reliable narrative, all suggest that the kingdom was fast approaching disaster. The power struggle among Castile, Barcelona, Denia, and the Cid over *Sharq al-Andalus* was taking its toll. Local elites sensed the unpopular al-Qadir's vulnerability, and began to plot an uprising. They may have assumed that the Cid, like Alfonso, was too absorbed by problems in the north to be able to protect him. With discontent pervading the region, the Almoravids moved in. It is a measure of the Cid's stature that Yusuf ibn Tashufin reputedly dispatched letters addressing him personally, to warn him away from Valencia. Not all the local Muslims regarded the Sanhaja as saviors, however, and many were said to be enlisting in the ranks of the Cid's forces stationed just outside the city, in Alcudia, in support of Rodrigo's trusted Muslim lieutenant and *wazir*, al-Faraj.

In 1092 a party headed by the *qadi* of Valencia, Ibn Jahhaf, along with other local leaders conspiring against al-Qadir, sent messages in secret to Yusuf ibn Tashufin's son, Da'ud (David) ibn 'A'isha, who was commanding the Sanhaja forces in the northeast. They promised to hand over control of the city to him. Da'ud's Almoravids moved on Denia, where the townsfolk opened up their gates to welcome them, and then the cautious commander sent a small contingent (five hundred men, according to the perennially exaggerating chroniclers) to Valencia. Ibn Jahhaf's fifth column struck. His supporters in the city attacked al-Qadir's palace guards, set fire to the city gates, and arrested al-Faraj. The Christian garrison in Alcudia and the native Christian population of the city fled. In the chaos, al-Qadir tried to escape disguised as a woman, his *jubba* stuffed with as much gold, jewelry, and coins as he could carry. But he was discovered, arrested, and sentenced to death as a traitor to Islam by Ibn Jahhaf. The crowds cheered as the king's head was paraded around the city on a lance. As most Muslims in Valencia saw it, with his death a long period of oppression had come to an end.

The Cid saw not justice but rebellion in these events. Having learned of Valencia's fate from the refugees who reached Zaragoza, he hastened to the city with all his soldiers and made camp on a small hillock just to the north of the city walls. Without a navy, Rodrigo could not blockade the city, so he launched a series of attacks on the surrounding towns, to bring the countryside under his control, extract money to pay for his campaign, and terrify the inhabitants of Valencia into submission.

Ibn Jahhaf had restored religious law in Valencia, purged al-Qadir's corrupt supporters, and paid its civil service and soldiers, all in an attempt to legitimate himself as the ruler of an Islamic republic. Growing in confidence, Ibn Jahhaf came to see the presence of the Almoravids as an inconvenience. He began to steal from the treasury al-Qadir had filled at the expense of the various *taifa* rulers who had sought refuge with him, but the people of Valencia intervened, seizing most of this money and sending it to the Almoravids, in the hope that the foreigners would raise a force to attack the Cid. Aware of the different aims of those behind Valencia's walls, Rodrigo began to send overtures to al-Jahhaf, suggesting that he could enjoy the same relationship al-Qadir had previously had with him. The *qadi* responded discreetly but optimistically, and Rodrigo led him on. Rodrigo's intent was to create discord and suspicion among the city's strongly pro-Almoravid populace. The gambit worked; as Syr ibn Abi Bakr's forces approached from the south, Ibn Jahhaf was arrested by his former supporters, and Valencia was left leaderless.

In early fall of 1093 a major battle appeared imminent. Rodrigo prepared his men to face the brunt of the Almoravid army in open battle, determined to succeed where every previous challenger had failed. The people of Valencia laid plans to attack the Cid's rear. The Almoravids conquered town after town in their march up the coast, and soon the smoke from their campfires could be seen rising from the plain just south of the city. Through the night both the citizens of Valencia and the Cid's forces primed for battle, sharpening their weapons and praying to the God of Abraham, each man steeling himself to meet the fate He had decreed. But when dawn broke, the people of the city saw that all that remained of Ibn Abi Bakr's army was the smoldering ashes of its campfires. The Almoravids had withdrawn. Why they did so remains a mystery, although they had on a number of earlier occasions failed to press an advantage for fear of suffering losses. Perhaps the reason was undependable supply lines, as their commanders would claim. Or maybe Syr ibn Abi Bakr had decided instead to buttress Almoravid holdings in the west by attacking Badajoz, the last great *taifa* kingdom in that region.

Whatever the reason for the Almoravid retreat, it left the Valencians reeling in disbelief and Rodrigo's men thanking their good fortune. They once again threw their energies into the siege. The Cid ordered anyone who tried to leave Valencia to be executed. With no alternative the people reinstated Ibn Jahhaf as their king. Over the next ten months he vacillated between negotiations with the Cid and resistance. As the people of the city suffered, and as winter turned to spring, they faced the very real possibility of starvation. No sign of relief from the Almoravids appeared. From the city's battlements, the people of Valenica looked with despair upon the Breughelesque carnival of the Cid's siege camp, where loot and prisoners from the Cid's attacks on the countryside were brought to be haggled over, bought, sold, and (in the case of women) raped.

By May 1094 the city was gravely low on provisions, though the chronicler Ibn 'Alqama was perhaps exaggerating when he wrote of cannibalism in Valencia. The qadi ruler attempted to maintain order, outlawing food hoarding and acting against speculation and price-gouging, but to little effect. Finally, Ibn Jahhaf agreed to parley. Rodrigo was not inclined to extend terms. Instead, he sent his treasurer Ibn 'Abduz to inform the qadi that he would be taking over the financial administration of the city, and that the Cid's wazir, al-Faraj, who had managed to escape his captivity, would be returning as governor. The latter arrived with a detachment of local Mozarabs to serve as a skeleton garrison and take control of the city's gates. Ibn Jahhaf requested a guarantee of safety for himself and his family, and the right to remain in power. It was agreed that he would send messengers to the Almoravids and Zaragoza, but if neither sent a relief force before the end of fifteen days, he would surrender. This was a common procedure in sieges of this type; it allowed both sides a chance to regroup, and paved the way for an orderly and swift surrender should the defenders realize that they would not be relieved. At this point the Cid evidently relaxed the siege, allowing merchants to enter the city with food. It was now in his interests to appear as a merciful and reasonable protector of the people of Valencia.

On June 15, 1094, Rodrigo Díaz de Vivar triumphantly rode into Valencia as its new lord, with Ibn Jahhaf installed as chief magistrate and the Cid's other Muslim officials managing the administration. On his arrival a delegation of the city's leading citizens came to "bid him welcome, and he received them very well and with great honor." If the thirteenth-century Castilian *Primera crónica general* can be trusted, the Cid was gallant and restrained, and made every effort not to offend his Muslim subjects. He is said to have assured the locals that the garrison consisted of men who had been "raised among Muslims," spoke Arabic, and were under orders to treat the populace with courtesy.* He would not allow his men to plunder the defeated city, and pledged not to levy any tax on the Muslim inhabitants higher than the 'ushr, the tithe ordained by the Qur'an, and to personally sit as judge twice every week to hear their petitions and complaints. They would always be welcome in his presence. He would be a "comrade," "friend," and "kinsman," and would not, unlike their previous kings, neglect them for women, singing, and drinking. In other words, Rodrigo—an infidel—would be the antithesis of a *taifa* king.

From the Cid's perspective, it was crucial to gain the confidence and support of the people, with the Almoravids again massing. The fall of the city had been an affront to Yusuf ibn Tashufin. In the words of the poet and historian Ibn Bassam, who lived through the events, "The fall of Valencia by the Cid was a thunderbolt on the Muslims of the Peninsula, and covered everyone of every social class in pain and shame." For Yusuf, "it was a poke in the eye, and he thought of nothing else."

By September 1094 the Almoravid army had returned to the city. Composed of the bulk of the Almoravid forces, as well as North African and sub-Saharan contingents and the armies of the remaining *taifa* kingdoms (except for those of Albarracín and Zaragoza), the host was a formidable one. Rodrigo was prepared: he had stocked the city, disarmed the local Muslims, and expelled all of those, including women and children, who were suspected of Almoravid sympathies. The refugees overwhelmed the Almoravid camp; and the foreign soldiers, who had little sympathy for the Andalusis, abused them, robbing the men and raping the women. Rodrigo spread rumors among the enemy that reinforcements were on their way from Castile and Aragon, and that he had read his own victory in the omens of the birds. He also made it known that once he had defeated Yusuf's army he would carry out brutal and exemplary reprisals against any collaborators. News soon reached him that the attackers' morale was wavering and that some regiments had withdrawn.

* Underlining the Cid's supposed gallantry and sensitivity, the Castilian chronicle claimed that Rodrigo ordered the windows of the towers that overlooked the town covered, so that the Muslims would not have to fear that his soldiers might peer through their windows to glimpse their women and offend their honor.

As was his habit, the Cid took the initiative, opening the city gates early on the morning of October 21 and sending out a detachment of light cavalry against the front lines of the waking enemy camp. The Almoravids rose to respond with their heavy cavalry, confident of their chances against what appeared to be a pathetic Christian force. Before the two sides could clash, though, Rodrigo's horses turned and galloped back toward the city, with the jubilant forces of the amir in hot, undisciplined pursuit. The tactic was called "turn and flee" (*al-qarr wa'l-farr* in Arabic, or *tornafuye* as the Latins called it); the Cid had learned it from his Muslim allies. After the false retreat came the ambush.

The effect was devastating. Rodrigo's fleeing cavalry enticed the disordered Berber vanguard into volleys of crossbow fire from their flanks. But there was worse to come for the Almoravids. The previous night the Cid had sent the bulk of his forces on a long route around the Almoravid lines, to pose as the Castilian relief force, a sight that would only further sap the enemy's morale. As the diversionary charge was under way, these men swept into the Almoravid camp, putting the defenders to flight and capturing their baggage train, including the treasure-filled royal tent of Yusuf's kinsman Muhammad ibn Tashufin. Once again the Cid had faced likely defeat and emerged victorious, humiliated his enemies, and captured a king's ransom.

Now that he was secure as ruler of Valencia, his Muslim subjects would see another side of "Prince Rodrigo Campidoctor." The leading citizens were ordered on pain of torture to hand over the treasures they had hidden prior to the conquest. The Cid charged Ibn Jahhaf with regicide—he had ordered al-Qadir executed—and had him put to death.

According to a later compilation, the *Bayan al-Mughrib*, Rodrigo soon after created a fiscal administration led by a Jewish *wazir*, who was given full judicial powers, including the ability to mete out corporal punishment to lawbreakers.

Rodrigo set out to remake Valencia as a Christian city, seizing a number of sites of Muslim worship and converting them into churches.

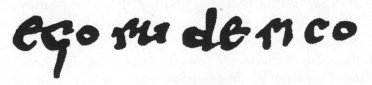

"ego ruderico" (I, Rodrigo), the Cid's signature

The great congregational mosque was consecrated as the Cathedral of St. Vincent, and the Cid appointed a French monk, Jérôme de Périgord, as bishop. Rodrigo surely hoped to attract loyal Christian settlers to the city, though it proved a futile cause, as in the 1090s there was simply no Christian interest in colonizing the unstable Andalusi frontier. Rodrigo also sent for his long-suffering wife. Ximena probably came with their two daughters, although it is possible that the eldest, Cristina, had already been married to Ramiro Sánchez, a Navarro-Aragonese prince. Soon after, the younger daughter, María, would be betrothed to Ramon Berenguer III of Barcelona, a marital alliance intended to contain the aggression of the nephew and successor of the Cid's old enemy, Berenguer Ramon II.

In 1096 Rodrigo would face his last challenge from the Almoravids. He was lured south to a place on the coast called Bairén, where it appeared that his luck had run out: he and his men found themselves surrounded in a narrow defile by a far superior force under Muhammad ibn Tashufin. But once more Rodrigo personally rallied his troops in a charge through the Almoravid lines, throwing the enemy into disarray and capturing and looting the commander's camp.

THE END OF AN ERA

Rodrigo spent the final years of his life fending off Christian rivals and stamping out Muslim resistance in *Sharq al-Andalus* with his customary mercilessness. Near the turn of the century, Rodrigo would have been in his late fifties, old by the standards of the day. He would have been physically worn down after forty years under arms and on a horse. Across the Iberian Peninsula, and in France and the Maghrib, his name had become legend. As Ibn Bassam put it, "this man, the scourge of his time, by his appetite for glory, by the prudent steadfastness of his character, and by his heroic bravery was one of the miracles of God." He died sometime in 1099. Much later stories, including Anthony Mann's cinematic potrayal, had him saving the widowed Ximena and Valencia from an Almoravid attack posthumously—his stiffened corpse strapped atop his faithful steed, Babieca, and sent charging into the enemy host. Only slightly more believable is the claim that he passed away on July 15, the same day that the city of Jerusalem fell to the Christian armies of the First Crusade—too neat a coincidence to give credence to.*

Whatever the exact date, by the time Rodrigo died the world was changing, not the least for the Christian and Muslim rulers of the *taifa* period. In the west the last great *taifa* kingdom, Badajoz, had been conquered by the Almoravids in 1094. Al-Mutawakkil, who had briefly ruled Toledo and had faced Alfonso VI at Zallaqa, was arrested and executed, as were his sons al-Fadl and Sa'd. A third, al-Mansur, established a rump principality on the frontier of Castile before finally deciding to join Alfonso and convert to Christianity. In this respect if no other, the Cid's fortune was little better than al-Mutawakkil's. Apparently, Rodrigo had a son, Diego, who also fought in the service of Castile but who was killed in battle in 1097 and did not live to inherit Valencia. His daughter María's marriage to Ramon Berenguer III would yield only daughters. And while Cristina would give birth to a boy who would ascend to the throne of Navarre in 1134, Rodrigo's line would die with him.

The year after Rodrigo's death, the Almoravids returned in force to Castile and Valencia, and it became clear that the city could not be held. In 1102 Alfonso rode south and evacuated Ximena and the city's Christian inhabitants. In late April or early May, after Alfonso's departure, the Almoravid general entered the smoldering city. As a Muslim chronicler wrote, "God took Valencia from the hands of polytheism, and from the power of the Christians; he cleansed it, and rekindled in it the light of Islam and the religion of Muhammad after eight and a half years, and the command of Destiny, as foreseen by the wisdom of God."

Yusuf ibn Tashufin would not have long to savor the victory. By 1104 the great amir was ill. As his condition declined he summoned his sons and began to prepare for the succession. His title would go to his son 'Ali ibn Yusuf, whereas power in the empire would be shared among the various members of his clan. By 1106 portents were appearing in the skies, including a comet that remained visible for three months. On September 2

---

* On the other hand, Count Berenguer Ramon, "the Fratricide," may well have died on that day. He had abdicated in 1097 and taken up the Cross, perhaps hoping to escape the opprobrium heaped upon him in his homeland for his brother's murder. According to certain accounts, he died in one of the assaults on the Holy City's walls.

he died. As one eulogy put it, "The prince had the determination and energy to defend the religion, proclaim his word, and aid Islam."

His old enemy "Aldhufunsh" (an Arabic corruption of the Latin *Ildefonsus*, or Alfonso) would survive him by three years, dying in 1109 at age seventy-one, his fate ultimately mirroring that of his rebellious vassal, Rodrigo. Alfonso's beloved heir, his only son, Sancho—born of Sayyida, the Muslim princess—had been killed in 1108 as he fled from a stunning defeat at the hands of Yusuf ibn Tashufin's son, Tamim, at the Battle of Uclés. As for Alfonso, even in his last year he went on campaign, ranging up and down Castile, rallying his defenses against the impending Almoravid offensive, until in June he collapsed under the care of his trusted physician, Joseph ibn Ferruziel, *Nasi* of the Jews of Castile. He would last no more than a month. In recalling the king's death, an anonymous Cluniac monk evoked scenes of his Muslim, Jewish, and Christian subjects wailing in despair, before concluding, "Today, on this day, the sun has risen over the Muslims and infidels, has darkened greatly over the Christians." Alfonso's realms would be quarreled over by his two surviving daughters, the illegitimate Theresa, who founded the Kingdom of Portugal, and the widowed Urraca, who would rule over Castile-León.

The last *taifa* kingdom, Zaragoza, ceased to exist in 1110; the populace had tired of the heavy *parias* payments and opened their doors to the Almoravids, having cast out the Banu Hud dynasty, who took refuge in Christian Castile. But Almoravid rule soon lost its appeal for the Andalusis. What had first been lauded as an Islamic revival was now viewed as an invasion by a haughty Sanhaja clique. Andalusis had seen their culture and religious traditions trampled on, and their local clergy disempowered. The Almoravids had failed to defeat the Christians, and had begun to levy outrageous taxes in the manner of the *taifa* kings. In 1144 Sayf al-Dawla, a grandson of Rodrigo's old patron, al-Musta'in, would lead a peninsula-wide native Muslim uprising against the now hated Almoravids, briefly occupying many of the major cities of the south. He took Valencia, thereby fulfilling his forefathers' ambition, before being killed in battle in 1146. The Almoravids faced trouble at home as well; that same year their capital, Marrakesh, fell to the Almohads, their Masmuda Berber nemeses.

By this time Zaragoza had been a Christian city for over a generation, having been conquered by Alfonso I of Aragon in 1118. The great library of al-Muqtadir and al-Mutaman had been scattered. Most of it ended up in Toledo, a city that, thanks to this, became the major center of the translation of works of Arabo-Islamic science and philosophy into Latin. Here, in 1142, the English clergyman Robert of Ketton was commissioned by Peter the Venerable, Abbot of Cluny, to carry out the first translation of the Qur'an into Latin—as a weapon for the order's arsenal in its war against Islam.

In a way, then, it was the Cid who outlived all his contemporaries and rivals, if not as a man, then as a legend. In the centuries following his death he would become an inspiration for Crusaders; later, a symbol of the Christian "Reconquest" and a personification of Spanish nationalism; and finally, as Hollywood hero, an open-minded, noble Everyman. And he remains attractive to this day, precisely because, for all we seem to know about him, his true character, motivations, and beliefs are elusive.

PART III

❋

Kings of Sicily, Kings of Africa

5

A Norman Conquest

One can imagine the fading sun of a late autumn day in Palermo, Sicily, in 1153.* It may have been early November; Ibn al-Athir, the great Arab chronicler, writing some three generations later, placed the day in the holy month of Ramadan. Hard by the ceremonial southern gate of the city, with the great walled palace of Roger II looming on one side and the city's former great mosque (by then, the Church of St. Gregory) on the other, would have been a solitary figure. Philip of Mahdia was the admiral, chamberlain, and confidant of the Norman king. He had stood in that spot many times before, as the cheers of the citizens of Palermo washed over him. But today they were not here to sing the praises of this commander, who had only recently captured the North African city of 'Annaba (modern Bône), completing Roger's conquest of Tunisia and

---

* The Islamic (*Hijri*) calendar consists of twelve months that correspond to lunar cycles. Because the year has only 354 or 355 days and there is no intercalary month to make it correspond to the solar year (as in the Jewish calendar), each Islamic month "moves" in relation to the Gregorian, or Western, calendar, occurring about ten days earlier with each coming year. The Islamic month of Ramadan of the year 548 corresponds to mid-November to mid-December 1153.

enabling him to claim the title King of Africa. Nor was it likely that Philip was dressed in his official finery that day. More probably he was wearing the unadorned shift of a supplicant or penitent, his dark brown skin a contrast to the plain white cotton. Tall, with the delicate features and long graceful limbs characteristic of a man castrated in prepubescence, he may have appeared almost angelic. Gone would have been any glint of pride or spark of arrogance from his countenance. Instead of being honored, he had been put on trial.

Scanning the crowd, he may have focused on the veiled features of the women, their hennaed hands clutching silk gauze across their faces, as he tried to guess which were Muslim and which Christian. The grim, bearded Orthodox priests, staring impassively beneath their chimney-pot hats and clutching crucifixes, would have offered little solace. Turning away from the gaggle of his fellow eunuchs in nervous expectation, Philip may have looked toward the scattering of turbans, and tried to meet the uneasy, downcast glances of local Muslim men. But these would have been outnumbered by the scowling Latin Christian throngs.

His attention and theirs would soon turn to the nearby dais and the dignitaries perched upon it. No less a figure than the aging King Roger himself would have stepped forward, and if Philip had any hopes that his boyhood patron and protector would save him, these were soon dashed. According to the only contemporary Christian account of what followed—the *Chronicon*, attributed to Archbishop Romuald of Salerno—the king addressed the crowds with these words:

May you know by your faith, dear subjects, that My soul has been pierced by the greatest pain, and goaded by great stabs of anger, because this, My minister, whom, once his sins had been cleansed, I raised from a boy to be Catholic, has been revealed as a Muslim, and this Muslim carried out works of faithlessness under the guise of faith. Yet, had he offended Our majesty in other ways: had he carried off even the greater part of Our treasury, he would have certainly found forgiveness before Us, and would have obtained mercy in recollection of all of his good service. But, because by his deeds he has principally offended God, and he provided others with the opportunity and example to sin, I should not remit such injury to Our faith and offense to the Christian religion even to My own son, nor should I pardon any other kin.

The noblemen and dignitaries who flanked the king withdrew, and after huddling for a brief discussion, stepped forward to pronounce their verdict:

> We order Philip, a derider of the Christian name and agent of the works of faithlessness under the guise of faith, to be burned by vengeful flames, so that he who rejected the fire of charity, may know the fire of combustion, and that no relic of this most evil man might remain, but that, having been converted into ashes by temporal fire, he may go on to be burned in perpetuity by the eternal fire.

Guards would have pounced on Philip, bound him, and tied him to a brace of wild horses that then dragged him to a well-stoked lime kiln. Here the battered and bloody Philip was apparently cut loose, and without further ceremony thrown into the white-hot flames. The eunuch Philip of Mahdia—an African Muslim slave acquired as a youth by Roger, converted to Christianity, freed, and raised as the king's protégé and prime minister—had been condemned to the most humiliating, disgraceful, and public death possible.

The kingdom had been cleansed. Or had it? Also looking on would have been Philip's onetime comrades: servants and officials of the king, who like Philip were former slaves, and Muslims who had converted to Christianity and wielded great influence in Roger's kingdom.

By 1153 the Crusading movement formally set in motion by Pope Urban II in 1095 had expanded into a global struggle against any and all enemies of the Church. And yet, although Jerusalem had been conquered a half century earlier by the knights of the First Crusade, the enterprise was in danger. The Crusader County of Edessa had fallen to Muslim armies, the Second Crusade had failed, and the great sultan Nur al-Din was at the height of his power and had his eyes on the Holy City. What kind of a kingdom, then, was Sicily, where Latin Christians, excommunicate Byzantine Orthodox, and infidel Muslims lived side by side? Where a Christian king raised ex-Muslim slaves to positions of command and aspired to be king of Muslim Africa? What would possess Roger to turn against one of his most faithful servants? And who was Philip of Mahdia? The answer lies with the men responsible for his rise, and with the origins of Norman Sicily.

"1061 AND ALL THAT . . ."

The term "Norman Conquest" usually calls to mind the history of medieval England—specifically the Battle of Hastings, and the image of the unfortunate Saxon king, Harald Godwinson, shot through the eye with an arrow. With that battle a family of French counts under William of Normandy, now "the Conqueror," seized the English throne and changed the course of Western history. But there was another Norman conquest of an island. It had begun five years earlier, and at the time would have appeared far more impressive and consequential. Whereas England was a poor and uncivilized land of wooden fortresses and scrubby hamlets, and London a clutch of huts surrounding a single stone building, the first St. Paul's, Sicily was populous, rich, and culturally sophisticated. The wealth of its capital, Palermo, alone far exceeded that of William the Conqueror's entire Kingdom of England; strategically and economically the city was at the center of the Mediterranean. And in 1061 a band of rapacious Normans arrived there.

The term "Normans" comes from "Norsemen," in reference to the clans of pagan Vikings who had settled in the misty Cotentin Peninsula in the northwest of France after striking an accord with King Charles the Simple in the 900s. In exchange for stopping their raiding, they were recognized as the lords of Normandy. They took up Christianity and served the French kings as knights. Tancred de Hauteville was a descendant of one of these clans, a minor lord who had no less than a dozen sons, eight of whom, beginning in the 1030s, set out—like many of their fellow countrymen—for Italy, in search of their fortune.

Southeastern Italy and Sicily had long been ruled by the Byzantine Empire, although since the late 800s Muslim raiders from North Africa had established a string of city-states along its shores. Muslim forces would complete the conquest of Sicily in 902. However, Muslims were not the gravest threat from Byzantium's perspective. By the late 900s the empire had recovered from the disastrous losses it suffered during the Arabo-Islamic expansion of the late 600s, and reemerged as a world power. Key to this revival was the long reign of Basil II, "the Bulgar Slayer," the conqueror of the Balkans, whose fifty years on the throne brought prosperity and security to Byzantium.

Yet the death of the childless emperor in 1025 provoked a series of crises. The crown first went to his younger brother, Constantine VIII, a reprobate whose response to the growing unrest of his nobility was to take refuge in worldly pleasure. On Constantine's death in 1028, the empire passed to his feuding daughters, Zoe and Theodora, and to their various husbands and relatives. A succession of plots, drownings, poisonings, exiles, and returns ensued. The weakening of Byzantium coincided with the rise of new political forces in Italy, notably the trading republics Venice, Pisa, Genoa, and Amalfi—towns that were tapping into the thriving commerce of the Greco-Islamic Mediterranean—and the efforts of local "Lombard" strongmen to shake off imperial rule.

But the empire would have been most unsettled by the transformation of the Latin Church, which was then becoming a coherent ideological and institutional body under the authority of the papacy. Until that point the popes had been little more than the bishops of Rome, an office held hostage by notoriously corrupt local families locked in petty struggles to control the city and the papal provinces. But in the mid-eleventh century, driven by currents of reform originating in northern France and spearheaded by the Order of Cluny, the popes began to pursue the authority due to them as the "Vicars of Christ on Earth," and to transform the Church. This movement was most clearly articulated under Hildebrand, a Tuscan priest of peasant origin who went on in 1073 to become Pope Gregory VII. The Gregorian Reform, as his innovations were called, put the election of popes in the hands of the cardinals instead of the people of Rome, required the clergy to remain celibate, forbade the purchase of Church offices, and declared the pope the ultimate authority on Earth, who possessed the power to depose emperors. The reform, in turn, laid the foundation for the Investiture Controversy, the long struggle between Church and empire sparked by the papal prohibition against kings and emperors appointing bishops and other Church officials in their lands.

The reformed Latin Church would challenge not only the claims of political and religious superiority of the German-based "Holy Roman Emperors," but those of the true Roman emperors in Constantinople.* As early as 1054 legates of Pope Leo IX and Michael Cerularius, the patriarch

---

* What came to be known as the Holy Roman Empire was a political fiction created by Charlemagne in 800 C.E., with the collusion of the papacy. The Latin world coveted the title Emperor of Rome, but it was still held by the successors of Constantine. In the view of contemporaries, both Christian and Muslim, what historians refer to as the Byzantine Empire was, in fact, the true Roman Empire.

of Constantinople, had excommunicated each other—marking the beginning of the East-West Schism—and by 1076 the Holy Roman Emperor, Henry IV, and the pope, Gregory VII, would declare each other deposed. Though the Gregorian Reform also included the "Peace and Truce of God," a series of Church mandates limiting the right of Christian noblemen to wage war against peasants, clergy, and one another, its immediate effect was a series of wars between the papacy and the two empires, wars in which the popes were at a decided disadvantage, given that they had no army of their own.

The papacy needed professional warriors, and the predatory de Hautevilles wanted land. In exchange for their allegiance, the Church would legitimize their authority as lords, so that their vassals could not rebel against them; legalize their rule over lands they conquered; and justify their waging war against fellow Christians. But the inauguration of this relationship was some decades off; until the 1070s the papacy and the Normans coexisted uneasily, or in open and belligerent opposition. For all their rhetoric about defending the Church, the de Hautevilles were driven not by religion but by the prospect of land and wealth, and would serve any master to further their own ends. Geoffrey Malaterra, a sympathetic near-contemporary chronicler, admiringly described them in these terms:

> This was an inborn trait of the sons of Tancred: they were always avid for domination. Whenever they were in a position of power, they suffered no one to have lands or possessions near their own without being jealous of them, so that either they would take possession of everything for themselves or they would immediately make their neighbours serve them as subjects.

One of their first military actions upon arriving in Italy was, in fact, in the service of the Byzantines, under the renowned admiral George Maniakes.* The object was Muslim Sicily, the former Byzantine territory

---

* George Maniakes had cut his teeth fighting Arabs and Saljuq Turks in Asia Minor, but his greatest successes were against the Muslims in Sicily in the 1040s, where he commanded the Viking soldiers of the Byzantine Varangian Guard. Having been discredited by the intrigues of his enemies at the imperial court, George would be proclaimed emperor by his troops when they rose up in rebellion in 1042, although the following year he was killed in a clash with the forces of the emperor Constantine IX.

now ruled by the Banu Kalb family, who were governing in the name of the Fatimid Caliphate of Egypt. For their part, the Byzantines made a show of fighting on behalf of a Muslim ally, al-Akhal, who was the amir of the island, but who had been ousted from power and whose kingdom had been invaded by the Zirid king of Ifriqiya in support of the rebels.* Undoubtedly, however, the Byzantines wanted to retake the island for themselves.

Though the campaign failed, Tancred de Hauteville's eldest son, William, distinguished himself, gaining the sobriquet "Iron Arm" for killing the governor of Muslim Syracuse in single combat. Soon after he was acclaimed leader of the Norman clans in Italy. In the next decades, as Byzantium faltered, his family would seize control of Apulia, a territory comprising much of southern Italy, from the empire and from local Lombard nobles.† Four of Tancred's sons would hold the title Count of Apulia in quick succession. After William came Drogo, and after the latter's assassination in 1051, Humphrey. The Norman barons were a fractious lot, and indiscriminately attacked the Byzantines, who still held the heel of Italy; local Christian lords; and the papal territories. By 1053 Leo IX, the noble-born German pope, had tired of the unruly Normans to his south. Unlike most of the reforming popes, he was a close ally of the Holy Roman Emperor, Henry the Pious, whom he called on for support. Gathering a coalition of Lombard and imperial forces, Leo met Humphrey in battle near the town of Civitella sul Fortore, northeast of Naples; but the papal forces were routed, and Leo himself was captured and imprisoned by the Normans, who took advantage of the resulting disarray to expand and strengthen their grip on southern Italy.

The last of Tancred's sons to rule Apulia was Robert "Guiscard" (the Cunning), a brave and wily fighter, a man—according to the Byzantine princess Anna Komnene—of "immense stature," whose "bellow, so they say, could put tens of thousands to flight." He had served with great distinction at the Battle of Civitate and, after Humphrey's death in 1157,

* These Zirids were the same Banu Ziri who had expelled their kinsman, Zawi ibn Ziri, the founder of Granada, from Ifriqiya (as recounted in chapter 1, "An Ornament, Tarnished," p. 25).

† "Lombard" refers broadly to the native Christians of the peninsula, and more specifically to those of Tuscan origin. The term originates with the Germanic "barbarian" tribe that established a kingdom in the north of Italy in the early Middle Ages.

took the title Count, and then Duke, of Apulia. The Norman barons' respect for Robert was based on his savage conquest of Calabria, during which, in the words of an admiring poet, he ordered his men "to burn, pillage and ravage all those lands which he had invaded, and to do all they could to instill terror in the inhabitants." At his side in this endeavor was Roger, his youngest brother, a man who was not only Robert's match as a warrior but had good looks and charm to boot. In 1062, out of a mix of mutual respect and fear, the two brothers arrived at a compromise for their future campaigns: they would divide and share equally each castle and town they conquered. Their forces now joined, they would be unstoppable.

New opportunities lay in southern Italy, but also farther south, in Sicily. The island had descended into chaos in the decades since the failed Byzantine campaign. In 1053 al-Hasan, the last amir of the Kalbid dynasty, had been thrown out of Palermo by its citizenry, who founded a republic controlled by the town council. The rest of Islamic Sicily became fragmented, as local military commanders each declared their independence and set out to make the island theirs.* In the east, the three strongest warlords were Ali ibn al-Hawwas, lord of Agrigento; his brother-in-law, al-Maklati, of Catania; and Muhammad ibn al-Thumna, of Syracuse. By 1060 Ibn al-Thumna had killed al-Maklati, but then was defeated by Ibn al-Hawwas. Desperate, and with no Muslim allies to call on, Ibn al-Thumna turned to the most feared and famous mercenaries in the region—Robert Guiscard and his brother, Roger.

Ibn al-Thumna evidently did not foresee the eventual outcome of his invitation. As the geographer and chronicler Muhammad al-Idrisi would write nearly a century later:

> It was in the year 453 of the Arabic reckoning [1061 c.e.] that the illustrious, wise, excellent and powerful ruler, Roger, son of Tancred, conquered most of this land, and with the help of his companions came to humiliate the pride of the rebels who opposed his domination and resisted with arms . . . Once the land was under his command and he had established his power on a firm foundation, he spread the benefits of his justice over the inhabitants, reassuring them in the practice of their

---

* The Kalbids, or Banu Kalb, were installed as governors of Sicily by the Fatimids in the 930s, eventually becoming functionally independent kings.

religions and the observation of their laws; he assured them the protection of their belongings, their lives, their women and their children.

Ibn al-Thumna should have known better. Robert and Roger had had their eye on Sicily for some time. In 1059 the newly elected Pope Nicholas II, in need of an army to deal with his rival, the antipope Benedict X, had approached the Normans. In exchange for their aid, he formally invested Robert "by the grace of God and Saint Peter [as] Duke of Apulia and Calabria, and in future, with the help of both, of Sicily." And Roger had already raided the island in 1060 and early 1061 with the help of Muslim forces recruited on the Italian mainland.

But the Norman conquest of Sicily did not happen the way al-Idrisi recounted it. The Muslim historian was in the employ of Roger's son and Philip of Mahdia's master, Roger II, King of Sicily, and therefore had an interest in presenting the conquest in the best light. In reality, the campaigns in Sicily extended over three decades, and were as fine an example as any of Norman brutality, opportunism, and guile.

THE BEGINNINGS OF NORMAN SICILY

After Ibn al-Thumna called for their help, Robert and Roger crossed over to Sicily, quickly seized the port of Messina, and drove southwest toward Ibn al-Hawwas's territory, taking the towns of Troina and Rometta in the interior. But, unable to defeat al-Hawwas, they halted their advance. Not long afterward, Ibn al-Thumna was killed—by his own subjects, who were outraged that he had gone to the infidel Normans to save himself. Robert and Roger turned this apparent setback to their rhetorical advantage, claiming that, since Ibn al-Thumna had been the legitimate ruler of Sicily and they had been his allies, they were now duty-bound to avenge his death by conquering the island in his name.

It may seem curious that the de Hautevilles would manufacture a formal pretext for their invasion; after all, they were Christians, and Sicily was ruled by Muslims. But at this time, a generation before the First Crusade had been conceived of, in practice conflict in the Mediterranean world was not a function of religious difference. The Normans may have been the most ruthless warriors on the island, but they were small in number and had few allies (even among their countrymen, such was their belligerence). They had to tread gingerly. The native Latin Christians of southern Italy regarded them as usurpers, and were continuously on the brink of revolt. The papacy was a fickle supporter, never hesitant to call in the Holy Roman Empire or threaten excommunication. The Byzantine Empire (the "effeminate Greeks" to the Norman chroniclers), though riven by internal conflict and facing new challenges from the papacy and the Holy Roman Emperor, still held important cities on the Italian mainland. And although the power of the Zirids of Ifriqiya had been crippled by the predations of the Banu Hilal—a Bedouin tribe unleashed against them by the Fatimid Caliphate—they, unlike the Normans (and like the Byzantines), had a sizable and experienced navy.

The Normans could call upon their unmatched bravery and appetite for violence, but even in an age of primitive, face-to-face combat, these alone were not enough. It was one thing to defeat an enemy, but quite another to win his loyalty and service. The prosperity of Sicily was a consequence of its agricultural and its artisanal output, as well as its role as a commercial hub of the Central Mediterranean. The Normans, much like Alfonso IV contemplating al-Andalus, understood that conquest would mean little if it involved the destruction of the economy of the conquered lands. But Sicily was a more complex environment than even al-Andalus. The Normans had to prove themselves to be fair rulers in a place where Byzantines, Latins, and Muslims had no choice but to adhere to a mutually recognized code of political conduct. Roger and Robert would set out to persuade Sicily's Muslims to recognize Christian overlords—something that was virtually unprecedented at that point not only in Sicily, but across the Mediterranean—and to assure the substantial Greek Orthodox population, which would have been ambivalent about Norman rule, of their goodwill.

But the Normans were not the only foreigners who coveted the island. In the late 1060s the Zirids sent a force to Sicily with the stated goal of relieving the beleaguered Banu Kalb, but they seized Palermo and claimed the island for themselves. This occupation, however, was ended shortly after by the combination of a Norman counterattack and the resistance of local Muslims, who saw the Zirids as no better than the Christian invaders. At the same time, Robert and Roger dealt with revolts on the mainland by their Norman underlings and local Lombard lords, which were supported by the new Doukas dynasty of Constantinople. They viciously put down these rebellions, with public executions and violent reprisals, and next took the port towns of Brindisi and Bari, Byzantium's last mainland possessions in Italy. Only then did the two brothers focus their efforts on Muslim Sicily. In 1071, less than eight months after the surrender of Bari, the city of Palermo found itself facing a Norman blockade, by land and sea.

Palermo would have been like no other city the Normans had seen, except for those very few among them who may have journeyed to Constantinople. Even though it was nearly a century past its peak and had endured more than fifty years of misgovernment, Palermo remained somewhere on the order of ten times larger and wealthier than Bari, Genoa, Pisa, Venice, and even Rome. Under the Kalbid dynasty in the late tenth century, its population reached approximately 350,000.* It was a bustling metropolis, where Muslim converts and colonists rubbed shoulders with Byzantine Orthodox natives and numerous slaves of African and Eastern European origin, and where visitors from across the Arabo-Islamic world encountered Arabo-Judaic traders from Alexandria and the Maghrib, as well as enterprising merchants from Latinate Italy.†

Under the Kalbids, Sicily had become a center of trade famous for the manufacture of silk, textiles, and ceramics, and a breadbasket for gold-rich Muslim Ifriqiya. Commerce enriched the island's governors, enabling them to patronize Arabo-Islamic literature and art. It also financed the construction of a ring of lavish palaces and lush garden estates around Palermo. The geographer Ibn Hawqal, who visited Sicily in the 970s, claimed that Palermo had some three hundred mosques, second only to Córdoba, including a grand mosque that could hold seven thousand worshippers. Here he was shown a casket suspended from the ceiling that was said to contain the body of the philosopher Aristotle, and to which local Christians would pray in times of drought. Still, Ibn Hawqal decried the religious laxity and hypocrisy of the city's inhabitants—a reaction, perhaps, to Palermo's cosmopolitanism.

---

* By way of comparison, contemporary Rome had about 50,000 inhabitants, and London 12,000. Constantinople's population likely exceeded a half million, with Cairo and Córdoba not far behind.

† "Arabo-Judaic" refers to the culture of the Jews of the Islamic world who, like the Christian Mozarabs of Spain, had adopted Arabo-Islamic customs and styles of dress, and for whom Arabic was the preferred language.

Decades into the Kalbid decline, Palermo remained a prize for any would-be conqueror. Much of the city was unprotected by walls, but there were two strongly fortified quarters, one inland, around the central fortress, and the other on the sea. Siege warfare was relatively new to the Normans. Like other contemporary Latin military elites, the Normans practiced a style of fighting based on professional medium-to-heavy cavalry trained to charge in unison with fixed lances. The goal was to break a line of opposing cavalry forces or sword- and ax-wielding infantry. Norman knights were the superiors of any others, but their tactics and arms were ill-suited to attacking walled cities, which were common in the Mediterranean, unlike in the less prosperous north of Europe. Large cities, or their core neighborhoods, were typically fortified with stone and rock walls many stories high and many meters thick, and girded by towers, moats, and other defensive works. The walls of Central and Eastern Mediterranean cities often dated back to the time of the Romans, and had been reinforced and expanded over the previous thousand years. Assaults on such walls with ladders were relatively easy to repulse, wooden siege towers were cumbersome and vulnerable, and it was often impossible to dig tunnels under city walls that would cause them to collapse. Sieges frequently devolved into a waiting game in which the defenders enjoyed a clear advantage.*

Defending walls, on the other hand, did not require a large professional army, particularly because all able-bodied citizens, including women and children, would be called on to serve in such a situation. Defending against betrayal—the bribing of a disloyal guard or the revenge of a discontented citizen—was perhaps more difficult. Medieval chronicles abound with such tales. According to contemporary sources, for example, during the 1098 Siege of Antioch, the first great victory of the First Crusade on its way to Jerusalem, the Latins only took the city because a certain "Firuz," an Armenian Christian, unlocked a gate for them. But whether this and similar episodes were fact or fiction, the besieging army could not count on such an opportunity. Instead, they attempted to starve the inhabitants of the city into submission.

Many Mediterranean cities, however, unlike those on the Iberian

---

* Few attackers had the good fortune that the Cid enjoyed at Valencia, which he took only with great difficulty and good fortune, after having successfully sowed despair and division among the inhabitants.

Peninsula, could hold out almost indefinitely if there had been adequate time to prepare, and if they were not completely blockaded. Many were equipped with vast underground cisterns built to supply water during lengthy sieges; others, like Palermo, were supplied by wells. The rulers of rich Islamic cities were also often able to maintain substantial reserves of olive oil, grain, and other foodstuffs as a bulwark against both famine and attack. Even if a city's food supplies were exhausted, the inhabitants could turn to consuming their animals, and, if necessary, their clothing and their dead, even their children—anything to forestall the pillage, rape, massacre, and enslavement that so often followed the conquest of a city.

At Palermo, this would have seemed to be an unlikely outcome. It took a considerable army to quarantine a large city effectively, and if Roger's chronicler, Geoffrey Malaterra, is to be trusted, the brothers had mustered only five hundred knights for the campaign against the capital. Food and information would have trickled into the city through tunnels, secret gates, and gaps in their line. And they would have faced difficult challenges of their own. Besiegers, too, had to provision themselves, and were furthermore vulnerable to debilitating and fatal illnesses while camped outside a city's walls, exposed to the elements and in crowded, unsanitary conditions. Dysentery spelled the messy and ignominious end of more than one Crusade. Moreover, in the Northern European tradition, warfare was essentially a private enterprise. Knights and noblemen followed their lord into battle, but they were responsible for their own upkeep. Campaigning drove them into crippling debt; it was a worthwhile proposition only because, if victorious, they would enjoy the right of pillage, or perhaps be apportioned new lands from the conquered territories. Yet even if they grew rich in gold or lands, warriors would still have to worry about what was happening on their own estates, which they often had no choice but to leave in the hands of vulnerable wives, untrustworthy relatives, or scheming subordinates. At the Siege of Lisbon in 1147, the Muslim defenders famously taunted the knights of the Second Crusade with the prospect of the sexual infidelity of the wives they had left back in Flanders and England.

It fell to commanders like Robert and Roger to maintain the morale and resolve of their men for the duration of a siege, and to prevent them from giving up and returning home. A failed siege could destroy a warlord's reputation and undermine his authority. Given the pressures on defenders and attackers alike, many sieges were resolved by negotiation—

either a promise from the city to pay tribute in exchange for the attackers' withdrawal, or an agreement to surrender the city and guarantee the lives and at least some of the property of the defenders.

In 1071, as the Norman Siege of Palermo wore on through the fall, provisions and spirits in the city would have begun to run low. The prospect of relief from the Zirids, the only possible saviors, became increasingly remote. Not only had the Normans crippled the Zirid fleet, they had seemed to reach a diplomatic understanding with the Muslim kingdom: Robert and Roger could have Palermo. Beyond the immediate hardship of the siege, the city's residents, especially the merchants, would have grown more and more worried about the toll of the blockade. Palermo's Christian minority may have also been a cause of concern for the city's rulers; there was always the chance that one among them might cut their own deal with the Normans and betray the city. In this siege of a Mediterranean city, however, time may have been on the Normans' side; aside from the city's internal troubles, Robert and Roger's knights could raid the countryside for food, and the duke and his brother could bring in reinforcements and supplies from the mainland.

Nevertheless, by the turn of the year 1072, the two brothers felt it was time to act. In the early days of January they mounted a coordinated assault on Palermo's harbor and walls. Norman troops broke into the city on both fronts, and, in the looting and killing that followed, the city's leading citizens took refuge in the fortress. On either January 9 or 10, a delegation representing the authorities of Palermo agreed to parley. They would surrender, although not unconditionally. As Malaterra wrote:

> they were unwilling to violate or relinquish their law . . . but [said] that under the present circumstances, they had no choice but to surrender the city, to render faithful service to the duke, and to pay tribute. They promised to affirm this all with an oath according to their own law.

The offer was a calculated risk. There was no guarantee Robert and Roger would accept, and no guarantee that if they did they would then keep their word. Only eight years earlier, another Norman-led force had accepted the surrender of the Muslim town of Barbastro, far off in the foothills of the Spanish Pyrenees. The Christian forces had granted the Muslim inhabitants safe-conduct to leave their town and take with them whatever they could carry. But as the populace left the safety of their walls, the Christians could not restrain themselves at the sight of their abundant wealth, and swept down on them, massacring the men, looting their belongings, and carrying off the women as slaves and concubines. Though they may have known of this event, the Muslims of Palermo did not see another option. They could not hole up in the fortress indefinitely, and they would have felt reassured by the fact that over the previous decade a number of towns in eastern Sicily had surrendered to the Normans, and thus far their treaties had been honored.

Robert and Roger likely did not have the stomach for the sort of drawn-out fight that taking the fortress of Palermo would have required, and were probably eager to agree to the city's offer. Unrest was again brewing back on the mainland, and they did not want to disturb the economy of their new prize any more than they already had. They would need Palermo's resources to complete the conquest of Sicily.

Upon the conditional surrender of the Muslim leadership of Palermo, Robert made an unprecedented move for a Christian, declaring himself before the city's Muslims to be the new *malik*, or king. Roger, for his part, began referring to himself as "count" (*qumis*) or "sultan" of Sicily. He had new coins struck at the city's mint, on one side bearing the Islamic profession of faith, "There is no god but God, and Muhammad is His Messenger," and on the other a stylized *T*, signifying, perhaps, "son of Tancred." There was no Christian imagery on the coins, but they bore a clumsy Arabic transliteration of Guiscard's name—"Arbart"—along with his new title, King of Sicily. The message for the Muslims of Palermo was clear: Robert and his Norman knights would provide peace and stability in exchange for submission and loyalty. The Normans would not infringe on the Muslims' religious rights or freedoms, nor would they undermine the civil and religious authorities within their community.

Robert Guiscard took most of the men under his and his brother's command back to Italy, to stamp out the various rebellions in his lands. Though he maintained a nominal half share of the Sicilian territories he and Roger had conquered, he would never again return to the island. Guiscard and his heirs would remain the rulers of Apulia, and it would be left to Roger, with a handful of his close family members and dependents, to establish a new realm in Sicily. This would take a full twenty years, and Roger's ultimate success would see him acquire the epithet "Bosso," or "the Great Count."

"O FORTUNATE CITY, ENDOWED WITH A TRILINGUAL PEOPLE!"

With Palermo at least nominally under his control, Roger set out to subdue the rest of Sicily, an island studded with castles and fortified towns, each ruled by a Muslim leader determined to protect his own independence. After visiting in the 970s, Ibn Hawqal had remarked on the stubborn nature of Sicilian Muslims, while sneering at the *mujahidin* he encountered, whom he characterized as "freeloaders, scoundrels and renegades . . . pimps and perverts . . . low-life and rabble." He was right on at least one count: Sicily's Islamic society was notably heterogeneous, in both ethnicity and creed. Some of the island's Muslims would have identified as "Arabs," and some were the descendants of native converts to Islam, but most had arrived in the ninth and tenth centuries from Tunisia or elsewhere in North Africa. This last group was itself a mixed lot, made up as it was of Berbers who saw family and tribal ties as far more important than religion. And unlike in al-Andalus, where Muslims were uniformly Sunni and Maliki in religious orientation, in Sicily the majority may have been Sunni, but all four of the major legal schools of orthodox Islam were represented.* There was also a strong Shi'a element, owing to the influence of the Fatimids, and even a significant presence of Kharijites—the radical denomination that denied the authority of the caliphs and called for a literal reading of the Qur'an. Such divisions would work in Roger's favor, as they made a unified Muslim response to his campaign improbable.

Muslims probably made up no more than half of the island's population, however; most of the rest were descendants of the native Byzantine Christians. These Greek-speakers lived in the major towns and cities, and seem to have dominated the rural areas in the eastern half of the island, where monasteries had quietly persevered under the benign indifference of the Muslim rulers. Rounding out the mix of peoples in Sicily were small populations of Arabic-speaking Christians and Jews—the latter present in both the towns and countryside—as well as slaves and

---

* In the Middle Ages, Sunni Islam recognized four distinct brands of Islamic law, or "schools" of religious interpretation, named after their founders: Maliki (after Malik ibn Anas), Hanifa (after Abu Hanifa al-Nu'man), Shafi'i, (after Abu 'Abd Allah al-Shafi'i), and Hanbali (after Ahmad ibn Hanbal). Each was considered legitimate throughout the Islamic world; individual believers could choose which one they would subscribe to.

**Multicultural Palermo, from the twelfth-century *Liber ad honorem
augusti sive de rebus siculis* of Peter of Eboli**

former slaves of both "Slavic" and sub-Saharan origin. Roger's conquest
introduced Latin Christians as a third major ethno-religious group. Aside
from the small Norman elite, among them were many other Northern
Europeans, and eventually, Lombard colonists from the Italian mainland.

The Normans would remain a powerful but vulnerable minority; as
Roger swept across the island, he was required to subtly manipulate his
new subjects' sensibilities and expectations. Eventually, under his successors, most notably his son, Roger II, a deliberate policy was instituted
to foster the creation of a "Sicilian" identity out of the kingdom's Muslim,
Catholic, and Orthodox constituents—a "happy trilingual people," to
paraphrase the late-twelfth-century chronicler, Peter of Eboli.

At first Roger had precious few resources to support his bid for the
island. His Norman knights were habitually unreliable; they might serve
him with valor, but would turn on him the moment he showed any weakness. And while Palermo had been taken, several other important port
cities, notably Syracuse, remained firmly in Muslim hands. Moreover,
the Zirids were regrouping, and in the years following the fall of Palermo

they not only invaded Sicily but sent a fleet to attack Roger's mainland territories in Calabria.

But he would succeed nevertheless. The Greeks he attempted to win over by offering them the chance to have the upper hand over their Muslim neighbors for the first time in two centuries. He endowed them with lands he had conquered and assigned them Muslim peasants as serfs and tenants. Areas that resisted, whether Muslim or Greek, were subjected to terror, including attacks on noncombatants and scorched-earth policies designed to starve and terrify the common folk and break their will to resist. Even so, progress was slow.

Syracuse proved to be another obstacle. An ancient, well-fortified city, it occupied a small peninsula connected to the mainland by a narrow spit. It was here that twelve hundred years earlier the inventor Archimedes had helped hold off a Roman attack. In Roger's time, the city had become the base for a powerful Muslim commander named Ibn 'Abbad. "Benavert," as he was referred to in the Christian chronicles, became, by default, the leader of Sicilian Muslim resistance to Roger. He organized the defense of his city, and even launched inspiring assaults against the de Hautevilles' possessions on the mainland. Roger's task might indeed have proven impossible had Ibn 'Abbad not been killed in a shipboard battle in 1086 as he defended Syracuse against the Norman fleet. With his death, the spirit of the Muslims of Sicily seems to have been broken, and in the years that followed the remaining Muslim communities gave up the fight. The Zirids, too, seeing that Roger's victory was assured, and more concerned about the grain trade with Sicily than the fate of the island's Muslims, signed a treaty with the Normans in 1087.

Roger's own people were a source of trouble throughout this period. In the mid-1070s Roger returned to Calabria to join Robert in suppressing a revolt by their nephew, Adelard, and in the early 1080s he was summoned by Robert again to join the papal forces against the Holy Roman Emperor Henry IV. In his second absence, Roger's own son, Jordan—an illegitimate child, and at that point Roger's only viable heir—rose up against his father, backed by a group of Roger's knights. The revolt, however, came to nothing: Roger returned and blinded the leading rebels, but pardoned his son. The island's Muslims were aware of such divisions and did their best to exploit them; there are indications that Jordan himself was considering converting to Islam. Other Muslim leaders professed fealty to the Normans and converted to Christianity. Some merely pretended to. Another nephew of Roger's, Serlo, was lured to his death by a Muslim warrior who had made a false "pledge of brotherhood" to him. A sincere pledge might have been more dangerous; a commander and trusted lieutenant of Roger, a Christian convert, Elias Cartomensis, was executed when his former coreligionists captured him.

If religion was a factor in the Normans' struggle to conquer Sicily and in the Muslim resistance, it was as often as not disregarded by individuals and communities pursuing more worldly agendas. Perhaps the most surprising example of this was Roger's use of Muslim soldiers. There were Muslims in Robert and Roger's army that took Salerno in 1076, and in 1098 they were present in large numbers at the Siege of Capua, where they helped Roger reinstate his kinsman Richard as prince in that city, a siege and outcome supported by the pope himself. All the more remarkable is that at the same moment the forces of the First Crusade, launched by the same pope, Urban II, were seven months into the grueling Siege of Antioch, the first major stepping-stone on the way to Jerusalem. And in fact, Urban was with Roger at Capua, as was the great philosopher and theologian (later saint) Anselm, Archbishop of Canterbury. Anselm's biographer claimed the English archbishop drew the admiration of many of the Muslim troops, who began to show an interest in converting to Christianity, until Roger made it clear that this would be strictly forbidden. This may well be an embellishment of his biographer, but if true, not only was the original Crusading pope giving tacit approval of Roger's use of Muslim troops against a Christian city, but he evidently consented to Roger's specific prohibition against any attempts to convert them.

Whether or not Roger gave such an order to Anselm, and whether or not Urban knew about it, there was good reason for the count to forbid the conversion of his Muslim soldiers. We can be reasonably certain that, as a matter of policy, Roger had agreed to respect his Muslim subjects' religious rights and to uphold the precepts of their communities. In Islam, as in Christianity, there was hardly a sin greater than apostasy. Leaving one's religion cast one's own soul into peril, and was seen as a betrayal of and a threat to the salvation of one's former community. If he had indeed faced the choice at Capua, Roger could not have afforded his Sicilian soldiers returning home as Christians, as this would have constituted a serious breach of the spirit, if not the letter, of his agreements with them and their communities. Moreover, Roger would have seen the clear advantages in his soldiers' and their communities' remaining

Muslim. As non-Christians living in a Christian-ruled society, they were dependent on Roger's protection and approval, and provided a much-needed counterweight both to the Greek community and to Roger's own Normans. Roger, consciously or not, emulated the famous dictum of the most famous Italian general and dictator, Julius Caesar: "Divide and rule." It was a principle Roger's Muslim subjects would have understood well. Since the age of the Arabic conquests of the seventh century, Muslim rulers from Persia to Spain—the Granada of Samuel ibn Naghrilla was a clear example—had cultivated and protected minority religious communities, whether Christian, Jewish, or Zoroastrian, playing them against one another and against potentially rebellious factions among the Muslim majority.

Roger was still a Christian, of course. He probably saw himself as virtuous, and perhaps believed that he was doing God's work. He was certainly prepared to support the Latin Church. Immediately after the conquest of Palermo, he and Robert ordered the city's Friday mosque consecrated as the new cathedral, and—in an act that would be echoed in the Crusader principalities of the Near East—he displaced the local Orthodox clergy in favor of new Latin appointees loyal to the papacy. The saintly and popular Bishop Nicodemus was quietly deposed and sent into unofficial exile in a hamlet outside the city. Across the rest of the island, Roger endowed Latinate churches and monasteries, and replaced indigenous Church officials with Latins from the mainland.

Sicily's Muslims, at least the more pious and educated among them, harbored no illusions regarding Roger's Christianity. The Norman conquest launched a diaspora that saw the wealthiest Muslims and the overwhelming majority of 'ulama', poets, and scientists flee to the Islamic world. Ibn Hamdis, the greatest Arab poet of Sicily, who left the island in the late 1070s, evoked his countrymen's despair in a series of laments. Recalling his hometown of Syracuse, he wrote:

> I console my soul, since I see my land
>   fighting a losing battle against a venomous enemy.
> What else, when she has been shamed, when the hands
>   of Christians have turned her mosques into churches? . . .
> Oh, Sicily! Destiny has deceived her . . .
> I see my nation—the Christians have imposed disgrace upon it . . .

Many of those who fled ended up in Ifriqiya and Egypt, as attested by the frequence of learned Muslims there bearing the surname "al-Siqiliyyi" (the Sicilian). Some of them left because they practiced vocations and had skills that were in high demand in Islamic lands but were of little use in a Christian court. Muslim poets and religious authorities could not count on the patronage of a Norman ruler. Others would have left on principle. The law was quite clear: Muslims should not live as willing subjects of non-Muslim kings. To do so would be to live in an unjust and impious society. It would constitute, in essence, a form of apostasy. *Fatwas* making this charge go back at least to the late ninth century, when in the course of a rebellion against the Umayyads of Córdoba in the 880s, Ibn Hafsun, a Muslim lord in the south of al-Andalus, declared himself a Christian, and Islamic jurists decreed that Muslims should not live under the rule of an apostate.* Roger went to lengths to assure his Muslim subjects that they could continue to live under Islamic law for precisely this reason, and his concessions provided those wealthy and educated Muslims who did not wish to leave their homes with a rationalization for staying. And many did.

On the whole, the Normans' religious rhetoric had been, from their arrival in Sicily, somewhat muted. Unlike the kings of León and Castile in Spain, they could not claim that they were reconquering land that was theirs by birthright. Though Sicily had once been a Christian land, its history was simply too contested for the Normans to convince anyone that their conquest represented a return of any kind. They were also too clearly pragmatic to acquire the halo of saintliness that was eventually attributed to some of the Christian kings who conquered Islamic Spain. Even the histories written by the monks and clerics loyal to the de Hauteville cause are restrained in their emphasis on the role of religion in the clan's conquests. Whereas the Castilian-Leónese *Reconquista*

---

* Ibn Hafsun was a *muwallad*—a member of a noble family of Christian origin that had converted after the Islamic conquest to preserve its position. In the late 800s, as Córdoba strove to centralize and undermine the power of these local dynasties, many rebelled. Ibn Hafsun's conversion may have been a gambit intended to draw support from the Christian principalities in the north of Spain. However, it failed; most of his supporters, scandalized, deserted him and he was declared an apostate, allowing the Umayyads to declare the war against him a *jihad*. Between this time and the late eleventh century and the Latin expansion in Iberia and Sicily, there would be no other instances of Muslims being put in such a situation.

was imagined as taking place under the heavenly banner of Saint James "the Muslim-killer," whose celestial host of knights could be counted on to intercede in battle and snatch victory from the Muslim hordes, saintly intervention was something the Normans almost never enjoy in the chronicles from the period. Aside from the singular appearance of Saint George mounted on a white horse at the Battle of Cerami in 1063, the only Providence the Normans could depend on was that derived from their own bravery and shrewdness. In the late 1090s, just as the bards of Christian Spain were working to turn the Cid from a gritty mercenary captain into a gleaming paladin of the Reconquest, an obscure poet, William of Apulia, wrote a verse song lauding the career of Robert Guiscard. But for all the references to God and the Virgin he put in Robert's mouth, the de Hauteville brothers were too ambiguous and too resented by their own people to be popularly viewed as Christian heroes in an epic struggle against Islam.

As Robert Guiscard's focus shifted to the Byzantine Empire, any portrayal of him as a religious hero became even more far-fetched. Whether he coveted the throne in Constantinople is uncertain, but he and his sons waged a relentless war against the empire, launching invasions of Byzantine Corfu and Durazzo (now Durrës, in Albania). After his death in 1085, his disinherited son, Bohemond of Taranto—later famous as the Crusader who seized Antioch in 1098 and claimed it as prince—continued these campaigns.

Roger, for his part, defeated the last enclave of Sicilian resistance, in the Noto Valley in the far southeast of the island, in 1091. He took direct lordship over its wealthiest regions and assigned other territories to his illegitimate sons. It was not until 1093, after siring a dozen daughters by his first two wives, that Roger's third wife, Adelaide de Vasto, bore him an heir, baptized as Simon. Two years later, a second son, Roger, would follow.

By the turn of the century, at somewhere between sixty and seventy years of age (his precise year of birth is unknown), Roger was firmly ensconced as Count of Sicily, ruling over a now quiescent population of Muslim and Greek subjects, a scattering of Lombard settlers (mostly in the northeast, around Catania), and a contingent of Latin clergy and Norman noblemen and knights. Sicily was a Christian county, but one that was deeply entangled with the Islamic Mediterranean. Ifriqiya remained Sicily's most important trading partner, and Fatimid Egypt one of its most constant allies. So strong were Sicily's ties to Muslim North Africa that—according to the historian Ibn al-Athir—in 1097 when Frankish envoys came to Palermo to enlist Roger's help with a Crusade against the Zirid capital of Mahdia, the count, by way of a reply:

> lifted his leg and farted a great fart. Then he said, "Strewth! That makes better sense than what you propose!" and sent them on their way.*

FROM COUNTY TO KINGDOM

Roger died on June 22, 1101, not in Sicily, but in Mileto, his stronghold on the Italian "boot." He left behind a vulnerable young widow in her mid-twenties, two small boys—Simon was eight and Roger six—and a clique of Norman warriors, none of whom would feel any moral compunction over seizing the county and putting a violent end to the Great Count's line. It is telling that Roger had felt little need to live in Palermo, which essentially ran itself under the care of the local Byzantine and Muslim elite and the *amiratus* (from *amir*, "prince") he had appointed. Instead, he had stayed in Calabria and northeast Sicily, to better keep watch over his troublesome Latin Christian subjects.

Roger's canniness ensured the future of his life's work and his family. Harboring few illusions about either the trustworthiness of his Norman followers or their capacity to run a complex, commercial economy, he had created a large and capable bureaucracy not made up of his own people but drawn from the Orthodox and Muslim administrative elite he had conquered. Most of the county's internal business was recorded in Greek, and some in Arabic, which effectively curtailed the ambitions of Roger's Latin Christian clients and vassals. The non-Latin elite had correspondingly benefited from Roger's patronage and support, and would have been loyal to his family, if only out of self-interest.

With Roger's death Adelaide became the regent of Sicily, ruling in the

---

* The flatulence, we can be sure, was the creation of the Muslim chronicler, who by adding this detail underlined the barbarous and uncivilized nature of the Christian Normans. Breaking wind is generally considered extremely impolite, but in Arabic culture it is also taken as a sign of incontinence and a lack of self-control and carries a connotation of sexual effeminacy.

name of her eldest son. When Simon died only four years later at age twelve, the title of count passed to her younger son; and by 1112, when the sixteen-year-old could formally be knighted and invested as Roger II, "Count of Sicily and Calabria," she had made Palermo the official capital of the realm. A woman ruling in a man's world, Adelaide needed the allegiance of a capable commander, one who would be in no position to overshadow or usurp her, and whose interests would be tied to those of her son. As early as 1105 she had settled on Christodoulos, whose name ("The Servant of Christ") was translated literally in Arabic sources as 'Abd al-Rahman al-Nasrani, and who may have been originally a convert from Islam.* This Greek Orthodox magnate from Calabria had served Roger I since the 1090s; under Adelaide he became the most powerful man in the county. Whatever his origins, he was very well connected in Calabria and in Sicily, where Adelaide appointed him *amiratus*, as well as in Byzantium, where he had been accorded the ceremonial title of *protonobilissimos* by the emperor Alexios I in 1109.† By that same year he was referred to in Sicily as *amiralius* or "admiral," and was evidently commanding the now impressive Norman fleet and very likely ruling the kingdom in all but name. Although we know little of Roger II's childhood, Christodoulos would have been a towering figure in the life of the fatherless boy.

When Roger came of age, Adelaide's life took a new turn. The Crusaders had taken Christendom's Holy City in 1099, and had, without much forethought, established a new "Kingdom of Jerusalem," with Godfrey of Bouillon, a northern French nobleman, at its head. Upon his death the following year, his brother, Baldwin, had been acclaimed as the first King of Jerusalem. Childless and critically short on funds, Baldwin cast about for a wealthy heiress. Adelaide caught his eye, and a deal was struck: as the new Queen of Jerusalem, she would put her considerable dowry at his disposal, and in return he would name her son, Roger, heir to the kingdom in the event their union produced no child. The fact

* 'Abd al-Rahman is, of course, a common Arabo-Islamic name, hence the additional suffix "al-Nasrani," which means "the Christian."
† The title *nobilissimos* (most noble) had originally been accorded to the highest officials of the Roman and Byzantine empires, but it gradually became a more common honor. Under Alexios, the title *protonobilissimos* was created and granted to important foreign dignitaries and allies, including Muslims.

that Baldwin was already married was no impediment; his present wife, the daughter of the unfortunate T'oros, was sent to a convent, and in 1113 Adelaide moved to Jerusalem, where she would spend four unhappy and barren years before the bigamous king consented to the annulment of their marriage at the insistence of Urban II's successor, Pope Paschal.* Returning to Sicily heartbroken and disillusioned, Adelaide retired to a convent, where she died in 1118. It was an injury Roger II would not forget.

While Adelaide was in Jerusalem, Christodoulos and young Roger oversaw the beginning of a new era for the island. Wielding his formidable navy, Roger began to take a much more aggressive approach toward Muslim Tunisia. The Zirid king, Tamim ibn al-Mu'izz, had managed to keep Ifriqiya under his control even though he was forced to pay substantial tribute to his Christian rivals. After he died in 1108, his successors began to strike back at Sicily. The count was obliged to reply in kind, as Sicily needed stable markets for its wheat. The budding conflict with the Zirids was one dimension of the larger challenge facing Roger: to stamp out all opposition within Sicily, and to expand and defend it against its various Latin, Byzantine, and Muslim enemies.

Roger swiftly accomplished these goals. He consolidated his dominion over southern Italy through aggressive military action: first against the Byzantines and then against the various other members of the Italo-Norman nobility. To the growing consternation of the papacy, which needed a Norman presence in Italy as a counterweight to the Holy Roman Empire—but only if the Normans did not become too powerful in their own right—Roger II campaigned to bring Apulia and Calabria under his power, and by 1127 had succeeded. Three years later, he forced Anacletus II—one of the two reigning popes at the time—to grant him the

---

* T'oros was of Armenian origin, but an adherent to the Byzantine Orthodox faith. He had originally been an official in the empire, but after the Saljuq Turks took Edessa in the 1090s, they installed him as governor. Plotting independence, in 1098 he called on Baldwin, who was passing by on his way to Jerusalem with the First Crusade, to aid him against the Turks. Baldwin complied, but then seized Edessa for himself. T'oros was killed by a mob soon after, possibly with Baldwin's connivance. As in the case of two other notable childless Crusading kings, England's Richard the Lion-Hearted and Aragon's Alfonso the Battler, historians and contemporaries have suggested that Baldwin's sexual preferences leaned more toward men than women.

title King of Sicily.* In the Middle Ages, a time when novelty was looked on with suspicion, the declaration of a new kingdom was a jarring event. The rival pontiff, Innocent II, was so alarmed by Roger's victories that he enlisted the emperor, Lothar III, as an ally against the Norman prince.

No sooner had an undeterred Roger received Anacletus's blessing than he arranged for his own coronation, and on Christmas Day, 1130, he was made King of Sicily in the cathedral of Palermo, anointed by a cardinal sent by the schismatic pope and crowned by his noblemen. At his side would have stood Elvira, his beloved queen, the mother of his three young sons. As the daughter of Alfonso VI of Castile, and born in cosmopolitan Toledo, she would have felt at home in a city of Christians, Muslims, and Jews. Indeed, her mother may have been Sayyida, the Muslim princess the Castilian king had taken as a lover in the 1090s. Few outside of Roger's circles were pleased by his new title, and from 1131 to 1139 the king repelled invasions of southern Italy, until Innocent II himself fell into his hands and was forced to recognize his title.†

The Fatimid Caliphate—ruled by a dynasty of messianic Shi'a Muslims—was by this point Roger's single most important ally. In 910 they had formally declared a new caliphate in Tunisia in defiance of the 'Abbasids of Baghdad, and had conquered Egypt and established their new capital, Cairo, in 969. With its tremendous agricultural and industrial output, and its connections to the gold routes of East Africa and the spice and gem reserves of the Indian Ocean, Egypt was during Roger II's time the center of the wealthiest empire in the West. Like the Normans, the Fatimids had long been rivals of Byzantium, although the establishment of the Frankish Kingdom of Jerusalem in 1099 had led to a rapprochement in response to this common enemy. In the early eleventh century the Fatimids' greatest strategic concern was over the far Islamic West, now ruled by the Berber Almoravids. By the mid-1130s, the Almoravids had been overtaken by a revolutionary faction that would soon

---

* Anacletus, the grandson of a Jewish convert, and Innocent had both been elected pope on the same day in 1130 by rival factions within the Papal Curia, and neither had a clear mandate. Innocent was only fully vindicated as the legitimate pontiff after Anacletus's death in 1138.

† This came only three months after Innocent had formally decreed the excommunication of Roger II at the Second Lateran Council.

threaten both the Fatimids and the Normans. These were the aggressively pious and militant Almohads, who combined an even more strin-
gent Berber "nationalism"—going so far as to translate the Qur'an into
their own language—with a strict, millenarian Islam, and who would
eradicate the Almoravid empire in the 1150s. Bound by trade, a common
interest in the stability of Muslim Ifriqiya, which, like Sicily, had formerly
been under direct Fatimid rule, and a shared fear of the Almohads,
Norman Sicily and Fatimid Egypt became natural allies.

By the early 1100s, the Fatimids' port city of Alexandria had become
the central hub of Mediterranean trade, and commerce between Sicily,
Ifriqiya, and Egypt was brisk. The documents of the Cairo *Geniza*—
receipts, contracts, correspondence, and miscellany stashed away in a
synagogue storage bin by Jewish traders who did not want to profane the
written name of God—attest to the density of movement, communica-
tion, and interchange among these empires.* Their similarities are striking. Fatimid Egypt was an Islamic land, but its population may have been
majority Christian. The largest of the Christian groups was the native
Coptic Christians, who traditionally held key positions in the caliphate's
financial administration. There were also Armenians, whose fathers had
come to serve in the Fatimid military a century previous, and who had
dominated the armed forces since the 1060s. They had maintained their
own language, culture, and brand of Christianity, despite having been
"stateless" and living under the rule of Byzantines, Persians, and Turks
for some six centuries. In short, Fatimid society was a near mirror image
of Sicilian society.

Roger received many gifts from the caliph, including the ceremonial
parasol and other regalia that had come to symbolize authority and majesty in the Islamic world, and that would have resonated with the Normans' Muslim subjects and awed their Christian ones. Roger's parasol
was evidently a large canopy, probably silken and bedecked in jewels. On
public occasions it would be held aloft over the king's head by one of his

---

* According to Jewish custom, the Hebrew language is sacred, and documents referring
to God should not be profaned by destruction, but rather kept in a storage bin (*geniza*).
In the late nineteenth century scholars became aware of a particularly rich collection of
documents in the Ben Ezra synagogue in Fustat (old Cairo). These consisted of hundreds of thousands of letters, receipts, and fragments, many dating to between the tenth
and thirteenth centuries, and relating to trade and family matters involving Jews living
across the Mediterranean and in the entrepôts of the Indian Ocean.

Arabic, Greek, and Latin scribes in the Norman court of Sicily, from
the twelfth-century *Liber ad honorem augusti sive de rebus siculis*
of Peter of Eboli

leading knights. The parasol was, in fact, a universal emblem of power; it
had originated in the ancient Near East, or perhaps with the royal palm
fronds of the Egyptian pharaohs, but by the eleventh century was sported
by popes, emperors, and caliphs alike.

Roger adopted more than just the symbols of Fatimid power, though.
At his request, the Fatimid Caliphate dispatched secretaries to Sicily,
where they introduced Fatimid administrative and chancery culture to
Norman Palermo. Roger understood that if he was to establish an imperial dynasty in the Islamic- and Byzantine-dominated Mediterranean,
he needed to be able to present himself as an emperor. Latin Christian
culture at the time was too primitive to impress his subjects or the rulers
and subjects of another empire. It made merely engaging with other
empires difficult. In 1135, for example, one of Roger's scribes committed
an error of protocol or unintentionally communicated disrespect in a letter in formal Arabic to the Fatimid caliph al-Hafiz. A controversy was
narrowly avoided because a Fatimid chancery official stepped in and
corrected his Sicilian counterpart.

As for the Fatimids and the Byzantines, both saw Norman Sicily as a rival and a threat. For Egypt, lending Roger II the tools with which to govern was an exercise in soft power. Their aim was to draw Sicily close in order to plant sympathizers and agents in the court at Palermo. By embracing Norman Sicily, they could hope to contain and, possibly, control it.

6

Don't Ask, Don't Tell

Roger II eagerly returned the Fatimids' and Byzantines' overtures. Though he may have looked in awe on their wealth and sophistication, he was not naive. He was driven by the same Machiavellian spirit as his allies and enemies, and needed to be able to compete on equal terms with these venerable empires. At home, he had to impress his Byzantine Orthodox and Muslim subjects, and, like the Muslim rulers of his era, whether in Fatimid Cairo or Zirid Granada, he had to worry about the threat posed by powerful elements within his community. The result of Roger's ambitions and strategies was perhaps the most dramatic episode of cultural transformation in the history of the medieval West. Roger became, in essence, a king to three nations: a Latinate *rex*, a Byzantine *anax*, and an Arabic *malik*.

Roger's identity as a faithful Latin Christian king was in some ways the most problematic of the three. This side of Roger was on display to his subjects on the Italian mainland, to the papacy, and to his fellow kings of the Latin West. Unimpeachable Roman Catholic faith was an absolute prerequisite for kingship in this context. If Roger's Christian identity was in any way questionable, it would spell disaster. His Christian vassals would be free of any bonds of loyalty or duty to him, and they would have the legal and moral right to rebel. A charge of apostasy might not only make Roger the potential target of a papally authorized Crusade, but would mean the deaths of his children and the end of his kingly line.*

Around the time of Roger's self-coronation, the clergy still exercised a near monopoly on literacy and numeracy in the Latin world. Hence, should the support of the Church be withdrawn, Roger would lose the services of the monks and other clerics on whom the administrations of his principalities on mainland Italy depended. To this audience, Roger made it clear that he was a vassal of the papacy and the Latin Church, and that his campaigns in the Islamic Mediterranean, if they were not explicitly Crusades, were fought on behalf of the Christian cause. The risk for Roger was that the advocates of the aggressive, chauvinistic piety who were becoming so vocal in Latin Christendom in the late eleventh century would view the religious diversity of his island kingdom as an intolerable offense to God and the Church. Fortunately for Roger, in Sicily Latin settlement remained restricted largely to the northeast and the area around Messina, where Roger II, like his father, founded and endowed Latin-style churches and monasteries, becoming a patron to the Catholic clergy so influential in Rome and across Western Europe. The most enduring example of this effort was the Norman cathedral at Messina, a hulking Romanesque church styled with the black-and-white-striped stonework that would become the hallmark of high medieval Italian monumental architecture.†

Sicily's substantial Greek Orthodox population required Roger's attention as well. The loyalty of these subjects became increasingly important as the Byzantine Empire recovered its equilibrium under the capable rule and expansionist policies of the emperor John II Komnenos. Roger was not overly worried about the Greek-speaking peasantry, even if they had become the clear majority in the eastern half of the island, as Muslims in the region had moved to the almost homogeneously Islamic western

---

* Indeed, in 1199 Innocent III would call a formal Crusade against Markward of Anweiler, the rebellious guardian of the boy-king Frederick II of Sicily.

† Both the horizontal black-and-white-striped stonework so typical of the exterior of Latin churches in Italy and the red-and-white-striped masonry of Spanish mosques were imitations of the ancient Roman technique, *opus mixtum*, which involved alternating horizontal bands of brick and stone.

Roger II crowned by Jesus, twelfth-century mosaic in George of
Antioch's Matorana Church, or Church of Santa Maria
dell'Ammiraglio, Palermo

side. Of more direct concern was the Byzantine elite. The early policies of
Roger II's father had left him with a royal bureaucracy dominated by
Greek functionaries, and the Arabic of the preconquest and conquest pe-
riods had fallen into disuse as an administrative language. Likewise,
Roger's navy was also rife with prominent Byzantine Christian com-
manders, above all Christodoulos.

Nor could Roger fail to be impressed by the refinement of Byzantine
culture, from the still-resonant grandeur of the title Roman Emperor to
the stunning, mosaicked interiors of Byzantine churches, which represented a higher order of opulence than any church in Frankish Europe.
Roger and his court would adopt Byzantine architectural styles with
deliberate enthusiasm. The nave of Palermo's Church of Santa Maria

dell'Ammiraglio—built by Christodoulos's successor, George of Antioch, in the 1140s—features a large gilt mosaic of Roger II, garbed in Byzantine senatorial robes and inclining his head as a levitating and haloed Christ sets the crown of Sicily upon it. The city's Orthodox faithful would have contemplated this image as they entered the church. The Andalusi traveler Ibn Jubayr, returning from his pilgrimage to Mecca, visited the church in 1185 and called it "beyond dispute the most wonderful edifice in the world . . . all embellished with gold," with a bell tower that is "one of the most wonderful constructions to be seen." In order to fund projects of this kind, Roger II endowed the Greek Church in Sicily with land and tenants, including Muslim farmers who, once installed as laborers for the Church, did not have the freedom to leave their new lords' estates.

But it was Roger's patronage and appropriation of Islamic culture that was the most exceptional aspect of his kingship and of his attempts to manage his multicultural realm. Whether as a counterweight to Byzantine influence, in recognition of the importance of Sicily's trade with the Islamic world, or as a consequence of his ambitions in Islamic North Africa, Roger II fostered a stunning Arabo-Islamic renaissance in Sicily. Quite early in his reign, he initiated a transformation of the palace administration, and began to acquire educated and skilled slaves from the Muslim world to serve in both his household and his bureaucracy. Members of the still-wealthy native Muslim elite also found themselves in a more visible and active role in running the kingdom, as the leaders within their own community and in the kingdom more broadly, and as diplomatic intermediaries with Egypt and Ifriqiya. In 1132, two years after his coronation and more than twenty since his father had subordinated Arabic to Greek as the official administrative language of Sicily, Roger II began to institute a formal bureaucratic structure in direct imitation of those of the contemporary Muslim world, in which official business was carried out in Arabic, by officials bearing Arabic titles and working in Islamic-style *dawanin* (the plural of the *diwan*, or "administrative department"). These officials were either themselves Muslims, or slaves or former slaves who had been obliged by Roger to convert to Christianity.

Why would Roger shift to Arabic as an administrative language? It may have been a move to weaken Byzantine Orthodox officials, without granting additional power to the Latin Christian elite. It may also have been a way to protect the royal accounts from intrigues, since most of his subjects did not know Arabic. The only ones who could work in the financial bureaucracy would be either Roger's Muslim subjects or his slaves and servants; both groups were dependent on the king for their position and security, and therefore could be relied upon to remain loyal. Indeed, if installing Muslims in crucial positions provoked bitterness and indignation among his Christian subjects, it was all for the better, as his Muslim bureaucrats would become even more in need of Roger's protection.

There were perhaps other, more basic reasons for Roger's decision. The Fatimid chancery provided a proven model for managing royal finance, and made use of revolutionary innovations from the Islamic world. The most notable was the so-called Arabic numeral system, the precursor to the decimal number system (1 through 9, plus 0) that we use today and that Muslim mathematicians had adapted from Indian models in the 800s. Until Arabic numbers were introduced and adopted by Latin Christians, the latter continued to rely on Roman numerals, which made complex calculations all but impossible, and which had no zero.

Roger II's move toward Islamic culture went far beyond administrative practice, however. It is not surprising that the de Hautevilles were seduced by the allure of Islamic civilization. The Islamic world, in combining Greek intellectual traditions that had been forgotten in the Christian West with Mesopotamian and South Asian innovations, had achieved many new breakthroughs in science, medicine, philosophy, and engineering. At a time when Latin Europe was still groping its way out of the "dark ages," the Islamic world had been home to open, literate societies for centuries. Religiously and ethnically diverse, driven by a dynamic commercial culture, and supported by public investment on the part of its rulers, the lands of medieval Islam were ruled by men steeped in notions of knowledge as a source of power, and of culture as an emblem of success. They founded libraries, hospitals, and academies; encouraged technological and intellectual research on a scale previously unknown in any era of human history, even Greek Antiquity; and patronized poets, musicians, and dancers. Through their Muslim subjects and their contacts with the Zirids and the Fatimids, the Normans were drawn into a dynamic and cosmopolitan civilization of almost global reach.

Roger II and his successors adopted elite Islamic culture. They ate the elaborate and flavorful foods of his Muslim subjects, wore the silken robes and the regalia of Muslim rulers, and constructed Islamic-style palaces and estates, with carefully tended gardens, exotic animals, and fountains and canals. In 1185 Ibn Jubayr would liken the Arabo-Islamic-styled palaces surrounding Palermo to "pearls encircling a woman's full throat." The slaves who served Roger, former Muslims thinly disguised as converts to Christianity, prepared his banquets, sang and danced for him, and ministered to his family members when they were ill. While a regal table in Northern Europe would have been lucky to see pepper, Roger would have dined on saffron- and tamarind-spiced delicacies and a range of fresh fruit unheard of in his family's ancestral lands. His attire and that of his family and closest clients was produced by his own *tiraz*, or royal silk workshop, which his father had inherited from the Kalbids. The genius of its artisans is manifest in the so-called coronation mantle: a red, gem-studded, silken cape measuring eleven feet by four and a half feet, and embroidered with the image of a lion pouncing on and devouring a camel—a clear metaphor for Roger's ascendance over his Islamic neighbors. Along the border of the cape are words in Arabic calligraphy praising the king's wealth. Roger would have donned the cape (together with the matching silk gloves and slippers) to receive potentates and envoys.

At his court, Roger surrounded himself with Muslim courtiers, poets, and scientists, both locals and foreigners, who flocked to Palermo after he showed his intent to support Islamic art and literature, and especially in the 1130s, when the Islamic West began to unravel. In Ifriqiya the situation was particularly grave, and food shortages sent refugees to Sicily, some of whom would have been the children of refugees who had fled the Norman conquest decades earlier.

The most famous among the human adornments of Roger's court was the geographer Abu 'Abd Allah Muhammad al-Idrisi. Born in Morocco, al-Idrisi had studied in Córdoba before finding his way to Palermo. There, during the reign of Roger II and his son and successor, William I, he produced the first accurate "world" map, a silver planisphere (a type of globe), and an encyclopedic geographical treatise, known as the *Kitab Rujjar* (The Book of Roger). Muslim poets, both foreign and Sicilian, also flocked to the Norman court, and wrote odes extolling Roger and his sons.

Common Latin and Greek Christians in Roger's kingdom also felt the allure of foreign ways. When Ibn Jubayr visited Sicily, his heart was lifted by the courtesy of Christians who greeted his party (evidently in Arabic) and by the sight of the Christian women of Palermo in Muslim-style

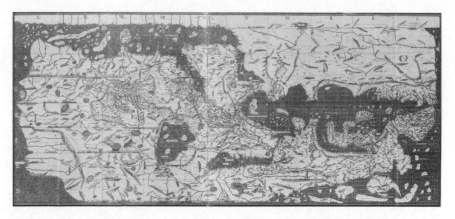

Muhammad al-Idrisi's twelfth-century world map, oriented with
the south at the top

veils and cloaks and jewelry, and with their hands painted with henna.
Many Christians in Sicily evidently spoke Arabic even in the 1180s, including Roger's grandson, William II, as well as the palace officials, and
some commoners. Further evidence of Sicilian Christians' attitudes
toward their Muslim countrymen can be seen in the memorial stones
placed in Palermo's Church of St. Michael during Roger's and William's
reigns. One commemorated two clerics, the Byzantine Grisando (Chry-
santhos) and the Latinate Drogo, with inscriptions in Greek, Latin, and
Arabic, while the other, for Grisando's mother, was additionally inscribed
in Judeo-Arabic.*

The most dramatic example of the cultural synthesis Roger II enacted
was his royal palace—especially the dazzling chapel at its heart. This
great chamber reflects an eclectic, if not necessarily harmonious, integration of Latin, Byzantine, and Islamic elements. The palace was completed by the early 1140s, although what one sees today is not quite as it
was during Roger II's reign. In his time it seems to have consisted of two
linked but independent spaces. At one end was a small, domed Byzantine

---

* The vernacular and principal literary language of Jews of the medieval Islamic world
was Arabic, Hebrew being restricted to liturgical, high literary, and theological works,
to inscriptions, and sometimes to confidential written correspondence between learned
Jews. Judeo-Arabic refers to the particular variations of Arabic spoken by Jews, and
Arabic written in the Hebrew script (Hebrew and Arabic share a three-consonant mor-
phology, unwritten or diacritical vowels, and closely corresponding letters).

A king (Roger II?) as sultan, from the chapel of the royal palace in
Palermo, twelfth century

chapel decorated floor to ceiling with gold leaf, mosaic, and marble inlay,
overlooked by a balcony from which Roger would observe Mass. Extend-
ing away from the chapel was a long, colonnaded, Islamic-style reception
hall, where the king held court. This room is most notable for its painted
ceiling, pocked by *muqarnas* stalactites, and featuring painted floral and
animal motifs as well as scenes of Islamic courtly life, including warriors
on camels, dancers, gamblers, and courtiers. Roger II himself appears to
be present in this scene, depicted in the style of a Fatimid caliph: robed,
cross-legged, and with a whisk—an emblem of power in Africa—in his
hand.* Legends in florid Kufic script bordered the palace doors, lauding
Roger's reign and urging visitors to "make haste and kiss" the king.
Another sign of direct Fatimid influence is the covered passageway that

* Its origins are uncertain, but the fly whisk, a handheld brush with long, soft, hairlike
bristles, has been a symbol of royal power in sub-Saharan and Nilic Africa and parts of
Asia since the dawn of history.

once connected the palace with the cathedral, and enabled the semidi-vine sovereign to pass safely and unseen to the kingdom's main church.

Outside of the confines of the palace, Roger did more to calibrate his image for his other constituencies. For instance, he minted silver ducats and third-ducats that, on one side, depicted Christ holding the Gospels, and on the other, Roger and his first son, Duke Roger of Apulia, dressed in Byzantine and Frankish costume and holding a crucifix. More com-mon, however, were Roger's Islamic-style coins, minted in imitation of the Fatimid *dirham* or quarter-*dirham*. On them Roger is styled as *al-Malik Rujjar al-mu'azzam al-mu'tazz bi-Llah*—"the exalted King Roger, mighty by Allah."* Later coins were struck with a crucifix on the reverse side and the Greek legend *IC XP NIKA*—"Jesus Christ conquers." Roger knew that he had to be a king for all seasons and all subjects. But as the 1140s wore on, his Islamophile side dominated, largely as a consequence of the fact that trade with the Islamic world had made him and his king-dom wealthy. Another reason was that as Ifriqiya tilted into anarchy, Roger had no choice but to intervene, and as a result needed to become a legitimate sovereign in the eyes of his newest Muslim subjects.

"KING OF AFRICA"

Politics, like nature, abhors a vacuum, and in the early and mid-1100s a political vacuum existed in what is now Tunisia. Rivalries within the Zirid clan had resulted in civil war, the economy had suffered from Bed-ouin raiding, the Fatimids were on the decline, and the urban elites were becoming restless and disenchanted under their Berber leaders. The vio-lent irruption of the Almoravids and then the Almohads onto the scene alarmed Zirids, Fatimids, and Normans alike, while giving hope to the more pious-minded of the upper classes of Ifriqiya.

Because the wealth of Roger's Sicily was based largely on exports of food staples to the region, which were exchanged for the cheap and plen-tiful gold obtained by Muslim traders in Central Africa, intervention in Ifriqiya was to him both a necessity and an opportunity. In a major change to his foreign policy, he would set out to conquer the Muslim cities of the coast, and establish himself as *malik Ifriqiya*, or "King of

---

* *Mu'azzam* translates as "august, serene, revered, glorious, resplendent."

Africa"—a step further than even the Cid or his liege lord, Alfonso VI of Castile, "the King of the Two Religions," had gone. The key to Roger's mission was a people who were neither Latin, Byzantine, nor Arab, who originated in the eastern reaches of the Mediterranean world, and who had learned to straddle Islamic and Byzantine society: the Armenians.

Armenian culture came into its own on the Anatolian plateau (modern Turkey) in Classical Antiquity. Caught first between the empires of Persia and Rome and later, from the seventh century through the Middle Ages, between the caliphate and Byzantium, Armenian kingdoms emerged, disintegrated, and reappeared almost cyclically. One such kingdom, under King Tiridates III, was the first state to become officially Christian, converting in 305, two decades before Constantine the Great made Christianity an official religion of the Roman Empire. By the end of the century, Armenians had developed a distinct alphabet, and by the early 500s the Armenian Church had formally separated from the "Catholic" or "Orthodox" Christianity of the empire, which had deemed it heretical.* By the 800s and 900s, Armenians could be found across the Eastern Mediterranean and Persia, serving the regions' empires as mercenaries, warlords, governors, and proxies, particularly in the contested no-man's-lands of Syria and eastern Anatolia. In the 1080s there were at least three Armenian "kingdoms": one based in Edessa, another to the west at Marash (modern Kahramanmaraş), and the last farther west, at Tarsus. Armenians were also scattered about the Eastern Mediterranean, seeking their fortunes as soldiers, administrators, and merchants in both the Greek and Islamic worlds. They had become especially powerful in the Fatimid Caliphate of Egypt.†

---

* The Latin Church and the Greek Church had yet to develop distinct identities. They were considered the same, united denomination: the Imperial Church, which was considered by its adherents to be both catholic (universal) and orthodox (correct).

† "Armenians" was a name given by the ancient Persians to a people who referred to themselves as the "Haik," who spoke a language distantly related to Greek, and who occupied the plateaus and mountains stretching from the middle of what is now Turkey eastward to the Caspian Sea. Not unlike the Arabs, they found themselves occupying a buffer zone between the two empires of Rome/Byzantium and Persia, and were drawn into each politically, culturally, and religiously, serving as mercenaries and establishing small, local kingdoms that occasionally were able to shake off their clientage to the great powers. While the Armenians in the west adopted Christianity and were Hellenized, the Armenians in the east were drawn toward Persia and its religions, Zoroastrianism and

The foundation of Roger's conquest of Ifriqiya was laid by Christo-doulos, but it would be George of Antioch, an Armenian who succeeded him as Roger's admiral and *wazir*, who would do the most to realize it. Another Armenian, the Fatimid *wazir*, Bahram, would provide the all-important link between Palermo and Cairo. George and Bahram had a personal connection: both of their families had originated in northern Syria and had served the Byzantines and the Turks.* It was their friendship that would draw the courts of Norman Sicily and Fatimid Egypt together, facilitating Roger's transformation from Norman king to Mediterranean sultan, and thereby making his domination of Islamic Ifriqiya conceivable.

Bahram's uncle, Vasak Pahlavuni, had ruled Antioch for the Byzantines in the 1060s, and prior to George's birth, his family had been in Vasak's employ. Both families went into exile after the Battle of Manzikert of 1071, where the Saljuq Turk sultan, Alp Arslan, had destroyed the Byzantine army, taken Emperor Romanus Diogenes prisoner, and swept away Byzantine power in Anatolia. Within ten years Asia Minor was transformed. The Turks now ruled Anatolia, with Nicaea as their capital, a city only fifty miles from Constantinople, where a Byzantine general, Alexios Komnenos, had seized the imperial throne. According to Latin lore, as a consequence of Manzikert Alexios sent word to Pope Urban II, via the nobleman Robert of Flanders, begging for military help against the Turks—and his letter inspired Urban to launch in 1095 what would become known as the First Crusade. Meanwhile, as Byzantine Anatolia plunged into anarchy, Vasak was assassinated by Vahram Varajnuni, the Armenian strongman of Marash who coveted Antioch.† Both Bahram's and George's families fled, the former to Cairo, the latter to Mahdia.

Mahdia, the capital of Zirid Ifriqiya, was a bustling port city with a

---

Manichaeanism; after the Islamic conquest many converted to Islam. However, these divisions were not always clear; some groups straddled the religious divide, and others developed hybrid, "heretical" faiths, such as Paulicianism—a religious movement that, like Isma'ilism, was also political and military in nature.

* Bahram is the subject of chapter 7, "After the Messiah."

† Better known by his Greek name, Philaretos Brachamios, Vahram Varajnuni was a general in the Byzantine army. After Manzikert he raised an army consisting largely of Norman mercenaries, and carved out his own state in southern Anatolia, ruthlessly taking on his fellow Christian rivals and attempting to harness the aggressive power of the Saljuqs and those Armenians who had converted to Islam. He died in 1086 or 1087, more or less universally despised.

well-defended harbor. Given the kingdom's position between Latin Sicily, Byzantium, the Fatimids, and the Almoravids, someone like George's father—a Byzantine, or "Melkite," Christian of Armenian descent, and an experienced administrator fluent in Greek and Arabic—would have been in high demand.* He was invited to serve as a functionary in the treasury of the Zirid king Tamim, and in due course, George followed in his father's footsteps. After Tamim's death in 1108, his son and successor, Yahya, took a more aggressive stance toward the Christian powers, and George fell out of favor in the Zirid court. He began discreetly looking for a way out of North Africa. It seems that he managed to get in touch with Christodoulos, and in 1114, with the admiral's collusion, he secretly boarded a Sicilian merchant ship bound for Palermo.

George became a vital cog in Roger's royal exchequer and amassed great personal wealth, before Christodoulos selected the eminently capable Armenian exile for greater tasks. He would serve Christodoulos as an envoy to the Fatimid court, which allowed him to forge the crucial diplomatic connection with Bahram. And he would serve, with nearly as great an impact, as a naval commander. George led a failed amphibious mission in 1123 on his hometown of Mahdia; after seizing a small fortress near the city, the attackers were overwhelmed by Zirid forces and withdrew, leaving the Norman landing party to be slaughtered. But the defeat does not seem to have affected George's career. By the time of his master Christodoulos's death (around 1127), he had attained the rank of *amiratus* and displaced his former superior. George's navy helped to subdue Apulia and Calabria, after which he was rewarded with the official title of *amiratus amiratorum* (supreme commander) in 1132. Although he failed in a second attempt on Mahdia in 1142–43, George did conquer the island of Jerba in 1134–35 and established Norman authority over Tripoli in 1146. Two years later he finally took Mahdia, forcing the Zirid king, Hasan ibn 'Ali, to retreat from the city. Mahdia having fallen, the way was cleared for the conquest of the other major cities of the Tunisian coast, including Sfax and Sousse. The following year George's fleet reached Constantinople. He died in 1151, after a long and glorious career.

This Byzantine Orthodox man of Armenian extraction, who was an exile from the Zirid court, had done more than anyone else to make

---

* "Melkite," meaning "royal" or "imperial," was the term used to refer to Byzantine or Greek Orthodox Christians living outside of the empire.

Roger II "King of Africa." But the Ifriqiya of the 1140s was not the Sicily of the 1070s, and Norman dominion there was tenuous. Whereas some cities, like Sousse, surrendered willingly, others had to be taken by force. The "conquest" of Gabès and Tripoli, for example, required Roger to suppress popular discontent, and to rule through local Muslim puppet princes watched over by his Norman troops. The people of Sfax had put up fierce resistance, and Mahdia's prince, Hasan, to Roger's great displeasure, managed to escape with his treasure. Mahdia's sister city, Zawila, acknowledged Norman rule but remained in Muslim hands. In most cities the Normans took, the local religious elite chafed under Christian rule, even as they recognized that the Norman rule had actually brought a measure of stability to the region.

The Norman presence in Ifriqiya would be fleeting, and ultimately George's most lasting legacy was the Greek Orthodox Church of St. Mary of the Admiral (Santa Maria dell'Ammiraglio), located in the heart of Palermo, and one of the greatest monuments of the city's medieval era. The church survives to this day and contains not only the gilt mosaic image of Roger being crowned by Christ, but another of its patron, George, prostrate at the feet of the Virgin. George also seems to have been responsible for another legacy, not of stone and gold leaf, but rather through his choice of successor: Philip of Mahdia, whom Roger would try and execute for religious treason in 1153. In his contemporary *Chronicon*, Archbishop Romuald claimed that Philip had been "placed . . . in charge of the whole palace and established . . . as master of his entire household." As George's life and career came to a close, Philip became the king's *camerarius*, or chamberlain, a trusted officer and intimate in the royal circle, as well as an *amiratus* and commander of a fleet. It was he who completed Roger's short-lived conquest of Ifriqiya. But who was Philip of Mahdia?

PHILIP OF MAHDIA ON TRIAL

Some early historians assumed that Philip must have been of Greek origin: that he was the same Philip who served Roger II as *logothete*, or chancellor, from 1125 to 1132, and that, as an already prominent adviser, it is no surprise that he suddenly appeared as *amiratus* and *camerarius* in 1152, a year before his death. But the Greek Philip was the son of Leo, a

A dying William II attended to by a Muslim physician and astrologer,
from the twelfth-century *Liber ad honorem augusti sive de rebus
siculis* of Peter of Eboli

Byzantine Christian, who had been chancellor to Roger I, which would
make the revelation of Philip as a Muslim somewhat odd, though con-
versions to Islam (or Judaism) in the Christian lands of the Mediterranean were not unknown, particularly among educated, elite courtiers.
Philip might have been drawn to identify with the Muslims slaves of the
Norman court because he, like many of them, was evidently a eunuch,
and this affinity might have paved the way for his conversion.

Could the son of a powerful Christian magnate have been made a
eunuch in the first place? The short answer is yes. Eunuchs had occupied
important court positions in the Romano-Byzantine Empire since the
reign of Theodosius in the fourth century, serving as administrators,
trusted servants, and generals. In the eleventh century their influence
grew as they provided administrative stability during the succession
crises that followed the reign of Basil II. They served both as naval
commanders and in the post of great chamberlain; in fact, many of the
highest posts at court were reserved by imperial law for eunuchs. Because Roger I had adopted Byzantine court practices in addition to Fatimid ones, he would have likely employed palace eunuchs.

For the Byzantine emperors eunuchs were "perfect servants" and comprised a socially accepted "third gender." Given their ambiguous sexual status and their incomplete nature, they were not perceived as a threat either to the power of the emperor or to the integrity of his household. In practical terms, eunuch administrators functioned like members of ethnic and religious minorities: they could not present a political challenge to their masters (because they lacked the requisite masculine attributes), and they could be used to implement unpopular policies and to serve as scapegoats if necessary. Nor could they have children whom they might hope to pass their wealth and position to. In Byzantium up-and-coming families sometimes castrated their younger boys in the hopes of landing them a coveted place in the imperial hierarchy. Somewhat mercifully, complete castration, in which the testicles and penis are entirely removed, seems to have been rare; instead prepubescent boys would have their testicles removed by incision, or by processes referred to as "compression" or "dragging." Either way, this would have been a painful, traumatic experience. When the sixth-century emperor Justinian investigated the mortality rate of castrati, he found only four survivors among ninety cases surveyed.

If the Latin account of Philip's trial has any truth to it, however, he could not have been of Greek origin. Instead, he must have been an ex-slave from the *dar al-Islam*, who was converted to Christianity as a youth. As Romuald reported, Roger had personally raised Philip from boyhood to be a true Christian, and in the process young Philip's "sins . . . had been cleansed."

To a greater degree than in the Greco-Roman and Byzantine traditions, slaves in Islamic life were integrated into the families they served. Slaves' rights and protections were enshrined both in Scripture and in Islamic law. Female slaves who produced male children were not uncommonly manumitted and legitimized as wives, whereas freed male slaves typically remained with the family of their former master, even adopting his family genealogy. Former slaves, once freed, could become respected men of religion and powerful officials, even princes. Even as slaves, they could rise to occupy the highest administrative positions in the Islamic world. In many circumstances, they were preferred over free men. Because Islamic law forbade the enslavement of Muslims, slaves had to be obtained from foreign lands. Prior to the twelfth century, the export of pagan Central and Eastern Europeans through Italy and Spain to the Islamic Mediterranean, and of Caucasian peoples through Byzantium, had been a major trade. But by the eleventh century, sub-Saharan Africa—the *Bilad al-Sudan* (the land of the Blacks)—was the main supplier. Black slaves, or *'abid*, came to form the bulk of the Fatimid army and of the empire's overall slave population.

Muslims apparently borrowed from Byzantium the custom of employing eunuchs, but their use became far more widespread in the *dar al-Islam*, in large part because upper-class women were often sequestered in harems, which were frequently very large, due to the practice of polygamy and the custom of keeping concubines. To avoid the possibility that male slaves might have sex with the women of the household, Muslims preferred eunuchs who had had their entire genitalia removed. But because Islamic tradition forbade the mutilation and physical abuse of slaves, pagan boys, usually between six and nine years of age, were rounded up and castrated before they were brought to market. Castration took place at specialized facilities at the margins of the *dar al-Islam* often run by Christians or Jews. The main castration center for the African slave trade was at Asyut on the middle Nile, where Christian monks grew wealthy performing the surgery well into the eighteenth century—a practice they rationalized as an act of charity.* By the time their journey to the slave markets of the North African coast was complete, the relatively few boys who were lucky enough to survive the procedure would have been converted to Islam and were ready for sale.

The Fatimid state has been described as "saturated" with eunuchs in the twelfth century, the same time that Roger II began to emulate his ally, the Fatimid caliph, al-Hafiz, and that Philip came on the scene at Palermo. The Arabic accounts of Philip's trial indicate that there was a substantial contingent of castrated slaves in the palace. This was certainly true a generation later, when Ibn Jubayr remarked at length on the number of eunuchs in the court of William II, Roger II's grandson. As for Philip, after his arrival in North Africa, he had likely lived in Muslim households long enough to become Arabized as well as a convinced Muslim, before being acquired by whoever would go on to sell him or present him as a gift to Roger. In view of what lay ahead for Philip, his first owner may well have been George of Antioch himself, who would have acquired him after the conquest of Mahdia in 1148, or perhaps as early as the raid

* The rationale was that by providing a relatively safe and sanitary procedure, the monks were benefiting the boys, who would be castrated in any case.

of 1123. Philip's conversion to Christianity as a young adult would be consistent with the allegation that he was a crypto-Muslim, which surfaces in the accounts of his trial. *Taqiya*—the deliberate dissimulation of faith—was considered a legitimate tactic for Muslims who would be subject to oppression or persecution if they revealed their true convictions. It was particularly important in Shi'a thinking, and the Fatimids were Shi'a Muslims.

All this makes for a strong argument that Philip of Mahdia was an individual of Central African origin, who had been enslaved as a boy, castrated, and converted to Islam before being sold in a Zirid or Fatimid market. As such, he provides a rare glimpse of the obscure and unwritten history of black Africans in the history of medieval Europe.

That Philip was of African, and not Greek, provenance aligns with the charges against him, which, as described by Romuald, reveal his religious affiliation. Romuald tells us that Philip's treason against Christ and the king was the core of his offense, and the reason for his execution. But the Latin account's detailed inventory of Philip's crimes is not a catalog of stock accusations; rather, it specifically outlines his connections with the Islamic world. Among the charges against Philip was that he "sent his envoys with offerings to the tomb of Magumeth [Muhammad], and commended himself to the priests of that place with many prayers." While it was unlikely that Romuald would have known it, the shrine of Muhammad's burial place at Medina was guarded by a prestigious corps of forty castrated slaves known as the Eunuchs of the Prophet. This esteemed "priesthood," in turn, was patronized by the court eunuchs of Cairo—a group Philip would have been in contact with as a Sicilian diplomat, and which would have been happy to convey his offerings to Medina.

Another of the Latin chronicler's allegations was that Philip donated oil for the lamps of the mosques of Palermo. This, too, rings true. For every courtier—and especially one as potentially isolated as a heretical, foreign eunuch—political advancement and personal survival depended on a network of patronage and affiliation. It would have been prudent for Philip to cultivate the Muslim community of the island, and an obvious way to do so would have been to quietly support their religious institutions. Indeed, Philip would have been following the same strategy as members of the Byzantine elite who supported local monasteries or of George of Antioch, who founded and endowed churches of the Greek rite.

Perhaps more telling is the accusation—which also surfaces in Ibn al-Athir's sparse account of the trial—that Philip did not fast with the king or refrain from eating meat on Fridays and during Lent. If Philip was not following the customs of the Church, he would have hardly been different from many members of the Christian elite, who also often ignored the Church's rules regarding fasting. But this accusation may be an indication that Philip was not so discreet about his religious ambiguity. As royal chancellor, admiral, and intimate of the king, Philip might have flaunted his sympathies for Islam or observed its customs openly, figuring himself above reproach. But in the Norman court it was one thing to be a Muslim and quite another to act like one. Roger and his successors were ambivalent regarding matters of conscience among their household servants and officials, and by the time Ibn Jubayr arrived in the kingdom, the Christianity of the palace slaves was widely recognized to be a fiction. But it was a fiction that existed for a reason: the stability of the realm depended on maintaining at least the appearance of Latin Christian dominance.

What is so striking about the Latin account of the trial is the absence of exaggerated accusations or a polemic tone. With the exception of a reference to mosques as "synagogues of the evil ones," there is little to suggest that Romuald saw Philip's tale as an excuse to launch a generic attack on Muslims. What aroused the author's and the king's indignation was that Philip was a turncoat—"a *secret* soldier of the devil." In the twelfth and thirteenth centuries, Christians and Muslims, members of the political and military elites above all, were more trusting of members of the other faith than they were of anyone who abandoned the faith they had been born into, even if they had converted to the "true religion."

However, if Roger II had concerns about Philip, they were probably political, not religious, and had to do with the admiral's greatest accomplishment for his king. Philip took the town of 'Annaba, completing Roger's conquest of Ifriqiya, with the same Muslim-inspired tactical approach the Normans had long employed: he laid siege to the city, while at the same time negotiating with the local elite, urging them to surrender the city willingly. However, Philip allowed the city's leading citizens to withdraw to their rural estates, which enabled them to save much of their property from ending up in Roger's possession.* In more secure times, Roger might

* 'Annaba (Bône), in eastern Algeria, had been known as Hippo in Antiquity. The pre-eminent theologian and Church father Saint Augustine (354–430) spent much of his

have done the same in order to win over new subjects, but at the time the king was facing a number of new threats. Manuel I of Byzantium had concluded an alliance with the Holy Roman Emperor Frederick Barbarossa and in 1153 was preparing to launch an invasion of Norman Italy. The Fatimid Caliphate, Roger's ally, was on the precipice of civil war. And the uncompromising and determined Almohads of Morocco were moving relentlessly eastward toward Ifriqiya, driven by a program of *jihad* that made them natural and implacable enemies of the Normans. Roger's hold on Ifriqiya was shaky; it was not a time for divided loyalties.

It thus may have appeared to Roger that Philip was playing a double game—taking the town at the behest of the infidel king, yet positioning himself as a protector of the city's influential Muslims. What was Philip's agenda? Was he hedging his bets? Was he planning to defect to the Almohads? Or plotting some greater treachery? Whatever the case, Roger may well have believed that he had to be removed and made an example of.

But when Roger put Philip on trial, it was not on vague charges of disloyalty, but rather of secretly practicing Islam. Philip could offer no defense to these, because he was demonstrably guilty. Conviction was guaranteed. It is difficult to believe that Roger would not have long suspected Philip's true faith. He may have been fully aware of it; according to contemporary accounts, Roger was an Arabic-speaker and familiar with Muslim practices. His indifference to the religious convictions of his subjects and servants was well known, and his enthusiasm for Arabo-Islamic culture and learning was such that he himself was rumored to be a secret apostate. As Ibn Shaddad, a Zirid prince who visited Palermo just after Roger's death, was said to have reported, "Roger treated Muslims with respect, took them as his companions and kept the Franks off them, so they loved him."

Roger also possessed another reputation, for merciless brutality. In his struggle to pacify Apulia and Salerno in the 1130s, he had more than once repaid rebellion in his Christian subjects with outright slaughter. Philip of Mahdia's execution was wholly consistent not with Roger's religious policies, but rather with his previous reactions to political disloyalty. In this calculus, Philip had to die. He had no natural allies who could

---

life there. After the conquest in the seventh century, the Muslims built a settlement beside the city that eventually came to be known as Madinat al-Zawi, after Zawi ibn Ziri, the founder of the city of Granada, who was at one time its lord.

plead his case to Roger, but even if he were innocent, Roger would have still gained from his death. By executing his prized confidant and admiral in a gory, public spectacle—the type of death Philip's crime called for—he would show his subjects that even a hint of sedition would draw the wrath of the king. And by executing an apostate, he could put to rest any insinuations about his own faith and his dedication to the Church in Rome.

THE RISE OF THE PALACE SARACENS AND THE DECLINE OF MUSLIM SICILY

Philip of Mahdia's trial and execution marked the end of an era in the Norman kingdom and the completion of Roger II's transformation into a sovereign king. For the rest of his reign there would be no more powerful admirals and prime ministers, no more foreigners with undue influence in his court, no more shadow rulers. No one, that is, like Christodoulos, George of Antioch, or Philip of Mahdia.

But Philip's death did not signal the end of Roger's use of Muslims in his administration. On the contrary, from that point forward, the management of the palace was placed almost entirely in the hands of the clique of baptized former slaves known as the Palace Saracens. Nor did the influence of Sicilian Muslims decline. As disquieting as the trial may have been from their perspective, Philip had been demonized as an individual. Islam, the community and the faith, had escaped being implicated in his downfall. And unlike the killing of Yusuf ibn Naghrilla, the execution of Philip did not involve a violent riot against a minority religious community—there was no broad popular resentment of Philip, and his service to the king had not generated jealousies or anxieties among the Latins.

As Roger's and his successors' imperial dreams focused ever more on Ifriqiya, they needed officials who could act as effective intermediaries with North African Muslims and yet would be loyal to the Norman king. No Latin could fill such posts. The Norman conquest and domination of the Tunisian coast required commanders who could manage the subtleties of negotiating in Arabic with Muslim princes and populations; recruit and control the Bedouin mercenaries upon whom the Normans relied for additional cavalry in the field; and administer subject populations who would not readily accept a Christian king. The volatility of the situation became clear only a few years after Philip's death, when popular uprisings in anticipation of the Almohads' imminent arrival saw Norman colonists put to the sword.

Sicily itself was hardly less unstable. After Roger II's death in 1154 and the accession of his only surviving son, William, Lombard and Norman elements at court and in the countryside attempted to seize power. Philip's successor as chamberlain and chief admiral under King William, the Latin Christian Maio of Bari, was unable to effectively keep the various factions at bay, and was assassinated in 1160 as part of a larger revolt. This episode involved the murder of many palace slaves, who were seen as William's core loyalists, and attacks on Muslim subjects in eastern Sicily, where Latin Christian colonization had accelerated.

Once William had regained his grip on Sicily, the Palace Saracens took their revenge on the rebellious Norman noblemen and Latin courtiers in an officially sanctioned purge. Thereafter, the title of chamberlain, renamed "cait" or "caid" (from the Arabic al-qa'id, "commander"), was reserved for the palace servants and eunuchs who were widely known to be secret Muslims, a policy that would continue through the reigns of William, known to his Arab-speaking subjects as "the Magnificent, the Guide by Order of God" (and to Christian posterity as "the Bad"), and his son, William II, "the Desirous of Power through God" or "the Good." After Roger II's reign, in other words, the codependency of the Norman kings and their Muslim subjects only intensified.

The Norman kings immersed themselves even more in Arabo-Islamic culture. Ibn Jubayr, who met William II in 1185, reported that the king not only spoke Arabic himself, but staffed his household with Muslim cooks, physicians, astrologers, and servants, including "a band of black Muslim slaves commanded by a leader chosen from amongst them." Many of these royal servants, according to Ibn Jubayr, had succeeded in converting Christians to Islam. While he may have been exaggerating the role of Muslims here in order to cast the condition of Islam in Sicily in a better light, one anecdote he relates is probably an accurate reflection of the atmosphere of religious accommodation between Muslims and Christians in the royal court of Palermo. When, in 1169, a powerful earthquake shook the palace, many of the king's panicked retainers, who were formally Christians, began to shout out Islamic invocations to "Allah." Seeing that the king had overheard, they became fearful for their lives, but William reassured them, "Let each invoke the God he worships, and those that have faith will be comforted." The line taken by the Norman kings with regard to faith was "don't ask, don't tell." Apostasy would only be an issue if the king or his servants chose to bring it to the forefront.

And yet this ethos would scarcely outlast William II's reign. Sicily and the world around it were changing. By 1160 the Almohad armies had reached Ifriqiya, their ultimate objective being the destruction of the schismatic Fatimid Caliphate. Norman 'Annaba fell, and soon after it, Mahdia, along with what remained of the Norman kingdom in North Africa. Christian colonists were massacred, and churches were transformed back into mosques. William would be the last "King of Africa." Aside from the occupation of the small islands off the Tunisian mainland by Aragon in the thirteenth and fourteenth centuries, and of the coastal cities by Spain and the Knights of St. John in the 1500s, Ifriqiya would enjoy seven centuries of nearly unbroken Muslim rule, until France installed a protectorate over Tunisia in 1881, and Italy's King Victor Emmanuel III occupied Libya in 1912.

As for the Normans' ally, Fatimid Egypt, it was in the midst of a civil war that would end in 1169, when Nur al-Din's Kurdish general, Shirkuh, seized power. Shirkuh died the same year, and was succeeded by his nephew, Yusuf ibn Ayyub, who under Nur al-Din's orders would dissolve the caliphate on September 13, 1171. Al-'Adid, the last Fatimid caliph, who had been raised to the throne in 1160 at age nine, died a few days after. In 1174 William II invaded Egypt in support of the Fatimid resistance. But he was routed in his first action, a siege of Alexandria, and unbeknownst to William, Yusuf, who would soon become a hero to the Islamic world as Salah al-Din, had already neutralized the rebels.

Back in Sicily, Lombard colonization was continuing unabated, and the settlers began targeting the island's Muslim inhabitants, stealing their lands. New trade patterns shaped by Venice, Genoa, and Pisa helped to reorient the Sicilian economy toward the Latin north, while trade with Ifriqiya declined. The end of the de Hauteville dynasty would soon follow. In 1184 William II had betrothed his half sister, Constance, to Henry, the heir to the crown of Germany and the Holy Roman Empire, in the hope of forging an alliance. When William died childless in 1189, Henry claimed the Kingdom of Sicily on the basis that Constance was the lawful heir to the kingdom. For five years the remnants of the de

Hauteville family warred against Henry with loyal Sicilian Muslims under their command. But Henry prevailed, and in 1194 was crowned king of Sicily in Palermo. By then, the Muslim population of the island had lost all position and influence.

Beginning in 1224, under Henry's son, the emperor Frederick II, the remains of Sicily's once vibrant Islamic society would be transported en masse to Lucera, an isolated colony in the far north of Apulia. In 1300 the vestiges of the community would be forcibly enslaved, and disappear entirely from the historical record.

The fate of Sicily's Muslims would have been almost unimaginable on that fall day in 1153, when Philip of Mahdia stood before his king and his people and heard his sentence pronounced. So it may appear curious that Ibn al-Athir—who was writing at about the time of the exile to Lucera—wrote of Philip's trial and execution as "the first blow which befell the Muslims in Sicily." Did he mean to imply that it was worse than the Norman conquest? That it signaled a new era of discrimination and oppression? Not at all. In Ibn al-Athir's opinion, Philip's fate had been sealed not by his apostasy but by his generous treatment of the wealthy Muslims of 'Annaba. We cannot be sure of Philip's motivations or of his intent at 'Annaba, but we can be certain that he failed to understand the delicacy of his position. If he had, he would never have returned to Palermo.

CODA: THE ONE THAT GOT AWAY

Thirteen years later, an even more powerful Palace Saracen, the eunuch Barrun, or Peter the Caid, found himself in a similar situation as Philip. By 1159 Peter, who had begun his career in the chancery of Roger II, had risen to the rank of admiral under William I. Sent in January 1160 to rescue Mahdia, then under siege by the Almohads, Peter retreated during a battle at sea, abandoning the Norman garrison, which was overrun and massacred. Although the mission had been a disaster, he continued to ascend the ranks of the Norman administration, and on William I's death in 1166, he became the trusted confidant of the queen, Margaret of Navarre, who was ruling as regent in the name of the eleven-year-old William II. Under Margaret, Peter became the most powerful man in the kingdom.

Within a year, however, resistance to him had gathered among the nobility. So one night, Peter sailed off with a handful of loyal eunuchs in a ship laden with his treasure chests. He never set foot in Sicily again. He had been so trusted by his intimates at the court that the queen and the members of her inner circle refused to admit his treachery, and at least one Christian nobleman was prepared to defend his honor in a duel to the death.

Peter landed in Africa and commended himself to the Almohads, journeying to their capital in Morocco and receiving the blessing of the Commander of the Faithful. 'Abd al-Mu'min not only showered him with gifts, but appointed him admiral, and Peter, or Barrun, now bearing the name Ahmad al-Siqilli ("Ahmad the Sicilian"), led the Almohad fleet to victories against both the Christians of Spain and the last Almoravid and Zirid princes in North Africa. If anyone deserved to go to the stake by the standards of the day, it was Peter, but unlike Philip of Mahdia, he was astute enough to be the one that got away.

PART IV

Infidel Rulers of a Heretical Caliphate

7

After the Messiah

Indifferent to the cold morning drizzle, crowds gathered before the Great Palace that was the heart of al-Qahira—Cairo—on this wet December day in 1140. Dawn, barely perceptible through the shroud of gray cloud, would have been greeted by the muezzins' call of *Allahu akbar! . . . Allahu akbar! . . .* , singing with all their strength to drown each other out, as the Shi'a and Sunni calls to prayer diverged. "I bear witness that 'Ali is the representative of God!" proclaimed the former. "Prayer is better than sleep!" cried the latter.

In the broad plaza known as Bayn al-Qasrayn (Between the Two Palaces), the crowds gradually took the shape of a procession. Near the front, bearing gold crucifixes and his pastoral staff, would have stood the bearded, black-robed catholicos, head of the Armenian Church in Egypt, attended by a group of clergy, notables, and a large company of officers and soldiers. All would have been sullen, whispering nervously to one another in their native tongues, their swords poking out from under their cloaks. Near the catholicos would have been two other bearded and bejeweled dignitaries: the Coptic Christian Pope of Alexandria and heir to Saint Mark the Apostle, his ceremonial crown sheathed in a black turban; and the Melkite Patriarch of Alexandria. Each would have had his entourage of bishops, monks, and priests, some having come from as far away as the Black Sea and the highlands of Ethiopia. There would have been high-ranking Muslims and Jews in attendance, as well as many other courtiers, clerics, and eunuchs: Slavs, Turks, Arabs, and Central Africans. But aside from these various factions and officials, and aside from the paid mourners, the large crowds of common folk who filled the side streets would have been overwhelmingly Christian, and their tears and dismay would have been genuine.

They had turned out to pay their respects to the man who had gone by the titles *Sayf al-Islam* (the Sword of Islam) and *Taj al-Dawla* (the Crown of the Dynasty), who had recently held the post of *"wazir* of the Sword," and who had died three days before. His name was Bahram Pahlavuni, and he, an Armenian Christian, had been for a brief two years the commander in chief and prime minister of an empire that stretched west to Ifriqiya, east to Ascalon, and south into Arabia and Nubia. Bahram had ruled in the name of the Fatimid caliph: the Imam of Islam and the living embodiment of Prophecy.

Just as the day's proceedings were about to start, a wave of astonishment would have run through the crowd. There, sitting on a donkey and robed in a simple green headdress and cloak, was the caliph al-Hafiz. This was exceptional. The caliph rarely appeared in public, and when he did, it was always in highly choreographed rituals designed to demonstrate his divinity and splendor. For the Shi'a Muslims who venerated him, al-Hafiz was the heir to the Prophet, the voice of Islam, and the manifestation of Revelation. But today he came in grief, as a simple man, his face unveiled as he slumped in the saddle and took his position behind the coffin. As the city's muezzins called the Muslim faithful to the noon prayer, the procession finally lurched forward, and began to make its way past the shuttered shops and offices of the imperial city. Priests girded the mourners, swinging censers from which wafted plumes of fragrant aloe and dhawa smoke and loudly chanting verses of the Gospels in repetitive plainsong. Only the caliph was allowed to ride; all the others walked.

Fatimid caliphs did not make a habit of attending the funerals of Christians or foreigners, but Bahram was no ordinary *dhimmi*. He had come to Egypt at the behest of al-Hafiz himself, in order to save the caliphate and the caliph's life in the empire's darkest hour. Al-Hafiz had rewarded him with titles and powers no Christian had ever held in the caliphate, and had, despite their differences, come to esteem him deeply. Al-Hafiz rode slowly as the mass of mourners left the fortress city through the great Bab al-Futuh, the "Gate of Conquest," and entered the northern suburbs. Passing under the arches of the gate, constructed half a century earlier for the caliph's forebear, al-Mustansir, they could have read the inscription praising its builder, Badr al-Jamali—another Armenian *wazir*, but a Muslim—as "the very illustrious lord, commander of the armies, sword of Islam, defender of the Imam, guarantor of the *qadis*, and director of the missionaries of the believers."

A mile or so later the cortege stopped at St. George of the Ditch, a monastery complex that was the seat of the Coptic bishop and the main Armenian church in Cairo. A tomb had been prepared in the cemetery, not far from the burial place of the monastery's founder, the illustrious Jawhar, conqueror of Cairo and perhaps the first Armenian *wazir*. Here, wearing the robes of the monk he had become, Bahram Pahlavuni was laid to rest. According to the thirteenth-century chronicler Ibn Muyassar, al-Hafiz, who "had been plunged into deepest sadness" by the death, "then dismounted his donkey, and stood by the edge of the tomb weeping hot tears."

The services would have continued long into the night and the days that followed, and many of the tens of thousands of Armenians as well as the Coptic and Greek Christians who lived in the city would have passed to pay their respects. The day after Bahram was buried, the offices of the imperial bureaucracy were reopened, having been closed since his death by order of the caliph. But the demise of the former *wazir* did not signal a return to normalcy in the caliphate, for these were turbulent times. The story of the Christians and Armenians in the capital was at a crossroads, and the days of the dynasty were numbered.

A century and a half earlier, 'Ubayd Allah, a refugee from Persia who was held by his followers to be the Imam of Islam, had established a state in Ifriqiya centered on Mahdia. In 909 c.e. he declared the 'Abbasid caliph in Baghdad to be an impostor, and himself to be the true *khalifa*, or "successor," of the Prophet Muhammad, thereby shattering the idealized unity of the Islamic world. 'Ubayd Allah became the *Mahdi*, or "the Rightly Guided One," a messianic figure who would restore justice to the world as a prelude to the end time. Sixty years later his great-grandson, al-Mu'izz, sent Jawhar al-Siqilli (the Sicilian), a general of obscure, possibly Greco-Armenian origin, as his viceroy and commander to conquer

Egypt. Jawhar succeeded, and in 969 C.E. laid the foundations of a new capital, al-Qahira, "The Conqueror," named in honor of the caliph and the war god Mars (al-Qahir), whose planet was ascendant.* Cairo would become the greatest city in the West, and for the next two centuries, the Fatimid caliphs would rule over an immense empire of orthodox Muslims (who considered them heretical), Christians, and Jews, and of Africans, Asians, and Europeans. But in al-Hafiz's time, the fissures were showing; torn by tensions, the caliphate—the diversity of which epitomized contemporary Mediterranean society—would soon spiral into disarry, to be destroyed in 1171 by the legendary sultan and holy warrior Salah al-Din.

HERETICS FROM THE EAST

Modern pundits and political commentators tend to speak of Islam as either a monumentally unified religion (as in "Islam says . . ." or "Muslims believe that . . .") or as a faith ruptured by a division of insurmountable and visceral hostility. On the one side are the Shi'a, who tend to be portrayed in the Western media as ecstatically irrational violent extremists, and on the other Sunni, who are presented as retrograde but rational violent ideologues. The reality is rather more complex.

Both historically and today, the vast majority of Muslims identify as Sunni: those who follow the tradition (*Sunna*) of the Prophet, and who in early Islamic times believed that the succession of leadership of a unified and single Islamic community (*'umma*) was to be determined according to Arab tribal tradition, which meant, in those times, by the consensus of the leaders of the Banu 'Umayya, the most powerful clan of Muhammad's tribe, the Quraysh. Shi'a, however, believe that Muhammad had declared his beloved cousin and son-in-law, 'Ali ibn Abi Talib, to be his successor, and that the imamate (*imama* refers to "supreme religious leadership") was passed down through Muhammad's daughter, Fatima Zuhra, the wife of 'Ali.

---

* Jawhar was known variably as al-Siqilli, al-Saqaliba, and al-Rumi. *Saqaliba* means "Slav" but was used to refer to slaves, servants, or clients from the Caucasus or of European origin or aspect. *Rum* was the Arabic for "the Roman Empire," which by this time referred to the Greeks of Byzantium. However, because so many people identifying as Armenians were serving as mercenaries in the Islamic East, *Rum* became synonymous also with "Armenian."

Scuffling between the parties followed the death of Muhammad, until a compromise was reached, in which it was agreed 'Ali would become the fourth caliph. The first three, universally acknowledged caliphs led the rapid expansion of the Islamic world, conquering most of what had been the Roman and Persian empires. The Umayyad clan established the center of the expanding *dar al-Islam* at Damascus in Syria. 'Ali's base of support, meanwhile, was in southern Iran and Iraq. In 656, with the assassination of the caliph 'Uthman, 'Ali was recognized as caliph, but the Umayyads would not relinquish power, and a civil war began that would see the assassination of 'Ali (661) and the killing of Hasan (670) and Hussayn (680), his sons by Fatima. The Umayyad victory was the genesis of what would become the Sunni–Shi'a divide.

For a range of reasons, inhabitants of the former Persian Empire would be drawn to the esoteric, mystically infused, messianic Islam that focused on the figure of 'Ali and the line of imams believed to descend from him—an Islam that anticipated an apocalyptic transformation of the world. The Muslims of Arabia and of the former Roman provinces favored the Islam represented by the Umayyads, who came to articulate a system of law, based on the Qur'an and the traditions of the Prophet, that was intended to guarantee a just, ordered, and peaceful world under the rule of Islam. In the centuries of Sunni domination that followed the death of Hussayn and Hasan, Shi'a Islam would harden as a faith of the politically disenfranchised, the culturally marginalized, and the religious nonconformists of the Islamic East.

There was also a third way of interpreting the message of the Prophet: that of the Kharijites, a movement that originated with the Bedouin warriors who deserted 'Ali at the Battle of Siffin in 657. When 'Ali was about to crush the forces of the Umayyad rebels, their commander, Mu'awiya, had his men fasten pages of the Qur'an to their spears as they marched into battle. Thus shamed at the prospect of killing fellow Muslims, many of 'Ali's troops left the field, and the movement of the Kharijites, or "those who departed," was born. More than any others, they represented the tribal, nomadic roots of Islam, and recognized neither the Sunni nor the Shi'a hierarchy, taking the Qur'an as the only valid authority over believers. It was a Kharijite, not an Umayyad, who assassinated 'Ali. In the centuries that followed, Kharijism continued to appeal to individualistic Arab and Berber nomads, who saw themselves as the true Muslims and remained a thorn in the side of mainline Islamic regimes. A similar group, the Qarmatians, spun off from Shi'a Islam, and went as far in 930 as to raid Mecca, where they massacred pilgrims and locals and carried off to their base in Bahrain the venerated Black Stone of the Ka'aba, the focus of hajj pilgrimage and the cornerstone of the Islamic world. It would remain their captive for twenty one years.

The religious and ethnic diversity of Islam was typical of any faith that spans cultures, peoples, and regions, and that aspires to be a world religion, and Christianity and Judaism were no less diverse.* Yet unlike medieval Christianity, Islam did not emphasize obedience to authority in religion, but rather personal responsibility for one's salvation; within the framework of scriptural monotheism and the primacy of Islam, people were largely free to interpret the will of God as they understood it. Thus diversity within Islam was not seen as problematic. For the most part, Sunni and Shi'a in the Middle Ages coexisted with little friction. They intermarried and recognized each other's religious laws and traditions as legitimate (if incorrect) interpretations of God's message. This is also why Christians and Jews could be so well integrated into Islamic societies—their beliefs were regarded as wrong, but not beyond the pale. And while it is true that Muslim, Christian, and Jewish polemicists attacked rival creeds, the accusatory writings of medieval ideologues did not necessarily reflect the priorities of the ordinary folk they claimed to represent. Though religious identity was formalized in the law of each faith or denomination, religious affiliation was frequently ignored by common people, who at times even mixed and matched religious beliefs— they attended one another's services, prayed at one another's shrines, and took part in others' ceremonies and celebrations. It was only in those moments when religious belief, ethnic community, political agenda, and

---

* Despite the fact that they did not formally separate until 1056, the Greek Orthodox and Latin Catholic Churches had developed distinct cultures and traditions from the start. There were other Christian denominations that were no less venerable: the Syriac Church, the Armenian, the Georgian, the Coptic (or Egyptian), and the Ethiopian, to name the most important. In addition, there were many groups classified formally by the Orthodox Churches as heresies: Paulicians, Donatists, Arians, Nestorians, and a dozen more local variants scattered throughout the Mediterranean and Near East. In terms of theology and stated practice, the Christian denominations differed on matters such as the nature of Christ and the Trinity and in the particularities of their liturgies and services; but in reality ethnic, cultural, and local political affinities for the most part determined their membership and nurtured their rivalries.

economic forces aligned that quite suddenly religion and theology could move to the forefront of people's consciousness, with transformative, violent, and sometimes catastrophic consequences.

Such an alignment occurred in the Islamic world in the year 750, when an uprising by the supporters of the long-deceased 'Ali (the *Shi'at 'Ali*, or "the Party of 'Ali") tapped into widespread discontent with the Umayyad regime and launched a full-scale revolt. The caliphate was destroyed, and the caliph, Marwan II, and his family were murdered. Only a single prince, 'Abd al-Rahman, escaped. He headed west to his mother's people, the Nafza Berbers of Morocco, before crossing over to al-Andalus and creating the emirate that would eventually become the Umayyad Caliphate of Córdoba. Back in southern Iran and Iraq the revolution ended with the founding of a new dynasty of Sunni caliphs, the 'Abbasids (descendants of Muhammad's uncle, 'Abbas ibn al-Mutallib). They would be recognized by all Muslims as the holders of the title of caliph for the next two centuries, although in practice their power was negligible west of Syria-Palestine, and their authority only grudgingly acknowledged by the Party of 'Ali, which now comprised the majority of the Muslim population in the 'Abbasid heartland of Mesopotamia. Here, moderate Shi'a collaborated with and sought to control the Sunni caliphs, a relationship that worked as long as power between the factions was kept in balance. It was during this period, in the court of Baghdad and those of the Persian provinces, that Islam experienced its so-called golden age, the era of figures such as the great caliph Harun al-Rashid, the legendary Sinbad the Sailor, and the other characters of the tales of *The Thousand and One Nights*.

But a current of restlessness ran beneath the surface of the empire. Its source was the still-simmering discontent of committed Shi'a activists, who thought that the caliphate was a sham, called for rebellion, and were relentlessly persecuted by caliphal authorities—first the Umayyads and then the 'Abbasids. They believed that the true imams of Islam were the direct male descendants of Hussayn ibn 'Ali, the son of Fatima. When Ja'far al-Sadiq, the sixth of these imams, was poisoned in 756, Shi'a Islam splintered. Most believed—as do most Shi'a today—that his line continued through his son, Musa, until eventually the twelfth imam, Muhammad al-Mahdi, disappeared from the world in 824. This "occultation," as "Twelvers" believe, will persist until his eventual return, when, alongside Jesus (who in the Islamic tradition was not killed, but was also hidden), he will herald a new age of justice and peace. A smaller group, however, believed that Ja'far had passed the imamate on to his second son, Isma'il, who also went into hiding. These "Isma'ilis"—persecuted by both the Sunni 'Abbasids and the Shi'a majority—went underground, disguising their heretical beliefs and meeting clandestinely to worship. They developed a highly effective network of secret missionaries and agents who quietly spread the Isma'ili faith throughout the 'Abbasid lands, thereby laying the groundwork for the political and religious revolution to come.

The moment would arrive soon after the year 900, when the Isma'ili imam revealed himself. According to his followers, an individual named 'Ubayd Allah was the great-great-great-great-grandson of Ja'far al-Sadiq. In the late 800s he was living in an Isma'ili community in Salamiyya, on the western edge of the Syrian Desert, from where he was dispatching agent-missionaries (*da'is*) to the fringes of the caliphate. In 903, as the 'Abbasid authorities were closing in, 'Ubayd Allah made his move, hop-scotching across North Africa until he landed in Sijilmassa. His agents had prepared for his appearance by inciting the Kutama Berber tribes of Ifriqiya to rise up against their Arab governors, the Aghlabids. When 'Ubayd Allah arrived, with his Kutama forces he seized the Aghlabid capital of Raqqada and proclaimed the establishment of a new Shi'a caliphate in Ifriqiya. Over the next decades, these Fatimids (as they became known because of their claim to descend from the Prophet's daughter) carved out an empire through brute force, bribery, and diplomacy. They used the muscle of their Berber army to take on local Sunni and Kharijite resisters, and to attack the North African dependencies of the Umayyads of Córdoba. Their Christian-staffed navy conquered Sicily, invaded the Italian coast, and struck Byzantine territories, forcing the empire to pay them tribute and become their ally. The greatest success came in the 950s under Jawhar, the enigmatic commander who would change the course of the dynasty in 969.

In that year, Jawhar marched on Fustat, the capital of a province that included Egypt, Syria, and Palestine, and the holy cities of Mecca and Medina, bearing the full authority of the fourth Fatimid caliph, al-Mu'izz. The Fatimids had been probing Egypt for some time, preparing for the invasion by sending *da'is* to stoke anger toward the 'Abbasid-appointed governors, and to convert locals to the Isma'ili faith. They found fertile ground: the population had endured a series of famines and economic crises, and the governors could not keep order in the capital or in the more remote territories. As the Fatimid army moved east, representatives of Alexandria, Egypt's second city and its major seaport, intercepted Jawhar and offered to surrender. After giving them generous terms, which they accepted, he continued southeast to Fustat, overrunning the city after a brief battle. Ever the pragmatist, and understanding that religious revolution would come slowly, Jawhar issued a pledge of safety, or *aman*, to the people of the capital. His army would not be allowed to pillage the city, and the Sunni Muslims who bowed to Fatimid control would be granted complete religious freedom and security for themselves and their property. According to Jawhar, his caliph al-Mu'izz had come

> to deliver the Egyptians from the menace of the [Muslim] infidels who wanted to attack the country . . . and to reorganize the pilgrimage and secure liberty, to reestablish security in commerce by a sound currency, abolish illegal taxes, and assure the freedom of exercise of religion to all.

This was essentially the same arrangement and rationale the early Muslim conquerors had offered to the non-Muslims they conquered in the era of the first caliphs.

Al-Fustat, "the Tent," had been founded by 'Amr ibn al-'As, the Muslim commander who conquered Babylon, a city on the Nile that had once been key to Roman Egypt, in 641.* Fearing his troops might be contaminated by contact with non-Muslims, 'Amr built a garrison town (a *misr* in Arabic)—a tent city—just to the north of Babylon. By the time Jawhar arrived in 969, Fustat had effectively absorbed its older neighbor; he encountered a dusty and crowded metropolis populated by Sunni Muslims, Christians, and Jews. Lining its riverside were fetid slaughterhouses, dye works, and mills, while cemeteries stretched across the flatlands in three directions. Clearly, this was no place for the Imam of Islam. Consulting his astrologers, Jawhar decided to found a new capital that would be a showcase of Isma'ilism and a worthy center for the dynasty of caliphs whose destiny it was to rule the world. He settled on a site a mile or so north of Fustat and about a mile east of the Nile. There he began to build a city that would be called "The Conqueror," and from which the Fatimids would rule their growing empire.

---

* Babylon in Egypt is not to be confused with Babylon in Mesopotamia. The Egyptian city's name was likely a Greek corruption of its ancient Egyptian name, Pi-Hapi-n-On.

THE MOTHER OF CITIES

The foundation of this new capital was not meant to signal the end of Fustat, which would remain a sprawling metropolis. It was, rather, to be a fortified palace city that would supplant 'Abbasid Baghdad as the center of Islam, not unlike Madinat al-Zahara outside Córdoba, which the rival Umayyad Caliphate had finished only a few years before.

Laid out alongside a canal connecting to the Nile, the palace city's rectangular plan covered half a square mile. Thick brick walls soon rose to seal it off from the outside world, and none but the caliph and his *wazir* were allowed to enter its gates mounted or without a written permit. Two great palaces were constructed inside the walls, adjacent to a large park: the Great Eastern Palace, for the administration, and a smaller one for the royal household, with the two connected by an underground passage. Between them was a massive plaza, Bayn al-Qasrayn, that could accommodate crowds of more than ten thousand. The rest of the palace city was divided into quarters for troops, including various Berber groups, "Blacks," Kurds, Byzantines, Turks, and Persians, all quartered based on their tribal, ethnic, and religious affiliation. According to Naser-e Khosraw, a Persian who visited in the 1040s, the city was patrolled day and night by a thousand guards, and the palace employed twelve thousand servants and another ten thousand female slaves and eunuchs; while in the city's port a fleet of six hundred newly launched ships lay anchored. In 970 Jawhar began construction of the great mosque, al-Azhar (the Brilliant One), which would be Cairo's main place of worship and a hub of Islamic learning and base for the development and dissemination of Isma'ili doctrine. Today, the mosque houses the second-oldest continuingly operating university in the world, predating the University of Bologna, the oldest in Europe, by more than a century.

The masses of laborers who built Jawhar's al-Qahira had to be housed somewhere, and a sprawling city of huts, shops, bathhouses, and inns rose up outside the walls. The rents from the residences and businesses went directly to the caliphs, who were already wealthy from tax revenues. With these incomes, Cairo's palaces were appointed with gold and rock crystal fixtures, the finest porcelain, and seemingly limitless silk brocade, while storerooms were filled with jewels and precious metal so plentiful that the caliphs could not keep track of it all. In 1001, when the envoy of the Byzantine emperor Basil II was arriving at the court of al-Hakim, at the last minute the caliph's aunt, Rashida, recalled the existence of twenty-two gold-brocade silken tapestries that had been forgotten in storage since the Fatimids' arrival in Cairo. These were hastily hauled out and hung.

On those occasions when the imam appeared in public—for the major Sunni, Shi'a, and Christian holidays, and civic celebrations such as the annual "opening of the canal"—he usually rode a fine horse, wearing robes of red-and-white silk and the turban bearing the enormous diamond solitaire (*al-Yatima*, "the Unique One") that was the symbol of his power. Above him swayed his broad ceremonial parasol, gems dangling on cords from its fringe. As he processed through the streets, which were festooned with great banners proclaiming his glory and that of 'Ali, the cousin of the Prophet, the Muslims in the crowd, particularly those who subscribed to the Isma'ili faith—and likely not a few Christians and Jews as well—would anticipate the gaze of the "heir of the Prophet" sweeping over them, imparting his *baraka* (divine blessing).

The Egyptian economy of the late tenth century was perhaps unrivaled by that of any other Mediterranean land; in the first year of his rule alone, Jawhar was able to raise almost 3.5 million dinars for the caliphal treasury in rents, taxes, and other incomes. At a time when Christian Europeans lived in an illiterate, agricultural barter economy, in Fustat and Cairo entrepreneurs erected towering apartment buildings for profit, and—according to Naser-e Khosraw—even the humblest workers negotiated their pay on the basis of written contracts. The fertility of the Nile was the basis for tremendous agricultural output, which easily sated domestic demand for food, while sweeping cotton fields provided the raw materials for the greatest cloth industry in the West. Fustat was a booming industrial center, producing the highest-grade ceramics and other manufactured goods, as well as lower-quality items for everyday use in massive quantities.

The greatest source of the empire's wealth, however, was trade. Along the Nile and the caravan route ("the Forty-Day Road") that ran alongside it, spices, slaves, precious goods, and exotica were brought up from the "Land of the Blacks"—Nubia and Christian Ethiopia, which were Fatimid protectorates. Via Alexandria, Cairo was connected to the markets of the Mediterranean: Byzantium, Syria, Sicily, Ifriqiya, and the Maghrib. Muslim and Jewish traders plied these routes and brought exotic products to Egypt from their bases in the Indian Ocean and as far off as China. As a consequence, Egypt enjoyed a virtual monopoly on the trade of the rarest, most valuable, and most sought-after products. The Fatimid world was so interconnected that in 1149, Abraham ibn Yiju, a Jewish merchant based in Bangalore, India, could send a letter to his siblings in Mahdia with nothing more than their names and their city of residence as an address. (Remarkably, it reached them in Palermo, to where they had moved!)

Under the Fatimids, Misr ("the City"), or Greater Cairo—the massive agglomeration of al-Fustat, al-Qahira, and the various other suburbs clustered along the Nile—was the most advanced and cosmopolitan urban center of its day. It boasted a police force, a commercial bureaucracy, fire-prevention policies, and street cleaners, and a startling variety of peoples. Although there had been a wave of conversion in the 800s, Christians still comprised the majority of the population. Most were Copts, followers of the Church of Alexandria, a creed that had been regarded as heretical since the Council of Chalcedon in 451. Their liturgical and written language was Demotic, the spoken language of ancient Egypt. The next most numerous Christian group was the Melkites, adherents of the Byzantine Imperial Church (*malik* is Arabic for "king"), whose services were in Greek. Then there were Syriac Christians, Nubians, and Ethiopians (who owed allegiance to the Copts), and—after the 1070s—a significant number of Armenians. Each of these congregations identified as a denomination, a linguistic group, and a "people," and was recognized as such by the Muslim authorities. There were also many Jews: Rabbinical Jews of the Palestinian and Babylonian schools, Qaraites, and a few Samaritans. Some originated in the Maghrib or Ifriqiya, others in Palestine or Persia, and still others had been in Egypt for generations. The wealthiest were active in commerce and a range of crafts and professions. Arabic was their common tongue, although Hebrew was used sometimes for letters, contracts, and religious texts. The Christian and Jewish communities were each characterized by internal religious, cultural, social, and economic competition as much as they were by communal solidarity. In any case, most members of each group thought of themselves as Cairenes, notwithstanding their differences.

As *dhimmis*, or "protected peoples" of Islam, these non-Muslim "Peoples of the Book" were second-class citizens, in theory, but in practice they were integral to the regime. The caliphs worked to earn their loyalty, and non-Muslims became prominent in learned professions, such as medicine, and in key government posts. In contrast to the Islamic West, where Jews played a crucial role in the financial administration, in Egypt the Coptic Christians had maintained their hold over the state's complex fiscal system since the time of the Muslim conquest. Thus, the first Fatimid *wazir* of Egypt was a Christian, Abu al-Yumm ibn Mina. Eminent non-Muslims used their influence to protect their religious communities and to control their communities' religious leaders. For their part, the caliphs treated bishops, patriarchs, and *Nasim* as servants of the caliphate. Imams were known to marry strategically into the top Jewish and Christian families, bringing the non-Muslims and the Fatimid dynasty even closer.* Some highly placed non-Muslims converted. The third *wazir*, Yaqub ibn Killis, for example, was originally a Jew from Baghdad, but converted to Islam in 967 and eventually to Isma'ilism (although he remained suspiciously close to his former coreligionists). He served from 977 to 991, and when he died was mourned by the Coptic Christians on account of the favor he had shown them. Most non-Muslim officials, however, did not convert, and some were known for their piety. The caliphs could find no more loyal servants of the state. Non-Muslims and Muslim foreigners understood that their positions depended on the strength of the regime, and they worked tirelessly to promote Fatimid ideology.

As in every society of that era, Muslim, Jewish, and Christian women occupied a lower rung than men, and their public lives were limited. They were not, however, totally disempowered. Common women of all three religions could manage businesses and property and live autonomously. Higher-status Muslim women attended seminars at al-Azhar, whereas those of the Fatimid inner circle became imposing political players in their own right. Slaves, for their part, enjoyed rights enshrined in Islamic law, and their owners often allowed them considerable liberty, treating them as clients rather than chattel, and allowing them to acquire their own fortunes. Some of the royal wives in the caliphate had once been foreign slaves, and as in other Islamic societies, concubines, eunuchs, and other slaves were seen as members of their masters' households, and could wield tremendous power, thus adding yet another dimension to factionalism in Cairo.

* Intermarriage of this type was technically impossible in Christendom, where religious law forbade unions with non-Christians. In Islam, Muslim men could marry non-Muslim women as long as they were "People of the Book"; and they were not required to convert to Islam. Any children born to such couples were considered Muslim.

Foreigners also came to fill important roles and occupations in Fatimid Egypt. Most, whether Turks, Persians, Berbers, Byzantines, Greco-Armenians, or "Blacks," arrived as slaves or freemen to serve in the Fatimid military, with freemen often bringing their extended families. Tensions existed among and within these groups, as individuals and cliques competed for influence and the favor of the caliphs. Muslim or not, all tended to be mistrusted by the native Muslim and Christian Egyptians, who saw them as interlopers.

The peoples of Greater Cairo were conscious of the barriers that separated them from one another, but nonetheless transgressed these barriers continuously. They consciously embraced ethno-religious ambiguity and diversity by intermarrying, socializing, and dabbling in one another's rites and rituals. The success of the Fatimid caliphs lay in the skillful manipulation of these divisions and the exploitation of internal rivalries, a necessary approach to ruling for a regime that not only governed a land in which Muslims remained the numerical minority, but that itself represented a heretical group within Islam.

Although the Fatimids did their best to outwardly respect orthodox Muslim sensibilities even as they worked to convert their subjects to Isma'ilism, many among the Sunni population regarded their usurpation of the caliphate as an outrage. They resented the caliphs as occupiers, and for privileging non-Muslims and foreigners so openly. But the Isma'ilis were not hollowly Machiavellian in their pursuit of power; they remained sincerely committed to the spiritual and political transformation of the world. After being refined intensively at al-Azhar, Fatimid doctrine was brought by missionary agents dispatched to the rest of the Islamic world by the chief *da'i* in Cairo. The goal of the Fatimid ideological mission, or *da'wa* (calling), was the creation of a universal Isma'ili state. This undertaking had two major domestic consequences. First, Cairo continued to evolve as a leading center of religious learning, science, and culture (the caliphal research library alone had some 1.6 million manuscripts). Second, religion in Egypt became intensely politicized through the figure of the caliph, who, unlike in the rest of the Islamic world, was—as imam—held to embody a very clear and direct spiritual authority over Muslims.

The Fatimid ideology of messianic revolution would be carried to a terrifyingly logical conclusion in the figure of al-Hakim bi-'Amr Allah, who came to the throne at age eleven in 996, following a prosperous

Twelfth-century depiction of a Fatimid court scene

decade for the empire under his father al-'Aziz. Al-Hakim's mother was a local Christian, and al-'Aziz had strongly favored the Coptic Church. His son's time on the throne, however, was one of chaos and decline. It is difficult to untangle the truth about this enigmatic character, who was vilified by later historians, but it is clear that the young caliph was a victim not only of his times but of his personality. By age fifteen he had violently shaken off the tutelage of his early guardians by executing his leading courtiers, notably Barjawan, the eunuch slave who ran the empire while the imam was a boy.* Indeed, execution became a favorite tool for the young caliph, one he used enthusiastically and capriciously. Notable courtiers and their dependents were targeted; on his orders, for example, the family of Jawhar was massacred.

Al-Hakim, it seems, became convinced that he was the *Mahdi*, a god-king and incarnation of the divine. He set out to purge society of what he perceived as widespread religious hypocrisy, and pushed Christians and Jews into formal subjugation. Non-Muslims were ordered to wear distinguishing clothes, badges, and tattoos, public processions were banned, interfaith socializing was curtailed, the clergy was persecuted, and some churches and cemeteries were destroyed. Many Jews and Christians

---

* Barjawan's execution was evidently carried out at the instigation of another eunuch, the "Slav" Zaydan, who was freed afterward and became one of the caliph's key officials.

converted under duress, although apparently they were later allowed to return to their faith. The most infamous edict was al-Hakim's call in 1009 for the destruction of Jerusalem's Church of the Holy Sepulchre, on the grounds that the popular Easter-time Miracle of the Holy Fire had been proven to be a fraud orchestrated by local priests to deceive believers and generate donations.

Nor were Muslims spared his fickle rage. For the sake of the morality of the populace, he limited the sale of wine, restricted the public lives of women, imposed a nightly curfew, prohibited chess, outlawed certain foods, and twice ordered the killing of all of Cairo's dogs because their barking disturbed him. That many of these measures were repealed and then reenacted, or followed by conciliatory policies or acts of excessive generosity, has convinced most historians that al-Hakim was mad, or a megalomaniac. In his own view and that of his supporters, his zeal was nothing less than the proof of his divinity. And, to be sure, some of his policies can be seen as ostensibly consistent with a reestablishment of Islamic norms and justice, and some as measures to combat bureaucratic corruption. Many Muslims would have approved of his treatment of Christians and Jews. Still, for most of the people in the Fatimid Empire, his was a twenty-five-year reign of terror.

On the night of February 13, 1021, it all came to an abrupt end, when al-Hakim disappeared while wandering alone at night in the hills above Cairo. Later, his bloody and shredded robe was found, but his body was not. Most people then and now believe he was killed, while some claim he retired anonymously to a monastery, and still others—the adherents of the present-day sect known as the Druze—that he was "withdrawn" from the world by God, and will in due time reappear as the true imam and *Mahdi*.

A possible culprit in al-Hakim's death was his half sister, Sitt al-Mulk. The favorite child of al-'Aziz and herself a Christian, she, too, had suffered under her brother's rule, and it was she who stepped into power after his death by sidelining al-Hakim's chosen heir and securing the succession of his son, al-Zahir. Sitt al-Mulk ruled through her nephew, undoing much of al-Hakim's damage—patching up previously cordial relations with Byzantium, which had been undermined by his anti-Christian policies, and allowing the rebuilding of the Church of the Holy Sepulchre. Although she died in 1023, she set in motion a renewed diplomatic collaboration between the two powers, including combined

Byzantine-Fatimid military action (against the Druze, in 1032), and a treaty in 1034 that guaranteed, among other things, that if one of the empires were to suffer famine, the other would send food. Once he was of age, however, the new imam apparently became a drunk who neglected affairs of state in preference for cavorting with Sudanese slave girls. Over his sixteen-year rule, al-Zahir gave free rein to the factions within the palace and army, setting the groundwork for the fatal destabilization of the caliphate.

AFRICANS AND ARMENIANS

Unlike many other groups that emerged violently into the medieval Mediterranean—including the Normans, Franks, Burgundians, Saljuq Turks, and Sanhaja—the Fatimids represented an ideology rather than a distinct people. Their revolution did not involve a mass movement, but rather a small, motivated core; they had no hinterland populations to draw on, or distinct ethnic traditions to galvanize them; and they did not have strong internal ties of kinship, culture, or language with their subjects. They were a small sect, a religious group that might attract adherents, but that might just as easily lose them. To use a concept of the great fourteenth-century sociologist Ibn Khaldun, the Fatimids were not a people bound by *'asabiyya*, the group feeling or solidarity that could transform a fractious tribe into a cohesive and potent political power.*

This fact had important practical consequences. The Fatimids were not a broad, self-reproducing tribe or military elite, and were therefore dependent on allies, clients, conscripts, and mercenaries to carry out their foreign policy and uphold their regime. The Isma'ilis only founded their state in Ifriqiya by harnessing the energy and discontent of the Kutama Berbers, who were happy to join any revolution, and who initially constituted the main force of the Fatimid army. Once installed in Mahdia and starting to expand into the Maghrib and Sicily, the Fatimids attracted clients and mercenaries, including the *Rum* (Romans)—Byzantines and

---

* Wali al-Din 'Abd al-Rahman ibn Khaldun (d. 1382) was a pioneering historian, sociologist, and philosopher, who lived and worked in Ifriqiya and the Maghrib and wrote histories of the North African dynasties, as well as a universal history famous for its methodological foreword, *al-Muqaddima*.

Greco-Armenians—who would eventually have their own quarters and churches in Jawhar's al-Qahira. They were only two factions among many; the Fatimids, hoping to limit the power of any one of their dependent groups, recruited soldiers from dozens of distinct tribes and peoples, keeping them separate from one another in order to prevent them from allying among themselves. The strategy was to exploit their clients' ambitions, prejudices, and animosities, in order to ensure that their only loyalty was to the caliph.

Once the caliphate had moved to Egypt and the Fatimids had begun to expand into the East, the need for troops only grew. The empire recruited from among the nomadic peoples who were infiltrating the fringes of the 'Abbasid Caliphate. Large numbers of Saljuqs, Kurds, Berbers, and Arab Bedouin came to settle in Egypt. These provided a counterweight to the Kutama Berbers, who had never been strongly attached to Isma'ili doctrine, and whose foreign aspect and manners appeared barbarous to the native Egyptians.* Soon the Kutama came to be seen as a threat, and the Fatimids turned to Saljuq mercenaries for troops. However, to allow the Saljuqs to accrue too much power would have been no less dangerous. Fortunately for the Fatimids, the trade corridor of the Nile and the Sahara gave them a new source for military muscle: the Blacks of the Sudan. Central African soldiers had been recruited by the earliest Fatimid military forces and had been used by previous Egyptian regimes, but it was under al-Hakim and his successor, al-Zahir, that they were brought north in massive numbers and became the dominant ethnic contingent in the Fatimid army.

The Sudanese provided a potent force for the Fatimid rulers. They were foreigners who had no natural allies in Egyptian society, in part because they were visibly different and—despite the inclusive nature of the Islamic 'umma and the historical and religious place of Blacks within it—there was considerable prejudice in Middle Eastern Islamic society against dark-skinned Central Africans.† These 'abid (the plural of 'abd,

---

* The Kutama were certainly easy to spot. They were clad in the woolen burnuses typical of Berbers, and the men's heads were shaved, except for a distinctive braid or lock coiffed in a way that indicated the particular clan an individual belonged to. Despite the fictive tribal genealogy they concocted with the support of the Fatimids, they were clearly not Arabs, and spoke their own tongue, which was unintelligible to the Muslims of Egypt.

† Bilal ibn Rabah al-Halashi, a Black of Ethiopian origin, was a Companion of the Prophet Muhammad, and the first muezzin in Islam.

Thirteenth-century battle scene: Egyptian troops and Crusader forces

the Arabic word for "slave," which came to refer solely to Blacks) were purchased as pagans, and therefore also bore the double stigma of bondage and conversion. Such was the disdain they elicited that the Sudanese were the only group not given a neighborhood in al-Qahira proper. Instead, they were settled in garrison quarters in the suburbs. The unpopularity of the Black troops only deepened as they were brought up in increasing numbers by al-Hakim and became the visible instrument of his despotism. When, in 1020, the populace rose up against his excesses, the caliph turned his Sudanese troops loose on the city for three days of riot, plunder, rape, and abduction. Apparently, a third of the city was destroyed by fire. Thousands must have been killed. Only after the non-Black regiments of the army entered the fray to defend the populace and themselves did al-Hakim call off the Sudanese, personally appearing on his horse and riding between the lines of the two forces to prevent a bloodbath.

During al-Hakim's rule a number of Black eunuchs were elevated to offices in the palace. Sudanese soldiers were no longer restricted to serving as lowly infantry, and as they moved into the cavalry they acquired prestige, wealth, and political clout. Al-Hakim created a unit of one hundred black slaves, al-Sa'diyya, to serve as his personal cavalry escort and, most provocatively, began to appoint 'abid as officers of Saljuq regiments. Even so, racial hatred would not be the cause of the conflict between African and non-African troops that boiled over in the 1050s. It was, rather, a typical struggle between two of the many ethnic groups that made up the Fatimid military. Under al-Zahir, the status of the Sudanese only rose; and he unleashed them, as his father had, against domestic insurgents.

Al-Zahir's predilection for Africans was related to the fact that his favorite wife, Rasad, was a Sudanese girl. She had been sold to the caliph by the Qaraite Jew Abu Sa'd al-Turtusi, who was al-Zahir's supplier of Black concubines. Like other prestigious women of the Fatimid court, she was lavished with properties and incomes, and became independently powerful. When al-Zahir died in 1036, it would be her seven-year-old son, al-Mustansir, who would inherit the imamate—a Black caliph—with her pulling the strings behind the scenes until the 1060s. Placing her former master, al-Turtusi, in charge of her finances, she set out to consolidate her hold on the empire by concentrating power in the person of the *wazir*, whom she could appoint. Her first choice was Yusuf al-Fallahi, a converted Jew. But al-Fallahi courted the Saljuq regiments in order to undermine al-Turtusi and his Berber troops, and in 1048 al-Fallahi incited the Saljuqs to murder him. Rasad had al-Fallahi put to death, and appointed a new protégé, Abu Muhammad al-Yazuri, as *wazir* in 1050. He was also given the offices of chief *qadi* and chief *da'i* (chief magistrate and chief missionary), despite the fact that he was a Sunni rather than a Shi'a. With his precedent, future *wazirs* would also claim both positions.

By the 1060s, the caliphate was facing a series of major existential challenges. The Kalbids of Sicily were no longer respecting Fatimid authority, having established an independent emirate. The island would soon be conquered by the Normans. Ifriqiya had been lost when its governors, the Zirids, declared their independence from the caliphate in the 1050s. The Fatimids were powerless to regain the territory, and instead dispatched the Bedouin Banu Hilal and Banu Sulayman tribes to ravage the rebellious province. There was a revolt in Alexandria, and the Arab tribes of Upper Egypt also declared their independence. Back in Cairo, factional fighting within the army was threatening civil security; a series of low years for the Nile was causing famine and economic crisis; and al-Mustansir's manifest weakness was only encouraging his enemies in the barracks and the palace. In 1062, after *'abid* troops killed a Saljuq officer, skirmishes broke out between the two groups, and in response Rasad allegedly armed the Blacks, enabling them to defeat the Turks. This is the last we know of the queen mother.

Four years of relative calm followed until, in 1066, the Saljuq and Berber troops made their move against the Sudanese. The capital became the scene of an all-out civil war that would transform the caliphate. Large sections of the city were destroyed in the fighting, and the palaces of the royal family were looted. The inability of the regime to restore order encouraged revolt in the countryside, as local governors simply refused to send tax revenues to Cairo, and the income from rural estates and tax concessions plummeted. The seemingly bottomless caliphal treasury had been the foundation of Fatimid authority, and now that the dynasty was plunged into poverty they would no longer be able to maintain control. In the immediate aftermath of the civil war the Saljuq Turks, who had defeated the Blacks and Berbers, took over the wazirate and army.

The rise of the Turks worried the other political factions in the capital, not to mention its Shi'a population, who saw their own influence was tied to the survival (at least in name) of the Fatimid regime. Not only were the Saljuqs Sunni Muslims who did not recognize the validity of Isma'ili doctrine, but they were kinsmen of the same Saljuq Turks who had recently seized power in 'Abbasid Baghdad, purged the caliphal administration of its powerful Shi'a officials, and sworn to destroy the Fatimid Caliphate as part of their *jihad* to reunify orthodox Islam under the banner of the 'Abbasids. It was at this point that the ineffective caliph, al-Mustansir, attempted to revive the power of the imam and his dynasty. In order to do so, he elevated the Armenians in the caliphate, who as a group had been at the margins in the years since Jawhar's death and the murder of his family.

The Armenian officer Badr al-Jamali was the immediate beneficiary of the caliph's strategy. Badr had been born the son of a slave of the Fatimid governor of Damascus, and had at some point converted to Islam (whether genuinely or not) and been freed. As a young man, he had distinguished himself as an administrator and soldier, becoming governor of Damascus and then governor of Syria (al-Sham) and commander of its armies. This was at the time when the Fatimids were being attacked by the Saljuqs, and in the 1060s, as most of Syria-Palestine was lost, Badr managed the Fatimid withdrawal to Ascalon, over which he was then appointed governor. While in Ascalon he received al-Mustansir's summons to the capital.

Badr arrived in Cairo in 1073. His first action was the massacre of the Saljuq military commanders in the city, as they returned home drunk and at ease under escort of his guards from a dinner party he had hosted. After this the caliph appointed him "Prince of the Armies," "*Wazir* of the Sword," and "*Wazir* of the Pen"—commander in chief, prime minister, and secretary of state, respectively—as well as chief *qadi* and chief *da'i*. Al-Mustansir went so far as to formally adopt Badr as his father, and gave him full political authority in the caliphate.

From that point on he would be addressed as *sayyidi* ("my lord," the same epithet used for the Cid). Once in power, he set out to rebuild civil society in Cairo, and, with the support of the Sudanese troops, to subdue the provinces. Instrumental in the latter endeavor were the tens of thousands of Armenian warriors—Muslims, Armenian Christians, and Orthodox Christians—he had brought from Syria, one hundred shiploads in all. The best of these men were assigned to the new caliphal bodyguard, a function that would be fulfilled by Armenians for the duration of the dynasty. In 1075 Grigor Martyrophile Pahlavuni, the catholicos, or head of the Armenian Church, arrived in Egypt; the caliph prevailed on him to stay, and in exchange opened his borders to Christian Armenian refugees from Anatolia.* These refugees flooded into Cairo, and many joined Badr's private army.

Al-Mustansir's strategy turned out to be a wise one. Badr instituted far-reaching fiscal and organizational reforms in Egypt, and borrowed foreign money to relieve the famine. Under his care, tax revenues recovered, and the proverbial wealth of the caliphs was once again in evidence. Badr rebuilt and modernized Cairo, including its fortifications. The new walls, towers, and fortified gates he commissioned—including the monumental Bab al-Futuh—were designed by Christian Armenian architects who had fled the Saljuq conquest of Edessa. He renewed the diplomatic relationship with Zirid Ifriqiya and strengthened relations with Byzantium, as well as with Christian Nubia and Ethiopia. The recovery of Syria—which the convert Badr called a *jihad*—proved to be beyond his

---

* Grigor's birth name was Vahram; he took his episcopal name in honor of Saint Gregory the Illuminator, the first head of the Armenian Church. He was called Martyrophile, or "the lover of martyrs," for having written extensively on Church martyrs.

impressive capabilities; but at the same time that he tenaciously warred against the Saljuqs, he won over the communities in Egypt that might have been hostile to him: Sunni Muslims, certain Christian sects, and Jews. He would be remembered as "a friend to all Christians, whether high or low." Yet Badr could turn brutally on his allies, and even his own family. For example, he did not hesitate to have one of his own sons killed when the latter led an uprising in Alexandria in 1084, and he set out to exterminate the former officials of the caliphate and their families.

He also strongly supported Isma'ili doctrine, which he saw as crucial to the stability of the dynasty. But his posturing was a pretense for what was, in effect, an internal coup. While he promoted the imam as a religious figure, he isolated him, so that the caliphs would become dependent on the *wazirs*. To seal the relationship, he married his sister, Sitt al-Mulk, to al-Mustansir, thereby securing a direct stake in the royal family.*

Badr's religious identity was rather enigmatic. He was a great patron of the Coptic Church and its patriarchs, as were many Fatimid officials, Muslim and Christian. He built a number of monasteries and churches, and repaired others; he himself would be buried in his own unconsecrated chapel, next to the Church of St. James, which he had founded not far from his majestic fortified gate, the Bab al-Futuh. He was a close friend to the exiled King Solomon of Nubia, whom he welcomed to Egypt and treated to an official funeral at the Church of St. George of the Ditch, the prestigious Coptic church he had reassigned to the Armenians.

Badr died in spring 1094. Al-Mustansir would die soon after—too soon to be able to wrest the caliphate back from Badr's family. Though he tried, the Armenian contingents resisted and ensured that Badr's son, who bore the Persian name Shahanshah (King of Kings), was appointed to all of his father's offices. He was given the honorific al-Afdal, "He of Great Divine Grace."

Al-Afdal passed over al-Mustansir's son, Nizar, who had been selected as the next caliph by the Isma'ili religious authorities, and named his own nephew, Ahmad, al-Mustansir's son by Sitt al-Mulk, as caliph. He would rule under the name al-Musta'li. Immediately Nizar was arrested and locked in a dungeon, and the cleric who had championed his cause, Hassan al-Sabbah, fled east. He and his followers, who believed

---

* Badr's sister, Sitt al-Mulk, should not be confused with the half sister of al-Hakim who went by the same name.

that Nizar was the true imam and the rightful caliph, were called the Nizaris, but are better known in Western literature as the Assassins. Hassan al-Sabbah's attempted revolt in Egypt may have failed, but his movement would win the support of the Isma'ilis in the East. Meanwhile, the ideological edifice of the Fatimid Caliphate had begun to crumble. Each controversy over the succession of the imamate diminished the power of the Isma'ili message, and resulted in the splintering of a group that was already a smaller denomination within the Shi'a minority.

When al-Musta'li died in 1101, al-Afdal installed the caliph's five-year-old son, al-Amir, on the throne, and began to rule Egypt as a king. Unlike his father, al-Afdal was not a state builder, and he treated the caliphate's wealth as his own. His reign finally came to an end when al-Amir, at age twenty-five, overthrew his *wazir*, having him assassinated with the aid of one of al-Afdal's own protégés, an Iraqi Muslim who then rose to the wazirate under the name al-Ma'mun. Five years later, to reassert personal control over the kingdom, al-Amir had al-Ma'mun arrested and crucified; from then on he would have no *wazir*.* But only five years later, on October 7, 1130, Nizari assassins infiltrated the palace and killed al-Amir, who was to them a usurper and false imam.

THE MESSIAH'S DONKEY

Al-Amir left a seven-month-old son as his successor, but the boy disappeared soon after his father's death. With no better options, the Isma'ili authorities in Cairo appointed as regent the eldest male member of the Fatimid clan: al-Amir's cousin, 'Abd al-Majid. In the meantime, al-Afdal's son, who was known as Kutayfat, seized power with the backing of the Armenian officers. He imprisoned 'Abd al-Majid and declared the dissolution of the Fatimid Caliphate, proclaiming that Isma'ilism was no longer the religion of government. He claimed to be the true authority: the hidden imam whom the majority of the Shi'a, or "Twelvers," had been awaiting. But by the end of 1130 the Isma'ilis were back, thanks to

---

* Al-Ma'mun is remembered for his interest in astronomy, and for constructing an observatory with the help of Yusuf ibn Hasdai—a refugee from Zaragoza and a descendant of the great Jewish statesman Hasdai ibn Shaprut—as well as Muslims who had left Norman Sicily.

al-Yanis (*Hovannês* in Armenian, or "John"), a former slave of al-Afdal who overthrew and murdered Kutayfat with the aid of a private army he had raised. 'Abd al-Majid was freed and made imam under the name al-Hafiz, and al-Yanis became the new *wazir* and ruler of Egypt. Al-Hafiz's claim to the title was rather thin, however, as the imamate was meant to be transmitted from father to son. He and his *wazir* produced a set of dubious rationales to justify his authority. Unconvincing as these may have been, for the regime and its followers all that mattered was that Fatimid authority had been restored.

Though he had been saved by al-Yanis, al-Hafiz saw that the caliphate was held hostage by its *wazirs*. Al-Yanis was always surrounded by body-guards, so the caliph arranged to have the *wazir*'s personal ablution fountain filled with a poison that would kill him upon contact with his skin. On October 27, 1132, al-Yanis dropped dead after performing the ritual washing in preparation for prayer. Al-Hafiz then named his own son Sulayman as his heir and as his *wazir*. However, his other sons and their mothers resisted. One of these sons, Hasan, engineered a brief coup, until the Armenian-led army intervened and demanded that he be put to death. To keep his own hands clean, al-Hafiz had Hasan's trusted Coptic physician poison him. Through these three years of intrigue and chaos, two truths became evident: the Armenian military needed to be re-assured that it would retain its power and prestige, and a complex, popu-lous kingdom like Egypt needed a *wazir*.

Al-Hafiz hit upon the idea of appointing as his *wazir* the Christian, Bahram Pahlavuni. Bahram was a native of Tell Bashir in the Crusader-ruled County of Edessa, and, as we have seen, a member of one of the most illustrious Armenian Christian lineages. One uncle, Vasak, had been the Byzantine governor of Antioch in the 1060s, and another was Grigor Martyrophile, the Armenian catholicos who had visited Egypt in the 1070s just as Armenian Syria was descending into civil war. The Armenian Church was itself in crisis in the 1080s, in response to which Grigor responded by devolving his authority on six bishops, each of whom would be given the title of catholicos and wield full authority over their regional congregations. One was Bahram's brother, also named Grigor, whom Grigor Martyrophile had invested as the head of the local Armenian Church during his stay in the caliphate. However, the catholicos in Cairo faced opposition from rival Armenian factions in Egypt. To help him, Martyrophile returned to Syria, where he gathered the Pahlavuni clan, which had taken refuge in western Anatolia, and sent them to Egypt with a great force of warriors under the leadership of his three nephews, among them Bahram.

We know little about the early years of Bahram's service for the Fatimids. There are indications that he spent a period of time as governor of the western province of the Nile Delta, and that he fought at Acre in late 1098 against Crusader forces. It seems he left the Fatimids for a spell and worked for Baldwin I of Jerusalem, but ran afoul of the king and saw his property confiscated. Shortly after 1130, if not before, he was back in Egypt, perhaps summoned by al-Hafiz to help suppress Hasan's revolt. What is certain is that once in Cairo he became the leader of the city's Armenians, or at least of the very numerous Christians among them, and commanded the most powerful military force in the land. He was the best candidate for the wazirate, and a *wazir* was what al-Hafiz needed. Later, in a letter to Roger II of Sicily, al-Hafiz recalled Bahram's arrival in a different light, in which it was the Armenian, not the caliph, who was in need of a savior:

> You know . . . how he arrived in the Fatimid empire . . . a fugitive, banished, chased out of his country, pushed out of his own homeland, rejected by his land, without money or work, without family or friends. Our empire gave him the best welcome . . .

In truth, each needed the other. Only al-Hafiz's unequivocal support could place an infidel in such a position of command, and only an infidel would be unable to control the imamate's religious offices, as previous *wazirs* had done. Bahram could not serve as chief *qadi* or chief *da'i*, nor could he participate fully in the elaborate ceremonial occasions that publicly demonstrated the authority of the regime and its officers. He would be loyal to the caliph, and he would not threaten his authority. In 1135 Bahram was duly appointed "*Wazir* of the Sword," and given the honorifics Most Excellent Lord, Commander of the Armies, Sword of Islam, Helper of the Imam, and Succor of Mankind, in spite of the fact that he was not a Muslim. Al-Hafiz himself was close to both the Coptic and Melkite communities in his realm; having them in his camp was a way of striking at the authority of the Byzantine emperor, who considered the Copts and Armenians heretical, and claimed universal sovereignty over Christianity. Nor did the Muslim populace and religious authorities seem to object to having a Christian commander in chief. As long as he was not granted religious powers, the infidel Bahram would be the unclean vehicle for the realization of the divine mission of the imamate, not unlike the "Messiah's donkey" of the Hebrew Old Testament. Indeed, many Muslims praised him.

But in Islamic tradition it was not the *Mahdi* who came by donkey. It was, rather, al-Dajjal, "the Impostor," the false Messiah, a rough equivalent to the Christian Antichrist. And it would be *this* figure whom Bahram would come to resemble to his Muslim subjects. Though an effective *wazir*, he strove to reinforce his own power at the expense of the royal family's. Contemporary Muslim historians characterized the tensions during Bahram's reign as those of religious conflict, but in fact they were the product of yet another struggle among military and palace cliques.

Bahram's goal was to bring Egypt under Pahlavuni control, and he began by appointing family members to key posts. His brother Vasak, for example, was made governor of Qus, in Upper Egypt. Bahram also aggressively patronized the faction of the Armenian Church his family dominated, constructing scores of churches in and around the capital, to the discomfort not only of common Muslims and Sunni ideologues, but also of native Christians and those Armenians who were Muslim or adherents of the Orthodox Church. More disturbing might have been the growing influx of his countrymen, who upon arrival in the caliphate were immediately given high positions in the army and administration.

There was another reason Bahram's religion had made him a desirable choice as *wazir*: his ability to influence the court of Roger II. By the 1130s the Fatimids had given up any real hope of recovering Zirid Ifriqiya, resigning themselves to the fact that the king of Sicily would dominate the region, either directly or indirectly. The Fatimids thus tried to "manage" the Norman situation, and control Sicily through diplomacy. For al-Hafiz, Bahram's Christianity would allow him more easily to export Fatimid administrative practices and slaves to the Sicilian dynasty and thereby infiltrate the Norman court. Roger also saw the advantages of working with this Christian *wazir*, not only because of the importance of Sicilian-Egyptian trade and his burgeoning Islamophilia, but because with his kinsmen and soldiers in northern Syria, Bahram, Roger hoped, could help him wrest the County of Antioch away from its Crusader occupiers. Roger had not forgotten the indignities his mother suffered at the hands of Baldwin of Jerusalem, and for him, taking control of Antioch would be fitting retribution.

But Bahram's loyalties were to himself, whatever face he put on for al-Hafiz, or Roger, for that matter. Once an official under Baldwin I, he would reenter the good graces of the Franks and the native Christians of the Holy Land, who started referring to him as "the chief of the Armenians." In 1137 he interceded before al-Hafiz at the request of the Syriac Archbishop of Jerusalem to free three hundred Crusading knights, who had been captured by the Egyptians in 1103–04, and kept prisoner ever since. Among those freed was Godfrey of Esch, a knight of Lorraine and a relative of the reigning kings of Jerusalem.

In short, the rise in Egypt of the Christian Bahram and his brother, the patriarch Grigor, generated all sorts of anxieties. Al-Hafiz was anxious about Bahram's ambitions and foreign contacts, the Sunni majority (including many Armenians) about his affinities with Roger's Sicily and his public support of Christianity, and local Christians about the ascendance of the Armenian Church. The caliphate's military commanders, provincial governors, and palace officials saw Bahram as a threat to their own positions, as he displaced many of them with newcomers from the Pahlavuni network.

Bahram's most vocal opponent was a Sunni Muslim official, Ridwan ibn al-Walakshi. The two began to spar after Bahram's appointment. Bahram sent Ridwan to take up the governorship of Ascalon, but once there the Sunni began to abuse Armenians attempting to pass through his province on the way to Cairo. Bahram recalled him to Upper Egypt, thinking to rein his appointee in, only for Ridwan to begin to foment revolt by sending preachers to the capital to agitate against the *wazir*. Bahram's official powers and his policies violated the legal principles of the pact of *dhimma*. Al-Hafiz observed all this without involving himself, content that Bahram was being challenged and wary of openly supporting a Christian who had become so resented in ruling circles.

In 1136 Ridwan acted, marching his troops to the capital. Bahram mustered his army. At the time, George of Antioch's Sicilian fleet was wreaking havoc on the coast of Muslim Ifriqiya in the name of Roger II, making it easier for Ridwan to depict Bahram as an agent of Christian expansion. In order to turn this personal conflict into a larger religious one, Ridwan declared his uprising to be a *jihad*, and ordered his troops to fasten pages of the Qur'an to their spears, in emulation of the Sunni army of the Umayyads, fighting 'Ali at the Battle of Siffin. The gambit worked;

when the two sides met, Bahram was abandoned by his Muslim troops, and Ridwan won the day.

Bahram and his troops hastily boarded ships on the Nile and escaped to his brother's predominantly Christian-inhabited lands at Qus, four hundred miles to the south on the Great Nile Bend. But Ridwan's forces beat him there. When he arrived Bahram found Vasak's mutilated corpse cast on a dung heap and chained to a rotting dog carcass. The tomb of his brother Grigor had been desecrated. In revenge, Bahram turned his men loose on the Muslim populace, and they massacred a great number of them before departing southward for Aswan, perhaps bound for Ethiopia. Ridwan sent an army to apprehend Bahram, but he was unable to defeat him, and a compromise was agreed to. The now ex-*wazir* would retire to the White Monastery, an Armenian foundation just north of Qus, and take up the habit of a monk.

Back in Cairo, Ridwan's stoking of popular discontent against the Christian communities had flared into mob violence. Churches had been ransacked and Grigor's successor as patriarch, Anania, had been killed. Al-Hafiz was forced to recognize Ridwan as his *wazir*. Pushing his Sunni agenda, the new commander took the title of king (*malik*) and began to replace key Shi'a officials with orthodox Muslims. Al-Hafiz could only tolerate so much, and judging that Ridwan had gone too far, he invoked his authority as imam and caliph over all Muslims, and ordered the *wazir*'s private army to rise up and overthrow him. Ridwan fled to Sunni-ruled Syria. After a short time in exile he returned to Egypt and, having attempted a failed coup, was captured and imprisoned—only to escape. During a third attempt to seize power, Ridwan, who stood out even in this era of determined troublemakers, was finally killed.

In order to reassure his Christian subjects in the aftermath of Ridwan's rule, al-Hafiz devoted his energy and resources to reviving the Armenian community, rebuilding churches and once again elevating its elite members to high offices. The new Armenian catholicos became a personal confidant of the imam, and was given a visible and prominent role in state ceremonies. In spring 1139 the caliph recalled the aging Bahram, who was apparently very ill, and invited him to reside in the great palace in Cairo as his adviser. A year and a half later, Bahram died, and in his honor the caliph granted safe-conduct to any of his family members and followers who wanted to emigrate. Al-Hafiz had nothing to gain by showing such honor to the memory of his former *wazir*; whatever suspicions he had of Bahram evidently did not lessen his respect and affection for him, and the grief he showed at his funeral was clearly sincere. It is a testament to the esteem that Bahram was held in that when Roger II of Sicily wrote to the caliph in 1137, inquiring after the fate of the *wazir*, the imam crafted a generous and frank reply. He praised Bahram but said that his position as *wazir* had been untenable, in the face of broad opposition to the Pahlavuni faction. Because of his Christian identity, "Bahram and his followers," the caliph wrote, "appeared [to al-Hafiz's Muslim subjects] as a stain on a clear surface, and as a drop of oil in the waters of the ocean."

THE COMING OF THE FRANKS

Since Jawhar's founding of Cairo and the middle of the twelfth century, the Fatimid Caliphate and the world around it had changed profoundly. The apparent stability of the ninth and tenth centuries, and the uncontested power wielded by the Islamic empires and Byzantium, were giving way to a volatile period characterized by shifting identities and priorities, and by new, and newly militant, ideologies. By 1098 barbarians from the north calling themselves Franks had arrived in the Holy Land, had conquered Jerusalem, and were gradually turning toward Cairo and Constantinople. Sunni Islam was recovering from the challenge of Shi'ism, and a strict Islamic ideology was emerging in response to the Crusades and the challenge of Isma'ilism. After Bahram's death, the Fatimids would not last much longer. Egypt's Armenians, who had dominated the caliphate for nearly a century, would decline with them. As for the rest of the Christians in the realm, the Coptic majority most of all—their fate would also be drastically changed, as Egypt became a truly Islamic land, and as some among the Muslim majority came to see them as no less of a threat than the foreign Christians to the east.

8

Traitors and Spies

Then he turned to al-Malik al-Salih and said, "O Prince! Cleanse this noble state from the Christians in such a manner that none of them is assigned to work in the offices of the Muslims. Anyone who says that they are good accountants is a liar, for it is they . . . who make the number one to be three, when they reckon the One Unique as three . . . And Almighty God . . . said, *They do blaspheme who say: God is one of three in a Trinity: for there is no God except One God* . . . Then the *sheikh* Zayn al-Din said, "O My Lord, this really is their belief, so drive out the Christian—he who takes three out of the treasury of the Sultan for one, and thus dishonors God . . .

It had been some twenty years since the overthrow of Bahram, and since the anti-Armenian violence during the short reign of Ridwan ibn al-Walakshi. The caliph was al-Fa'iz, a grandson of al-Hafiz, who had succeeded to the imamate in 1154 at the tender age of five. He was now probably eleven. But al-Fa'iz was not the "prince" who was addressed that day by the sheikh, and the interview did not take place in the Emerald Palace of the caliphs. Zayn al-Din was presenting his petition in the audience hall of the *wazir*, who bore the title al-Malik al-Salih, "the Pious

King." His real name was Tala'i ibn Ruzzik al-Armani. He was a career soldier, the former governor of Qus, and the son of one of the thousands of mercenaries who had followed the great *wazir* and general Badr al-Jamali to Cairo in the late eleventh century. He was the master of Egypt; the young al-Fa'iz, nothing more than a puppet. The Armenians were back in power.

Zayn al-Din was an elderly Arab, whose Syrian accent would have marked him as a recent arrival in the caliphate, and as, very likely, a pious Sunni Muslim at least as hostile to the *wazir*'s brand of Islam than to the errors of the Christian he was denouncing. Tala'i ibn Ruzzik was, many scholars today believe, an Alawite, a member of a secretive Islamic sect viewed as brazenly heretical by mainstream Sunni and Shi'a alike. But the object of Zayn al-Din's vitriol and scorn on that day was a Coptic Christian, an individual known to us only as "Ibn Dukhan," who was a high-ranking official in the palace's financial administration. According to the account of the prosecution of Ibn Dukhan recorded about a century after the event by Zayn al-Din's great-grandson, the poet and chancery bureaucrat 'Uthman ibn Ibrahim al-Nabulusi, the charges the sheikh brought against the Christian included a laundry list of offenses against Islam and the Fatimid regime. Zayn al-Din did not attempt to prove the guilt of Ibn Dukhan on the basis of hard evidence, but rather on the presumption that these allegations must have been true simply because he was a Christian.

Ibn Dukhan may well have been present as the allegations against him unfolded, dressed in the ceremonial robes whose colors and cut signified his department and position: he was secretary of the imperial treasury. He was a rich, influential, and well-connected man. Did he stand in proud defiance as this foreign bumpkin launched into his denunciations? Or did he sense, as insubstantial as these accusations may have been, that his life was in danger? Could he have known that he was witnessing firsthand a gradual but dramatic shift in the fortunes of his community? As the story is told, Ibn Ruzzik was swayed by Zayn al-Din. Ibn Dukhan was seized and searched, and letters were found on him addressed to the Frankish Crusaders, in which he tried to persuade them to conquer Egypt. Ibn Dukhan was put to death as a traitor and a spy.

The story is perplexing. The Christian-Muslim relations it depicts are more belligerent than we usually associate with the Fatimid period. Although al-Nabulusi's story was widely repeated, there is no contemporary evidence that it unfolded as described. Nor do we know for certain the identity of Ibn Dukhan. But this is not to say that some version of this event did not take place; in all likelihood al-Nabulusi's account rests on a foundation of fact. The execution of a treasury official for malfeasance was hardly an unusual occurrence in the Fatimid regime, after all.

This episode—and al-Nabulusi's and others' retellings of it—are best understood within a broader context. To what extent can Ibn Dukhan's execution be characterized as religious violence? Does this event reflect widespread Muslim-Christian tensions, or only a Sunni-Coptic dynamic specific to the late Fatimid, Ayyubid, and Mamluk eras? Or is it an example of ethnic and religious anxieties harnessed in the pursuit of personal vendettas? One thing we can be sure of is that if al-Nabulusi's tale was even half true, the trial and punishment of Ibn Dukhan would have had a profound impact on Egypt's Christian communities.

CHRISTIANITY IN MUSLIM EGYPT

Egypt was a cradle of Christianity. In Antiquity, Alexandria was home to the library of the ancients, where, according to tradition, in the second century B.C.E. the Septuagint—the first Greek translation of the Hebrew Old Testament—was produced under King Ptolemy II. It was said that seventy scholars labored independently on the project, and all miraculously produced identical translations. Alexandria is the place where Saint Mark evangelized, as well as the site of his martyrdom. In the first turbulent centuries of Christianity, the city was the scene of conflicts among pagans, Jews, and Christians of various creeds. There were many heretics and nonconformist Christians in Egypt; Nag Hammadi, the place where the "Gnostic Gospels," which had been buried to save them from destruction by orthodox Christians, were discovered in 1945, is near Qus, on the Nile Bend. Egypt was also the cradle of Christian monasticism, the home of Saint Anthony of the Desert and Saint Pachomius. During the first three centuries after the death of Jesus many Egyptian Christians were persecuted and martyred by the Romans.

In the centuries after the Crucifixion, as Christians grappled with the import and meaning of the stories they had inherited—above all, the nature of the Trinity and of Christ—and as local, "national," and imperial interests clashed, two major traditions appeared in Alexandria: the Orthodox,

Greek-speaking "Melkite" Church, and the Coptic ("Egyptian") Church. They formally split after the Council of Chalcedon in 451, when the Imperial Church of Byzantium affirmed that Christ fully and simultaneously embodied two natures, human and divine, whereas theologians of the Syriac, Armenian, and Egyptian Churches held that Christ had one nature that fully embodied both the human and divine. The latter creeds—called "miaphysite" or "monophysite"—were thereafter regarded as heretical by the Latin and Greek "duophysites." Such theological niceties, however, were outside the concern or understanding of most of the faithful. Ordinary Christians were attracted to one or another Church for reasons that usually had little to do with dogma and far more to do with family traditions, regional loyalties, political views regarding the empire, and social connections and relationships to local authorities. After Chalcedon the Egyptian Church distinguished itself from the Orthodox through its rites and festivals, and by using Coptic, the common Egyptian tongue, rather than Greek, as its language of liturgy and theology.

The estrangement of the two denominations grew in the declining years of the Roman Empire, as the Church became more important as a branch of imperial government and the clergy acquired political power. Emperors, notably Justinian in the early 500s, inspired resentment for levying high taxes on the provinces, including Egypt, all the more because the revenues were used to fund foreign military adventures or opulent building projects in Constantinople. In the early 600s, when the Sassanid Persians, who were officially Zoroastrians but who counted many Christians among their subjects, invaded and conquered Syria and much of Egypt, they claimed to be the saviors of the local Christians. The empire would briefly retake Egypt and the Holy Land in the 620s, but would soon be swept away by the armies of Islam.

During the first great age of Islamic conquest under the caliph 'Umar, the Arab warrior 'Amr ibn al-'As arrived in Egypt in 639 with a force of only one thousand men, yet in only a few short years subdued the north of the country. It was a conquest by negotiation. 'Amr took advantage of discontent with Roman rule, offering generous terms of submission, including guarantees of freedom of religion and security for the inhabitants of the region, who, faced with the alternatives of conquest and enslavement, grudgingly accepted. Local political leaders, many of them churchmen, were soon brought into the new Islamic administration, and became willing collaborators with the Muslim regime. The Arabs were relatively uncultured desert warriors at the time, and could not hope to run a kingdom like Egypt, whose tremendous cash economy was based on techniques for controlling and distributing the water of the Nile that had been refined over millennia. For the first century or so of Islamic rule, little changed from the Byzantine period: Greek remained the language of administration and coinage, and the same local elites who had managed Egypt under the Romans continued to do so under the Muslims. Egypt's Christians were now *dhimmis*, whose political and religious rights were curtailed, and who were supposedly subject to Islamic authority. But they were so numerous and so necessary to the functioning of the state that they exercised significant power and influence over the slowly growing Muslim population.

While there was some Arab immigration to Egypt, those who arrived were for the most part nomads, and were settled in the provinces. In the cities, natives eventually began to convert to Sunni Islam. But, like their counterparts in Spain, even those who did not convert were drawn into Arabo-Islamic culture, and adopted the style of dress, music, dance, social habits, and language of their new lords. Such was the closeness of the Christian and Muslim communities from the time of the overthrow of the Umayyad Caliphate in 750 C.E. to the mid-ninth century, that when Coptic Christians led a series of uprisings in response to the high taxes levied by governors appointed from 'Abbasid Baghdad, many Muslims joined them. Throughout the period, Christian cliques, whether Copts or Melkites, as well as Jews, clung fast to their positions in the administration.

As the 'Abbasid Caliphate slowly fell apart in the late 800s, Egypt drifted toward independence under its governor at the time, Ahmad ibn Tulun, and the relationship between the regime and its Christian subjects that would persist through the Fatimid period was forged. It was a relationship of codependency; Muslims ruled, while *dhimmis* filled the important bureaucratic posts. As part of the arrangement Muslim rulers granted privileges to Christians far in excess of those sanctioned by Islamic law, a fact that only brought the minorities even closer to the regime.

Even so, when convenient, Christian and Jewish communities could be subjected to arbitrary taxation, confiscation, or violence. Or they could be used as scapegoats to diffuse popular tension among Muslims, or to placate the demands of religious hard-liners. Although relations between the Muslim and Christian populations were cordial and stable, that *dhimmis* served as tax collectors and in other offices was a source of tension.

Some pious Muslims, as well as some nonpious but poor Muslims, saw the *dhimmis* exercise of authority over the faithful as an affront to the divine order established in the Qur'an.

A sizable number of Egyptian *dhimmis* were indeed powerful. Bahram Pahlavuni had not been the first Christian to serve as *wazir* during the Fatimid period; the self-declared Messiah and imam, al-Hakim, had no less than three. Christians also regularly occupied some of the highest posts in the royal household. Though these positions entailed a certain amount of risk, this was not unusual in the cutthroat world of Fatimid politics; at least half of the scores of *wazirs* who served during the Fatimid period—Muslim, Christian, and Jewish—were executed or assassinated. The average life expectancy once in office was only about two years.

Many Christians served as *katib* (chief secretary) to the caliphs, including Abu Mansur Bishr ibn Severus, who drafted al-Hakim's order for the destruction of the Church of the Holy Sepulchre. Some of the men elevated to this office, such as the monk Abu Naja, who served al-Amir as *katib* (and was ultimately arrested by the caliph and executed), were clergymen. But the wazirate and the secretariate represented only the most visible sign of Christian influence in Muslim Egypt. Christians served as governors and deputy governors, as household administrators for caliphs, queens, and princes, and in the middle and upper ranks of the financial bureaucracy. Those in high positions did their best to place their relatives, friends, and fellow congregants below them. To an ordinary Muslim Egyptian, it would have seemed that there were Christians everywhere in the administration of his society, and that these Christians were frequently proud, powerful, and corrupt.

Upper-class Egyptian Christians won renown as scientists, astrologers, and physicians, while still others grew rich as merchants. The Persian traveler Naser-e Khosraw claimed to have met a Christian trader so wealthy he was able to supply wheat for the realm during six years of famine at the caliph's request. This is certainly impressive, but what went unsaid in the tale is that the caliphs had an interest in allowing Christians to become wealthy because they could, if necessary, appropriate their wealth, or extort them, or demand obligatory loans. Knowing that their gains might be temporary only encouraged Christian merchants, officials, and tax collectors to seek their fortunes by means honest and not—feeding the negative stereotypes of affluent Christians held by Muslims.

Several Fatimid caliphs took Christian wives, and as a consequence, their children sometimes sympathized quite openly with Christianity. At least one caliph's powerful daughter, Sitt al-Mulk (the daughter of al-'Aziz), chose to remain Christian even though her father claimed to be the earthly representative of Islam. According to Islamic law, she was a Muslim by virtue of having been born to a Muslim father; thus, for her to have lived as a Christian would have constituted a crime of apostasy, punishable by death, but as a princess, she was clearly above the law. Several caliphs were noted for attending church services, befriending high-ranking clergy, or visiting monasteries. Al-Hakim, it was said, allowed Christians who had converted to Islam during moments of persecution to return to their former faith—another scandalous affront to Islamic law.

The closeness of the Fatimids and the Christian high clergy encouraged the Coptic, Melkite, and Armenian Churches to play out their internal disputes in the caliphal court, whether they were conspiring against the other creeds or against competitors within their own denomination. Later, in the early 1200s, for example, when the sultan al-Malik al-'Adil was pondering the appointment of a Melkite as bishop to the Ethiopians, the Coptic patriarch warned him that a Greek Christian would "corrupt them, and he would make them Greek . . . and, perhaps, he would incite them to fight the Muslims." Competition within each community was no less intense; the anonymous successor as Armenian patriarch in Egypt to the murdered Anania—who was a close friend of the caliph al-Hafiz—died by poisoning. The culprit? The Armenian Patriarch of Jerusalem.

Eminent Christians and the Christian clergy became instrumental in Fatimid foreign policy. The Fatimids were the declared enemies of the other major Muslim powers in the West, and with the help of their Christian subjects, could hope to form alliances with Sicily, Byzantium, Bulgaria, Nubia, and Ethiopia, all of them Christian-ruled. Native Christian clergymen made effective and loyal envoys. Moreover, until the 1070s the Fatimids controlled Jerusalem, which meant they had the authority to name the Byzantine Orthodox patriarch there. In the late 900s al-'Aziz appointed one of his Melkite wife's brothers, and later his daughter, Sitt al-Mulk, appointed Patriarch Nikepheros, who restored Byzantine-Fatimid relations after the saber-rattling of al-Hakim's reign.

Clergy from the Coptic Church were also relied on by the Fatimids to secure Egypt's southern frontier, and to spread Fatimid influence in the Christian nations beyond it, which the caliphate had long failed to keep

A twelfth-century Egyptian lusterware bowl with the figure
of a Coptic priest

in line. In the 1080s Badr al-Jamali sent a force to subdue Muquarra (Nubia), known for its gold and slaves, and prevailed upon its king, Solomon, to open his borders to Fatimid subjects and to allow the construction of mosques. When, as a consequence, Nubia's Christians rose up and expelled Solomon, he settled in Cairo under the protection of the *wazir*, and retired as a monk. The Ethiopian Kingdom of Axum, a key trading link with East Africa and the Indian Ocean, had been Christian since 330 C.E., and had welcomed Muhammad's followers, who had been persecuted in Mecca prior to the *Hijra*. Formally, the Ethiopian Church was subject to the Patriarchate of Alexandria, which gave the Fatimids clout in the kingdom through their control of the Coptic Church. These relationships, however, were not always one-sided. The Axumite king could also help protect Egyptian Christians from their Muslim overlords. Because it was believed that he had the ability to physically cut off the flow of the Nile, which was thought to originate in his kingdom, he could intimidate the caliphs when they threatened the Coptic community.

Christian dignitaries in Egypt were accorded places of honor at the important Isma'ili ceremonies of state, and at "national" festivals, such as the opening of the Nile canal, and the caliphs even supported, and sometimes appeared at, the major Christian festivals: Nawruz, the Coptic New Year, which falls on September 11; Epiphany, or the Feast of Baptism; Christmas Day; and Palm Sunday. On each of these occasions, the caliphs distributed money and gifts to officials and their families or to the general public. The celebration of Nawruz involved a great procession of all the officers of the regime, Muslim and Christian, whereas on Palm Sunday Christian clergy marched to the homes of the leading Muslim magistrates and chanted out verses from the New Testament while swinging censers of pungent incense and calling down blessings on the *qadis* and their families.

To conservative Muslims the caliphs' sponsorship of Christian festivals was alarming, and the large-scale participation of ordinary Muslims even more so. Indeed, common folk of different religions often mixed with one another. Medieval Islam, Christianity, and Judaism shared the traditions of the Old Testament, and Islam and Christianity those of the New Testament. Figures like Elias and Saint George were prominent in the folk mythology of both of the latter religions. Members of each of the three major faiths, moreover, had common beliefs that sometimes defied the orthodox theology of their religious leaders: the efficacy of saintly miracles, the veneration of holy men, and the intercessionary power of Prophets. Muslims were frequently drawn to Christian rituals and places of worship and pilgrimage. Many, for example, visited the Church of St. George in Fustat, where the chains said to have once bound the dragon-slaying saint were on display. Christians and Muslims singing, dancing, and drinking together could lead to dangerously frank discussions of theology or to emotional and sexual liaisons across the religious divide. To attempt to head off such unwanted contacts, authorities enforced dress codes: Egyptian Christians were often mandated by law or by their own Coptic leaders to wear the *zunnar*, a traditional belt-like accessory, or tattoos of crosses.

There were periods of official persecution of Christians, notably during the reigns of al-Hakim and of the Sunni *wazirs*, al-Yazuri (1050–57) and Ridwan ibn al-Walakshi (1136–38).* To an extent the oppressiveness of these regimes can be explained by the personal whims of these rulers, but there was always a political component to anti-Christian policies. One rationale behind them was to publicly reassert the dominant position of Islam to both Christians and Muslims. For their part, non-Christian *wazirs* could be vindictive in their treatment of those Christians whom they saw as political competitors. Another reason for anti-Christian laws and actions was the simple fact that Christians were so numerous in Egypt. There was always some amount of fear that Christian functionaries and generals were plotting to overthrow Islam, and some degree of envy at the positions powerful Christians enjoyed. A sarcastic refrain by a late-tenth-century poet took aim at the power held by Copts in the Fatimid court—in this case, Fadl, the caliph al-'Aziz's military commander:

> Become Christian, for Christianity is the true religion!
> Our times demonstrate this.
> So recite the Trinity! [The Christians] are strengthened and exalted,
> Whereas that which is not theirs is neglected, and so it is ruined.
> Don't worry about anything else: Ya'qub, the *wazir*, is the Father,
>   and this
> 'Aziz is the Son, and the Holy Spirit is Fadl.

Al-'Aziz pardoned the poet for his indiscretion, but Ya'qub ibn Killis, the *wazir* of the poem (a Jew who had, at least in name, converted to Islam), had him put to death.

Resentment periodically boiled over among the populace, too. Many Muslims were sensitive to the importance of maintaining the world order ordained by God, an order in which they held a privileged position by virtue of their faith. Muslim mobs, at times incited by what they saw as an affront to their supposedly superior status, would take to the streets and attack Christians and churches. Sometimes this was done in defiance and rebellion against the Isma'ili imamate, and at other times with the support of the caliphs or their *wazirs*.

Many Christians lamented their subjugated status and the gradual decline of their language and culture, but there is no evidence that they

---

* Each of these *wazirs* died a violent death, and the rule of each was followed by a period of Christian-Muslim reconciliation.

were agents of foreign empires. The Muslim-Christian divide, however, was only one of the ways in which the people of Egypt defined themselves and the nature of their society. Every person belonged to a range of communities—religious, local, professional, and kin-based—and membership in any could result in that person crossing religious lines or ignoring religious affiliations. The Christians and Muslims of Egypt were deeply integrated, and it was only because the politics, ethnicities, communities, and religions of Egypt were entangled that mundane rivalries could be presented or imagined as epic religious conflicts.

THE SYRIAN CONNECTION

The largely peaceful coexistence of the many religious and ethnic groups in Egyptian society would be challenged in the early decades of the twelfth century, not so much by internal strife, but rather as a result of events in the cold reaches of the lands of the *Ifranj* (Franks). Pope Urban II's Call to Crusade of 1095 launched a phenomenon that would transform the political and religious environment of the Mediterranean world. In the 1080s and 1090s, the Armenian *wazirs* Badr al-Jamali and his son al-Afdal had been attempting to recover territory in Syria and Palestine (*Bilad al-Sham*, or "the Land on the Left") that had been conquered by the Saljuq Turks in the previous decades. In 1097 al-Afdal regained possession of the strategic port of Tyre, and in 1098 he marched victorious through the gates of Jerusalem—though the city was then a backwater of largely symbolic value. By this time, the Fatimids were exchanging envoys with the newly arrived Franks. At first the Fatimids mistook them for just another tribe of warriors seeking to carve out a piece of Mediterranean prosperity. Soon they would understand that these Christian warriors were, in fact, on a single-minded mission of a different kind.

The Frankish campaign of 1097–99 caught the Muslim rulers of *al-Sham* by surprise. They were not expecting such an attack, but the real shock was that their new enemy thought of them as religious enemies who deserved to be destroyed. To be sure, there was a notion of holy war in Islam—it was an important dimension of the larger moral mission of *jihad*, or "moral struggle." *Jihad* had been a key element in the dramatic initial phase of Arabo-Islamic expansion, the force that bound motley tribal warriors into a unified and motivated military, and spurred the campaigns that brought the former Persian Empire and much of the Mediterranean under Islamic rule between 622 and about 800 c.e. After that, Muslim rulers waged occasional wars of conquest, but for the most part the further expansion of the Islamic world was carried out through trade and cultural assimilation, and occurred in Africa and Asia rather than Europe. By the 800s the idealized notion that the world could be divided into two zones—the *dar al-Harb* (Abode of War) of the infidels and the *dar al-Islam* of the Muslims—had been set aside for the new concept of the so-called Zone of Truce (the *dar al-'Ahd*), comprising those non-Muslim powers with whom Muslims had peaceful relations.

Even in its classical glory, the *jihad* of the early caliphs was not aimed at exterminating non-Muslims, but rather at dominating them—subjecting them to Islamic rule so that they and their descendants would have the opportunity to convert freely to the true faith and live in peace. As unlikely as it may sound, *jihad* was not so different from the self-professed duty of many people in the West today to bring democracy and the free market to those parts of the world that do not have them. Yet *jihad* in the Middle Ages had an additional wrinkle. When, for instance, the Saljuqs embarked on their *jihad* against the Fatimids in the mid-eleventh century, and the Fatimids on their counter-*jihad*, each drew on a common spirit—the aim to reestablish what they saw as legitimate and righteous Islamic political authority—and as a consequence, they saw each other, rather than any Christian regime, as the true threat. For the rulers of each faction, the campaigns were really attempts to eliminate the other's political elite, not to wipe out the civilian populace, many of whom would have sympathized with their cause. Muslim rulers, like their Christian counterparts in the Near East, had long been fundamentally pragmatic. Compromise and negotiation were preferred over extremism and extermination, and princes and kings pursued their political goals with relatively little concern as to the religious identity of their allies and enemies.

This is why the First Crusade was so incomprehensible and so devastating to the Arabs, Turks, Armenians, and Byzantines who ruled in *al-Sham*. They were stunned by the fierceness and cruelty of the Franks, and baffled by their single-minded focus on Jerusalem, which to them was no prize compared to Cairo or Constantinople.

After conquering Antioch in 1098, the Frankish army moved south through Syria and into Lebanon. Those local rulers who could not buy off the Crusaders were attacked, and their civilian populations were given no quarter. In a notorious episode in late 1098, after the town of Ma'arat al-Nu'man was taken, the desperate Frankish victors gorged themselves on the dead bodies of the populace in the wake of their wanton massacre. A later French romance, *The Song of Antioch*, has the French knights re-marking, "This is most tasty, better than any pork or even cured ham," as they feasted on their Muslim foes. When Jerusalem fell to the Franks on July 15, 1099, the city's Fatimid commander and garrison were able to negotiate their own safe passage, but were either unable to save the city's inhabitants or indifferent to their fate. For three days the Crusaders butch-ered Jerusalem's Muslims (along with some Jews and local Christians) in an effort to cleanse the Holy City of the "pollution of the Saracens." Thousands were put to death, including hundreds of *'ulama'*.

The Muslim princes of Syria and Palestine were largely unmoved by the plight of the ordinary Muslims living in the Franks' path. During the First Crusade and in its aftermath, they negotiated treaties and alliances with the invaders. They simply did not yet grasp the Crusade as a war of religion. Those Muslims who escaped the massacre at Jerusalem and who fled into Syria may have, but they held no political influence. In 1105, when the Damascene preacher al-Sulami wrote *A Treatise on Holy War* decrying the Franks' vicious *jihad* against the Muslims, he was practically ignored. Four years later, when a delegation from Syria staged a noisy public demonstration in Baghdad to draw attention to the suffering of the Muslims of *al-Sham*, and to demand that the 'Abbasid Caliphate fight back against the Franks, they were threatened with arrest for disturbing the peace. Their protests had cast an embarrassing pall on the ceremonial arrival of the caliph al-Mustazhir's wife.

With the exception of the direct victims of Frankish aggression, Mus-lims in the Near East simply did not conceive of politics in terms of a grand Muslim-Christian conflict of civilizations; it did not correspond with their experiences. It is true that in the 1060s the Saljuq Turks had launched a war on Byzantium, and following their near-total victory at Manzikert, where they routed the imperial forces and captured Emperor Romanus IV Diogenes in 1071, they did overrun most of the Christian-ruled Anatolian Peninsula. But this was an unexpected opportunity, and they were not pushing on with the aim of annihilating Byzantium. It was not the result of a religiously inspired mission to conquer Christendom;

their larger goal was to overthrow the Muslim Fatimids. By the time Frankish Crusaders arrived in Constantinople a generation later, the Saljuq princes in Anatolia had built stable relationships with Byzantium; Turkic warriors could even be found in the imperial army. In 1092 the great warrior Malik Shah, who bore the title Grand Saljuq, and who had been the true leader of the 'Abbasid Caliphate, died, and in the wake of his passing the various Saljuq princes and governors of Anatolia, Syria, and Iraq claimed independence, and began fighting for supremacy within the 'Abbasid world. For them, at first the Franks seemed to be at worst a distraction, and at best another regional player to use against their Muslim rivals.

Whatever divine fury and religious solidarity had driven the Franks halfway across the known world, meanwhile, had begun to dissipate even before Jerusalem was theirs. The First Crusade resulted not in a united Christian-ruled Holy Land, but in four independent principalities: the Kingdom of Jerusalem, the Principality of Antioch, the County of Tripoli, and the County of Edessa. They became immersed in the world of Near Eastern politics, seeking out allies among local Muslim rulers in efforts to outmaneuver and undermine one another. The rulers of the three major cities in Islamic Syria in the period—Aleppo, Damascus, and Mosul—had no real interest in Jerusalem, which had been under Fatimid control, and eagerly responded to overtures from the Crusader states. Damascus and Jerusalem, for example, became crucial allies and trading partners.

Eventually, however, a Saljuq warlord named Nur al-Din started to promote an ideological program of anti-Frankish *jihad*—what historians have called a Counter-Crusade. His father, 'Imad al-Din Zengi, had been a formidable warrior and the 'Abbasid governor of Mosul in 1127, and had taken Aleppo in 1128. Yet Zengi believed his greatest accomplishment—before a Frankish slave assassinated him while he was passed out drunk—was the conquest of the Frankish County of Edessa in 1147. Edessa, formerly an Armenian kingdom, had been the first principality brought under Crusader rule in the East, and its fall to Zengi enabled him to style himself a hero of Islam. When word of the defeat reached Innocent II in Rome, the pontiff reportedly dropped dead on the spot.

After his father's death, Nur al-Din set out to complete his goal of conquering Syria. But the elite of Damascus resisted Nur al-Din's aggression with the help of their Frankish allies in Jerusalem. At this point,

Nur al-Din realized the value of portraying the Franks as enemies of Islam and the conquest of Jerusalem as a step toward his ultimate goal of dominating Baghdad and the 'Abbasid Caliphate. Presenting himself as a champion of Islam, he gained the allegiance of disaffected Muslim clergy who were dismayed at the princes' passivity in the face of the Crusaders, and who began to spread his message from their pulpits.

He got even more help from the Franks themselves. The crucial moment came in 1148, when Latin forces under King Louis VII of France and assorted other Christian kings and magnates arrived in the East determined to take revenge on the Muslims for the loss of Edessa. But instead of going after Nur al-Din in the north or moving on Edessa, the bickering and divided Crusaders targeted Damascus, not realizing how critical an ally the city was to Frankish Jerusalem. The siege was a debacle. Camped first in orchards west of the city, the Crusaders' heavy cavalry was slowed by the terrain and harassed by defenders sallying from the city. Moving to open ground east of the city, they were exposed to the heat of summer without a water supply. Nur al-Din and his forces soon arrived at the request of the Damascenes, and put the Christians to ignominious flight. As a result, Damascus opened its gates to Nur al-Din, and its inhabitants accepted his call to holy war against the Crusaders. To reconquer Jerusalem and to expel the Franks from Syria—these two quests would bind his fickle and independent followers to him in the name of a higher cause. No sooner had Nur al-Din assumed power in Damascus than he renewed the old treaties with the Frankish Kingdom of Jerusalem, but he would live up to his promises, battling the Franks elsewhere in Syria. In the 1170s, he was in a position to deal a death blow to the Kingdom of Jerusalem—and he may well have, had he not been betrayed by his governor in Egypt, a Kurdish commander named Yusuf ibn Ayyub.

The ideal of anti-Frankish *jihad* that Nur al-Din promoted was very much a Sunni Muslim phenomenon, and propelled mainly by one of the four "schools" of orthodox Islamic jurisprudence. Ahmad ibn Hanbal, a ninth-century Iraqi theologian, had argued for strict adherence to the Qur'an and the traditions of the Prophet. Out of his writings and those of his followers—the Hanbalis—grew today's strict Wahhabi school of Saudi Arabia, and the Salafist movement associated with modern-day violent extremist groups like al-Qaeda and al-Shabaab. Ibn Hanbal's unswerving emphasis on the Word of God encouraged his adherents to perceive right and wrong as absolutely clear and eternal categories. Christians, for example, were in the wrong, as were Muslims living under infidel rule. Muslims had a clear duty to eliminate the political power of Christianity. While the Hanbalis represented a minority within Sunni Islam, their views found traction among certain constituencies—for example, the people of Salihiyya, a suburb of Damascus settled by refugees from the Crusader massacre at Jerusalem. Another bastion of Hanbali support was Nablus, a town in Palestine that had surrendered to the Franks in 1099, before Jerusalem had fallen.

The population of Nablus, or Nabulus, located some forty miles north of Jerusalem, was a mix of Muslims and Christians. A nearby hamlet, Jama'il, was home to the Banu Qudama, an Arab clan headed in the mid-1100s by a sheikh named 'Ahmad ibn Muhammad Abu Qudama. 'Ahmad was a fiery Hanbali preacher and charismatic miracle worker who roused the people of the countryside against the local Muslim establishment, which represented, if indirectly, the interests of the Christian occupiers. After some time, 'Ahmad's agitating came to the attention of Baldwin of Ibelin, the Frankish lord of Nablus, who decided to get rid of the troublesome sheikh. But 'Ahmad got wind of Baldwin's intentions and fled with his family to Damascus. Here, they found a welcoming reception among the like-minded inhabitants of Salihiyya, where Banu Qudama preachers and holy men would flourish.

At about the same time that the Banu Qudama arrived in Damascus, Zayn al-Din, the accuser of Ibn Dukhan in al-Nabulusi's story, and also a Hanbali *qadi*, left that city for Egypt. We can't be certain of Zayn al-Din's origins, but he may have been connected to the Banu Qudama—his great-grandson's surname, al-Nabulusi, means "from Nablus," so the family had some connection to the town. Nor can we be certain of what prompted the move to Egypt, although al-Nabulusi tells us that his ancestor came at the express invitation of Tala'i ibn Ruzzik. Tala'i was certainly an admirer of the anti-Frankish rhetoric of the Hanbalis, and he was secretly working against the Isma'ili clerics. Inviting men of religion like Zayn al-Din to Egypt would have fit well with both of these agendas. Whatever was behind the invitation and whatever led Zayn al-Din to accept it, there were clearly kinsmen in Cairo waiting for him.

This is not surprising. Syria and Palestine had deep links to Fatimid Egypt, which had ruled much of the region until the Saljuqs' arrival on the scene. Al-Yazuri, famous for his persecution of Egyptian Christians during his short term as *wazir*, had been born in Palestine, and was the son of a line of wealthy and powerful Sunni *qadis*. After 1100, immigration to Egypt had increased, as the Franks completed their conquest of the coastal lands of *al-Sham* and Saljuq Syria plunged into internecine chaos. Almost all of those Muslims who arrived in the Fatimid capital would have been Sunni, and almost all would have been scarred by their experience of the Christian conquerors, and politicized by Nur al-Din's Counter-Crusade. Many would have been stunned by the situation in Cairo. Even those who were willing to tolerate the notion of an Isma'ili caliphate would have been scandalized by the cosmopolitanism of the capital, and the sight of Muslims, Christians, and Jews rubbing shoulders with an intimacy all but unheard of in their homelands. As Sunni religious authorities, poets, and political operators continued to arrive in Fatimid lands, they quietly committed themselves to the return of Sunni authority. During Ridwan's short time as *wazir* in the 1130s, he—a Palestinian Sunni—founded a *madrasa* in Alexandria, a religious academy whose purpose was to disseminate Sunni ideology and buttress Saljuq political claims. Ridwan also created a "Department of Holy War," which coordinated naval operations against the Crusader-occupied coast of Syria.

Zayn al-Din would have found that Muslim Egyptians' attitudes were changing even without Sunni provocation or exhortation. Before Ridwan, the troubled reign of Bahram—openly Christian and non-Arab—as *wazir* had coincided with the rising fear among native Muslims that elite Christians might be serving as agents of the infidel powers abroad. Indeed, there appeared to be an abundance of evidence. In the 1150s, with the death of Roger II of Sicily, Norman-Egyptian relations declined, and by the 1160s Norman fleets were raiding the coast of the Nile Delta. The Kingdom of Jerusalem was also on the offensive; freed from having to defend its eastern frontier thanks to a truce with Nur al-Din, Crusader forces laid siege to and conquered Ascalon, the last Fatimid port on the Syrian coast, in 1153. This conquest, which sent another wave of refugees to Egypt, only underlined the ineffectiveness of the Isma'ili regime. With the loss of Ascalon, the Fatimid navy no longer had the range to strike at the ports of the Kingdom of Jerusalem. The balance of power was shifting, and the caliphate was intimidated into paying tribute to the Crusader kingdom. In the West, the situation was no less auspicious for the Fatimids. The Almohads were sweeping eastward across the Maghrib and Ifriqiya, fostering a sense of Sunni triumphalism among Egypt's new arrivals and a corresponding uncertainty among the natives, who found themselves caught in the midst of the strong ideological crosscurrents of a dawning era.

CHRISTIANITY ON TRIAL

Soon after Zayn al-Din arrived in Egypt at the end of the 1150s, Ibn Dukhan, the royal treasurer in Cairo, was summoned to the court of the *wazir* to face the indignant old sheikh, who accused him of various misdeeds, including ordering a Muslim to convert publicly to Christianity, embezzling the caliph's fortune, and spying for the Franks to help them overthrow the regime. Zayn al-Din, a man well versed in "science and religion," was intent on bringing him to justice.

But the charges were rather vague, and Ibn Dukhan's guilt was far from a proven fact. It is quite unlikely that Ibn Dukhan would have induced a Muslim to convert; he would not have been so foolhardy as to commit such a brazenly outrageous breach of Islamic law. The second charge Zayn al-Din raised is more plausible. The officials of the financial bureaucracy of the caliphate were generally subject to little oversight. As long as the coffers of the state and those of its grandees remained full, they were unlikely to face scrutiny. Even so, they took steps to protect themselves, by appointing dependents to subordinate positions and by raising private armies, for instance. Embezzlement by a treasurer was quite common, a result of greed and the fear that he might be arbitrarily dismissed, or worse, at the whim of the imam or the *wazir*. Ibn Dukhan was probably skimming from the caliphal accounts, although not the unbelievable amounts that Zayn al-Din claimed.

The most sensational charge was that of spying, a charge based on allegedly incriminating documents said to have been found on Ibn Dukhan and in his house, where he was said to frequently have Frankish guests. But Frankish envoys were by this time a commonplace in Cairo, both in the royal court and in the houses of its functionaries, and there is no historical evidence at all of any Coptic Christian "fifth column." The Copts and the Catholic and Orthodox Christians of the Latin and Byzantine worlds did not see one another as allies engaged in a common cause against Islam. In Egypt, Copts and local Melkites competed for influence and actively subverted each other; and, as miaphysites, they were aware that both the Franks and the Greeks considered them heretics. Moreover, local Christians would have heard of the treatment of their coreligionists in the Holy Land by the Frankish Crusaders, who saw them as only slightly less irredeemable than infidels. The Franks dislodged their clergy as a matter of policy, and local Christians were assigned a second-class legal status. In their enthusiasm and ignorance, Crusader knights were known to occasionally slaughter native Christians along-side Muslim civilians. In fact, the Christians of Egypt tended to support the Islamic regime against the Crusaders. Before the arrival of the Franks, far from spying against the Fatimids, Bahram and other Christian officials had helped the caliphs infiltrate the Norman court of Sicily.

But Zayn al-Din's case against Ibn Dukhan was not argued on the basis of a modern conception of what constitutes evidence. Rather, Ibn Dukhan's religious identity was proof enough for the Hanbali sheikh. This is why he based his argument on Scripture:

> He began with reports of the Christians and their misdeeds, and the proscription against their employment. And he mentioned some statements regarding this found in the Book and the *Sunna*.

—and why he closed with a disingenuous jab at Christian officials based on the doctrine of the Trinity:

> And Zayn al-Din said, "How can any who insults God with the claim that He is three, when He is One claim to understand accounting?"

The notion that God is an indivisible One is central to Islamic doctrine, and Muslim polemicists traditionally pointed to the belief in the Trinity as proof that Christians were "polytheists." Along the same lines, they often viewed the veneration of saints and the prominence of icons and statues in churches as signs that Christians were "idol worshippers." These charges resonated with pious Muslims, since from the time of Muhammad himself, idolatry and polytheism were seen as the greatest affronts to God, and it was the mission of Islam to wipe them out. By framing Ibn Dukhan's alleged malfeasance in terms of his belief in the Trinity, Zayn al-Din transformed what might have been a mundane instance of official corruption into an existential threat to Islam.

As such, Zayn al-Din's confrontation of Ibn Dukhan would seem to signal the start of an era in which religious conviction would replace personal animosity as the primary motivation for political actors. But on the contrary, Zayn al-Din did, in fact, have a very personal hatred of Ibn Dukhan. According to al-Nabulusi, when al-Din's great-grandfather, the *qadi*, had come to Cairo, Tala'i ibn Ruzzik had assigned him a salary. This was a regular practice in medieval Islamic regimes, which cultivated the influence of men of religion to reinforce their legitimacy and authority before their subjects. And so one day Zayn al-Din turned up on the doorstep of Ibn Dukhan with a letter in hand that bore the signature of the *wazir* and authorized him to begin drawing a stipend from the royal treasury. The Hanbali firebrand was probably shocked to find that the individual facing him was a *dhimmi* who, in his view, had no right to exercise authority over Muslims, to say the least.

As for Ibn Dukhan, we can only guess at his opinions. He may have been a pious Christian, resentful of infidel Muslims who had usurped the authority of the true religion. Or he may have thought of himself as a proud Egyptian, who should have nothing but disdain for the uncultivated Syrian Arabs pouring into his homeland as refugees. Or perhaps he enjoyed exercising the petty tyranny of the bureaucrat. What is certain is that he was one of the most powerful officials in the kingdom, and would have been accustomed not only to interacting on equal terms with elite Muslims, but to being shown a certain measure of deference and respect. These, Zayn al-Din was not prepared to offer.

Not surprisingly, the meeting between the treasurer and the sheikh did not go well. As al-Nabulusi put it, instead of assigning Zayn al-Din the salary he had been allotted, Ibn Dukhan wrote his name down in the "register of neglect" and the "roster of disregard." In other words, he did not dispute Zayn al-Din's right to draw a stipend, but merely filed it away, as it were, in the wrong drawer. With no money forthcoming to fund his new life in the bustling and expensive capital, the proud Zayn al-Din would have been in an awkward position. Not only would he have to borrow from friends and relatives, he would have to explain to them that the reason why he was in such straits was that a Christian treasurer had chosen to ignore him. The *dhimmi* had humiliated the Muslim, and Zayn al-Din's humiliation would have only grown as word of the squabble spread. We learn from al-Nabulusi that Zayn al-Din began to send messengers to the offices of Ibn Dukhan, demanding he be paid, but the

Christian treasurer either refused to receive them or rudely dismissed them.

This ongoing affront to his honor and authority would have given Zayn al-Din no choice but to act. But when he appeared before the *wazir*, it was not to denounce Ibn Dukhan for something as trivial as delaying his salary (which the latter could have blamed on a heedless subordinate), but to attack the treasurer in such a way as to destroy him. This is why Zayn al-Din shifted the discourse from the particular crimes of Ibn Dukhan to the far graver errors inherent in Christianity.

But aside from his insinuations about Frankish envoys seen frequenting Ibn Dukhan's house, Zayn al-Din did not tap into the rhetoric of Counter-Crusade preached by the Hanbali *'ulama'* of Saljuq Syria. Rather, he called on traditions of anti-Christian polemic and a mistrust of Copts that stretched back centuries. For all the day-to-day cooperation among Christians and Muslims in Egypt and across the Islamic world, theologians on both sides had been waging polemical battle since the eighth century. In the folk traditions of Muslim Egypt, the notion that the Copts were attempting to subvert the Islamic administration can be traced back almost to the time of the Muslim conquest.

If Ibn Dukhan had been counting on his rank to protect him against such tired arguments, he would soon discover his mistake. According to al-Nabulusi, the *wazir* ordered him arrested and had him put to death. But we cannot be sure that this is how the episode ended. The only contemporary allusion to the event—a poem written by 'Umara of Yemen, a sycophantic courtier-poet who earned his keep by flattering Tala'i ibn Ruzzik—was evidently composed before Ibn Dukhan's fall, and urged the *wazir* to depose the arrogant Coptic official, and to "shave off [the Christians'] beards" in humiliation.

THE END OF THE ARMENIANS AND THE FATIMID CALIPHATE

The appeals of Zayn al-Din and 'Umara of Yemen could not have fallen on more willing ears. Tala'i ibn Ruzzik was an Armenian of eastern extraction, born to a family from the north of Persia that had converted to Islam generations before. He had spent his early years wandering the great cities of the 'Abbasid Caliphate, and studying under religious leaders of the Alawite sect. According to legend, Tala'i was in Mecca when his spiritual master instructed him to head to Egypt, a land that, in his teacher's prophecy, he would one day rule. Once there, he went on to distinguish himself as a soldier, commander, poet, and man of learning. Eventually he would marry his granddaughter to the son of the deceased *wazir*, al-Afdal.

In the 1150s, Egypt was once more in chaos. The Sudanese and Turkic military contingents had renewed their conflict, and the *wazir*, 'Abbas ibn Yahya, a descendant of the Zirid kings of Ifriqiya, was moving to seize power from the Fatimid family. 'Abbas had obtained his position in 1153 by assassinating the previous *wazir*, who also happened to be his father-in-law. This was done with the complicity of the dissolute caliph, al-Zafir, who had apparently taken 'Abbas's son, Nasr, as a lover. Once in power, 'Abbas and Nasr assassinated al-Zafir, and having charged the caliph's two brothers with the crime, had them put to death. Al-Zafir's five-year-old son, 'Isa, was named caliph.

The coup might have succeeded had it not been for the women of the palace—led by al-Zafir's sister, Sitt al-Qusur—who, in a potent symbol of their rage, cut off their hair and sent the locks to Tala'i ibn Ruzzik, then the governor of Qus. As the people of Cairo rose up against 'Abbas, Tala'i's forces arrived fluttering black banners—the color of the 'Abbasids—and bearing the hair of the royal women tied to the ends of their lances. In a panic, 'Abbas loaded up the treasures of the caliphal palace on a caravan of more than eight hundred horses and fled eastward, soon falling into the hands of Baldwin III, King of Jerusalem, who executed him and seized the entire Fatimid treasury. 'Abbas's son, Nasr, was sent back as a gift to Tala'i, who handed him over to the palace women for them to personally torture, before he was crucified on the palace gate.

Now *wazir*, Tala'i fulfilled the long-standing ambition of his Armenian predecessors: he became absolute ruler of the caliphate. It was, however, bankrupt, and his first order of business was to put Egypt's finances in order—one reason that he would be sensitive to allegations of financial corruption such as the one leveled by Zayn al-Din against Ibn Dukhan. Moreover, Tala'i was an authoritarian ruler who punished any hint of corruption or rebellion in an exemplary manner. What truly set him apart from previous Armenian *wazirs*, though, was that he not only had little sympathy for Christians, but reserved his greatest hatred for the Franks. So intent was Tala'i on crushing the Kingdom of Jerusalem that he repeatedly courted his ideological enemy, Nur al-Din, in the hopes of forming a military alliance against them. Nur al-Din, however, demurred, aware that if he bided his time, both Egypt and Jerusalem could be his.

Tala'i's willingness to side with the Saljuqs was part of his religious program. He encouraged Sunni religious culture in Egypt in order to weaken the Isma'ili element, while subtly trying to win over the religious figures he had brought to Egypt—individuals like Zayn al-Din—to the Alawite faith. To demonstrate his authority and piety by executing a proud Christian official who had been accused of embezzlement, spying for the Franks, and overstepping the bounds of *dhimma*, would have served his purposes well. As for the ordinary Muslims of Egypt, struggling as they were to meet Tala'i's tax demands, the death of a leading figure in the financial bureaucracy would have been reason for celebration, but especially a Christian. With the bloody Sicilian attack on the seaside town of Tinnis in 1154 still fresh in their minds, many would have been content to see any Christian pay the price.

But Tala'i would not long outlive Ibn Dukhan. On September 11, 1161, he was assassinated by Sudanese soldiers in the pay of Sitt al-Qusur, the sister of the latest caliph, the young al-'Adid. But the Fatimid princess could not prevent Tala'i's son, Ruzzik ibn Tala'i, from succeeding his father. Ruzzik had Tala'i formally declared a "martyr" and continued his project of transforming the Fatimid state. However, it was beyond his capacity to hold Egypt together against the intrigues of the caliphal family, the insurgencies of rival Isma'ili groups, the rebelliousness of his own governors, and the actions of Nur al-Din's agents in the kingdom. In 1162 Shawar, a Bedouin Arab, whom Tala'i had installed as governor of Qus, rose up against him and marched on Cairo. Ruzzik fled the city but was caught, and in August 1163, the new *wazir* had him decapitated, afterward presenting his head, quite literally on a platter, to the leading officers of the realm. The age of the Armenians was over; that of the Fatimids would soon follow.

After Ruzzik's execution, the general Muslim populace unleashed its resentment on the Armenians, both Christian and Muslim, and the Franks launched a series of invasions. In 1163 a brief coup saw Shawar removed from office, only to be restored with the help of Nur al-Din. The Saljuq prince dispatched one of his trusted officers, a Kurd named Shirkuh, with a contingent of troops to prop up the faltering regime. Shirkuh was accompanied by one of his nephews, a young warrior named

Yusuf ibn Ayyub. In 1167 Shawar agreed to a truce with Frankish envoys that required him to pay a 400,000-dinar tribute. Nevertheless, the following year the Franks attacked the town of Bilbeis, some twenty-five miles northeast of Cairo, and slaughtered many of its residents. As the Crusaders neared Cairo in November 1168, a desperate Shawar ordered the city set alight to deny them their prize.

Soon after, Nur al-Din's forces intervened and halted the Frankish advance. When Shawar was assassinated in January 1169 by members of these forces, Shirkuh was declared *wazir* by the caliph, al-'Adid. When Shirkuh died, only two months after taking power, his nephew Yusuf succeeded him, and in 1172 proclaimed the Fatimid Caliphate abolished. A short time after, the isolated and effete caliph died, aged twenty-one. Officially, Yusuf continued to administer Egypt as Nur al-Din's governor, but he would rule as an independent king—a "sultan"—rather than an imam or caliph. This man of obscure origins would conquer Saljuq Syria and ultimately all but destroy the Frankish Kingdom of Jerusalem. He would become the greatest hero of Sunni Islam since the days of the first caliphs, and an object of admiration, fear, and romance for the Christians of Latin Europe, who mispronounced his throne name, Salah al-Din—which meant "Righteousness of the Faith"—as "Saladin."

THE TALE AND THE TELLING

Salah al-Din's termination of the caliphate may have heralded a new era for Egypt, but it did not mark the end of an era for the Coptic Christians or of their role in the kingdom's administration. Nor did the execution of Ibn Dukhan constitute a significant event at the time from either a Christian or a Muslim point of view. No Coptic source records the trial and execution. As for the poet 'Umara, who had accused the Copts of treachery: he was executed in 1174 by Salah al-Din for his role in a conspiracy to reinstate the Fatimid Caliphate, a conspiracy that also included descendants of Tala'i, and—irony of ironies—the Franks. Salah al-Din did make a show of removing *dhimmis* from office when he first took power, but he soon found, as the Fatimids had before him, that the Copts were a necessary element in the Egyptian administration. And he would have understood that Egypt's Christians did not see the Franks as their allies or saviors.

In truth, the tale of Ibn Dukhan tells us more about the time in which it was written than about the time in which it was set. The thirteenth century, the era of the Ayyubids (Salah al-Din's heirs) and the Mamluks who succeeded them, witnessed a Coptic renaissance. It was the golden age for Coptic literature written in Arabic, and, for the native Christian religious and social elite, a time of prosperity and stability. Foremost among this elite was a family known as the Awlad 'Assal (the 'Assal clan). Three brothers from this family, all writing in the mid-1200s, pushed for the reform of the corrupt Egyptian clergy and raised Coptic theology and canon law to new heights of sophistication. The eldest, al-Safi, even went so far as to compose anti-Muslim polemics, a blatant violation of Islamic law. Prominent Copts also began rebuilding churches, an activity prohibited under the precepts of *dhimma*. One of these luminaries, the sheikh Khassat al-Dawla Abu Fada'il, was also known by the epithet "Ibn Dukhan."* "Ibn Dukhan," it turns out, was a traditional name used by members of the Awlad 'Assal, and this Khassat al-Dawla was none other than the polemicist al-Safi.

With al-Safi ascendant, al-Nabulusi composed his *Kitab al-tajrid*— "The Book for Disarming the Sword of Ambition for Removing the Usurpations of the *Dhimmis*"—which includes the story of Zayn al-Din and Ibn Dukhan. Al-Nabulusi was a pious Sunni, and an official who had dedicated his life to the sultanate of Egypt. His cause was the elimination of bureaucratic corruption and incompetence. But when his outspokenness got him into trouble and landed him in prison, there were undoubtedly Copts among the rivals who had him deposed. In other words, he had a very personal beef against corrupt Christian officials. So, when he was eventually rehabilitated, he then sat down to write about a historical confrontation that was, if it happened at all, a religious attack motivated by personal interests. By telling it when he did, al-Nabulusi was sending a message directly to the Awlad 'Assal: "My great-grandfather killed your great-grandfather for being a dishonest Christian; watch yourself, or I might do the same to you."

The story of Ibn Dukhan struck a chord, and was repeated and exaggerated by other Muslim polemicists of the fourteenth century, until all

---

* *Sheikh* (or *shaykh*) is an Arabic term meaning "elder" or "wise man." Typically, it referred to Muslims, but respected Christians and Jews were also occasionally referred to as sheikhs.

manner of outrage and crime was attributed to him. Yet what emerges from the tale and the events it describes is not some eternal enmity between Christianity and Islam. Rather, what it reveals is the tendency for individuals then, as much as today, to frame their agendas in ideological terms, and to conflate what is good for them with the good of whatever higher cause they claim to represent. It reminds us that issues of ideology and identity always need to be considered in the light of power relationships, and that in times of fear, confusion, and vulnerability, people can easily turn against those who in normal circumstances they would consider neighbors, friends, and fellow citizens.

PART V

Ambition, Opportunism, and the End of an Era

9

A Heavenly Kingdom?

Writing about the Crusaders' capture of Jerusalem on July 15, 1099, Raymond of Aguillers, a monk from the monastery of Vézelay in northern France, recalled in lurid detail the watershed event he had taken part in:

> now that our men had possession of the walls and towers wonderful sights were to be seen. Some of our men (and this was more merciful) cut off the heads of their enemies; others shot them with arrows, so that they fell from the towers; others tortured them longer by throwing them into the flames. Piles of heads, hands and feet were to be seen in the streets of the city . . . But these were small matters compared to what happened at the Temple of Solomon, a place where religious services are normally chanted. What happened there? If I tell the truth, it will exceed your powers of belief. So let it suffice to say this much, at least, that in the Temple and the porch of Solomon, men rode in blood up to their knees and their bridle reins. Indeed, it was a just and splendid judgment of God that this place should be filled with the blood of the unbelievers since it had suffered so long from their blasphemies. The city was filled with corpses and blood . . .

Raymond recorded these scenes in his *History of the Franks Who Captured Jerusalem* shortly after the bloody work was done. His descriptions have an immediacy that many other accounts of the Mediterranean in this period lack, and are uncolored by hindsight or complex justifications. His is a stark moral vision, one that mirrored the certain and violent piety of the Franks. He believed the Franks were doing nothing less than transforming the world in the name of God:

> Now that the city was taken, it was well worth all our previous labors and hardships to see the devotion of the pilgrims at the Holy Sepulcher. How they rejoiced and exulted and sang a new song to the Lord! . . . This day, I say, will be famous in all future ages . . . this day, I say, marks the justification of all Christianity, the humiliation of paganism, and the renewal of our faith.

How did the representatives of a self-declared religion of peace, natives of the cold and damp north of Europe, find themselves a thousand miles away in the heat of the desert, slaughtering men, women, and children of a religion they did not understand and a culture they did not know? What drove them to abandon their homes and families, often at great cost to themselves? Where did this impulse originate? Did they all believe, as Raymond did, that they were on a mission from God? Were they cynical brutes, or paladins and martyrs? Were they defending their Church and their civilization against Islamic aggression? Historians continue to argue about the nature and significance of the Crusades, but the consensus has long been that together they constituted an anomaly, having no precedent in the history of either Europe or the Middle East.

Nevertheless, when seen from the Mediterranean, the only exceptional aspect of the First Crusade and the founding of the Crusader states was the zealous and unrestrained fury the Franks displayed upon their initial arrival in the Levant. For all the efforts of historians of the past to present the Crusades as a unified spiritual undertaking in the service of a larger calling, the fact is that Crusaders were no less riven by factional conflicts, personal agendas, and ideological inconsistencies than the peoples they were fighting. The motives of the Frankish warriors and pilgrims of the First Crusade were variously sacred and mundane, selfish and virtuous. Like Samuel ibn Naghrilla, the Cid, Roger II, and Bahram

The conquest of Jerusalem, from the twelfth-century *Rylands Beatus*

Pahlavuni, they became creatures of a diverse Mediterranean world, even as they set out to remake it.

GOD WANTS IT!

Traditional narratives of the Crusades usually begin with the Council of Clermont, an assembly of bishops called by Urban II in 1095 and held at the most northerly point the pope dared travel to, fearful as he was of being detained, or worse, by Philip I, the king of France. Urban, a former monk of Cluny, had convened the bishops of the Church to push the Gregorian Reform, the effort to rehabilitate the clergy, standardize Church ritual and practice, and achieve peace within Latin Christendom. Toward the end of the three-day conclave, as if as an afterthought, the pope added an unexpected codicil to the program: he called on the faithful of Latin Christendom to go to the aid of their Christian brethren in the East, who were suffering under the yoke of the Turks. He was referring to those subjects of the Byzantine Empire who had found themselves under Saljuq rule in the aftermath of the Battle of Manzikert in 1071. Writing in 1100, Fulcher of Chartres, a priest who went on the First Crusade and probably attended the council, recalled Urban saying:

> For as most of you have been told, the Turks, a race of Persians, . . . have penetrated within the boundaries of the Byzantine Empire . . . and have killed and captured [Christians], have overthrown churches, and have laid waste to God's kingdom.

Later chroniclers claimed that the clergymen, knights, and commoners who made up his audience were so moved by this appeal that, with a rallying cry of "*Deus lo volt!*" (God wants it!), they began to tear strips of cloth from their cloaks. They then sewed these strips back on in the shape of crosses, signaling their vow to liberate their oppressed fellow Christians. And so the "Crusade" was born.

What is curious is that an event that set in motion a process often credited with transforming the Christian and Islamic worlds went nearly unremarked by contemporary chroniclers. We have no record of Urban's words dating from the time of the speech itself; those few accounts we have that were written by individuals who claim to have been present that day at Clermont were, in fact, written years later, after the Franks had conquered Jerusalem. In these accounts Urban's instructions are precise—take back the Holy Land—and his evocation of the atrocities inflicted on the Eastern Christians are absolute fabrications. For instance, the version of Robert of Rheims, written around 1107, is pure, jingoistic fantasy:

> [The Turks] destroy the altars [of churches,] having defiled them with their uncleanliness. They circumcise the Christians and the blood of the circumcision they either spread upon the altars or pour into vases on the baptismal font. When they wish to torture people by a base death, they perforate their navels, and dragging forth the extremity of the intestines, bind it to a stake, then with flogging they lead the victim around until the viscera having gushed forth the victim falls prostrate onto the ground . . . What shall I say of the abominable rape of women?

Surviving copies of Urban's letters from just after the council show that his own conception of the venture was quite vague, even if they do include the idea that the faithful who journeyed to the East to rescue their oppressed brothers would be rewarded by God with the forgiveness of their sins.

Whatever Urban actually said at Clermont, his words unintentionally sparked an unprecedented popular movement: the People's Crusade. In the weeks and months after the council tens of thousands of poor, common folk—men and women, most with no experience as warriors and little or no money—embarked on foot across Europe, with no clear idea of where they were going, no maps, and no sense of what awaited them. They imagined the Holy Land a sort of magical paradise, literally running with milk and honey. Setting out from the north of France, these unruly mobs made their way through the Rhineland and on to Hungary, attacking and plundering Jewish communities along the way. By August 1, 1096, they had reached Constantinople, and less than a week later they had been ferried across to the Asian shore to continue their march on Jerusalem.

This movement sprang from hope and desperation, as most of the participants were landless vagrants: peasants who, with the recent breakdown of feudal institutions, had been freed from the manor to seek their fortune in towns and cities, but who found that with this freedom they lost any guarantees of safety and sustenance. The Church, the only possible source of comfort and aid, had no interest in ministering to them, and no institutions capable of supporting them. Compounding this restiveness was a strong dose of millenary anxiety—a belief that, since the thousand-year mark after Jesus's Crucifixion had passed, the time of his return was nigh, and that the corruption of the world needed to be swept away in preparation. In the years prior to the Council of Clermont, these near-revolutionary mobs of vagrant peasants had been causing no end of trouble in northern France, where the king had been forced to wield his troops against them on more than one occasion. Now, with Urban's call, they found a new sense of purpose and a vindication of their lowly position. The meek would not only inherit the Earth, but they—not the corrupt clergy or nobility—would miraculously restore Jerusalem to the Mother Church.

They were led by charismatic figures, each of them a charlatan of one kind or another. The most prominent were the penniless knight, Walter "the Have-Not," and Peter the Hermit, a self-proclaimed prophet who enthralled the faithful with visions of a paradisiacal Holy Land. It was all lies and false promises. Peter brandished a letter, said to have fallen from

The Siege of Antioch during the First Crusade, ca. 1200

Heaven, bearing God's pledge to these poor pilgrims that they would liberate the Holy Land, if only they were prepared to make the necessary sacrifices. Worse, it seems he knew well what likely lay in store for them; if contemporary sources can be believed, he himself had already visited the Holy Land on pilgrimage. It is little surprise, then, that the People's Crusade came to an abrupt and bloody end when the thousands of pilgrims who had survived the trek to Anatolia were slaughtered en masse by Saljuq forces on October 21, 1096, not long after their departure from Constantinople. Peter, for his part, survived and escaped.

The People's Crusade was not what Urban would have imagined when he made his appeal to his bishops at Clermont, as the last thing he or the Church wanted was an unruly and destructive rabble of commoners surging across Europe. What he had in mind was a disciplined military mission made up of knights and noblemen fighting under ecclesiastical authority. Just such an expedition was organized in the days after his speech at Clermont, and it is this that historians refer to as the First Crusade.

In some senses this Crusade was unquestionably something new; the Latin Church as an institution had never before undertaken a military venture of this type. But it was not necessarily understood as a radical innovation by the people of the time. They did not even bother to coin a new word for it.* From their perspective, the Crusaders, whether warriors, kings, or commoners, clergy or lay folk, were merely *peregrini*: "pilgrims" journeying to the Holy Land. The novelty was that they were participants in an "armed pilgrimage."

Indeed, the Crusade phenomenon emerged out of three well-established Latin Christian traditions: holy war, pilgrimage, and penance. Christianity presents itself as a religion of peace, but once any religion comes to be associated with political power, a theological justification of warfare becomes a necessity. Warfare in Judaism was justified by the divine imperative to acquire the Promised Land and to found the Kingdom of Judah. Islam, a political movement from the beginning, enshrined ideals of legitimate war (*jihad*) in Scripture.† In Christianity, Saint Augustine of Hippo formulated a doctrine of "just war" at the very time his faith was being established as the sole and official religion of the Roman Empire. By Urban's time the notion of Christian holy war was long established.

The second ingredient was pilgrimage. The desire to approach the divine by visiting places mentioned in Scripture or touched by God, or by coming into contact with the physical remains or earthly belongings of holy men and women, is likewise shared by the three religions. Jews journey to the Western Wall and to the tombs of sages such as Moses Maimonides in Tiberias; Muslims travel to Mecca and Medina, and to local holy sites; and Christians visit the places named in the New Testament narrative. Members of all three faiths travel to the tombs of the biblical Prophets and patriarchs in search of blessings. And for Christians especially, pilgrimage is bound up with penance: the inconvenience, danger, and expense of the journey to the tomb of a saint or to Jerusalem itself is part of the payment demanded by God in return for the forgiveness of one's sins; part of the process of absolution and redemption.

---

* The English term "Crusade" comes from the French *croisée*, which was not attested to until about 1300, and the Latin *crucisignatus* (bearing the sign of the cross) was not in use until well into the 1200s, by which time the Crusades in the Holy Land were effectively over.

† *Jihad* actually means something more than "legitimate war." The term refers to moral struggle in general and includes any attempt by a believer to better himself or the world. Since at least the eighth century, Muslim theologians have distinguished between the more virtuous "greater *jihad*" and the "lesser *jihad*," the former being the inward striving for individual spiritual or moral betterment, and the latter referring to attempts to improve the outside world, including through justified warfare.

In the century prior to Urban's call to Crusade, each of these dimensions of Christian devotion had risen in importance. Both in Spain and in Italy Christians had been clashing with Muslim adversaries, often rationalizing their aggression in terms of religious duty and virtue, particularly in the Iberian Peninsula, where warfare could be represented as a justifiable "reconquest" of lands that had rightfully belonged to Christians. By the 1060s, it seems, the Church was making a direct connection between personal salvation and waging war against Islam. The famous 1064 campaign against Muslim Barbastro was, if not a "proto-Crusade," as some historians have claimed, at least a taste of things to come. It appears that as an incentive to encourage Norman and Occitan knights to join the expedition, Pope Alexander II offered a remission of sins to those who participated. Shortly after the Council of Clermont, Urban II would grant the same indulgence not only to those who fought to recover and hold the Holy Land, but also to those who battled against Muslims in Spain.

At the same time, the determination of the Gregorian reformers to reduce violence among Christians led them to develop the "Peace and Truce of God," a legal and religious principle that limited the ability of the feudal nobility to wage war on one another and on common folk. Suddenly, it was no longer acceptable to fight on Sundays and holidays, to attack unarmed peasants, to kill people in church, or to raid the lands belonging to the monasteries of Cluny. The Church was not in a position to enforce these rules by force, but it could exert influence on the kings and noblemen of Christian Europe through the threats of excommunication and interdiction. An excommunicated lord was cast out of the Church, losing not only the chance for salvation but his authority to rule. His lands would be placed under interdict, an embargo of church services that denied all his subjects access to the sacraments and put their salvation in peril. In an era when many people, high and low, took the notion of Hell very seriously, and when nobles were eager to undermine the power of their king, the excommunication and interdiction of a ruler released his subjects from their bonds of allegiance and implicitly sanctioned rebellion. It could be a powerful weapon for the Church.

In early 1077, for example, when Henry IV, King of the Germans and Holy Roman Emperor, clashed with Gregory VII over who had the right to appoint the bishops in Henry's realms, the pope put the defiant emperor under interdict. Henry, with the prospect of an uprising of his own noblemen looming, begged Gregory for forgiveness. When the humbled emperor arrived at the papal castle at Canossa in Tuscany wearing the hair shirt of a penitent, the pope kept him waiting three days outside in the snow before he granted him an audience. It was a clear sign that the papacy was slowly refashioning itself into an imperial power. The Church lacked only an army.

As the reform of the Church led to the development of more sophisticated rituals and a more rigorous system of penance and absolution, pilgrimage moved to the forefront of many believers' minds. In Catholicism, people are born sinners, but God's forgiveness can be obtained by confession and the performance of penance. For most, this was not a great issue: smaller sins could be forgiven by one's parish priest. But more serious infractions—such as homicide, a mortal sin—required a higher authority, and for these, sinners were obliged to seek out the intercession of a bishop, the pope, or even a saint. This was particularly true of the nobility; the aristocracy of Europe was essentially a class of professional killers who committed mortal sins with regularity, and this created a healthy demand for high-level absolution. Saints became particularly popular agents of redemption; after all, if one asked the pope or a bishop for absolution, they might say no, or ask for something in exchange. Saints, on the other hand, could always be depended on. As a consequence, Santiago de Compostela and the Holy Land became ever more popular among the Christian elite in search of forgiveness or benediction.

Simultaneously, from about 1050 onward pilgrimage was becoming more feasible for Europeans of all social classes. This was a time of warming climate, increased agricultural production, growing population, and the stirrings of commerce and trade. The Latin West was becoming more town-centered and prosperous, and people were moving off the farm and setting out in search of education, opportunity, and fortune. As Europeans became wealthier, more mobile, and connected to the larger Mediterranean world, even ordinary people began to travel, and the churches where the relics of saints and martyrs were kept became the most popular destinations, whether for penance or simply for tourism. It was in this era that the first European guidebook appeared: the *Codex Calixtinus*, a sort of medieval Frommer's that provided a stage-by-stage itinerary for the trip to Santiago de Compostela, replete with practical insiders' advice for the traveler:

In a place called Lorca, towards the east, flows the river called Rio Salado. Beware drinking in its waters or watering your horse in its stream, for this river is deadly. While we were proceeding towards Santiago, we found two Navarrese seated on its banks and sharpening their knives: they make a habit of skinning the mounts of the pilgrims that drink from that water and die. To our questions they answered a lie, saying the water was indeed healthy and drinkable. Accordingly, we watered our horses in the stream, and no sooner had we done so, than two of them died; these the men skinned on the spot.

Pilgrimage would soon become big business, not only for the destination churches of Santiago and Jerusalem, but for the churches, chapels, and hospitals (what we would call hostels or hotels) along the routes that wound through Europe, and for those entrepreneurial monasteries and cathedrals that managed to acquire, by whatever means, some major relic—whether the finger or foot of an Apostle or notable martyr, a nail from the Crucifixion, a thorn from the Crown, a splinter from the True Cross, or even the Holy Foreskin of the Lord.* Such sacred items would bring pilgrims and patrons, power and money, to the churches that held them. Pilgrimage became inseparable from commerce—and both brought Christian Europe into contact with the Islamic world.

In the decades prior to the Crusades, lords, bishops, and even many common folk made the journey to Jerusalem. Local Muslim authorities, Fatimid or 'Abbasid, did not object to foreign Christian pilgrimage, since they, of course, considered Jesus a Prophet, and had their own Christian subjects. They were content to charge for visitors' visas and did not harass the pilgrims passing through their land, although they could not necessarily guarantee their safety. The increasing numbers of European Christians who trekked to the Near East must have felt as if their world had been turned upside down. Having seen the wealth and sophistication of Byzantium and the *dar al-Islam* firsthand, they must have found the poverty and primitiveness of Europe as striking as it was undeniable.

---

* As a Jewish boy, Jesus would have been circumcised, and his foreskin would have been the one part of his body that remained on Earth after he ascended to Heaven. The relic is first attested to with the claim that it was in the possession of Charlemagne in 800; by the late Middle Ages, several Holy Foreskins were being venerated in various sites around Europe.

The prodigious wealth of the Islamic lands, and their role as a gateway to the riches of Africa and Asia—silks, gold, and spices—attracted another kind of Christian visitor, too. The engagement of West and East in the decades previous to 1095 was driven primarily by the Italian trading states: the urban republics of Pisa, Genoa, and Venice, which had forged links among the trading centers of Byzantium, the Islamic empires, and the markets of Christian Europe. For the feudal nobility of Europe, who lived in an earthbound society of horses and carts, the fleets of the Italian states would not only be the means by which they could acquire the luxurious goods of the East, they also became indispensable as a naval force and merchant marine, and for seaborne transport to the Eastern Mediterranean.

And they would be crucial to the Crusades. In fact, it is not unreasonable to say that the Crusades started not with Urban's speech of 1095, but with a Pisan naval expedition half a century earlier. After having spent some decades in the business of ferrying Latin pilgrims to the Holy Land, in 1034 the Pisans hit upon the idea of combining such a voyage with a return-trip raid on 'Annaba in Islamic Ifriqiya, a raid in which the pilgrims would be invited to participate. Thus, the Pisans, who lacked ground forces, could pillage a Muslim town with the help of the pilgrims, while the loot the pilgrims carried off would help them recoup the cost of their voyage. Because 'Annaba was a Muslim town the attack could be presented as a virtuous act of piety, and all the participants would come away not only richer, but having redeemed their sins. The plundering of 'Annaba prefigured the mix of moral and material ambition that would, as much as any religious impulse, be both the cause and the essence of the movement that began with the First Crusade.

In 1096 the knights of the First Crusade, warriors on a divine mission under the aegis of the Church, were heading east close on the heels of the People's Crusade. But, regardless of the pope's aspirations, this was not a concerted effort by a single army of the faithful to liberate Jerusalem. Rather, the knights came from different parts of the Latin West, were driven by a range of motivations, and departed separately for the Holy Land. In fact, the knights and nobility answered Urban's call to the East only because so many were already heading in that direction, in search of fortune and glory. As with the desperate commoners of the People's Crusade, for some knights and noblemen of the First Crusade, an "armed pilgrimage" would have appealed in large part because it offered an opportunity to break out of the limitations they faced in a changing Europe. For others, such as the Normans of southern Italy, the Christian princes of the Iberian Peninsula, and the emerging merchant republics, Urban had merely officially sanctioned a process, or a series of processes, that had been under way for some time. For the Church the Crusade would provide the warrior class with an outlet for their violent energies, now that they were expected to respect the "Peace and Truce of God." As Urban II is said to have decreed at Clermont:

> Let those who are accustomed to wage private wars wastefully even against Believers, go forth against the Infidels . . . Now, let those who until recently were plunderers, be soldiers of Christ . . . now, let those, who recently were hired for a few pieces of silver, win their eternal reward . . .

Now Urban II took a deliberate step to creating that army that the papacy lacked by placing the entire venture under the nominal leadership of his deputy, Bishop Adhemar of Puy. But he would be unable to control the willful and divided Frankish nobility, who were dominated by three main groups. One faction was the Provençals, land-starved knights from the crowded southwest of France and headed by Count Raymond IV of Toulouse, who had been appointed the official military commander of the expedition. Another faction was composed of the Norman forces under Bohemond of Taranto, the son of Robert Guiscard, and his nephew, Tancred de Hauteville. Bohemond had cut his teeth fighting against and alongside the Muslims of Sicily, and had spent most of his career battling against Christian Byzantium. He and his men were no strangers to the ways of the Greeks, the Turks, and other peoples of the East; many had served as mercenaries in Anatolia.

Finally, there were the knights of Burgundy and northeastern France, led by the brothers Godfrey and Baldwin of Bouillon, both of whom were younger sons of Duke Eustace of Boulogne. Godfrey was Duke of Lorraine, and Baldwin had been living on the lands of his father-in-law in Normandy. Supporting them was a host of independent knights and noblemen, many having mortgaged themselves to the hilt to participate, in the hope of salvation or of acquiring the fame and prestige that would enable them or their sons to marry up when they returned to France. Drawn to the mission by Godfrey's and Baldwin's high standing, they trusted that the Bouillons' talents would result in victory and enable them to recoup their investments.

United, the three factions were formidable, but whatever lofty ideals appeared to bind them together as they set off for the East, it would soon become clear that they were as determined to weaken one another as they were to vanquish the Muslims of the Holy Land.

PROMISED LANDS

The Byzantine Empire, which the Crusaders had purportedly set out to rescue, had a thoroughly complicated relationship with the Latin West. Even from the time of the Caesars, the eastern and western halves of the Roman Empire had been distinct. The former was culturally Greek and heavily urban, the latter culturally Latin and overwhelmingly rural. In 325, when Constantine the Great adopted Christianity as an official religion of the empire and moved the capital to Constantinople, he exacerbated the sense of difference between the two halves, and the Latin and Greek worlds continued to grow apart. By the fifth century a dispute was brewing over who held the highest religious authority in the Christian world—the emperors, who claimed the title High Priest, or the bishops of Rome, who claimed, as the successors of Saints Peter and Paul, to be God's representatives on Earth. The Churches, Latin and Greek, developed divergent practices and theologies, and as the Latin West emerged from the isolation of the early Middle Ages, they clashed. In 1054, due to an ostensible dispute over the nature of the Trinity and the Holy Spirit that hinged on a single word in the Nicene Creed—*filioque*, or "and of the Father"—the two Churches split, with each declaring the other illegitimate, if not heretical. This coincided with a period of political and economic competition: the Normans began invading Byzantine territory, the Italian merchant republics started to compete for access to the empire's ports, and the kings of the Latin West began to covet the prestige and authority of the title Emperor of Rome.

In 1096, when the Frankish Crusaders appeared before the walls of Constantinople, the emperor Alexios Komnenos saw them not as his saviors but as a threat—not least because among their leaders were the same Norman commanders who had been attacking his lands for decades. And if a few years earlier, Alexios had been hemmed in by the

Saljuqs, by 1096 he had settled into a détente with them, and was no longer in need of saving, had he ever been in the first place. For their part, the Crusaders viewed the Byzantines with envy, suspicion, and disdain, considering them untrustworthy, "effeminate," and effete. Yet they could not help but be overawed by Alexios's capital. With its miles of sturdy double walls studded with towers, its immense gilt-mosaicked churches, its relics, and its palaces, Constantinople—the fulcrum of Europe and Asia—was a city of a size and splendor the warriors and clergy from the cold Latin north could not have imagined. Ten times the size of Paris, twenty times that of London, it would have been a hundred times as wealthy and refined as either.

Unable to turn back the Frankish Crusaders, Alexios granted them passage to the eastern side of the Bosphorus on the condition that they swear an oath of loyalty to him, and promise to return any formerly Byzantine lands they conquered to the empire. With no other means of reaching Asia from Constantinople, the Crusaders agreed, although many thought the emperor's avowed support for their mission was insincere. It was, in fact, worse: although the Crusaders would not discover this until 1105, even before they had left Constantinople, Alexios began plotting with the Fatimids to defeat them, once they had passed through Saljuq territory.

In the meantime they would see other evidence of apparent Byzantine treachery. Their first military action took place in May 1097, when they attempted to help Alexios retake the city of Nicaea from Qilij Arslan, Sultan of Rum ("Rome," as the Saljuqs called Anatolia), the warlord who had massacred the People's Crusaders. The Latins were eager to exact revenge on the Turks, and by now heavily in debt and running out of funds, they were counting on the spoils the town's defeat would provide them. But after they had laid siege to the city for some weeks, Alexios cut a deal with the defenders without the Crusaders' knowledge, promising not to allow the Nicaeans to be pillaged, if the townsfolk surrendered the city directly to him. Once they had discovered what had happened, the Crusaders were incensed, believing that they had been robbed of their legitimate rights to plunder and revenge.

Determined to continue to Jerusalem, they marched south, enduring attacks by the Turks and the broiling heat of the Anatolian summer. In July their spirits were buoyed when they won a stunning victory over Qilij Arslan at a place called Dorylaeum. But cracks within the Crusader enterprise began to show. In September 1097, as they were approaching the easternmost part of the Mediterranean coast, Baldwin of Bouillon's and Tancred de Hauteville's troops were clashing. The Crusade was breaking up.

News of the Franks' arrival and of their victory at Dorylaeum spread through the region, raising the hopes of the local Armenian and Greek strongmen who had been living under the shadow of Saljuq rule since the Battle of Manzikert. This was a full generation after Badr al-Jamali had brought his army of Armenians to Egypt, but many had remained in Anatolia, and a scattering of small Armenian principalities stretched from the Taurus Mountains eastward to Lake Van. Among these was Edessa, then ruled over by T'oros the Curopalate. T'oros was an Armenian Melkite who had formerly served both Byzantine emperors and the Armenian warlord Vahram Varajnuni, and who was now governing the ancient Armenian capital with the recognition of the Turks, and despite the resistance of his own subjects, who were affiliated with the Armenian Orthodox Church. T'oros saw in the Crusaders an opportunity to consolidate his independence, and invited Baldwin to his court to serve him under arms. Baldwin and his knights promptly abandoned the Crusade; once in Edessa, Baldwin coerced T'oros into granting his daughter to him and formally adopting him as his son.* The facts that Baldwin already had a wife back in France and was well into middle age were simply ignored. Only one month later, with Baldwin's complicity T'oros was overthrown and murdered by his subjects, and Baldwin declared himself "Count of Edessa." Thus, in 1098 the first Crusader state was founded. A principality with no biblical significance, it was taken not from the Muslim Saljuqs, but from a fellow Christian.

Baldwin's behavior was hardly exceptional among the Frankish Crusaders. To the west, Tancred had conquered the port city of Tarsus, and was attempting to bend the Armenian- and Greek-populated countryside to his will. But the Normans' ambitions would truly be laid bare at

---

* It was usually infants who were adopted and for whom the traditional Armenian rite was intended. Nevertheless, in order to make it official, the grizzled middle-aged Baldwin and King T'oros both stripped their shirts and donned a single large shirt, under which they rubbed their bare chests against each other, after which the ritual was repeated with Baldwin and the king's wife. One can only imagine what the grandees and warriors who had gathered to witness the ceremony thought.

Antioch, a city that had been evangelized by Saint Peter himself, and which had been in Byzantine possession as late as 1084. They would conquer the city, and their victory would represent the first major success that seemed to align with the Crusade's stated purpose. However, their refusal to hand it over to Alexios, as they had sworn to do, revealed their true motivations.

In October 1097 the Crusaders set up camp outside Antioch's well-defended walls. Both the Muslim defenders of Antioch and their Christian attackers then endured a grueling siege, suffering through a harsh winter. The siege camp was ravaged by famine and disease, and as the months dragged on, many Franks abandoned the Crusade, returning to Constantinople or home, exhausted and demoralized. As winter turned to spring, those inside Antioch found themselves in little better straits; the city was blockaded and supplies had been all but exhausted. Meanwhile their ruler, a former slave of Malik Shah named Yaghi-Siyan, sent appeals for help to the neighboring Muslim princes. But for eight months these went unanswered; none would risk weakening himself by coming to Antioch's aid, until finally the prince of Mosul relented and sent a relief force.

It was too late. Contemporary sources claim that Bohemond had made contact with one of the defenders, an Armenian officer named Firuz, who was in charge of the towers and who had offered to let the Franks in in exchange for a reward. On June 2, 1098, only days before the relief force from Mosul arrived, the Norman faction under Bohemond broke into the city, followed by the full Crusader army. Antioch was plundered and its inhabitants put to the sword. Claiming personal credit for the conquest, Bohemond defied his agreement with both Alexios Komnenos and his fellow Crusaders and claimed Antioch as his own. With the army of Mosul surrounding them, the Crusaders now found themselves on the other side of a siege. Attempts to negotiate a settlement having failed, on June 28 the Frankish forces burst out of the gates and after a hard-fought battle put the Muslim forces to flight. In this manner the second Crusader state, the Principality of Antioch, was founded. Its territory was inhabited largely by Melkite and Armenian Christians and belonged by right of law to the Byzantine Empire. It would not be ruled by the papacy or by the empire, but by Bohemond, a man whose cunning matched his bravery, and who was no stranger to the ambiguous and shifting loyalties of the Eastern Mediterranean world.

In the months that followed, the Crusade stalled as the de Hautevilles tried to impose themselves on their new principality. Baldwin was ensconced in Edessa and had lost interest in Jerusalem, while the rest of the Burgundians and the Provençal knights were both exhausted from the siege and weighed down with plunder, their resolve flagging and their motivation declining. It was then that Raymond of Toulouse, the notional leader of the Crusade, seized the initiative and the moral high ground, vowing to push on to Jerusalem as a penitent and pilgrim with any who would join him. As he departed, most of the Crusaders followed, including Bohemond's nephew, Tancred, who was dispatched by the new Prince of Antioch to make sure the Normans got a piece of whatever lands were taken in the south. Marching rapidly through the Orontes Valley and then along the Lebanese coast—both areas home to significant populations of native Christians—the Crusaders arrived at Jerusalem, establishing a siege on June 6, 1099. They had left a swath of destruction behind them; the cannibalism at Ma'arat al-Nu'man was only the most sensational episode in a string of massacres committed as the Frankish forces swept southward. Italian ships were soon arriving at the coast carrying much-needed supplies for the Franks. Even the ships themselves would be dismantled so their timber could be used for the construction of the siege machinery needed to take the city.

At Jerusalem, the weeks wore on and both defenders and attackers suffered in the heat. Finally, on July 8, 1099, Peter the Hermit, the same preacher who had marched at the head of the People's Crusade but who had escaped the disaster that befell his followers, led the near-starving Crusaders in a barefoot penitential procession around the city. They prayed and sang hymns as they circled the walls, imitating the biblical Joshua at the Battle of Jericho. Afterward, the assaults began, and on July 15 Tancred's disciplined Norman troops breached the walls. Heading to the Tower of David, the city's citadel, they negotiated the surrender and release of the Fatimid commander and his garrison, and took effective control of the city. The rest of the Crusader forces, in contrast, showed little focus and no restraint, plundering and massacring indiscriminately as they coursed through the city, hastily marking the doors of homes to claim their rights of pillage. According to Fulcher of Chartres, ten thousand Muslims, including women and children, were beheaded on the Temple Mount alone—in defiance of a guarantee of safety Tancred had personally given to those who had taken refuge there.

Plundering was normal practice in the Middle Ages, but what took place after the city of Jerusalem fell was nothing less than a deliberate act of genocide. After the initial orgy of killing, the looting was halted for three days while the city was scoured for surviving Muslims, who were rounded up and systematically put to the sword. The few who were spared were forced to carry off the remains of their coreligionists for burial, and then ransomed or sold off as slaves. Horrific as these acts may have been, the Franks sincerely believed they were performing God's work, that they were taking revenge for the desecration of this most holy city and cleansing it with the Muslims' blood. The city's Jews fared a little better: some were killed, but most managed to ransom themselves, winning their release by pawning their precious holy books to the Jewish community of Fatimid-ruled Ascalon.

After three hundred years of Muslim rule, Jerusalem was once again a Christian city. The mosques and synagogues were either defiled or reconsecrated as churches, and the Franks decreed that henceforth, no Muslim or Jew could live within the walls. Against all odds, the Crusaders had accomplished what they could only see as a miracle. In four short years Urban's audacious exhortation at Clermont (if this outcome was indeed what he had envisioned) had been fulfilled.

But the Crusaders had not prepared for success—there was no post-conquest plan and they faced a crisis of authority. Adhemar, the papal legate, had died, and the Crusade's official military commander, Raymond of Toulouse, had few supporters. A council was called, and Godfrey of Bouillon was elected as ruler by the leading Crusaders. The following summer, when he fell ill and died, his brother, Baldwin of Bouillon, was chosen to succeed him. Departing Edessa, Baldwin journeyed south to Jerusalem, where he was crowned on Christmas Day 1100 as the first King of Jerusalem.

Throughout the decade that followed, the future of the Kingdom of Jerusalem remained very much in doubt. Many of the Crusaders returned home, covered in glory and laden with loot, their vows fulfilled and sins absolved. Those few who stayed faced the challenge of repelling attacks from the Fatimids and the Saljuqs. Then they went on the offensive, and by 1109, of the cities on the Levantine coast and in the areas west of the Jordan River, only Ascalon and Tyre remained in Muslim hands. Tancred had taken Tiberias on the Sea of Galilee, as well as Nazareth and Bethlehem, the most important New Testament sites. The rest of the territory had fallen to the French, who were obliged to share the coastal cities with the Italian merchant states that had kept them supplied, and that were providing naval support to these new and distant European colonies. Raymond of Toulouse, whose integrity was apparently matched only by his naïveté, had been repeatedly outmaneuvered by his fellow Crusaders, and decided to conquer Tripoli for himself in 1101. He died outside its walls in 1105, and when the city finally fell four years later, the newly christened County of Tripoli—the fourth of the Crusader states—was claimed by his son Bertrand, Count of Toulouse, who had arrived in the Holy Land in 1108.

For the Muslim population of the Levant, the Frankish conquest was an unqualified disaster. Except for a lucky few, most city dwellers or townsfolk who were not murdered were expelled or enslaved. The fate of those in the countryside was substantially better, as the Crusaders soon realized that without a peasantry their domains would be worthless, and if they mistreated their rural Muslim subjects, the latter would either deliberately spoil their harvests or simply escape east into Saljuq territory. But Muslims would have made up no more than half of the native population, the majority of which was Christian, including Byzantines, Syriacs, and Armenians. Despite their common faith, however, the Franks did not see these fellow Christians as equals. To them the Eastern Christians were practically infidels. After all, they *looked* like Muslims, dressed like them, spoke strange and foreign tongues, and practiced strange and foreign rituals. Their experience under Crusader rule would be what one historian has recently characterized as "rough tolerance." The Franks took over their churches, pushed them out of positions of religious authority, and treated them formally as second-class citizens—arguably worse than their experience under Muslim rule. In 1105 the Armenian population of the town of Artah became so fed up that they expelled their Latin "liberators" and pledged their allegiance to Muslim Aleppo.

The states the Crusaders had founded in the Holy Land were not Christian, but Frankish. Just as the Berber Almoravids had subjugated Muslim al-Andalus in the name of religious revival, but had ruled as an ethnically defined clique and imposed their own narrow religious interpretations on their subjects, so did the Christian Franks rule in the Holy Land. Theirs was a society in which full participation was limited to the "Frankish race." The nobility and the military class were all Latins, as were the high clergy. And while some commoners came from the Latin West to the Levant, most of the nonnobility were merchants and tradesmen who tended to live in the cities and large towns of the Frankish states. Theirs was a colonial regime. Latins enjoyed special privileges and rights under law: the nobility was governed by the "High Court" and the commoners by the "Court of the Burghers," whereas all non-Franks, whether Christian, Muslim, or Jew, came under the jurisdiction of a separate and lesser "Court of the Syrians." Frankish society was effectively a closed system, designed to maintain the privilege of the conquerors. While it was conceivable that a Muslim might convert to Christianity, he could never become a Frank.

DEALS WITH THE DEVIL

Whatever the Crusaders' initial opinion of their Muslim adversaries, it was soon tempered by experience, expedience, and the demands of real-politik. In 1100 there were four Crusader principalities—Jerusalem, Antioch, Edessa, and Tripoli—and Frankish politics in the East were shaped by competition among them and the Byzantine Empire, which continued to regard Antioch as unlawfully occupied territory. With the ascent of Baldwin I to the throne of Jerusalem, that kingdom formed a bloc with Edessa and Tripoli, its vassal counties. Although Muslim Aleppo and Damascus sat like a wedge between Jerusalem and Edessa, the new king's main preoccupation was the south, and the danger posed by the Fatimids. But the French Crusaders soon learned the same lessons the Normans had learned in southern Italy: when dealing with Muslim neighbors, shrewd calculation and local knowledge would produce better results than blind trust in Providence and in their own righteousness.

The Fatimids had made diplomatic contact with the Crusaders as early as the Siege of Antioch; their envoys spent a month in the besiegers' camp, discussing a peace settlement. This came to nothing, but, along with the fact that the Normans' cousins in Sicily were on good terms with the Isma'ilis, it may account for the clemency offered to the Fatimid garrison by Tancred and his men when they took Jerusalem the following year.

After the fall of Antioch, while the idealistic Raymond of Toulouse was launching brutal raids against Muslim civilians, Bohemond and Tancred were making deals with local Muslim elites. Tancred, for instance, reputedly offered to turn Tarsus, his first conquest, over to a Saljuq garrison, if they would pledge loyalty to him.

In 1100 Bohemond was captured by the Turkic prince Danishmend, a local non-Saljuq warlord, and Tancred was left in charge of the county. The Prince of Antioch would be held in chains for three years, until Danishmend freed him after Bohemond had agreed to ally with him against their common enemies, the Saljuqs and the Byzantines. Bohemond then returned to the West, touring as a celebrity and raising a huge Crusader army. When he brought this army back to the East, however, he made war not on the Saljuqs but on the Byzantines, who had been clamoring for the Normans to hand over Antioch. Bohemond's army was defeated in 1108, and he was forced to sign a humiliating submission to Alexios—the Peace of Devol. He died soon after. Tancred, still in power in Antioch, now as regent for Bohemond's infant son, rejected the agreement, and from that point forward, Byzantium and Antioch were at war. This only drove the Normans and the local Muslims closer together, whether against the Greeks or their common Muslim enemies.

Norman-Muslim integration in the East reached its high point with Roger of Salerno, another member of the de Hauteville clan, who had succeeded Tancred as regent after the latter's death from illness in 1112. In 1115 Roger forged an alliance with two Muslim princes, Il-Ghazi of Mardin and Tughtikin of Damascus, former rivals who had been independently waging *jihad* against the Crusaders over the previous decade. Their target was Aleppo, which was ruled over by Ridwan ibn Tutush, a grandson of the great Saljuq Alp Arslan. When the armies rallied, a Christian chronicler recalled how the Christian and Muslim warriors greeted each other with "a welcome, even a bond of complete love, like sons and parents in companionship." The alliance would be fleeting, however. Only four years later, Il-Ghazi (who had by then defeated Ridwan of Aleppo) would wipe out the Norman army—more than a thousand Latin and Armenian cavalry plus several thousand infantry—at a battle known to the Crusaders as "The Field of Blood." He and Roger (who was an Arabic-speaker) had apparently been close friends, a relationship Il-Ghazi commemorated by having the dead regent's skull cleaned out and converted into a jewel-encrusted goblet for use at his table.* Norman Antioch survived only because Il-Ghazi did not press his advantage.

---

* This seems to have been a local rather than a Turkic tradition, given that Vahram Varajnuni, the Armenian strongman, practiced the same custom.

With the destruction of Antioch's army, Baldwin of Bouillon, King of Jerusalem, took possession of the county, ending Norman domination and poisoning Norman-Frankish relations for the next half century. By this time, the Franks of Jerusalem had adopted the Norman realpolitik, and had begun making alliances with Muslim princes while encouraging the natural divisions among the Saljuqs, the other Turkic clans, and local Arab warlords. As early as 1108, Jerusalem and Damascus signed the first in the series of treaties that would ultimately allow the Frankish kingdom to survive. Protocols for trade and peace were devised, and border zones became codominions. The 1108 treaty included an arrangement by which Jerusalem and Damascus would split the tax revenues for the lands just east of the Sea of Galilee. A similar arrangement was reached in the Golan. One benefit of these truces was that each side gained a secure frontier, permitting it to focus on its most dangerous enemies: for Damascus, Muslim Aleppo, and for the Crusaders, the Fatimid Caliphate and Christian Byzantium.

The trade networks that arose out these political agreements ensured that Muslim and Christian rulers would continue to work together. Goods and commodities (cloth, spices, and manufactured goods) originating in Damascus and points east arrived in the Crusader kingdom's ports, and were traded to Western merchants bound for the Latin world. Muslim traders and Italian merchants met in Acre and Antioch, which boasted Muslim-style customs offices staffed by individuals trained in Latin and Arabic, who facilitated exchanges and levied lucrative duties and fees for the kingdom. Even in times of open warfare this commerce continued. Ibn Jubayr, who visited Damascus in the 1180s, just as Salah al-Din was preparing to deal the death blow to the Kingdom of Jerusalem, marveled at the caravans of Latin merchants even as columns of unfortunate Franks were led into the city to be sold as slaves: "although the fires of discord burn between the two parties," he wrote, "Muslim and Christian . . . travellers will come and go between them without interference."

Outremer, or "the Land Beyond the Sea," as the French referred to the Crusader principalities, was thoroughly dependent on its port cities and the Italian merchants who traded in them. At the time of the conquest the Crusaders had no naval forces, and capturing the coastal towns would have been impossible without Italian blockades and actions against the Fatimid fleet. Italian ships brought much-needed supplies, including foodstuffs, weaponry, and timber, during the Franks' campaigns, and later brought people—those intrepid Latins who left Europe to colonize the Holy Land, or who made pilgrimages to now Christian Jerusalem, Nazareth, Bethlehem, the Sea of Galilee, and other biblical sites. After 1099, warrior-pilgrims became increasingly common in the Holy Land. Knights from across Latin Europe would journey east to spend time fighting for the kingdom in pursuit of glory, the forgiveness of their sins, and booty. As freelance warriors, however, they owed no obedience to the local Frankish authorities and frequently mistreated Muslim subjects or attacked Muslim allies, in these ways threatening the region's delicate equilibrium. They were roundly regarded as uncouth and uncivilized both by local Muslims and by the "Orientalized" Latin nobility of the East.

In many respects, the Italians were no better. As proto-capitalists, even if they may have had one eye on Heaven, the other was firmly on the bottom line. War profiteering was an important part of their livelihood. They would eagerly bankrupt Frankish siege camps by charging extortionate prices for food, and then turn around and lend the soldiers in those same camps money at obscene rates in exchange for a piece of the action to come. Their standard fee for assisting in the conquest of a city, for example, was one-third—which is to say, permanent political control over one-third of the city in question, with all the incomes that this entailed, and a monopoly on westbound commerce and rights to tariff-free trade.

In short, while they made possible the Christian Kingdom of Jerusalem, they also dramatically impaired it. They had no loyalty to the kingdom, the Crusading venture as a whole, or to one another. Pisa, Genoa, and Venice were locked in competition for the lucrative Eastern trade. This allowed the Crusader states and Byzantium to use the trading republics against one another, and it was Byzantium that gained the most from these tactics, as the empire was regarded by the merchant cities as the richest client. Constantinople was not only the most populous and wealthiest city in Christendom, but stood at the gateway to the grain-rich shores of the Black Sea and the terminus of the Silk Road, the great overland trade route that crossed the Asian steppes to China. Fatimid Egypt was the other target of Italian designs, for more or less the same reasons: it was the point of access for the Red Sea, East Africa, and the jewel- and spice-rich Indies.

The Crusades as undertakings were so dependent on the Italians for naval support, logisitics, financing, and trade that Byzantium and Egypt would eventually become the true objectives of the Crusading movement. After Salah al-Din retook Jerusalem in 1187, the Latins did not decisively return, seeing little financial gain in its reconquest. For the Italians the margins were too small, and as long as they enjoyed favorable trading rights, it mattered little to them if a city was ruled by Muslims, Christians, or heretics—an indifference that would contribute to the ultimate demise of the Crusader states. In Egypt, though, Italian and Crusader agendas would coincide: both had an interest in conquering the Fatimid Caliphate, and in the process securing Italian access to Indian Ocean trade and the fragile Kingdom of Jerusalem's western flank.

And while the Kingdom of Jerusalem suffered as a consequence of the Italians' apathy regarding its survival, Byzantium would be destroyed by their attention: Venice's determination to have exclusive access to the trade of the empire would lead directly to the Fourth Crusade's sacking of Constantinople in 1204. Before then, though, and quite independent of the Crusade movement, the nobility of the Latin West had been plotting to dismember the empire, and to claim for themselves the title Roman Emperor.

After the Franks' conquest of Jerusalem, the Italian city-states continued their practice of raiding the Byzantine coast in order to win trade concessions, while the Latin nobility infiltrated the imperial power structure by providing much-needed troops and commanders—particularly Frankish heavy cavalry—to the Byzantine army, and by marrying into the Greek elite, including the imperial family itself. Alexios and his successors were aware of the dangers the Franks and Italians represented, but for their part understood that incorporating Latin warriors into the military and into the leading families of the realm mitigated the chance of direct invasion by a Western king. And while the success of Italian commerce made it difficult not to concede the merchants a larger role in the empire, granting them commercial privileges was a means also of co-opting their support. In any event, the situation would hold through most of the twelfth century, with the Komnenos dynasty producing a series of long-lived and capable emperors who were astute enough to keep the various Latin, Muslim, and Italian factions in check.

The Byzantine strategy was helped by the fragmentation of the Christian and Muslim Near East over the twelfth century. The Muslims—

Saljuqs, Arabs, Armenians, and Turcomen of various stripes—continued to view one another, rather than the Latin Christians, as the principal threats, and the Saljuq warlords remained obsessed with their goal of taking power in Baghdad. Latins and Christian Armenians jockeyed for position and survival in northern Syria and central Anatolia, and the Frankish Kingdom of Jerusalem became ever more divided, as its unruly nobility intrigued against and disobeyed its kings, and sapped its military capacity by coercing these kings to reduce the obligations to serve in the kingdom's military.

The decline of the Kingdom of Jerusalem was not immediately evident; in fact, to all appearances it was on the offensive in the first half of the century. The Fatimids were in disarray and contained, and Damascus remained in check even as Frankish warriors moved into territories to the east of the Jordan Valley and the Dead Sea. They founded new Latin lordships in the distant Transjordan, wresting control of a crucial stretch of the ancient King's Road that connected Syria to the Arabian Peninsula. Most significantly, castles sprouted up along the perimeter and throughout the interior of the Crusader territory: Belvoir, Krak des Chevaliers, and Marqab were only the most imposing and famous. These were no mere feudal keeps, but massive and impenetrable fortresses that could hold thousands of troops, and that were stocked to withstand extended, years-long sieges. But they were not the creation of the anemic Kingdom of Jerusalem. Rather, they were built by a new type of entity that had emerged in the aftermath of the conquest of Jerusalem.

The Military Orders were the next logical step in the evolution of Catholic piety and Crusade ideology, embodying new notions of chivalry, the militarization of the papacy, and the advancement of that potent mix of holy war and penance. Fusing monasticism and chivalry, pious knights took vows of celibacy, poverty, and obedience, and swore to protect the Holy Land and Christian pilgrims. They followed no earthly lord, but pledged their service to the Church and the pope. In an age of millennial anxiety and religious awakening, the orders provided an outlet for landless knights and noble younger sons who lusted for blood and searched for a higher calling. These men, in turn, finally provided the papacy with the army it needed to fully pursue its imperial ambitions, after it lost control of the First Crusade.

The two most prominent orders were the Knights of St. John of the Hospital (the Hospitallers) and the Knights of the Temple of Solomon (the Templars). The Hospitaller Order was rooted in the institution of the pilgrim hostel, the foundations established to house and care for visitors to the Holy Land. In the 1120s a knight named Raymond of Provence, who was in charge of one such hostel in Jerusalem, assigned military escorts to protect pilgrims to the city, and soon knights flocked to join his order. The Templars had been founded in 1118 by another French knight, Hughes de Payens, who, together with a handful of companions, pledged to serve the Patriarch of Jerusalem under arms.

Both orders attracted droves of recruits from among the Latin aristocracy and generous donations from kings and lords across Europe, for whom contributing was a means of blending religious and political patronage, and for whom the orders constituted an alternative military force to their often unreliable and rebellious nobility. As these knightly orders grew in size and influence, it became incumbent on monarchs to increase their support in order to better influence and control these independent organizations. For the Kingdom of Jerusalem, the orders soon became a permanent standing army, and one that carried almost no direct cost to the monarchs; consequently, they were granted large tracts of territory to administer as lords. But the orders also expanded into Europe itself, forging networks of fortresses and lordships spanning the length and breadth of Latin Christendom. As a result of donations they received, the Templars and Hospitallers came to wield formidable power both in the Holy Land and in Europe, while their ability to transport large quantities of gold and silver securely put them in a position to become the bankers of Christendom.

But success is a dangerous tonic, and institutions, however virtuous their founding principles, inevitably develop self-serving agendas. While both orders shared stated ambitions and answered, at least in theory, to the same authority, they quickly came to view each other as rivals. And though they never clashed directly in arms, they carried out policies independent of each other and the kingdom, and engaged in a strategic competition for power and influence in Syria and Palestine. They became, in effect, simply two more regional players willing to compromise their ideological convictions in the pursuit of security and power. The most dramatic manifestation of this was the Hospitallers' and Templars' long-term alliance with another revolutionary group that emerged in the Levant in the twelfth century: the Assassins.

The Nizaris, or the Batini, as they were properly known, were an unforeseen bit of blowback from the coup by the Egyptian *wazir* al-Afdal ibn Badr al-Jamali in 1094, in which he placed his nephew, al-Musta'li, on the Fatimid throne. The *da'i*, Hassan al-Sabbah, loyal to the memory of the assassinated prince and rightful heir, Nizar, fled to northern Persia, which was fertile ground for Isma'ili missionaries. There he occupied the mountaintop fortress of Alamut, from where he would dispatch agents, or activate those who had already infiltrated the palaces of local rulers, to assassinate anyone he regarded as a threat. His assassins were prepared to die in what they saw as a righteous cause. An early victim was Nizam al-Mulk, the brilliant Persian prime minister who had been the architect of Malik Shah's Saljuq imperium, and had attempted to extinguish the Nizari movement in its infancy. After his death, prudent princes gave Hassan a wide berth. What his group lacked in numbers, they made up for by instilling fear. In the first half century of their existence, the Nizaris are recorded as having carried out forty-four assassinations. There was only one instance when they missed their target.

The Nizaris expanded into Syria in the 1150s, where they would stake out a base in the mountainous no-man's-land between the Franks and the Muslims. They had nothing but contempt for Sunni Muslims, who gladly reciprocated, calling them *Hashashiyya*, a disdainful term referring to the use of hashish (which locals saw as despicable), and from whence comes the English word "assassin." Yet even though they were despised by the Christian and Muslim warrior elites, who considered assassination a dishonorable and cowardly way to fight, the Assassins' services were in high demand in Levantine politics. They were treated gingerly, and often with respect. Such was their reach that Salah al-Din, who had also pledged to stamp them out, was said to have escaped no fewer than three attempts on his life before concluding a treaty with them. His biographer reported that in 1176, when Salah al-Din was campaigning against the Nizaris, he awoke one evening to a dagger on his pillow with a message from their leader, Rashid al-Din Sinan, "The Old Man in the Mountain"—fair warning that they had infiltrated his bodyguard and could kill him at will.

It is one of the ironies so typical of the era of the Crusades that the Assassins' most durable relationship would be with the Hospitallers and the Templars. In the 1170s, Sinan sent a mission to the king of Jerusalem with an offer to convert to Christianity, and the Templars, concerned this would mean an end to their alliance with the Assassins, scuttled the deal by ambushing and killing the envoys on their way home. Ideology aside, the orders and the Assassins were natural allies. They shared sovereignty over the lower Orontes Valley and the Golan, and each was, in some sense, an underdog. Moreover, none of them wanted to see an overly strong Frankish kingdom, nor a Syria united under a single Sunni ruler, either of which would result in the diminishment of their own power.

Indeed, the goal of every lord, principality, or institution was survival and expansion, and pursuit of this goal often required allying with infidels against coreligionists. As they settled in to life in the Levant, the Franks came to recognize how much they shared with the natives. They became, by their own admission, less and less Frankish. Late in life, Fulcher of Chartres would wax prosaic about his "Easternness," with magnanimity and empathy:

> We are all Orientals now . . . Consider, I pray, and reflect how in our time God has transferred the West into the East. For we who were Occidentals now have been made Orientals. He who was a Roman or a Frank is now a Galilaean, or an inhabitant of Palestine. One who was a citizen of Rheims or of Chartres now has been made a citizen of Tyre or of Antioch. We have already forgotten the places of our birth.

It was hard for the Franks not to be seduced by the culture of the East, and hard for them not to recognize the noble, even chivalric character of the infidel knights they rode against in battle, and entertained as guests in their courts.

One of those infidels was 'Usama ibn Munqidh, a scion of the last generation of the Arab lords of Shayzar, just southeast of Antioch. He was a poet, diplomat, politician, and *mujahid* who lived as an exile and knight-errant. Over his long career, he plotted in Egypt with 'Umara of Yaman in support of the traitorous *wazir* 'Abbas ibn Yahya, served as Nur al-Din's envoy to the Franks, and fought countless battles, both in the saddle and behind the scenes, against both Franks and Muslims. Born the same year as Urban's fateful conclave, 'Usama wrote an autobiography in his nineties, a few years before Salah al-Din would wipe the Crusader kingdom off the map. It is a unique account, and we are lucky to have it: a single copy was found in a Moroccan manuscript in the Spanish royal library of the Escorial. It is rife with amusing anecdotes, pithy observations, and distinctive characters. 'Usama has much to say about the Franks. In his most unguarded moments, he describes innocently uncultured and Orientalized Franks, sympathetic Templars, and crude but valiant Crusaders. Some gave him shelter and protected him while he prayed, and one, who referred to him as his "brother," even offered to take 'Usama's son back to Europe with him.

THREE PRINCESSES

It became a necessity for the Frankish principalities to make allies among the local Muslims because they faced, from their first arrival in the region, a serious disadvantage: a lack of men, at least of Latin men, the only kind that truly counted for them. They were short on settlers, short on knights, and short on noblemen who were willing to sacrifice their own self-interest for the kingdom. And because the kingdom was so new, with no history and no "custom" (the most powerful principle of feudal law), and with a royal line that had been founded through an election, the kings were weak. They were beholden to their magnates and lords, who did everything they could to reduce their personal obligations to the kingdom, to the point that the kings were left with what was essentially a volunteer military, and a rather capricious and mercenary one at that. The noble pilgrims who came to Jerusalem under arms and in search of glory and redemption helped little. They were not interested in defensive actions or strategic considerations. Each wanted to be on the front line, claiming his share of glory. The debacle of the Second Crusade and the disastrous attack on Damascus demonstrated how much havoc these committed but ill-informed Crusaders could cause.

But the shortage of men in the Crusader states had an even more dire consequence: the shortage of male heirs. When Godfrey of Bouillon, ruler of Jerusalem, died childless, his brother Baldwin of Edessa was elected and reigned as the city's first king. Baldwin was a strong and capable ruler, but either out of disinclination or disregard, he failed in that most important task of any monarch: when he died in 1118, he left no heir. This was not for lack of wives. Having apparently forgotten that he had left behind his first wife in France, Baldwin had married the daughter of the ill-fated T'oros of Edessa in 1098. By 1105, however, he was King of Jerusalem and she had outlived her use, so she was packed off to a convent and forgotten. In 1112 he contracted another marriage, this time to Adelaide del Vasto, the widowed mother of Roger II of Sicily. In her late thirties, Adelaide was close to if not already past childbearing age, and it was clear that Baldwin lusted after not her flesh but her dowry. Once he had obtained the latter, she, too, was ignored and then discarded.

Upon Baldwin I's death, the nobility of the kingdom elected his kinsman, Baldwin of Bourq, who had been appointed Count of Edessa by the former king. Baldwin II of Jerusalem, as he would be known, ruled for thirteen years. He faced many challenges: the Saljuqs and Fatimids took advantage of every opportunity to strike at the kingdom, while the plotting between Antioch and Edessa diverted him from capitalizing on his successes, which included his capture of Tyre in 1124 and a major victory over the Saljuqs at the Battle of Azaz in 1125. His lowest point had come in 1123. After Jocelyn of Courtenay, his deputy in Edessa, had been captured by the Danishmends, the king rode north to defend the county, but he, too, was taken prisoner. He spent sixteen months in captivity before he was able to raise his own ransom. He received little assistance from the nobility of his kingdom, and even once he had the gold to pay for his freedom, he was forced to leave his four-year-old daughter, Ioveta, as collateral for the terms of his release.

In Baldwin's absence, his strong network of kin, the maturing clerical bureaucracy of the kingdom, and his wife, the Armenian Melkite princess Morfia of Melitene, held the kingdom together. Morfia was the daughter of Gabriel of Melitene, who had been a lieutenant and successor of the Armenian strongman Vahram Varajnuni, and an unflagging oppressor of the local Syriac Christians. Morfia, whom Baldwin was evidently deeply attached to, had borne him four daughters, all of whom were forces to be reckoned with. The eldest, Melisende, would succeed her father as Queen of Jerusalem in 1131. Baldwin II foresaw that she would inherit the throne, and he supported her, but understood that she needed a king at her side, someone capable of riding personally into war, and who had the resources and reputation to bring men from the West to buttress the kingdom. He settled on Count Fulk of Anjou, a wealthy French lord and a seasoned Crusader. Fulk agreed to the marriage in 1129 on the condition he would rule Jerusalem with the title of king, and not merely as royal consort.* Baldwin acquiesced, but reinforced Melisende's position

* As part of the marital agreement, Fulk relinquished the title Count of Anjou to his eldest son, Geoffrey. In 1128 Geoffrey would marry Matilda, the daughter of Henry I of

by making her sole guardian over the son she had borne Fulk in 1130. Baldwin wanted the crown to remain in the control of his bloodline.

It was hardly an affair of the heart. Melisende, an independent woman, would not be dominated by a foreign lord she had married out of obligation. Her leading subjects—the second-generation Frankish nobility of the Holy Land—shared her prejudices. While Fulk did his best to curb the kingdom's restless nobility and bring the northern counties under royal control, he met with nothing but resistance. The native Frankish nobility treated him as an intruder, and, sensing the kingdom's instability, John II Komnenos, the son and successor of Alexios, brought pressure on the Franks to recognize the Byzantine Empire as the ultimate sovereign of the Crusader territories. Soon after the marriage, Fulk had tried to weaken his wife, and this provoked a rebellion by her kinsman, Count Hugh of Jaffa, who called on the Fatimids to join him in overthrowing the king. Hoping perhaps to dethrone his wife and lock her away in a convent, Fulk encouraged rumors that the queen and Hugh were lovers. Although the uprising came to an end through negotiation, with Hugh accepting exile, it was made clear over the course of the struggle that Melisende, rather than her husband, held power in the palace and had the loyalty of the kingdom's bureaucracy.*

Melisende's ambition did not abate with Fulk's death in 1143. As regent over their teenage son, Baldwin III, she became the unchallenged ruler of Jerusalem. Over the next decade, Baldwin would struggle to free himself from his mother's control. When he came of age, she refused to relinquish power. He defied her, having himself crowned king in 1152, which provoked a north–south split of the kingdom. The young king, backed by troops loyal to his cause, occupied Jerusalem. But he could not defeat his mother, and in 1154 they reached an understanding: Melisende would "retire" and recognize Baldwin as king, but would be allowed to exert her will backstage.

The queen's two eldest sisters were cut from the same cloth as she was, and their father, Baldwin II, used each of them well. Hodierna was married off to Raymond II of Tripoli, the grandson of Count Bertrand.

England, the first of the Plantagenet dynasty, the same line that would produce the Crusading king, Richard the Lion-Hearted.

* Hugh was leaving the kingdom when he was attacked by a knight from Brittany and gravely wounded. Fulk was suspected of arranging the attack. Taking refuge with his kinsman Roger II of Sicily, Hugh died not long after from his wounds.

She was no less spirited than her elder sister, and she and Raymond—who did his best to cloister her—fought constantly. It was widely rumored that her children, Melisende and Raymond, had been fathered by a lover. In 1152, after a particularly nasty spat in which Queen Melisende herself was forced to intervene, Raymond II was killed by Nizari assassins, leaving Hodierna as regent of the County of Tripoli in the name of their son, the young Raymond III. This Raymond would become one of the most principled and loyal defenders of the Kingdom of Jerusalem, achieving fame as a tireless warrior and a man of his word. In the 1160s he launched an assault on Byzantine Cyprus to avenge his sister's honor, after the empire had abandoned a marriage negotiation because of the rumors of her true parentage. He would later spend eleven years as Nur al-Din's captive in Aleppo, and in the 1170s would serve as regent for his nephew, Baldwin IV, the leper King of Jerusalem. As lord of Galilee, a position he held through his wife, he would conclude a truce with Salah al-Din, and was so highly esteemed by his Muslim foes that they tricked him into escaping the death that awaited his comrades at the Battle of the Horns of Hattin in 1187, in such a way that his honor or reputation would not be affected.

Alice, only slightly older than Hodierna, was sent by Baldwin to secure the County of Antioch, which was set to pass in 1126 to Bohemond II, the son of Bohemond of Taranto, on the former's eighteenth birthday. By arranging Alice's marriage to him, Baldwin would keep the county under Jerusalem's influence. Alice had plans of her own. When her young husband was killed in battle in 1130, she refused to hand over Antioch to her father, and allegedly attempted to strike an alliance with 'Imad al-Din Zengi, the Saljuq lord of Mosul and Aleppo, against him. At this, a pair of townsfolk opened the city gates to Baldwin's forces. Alice backed down, and father and daughter reconciled. It was agreed that the county would pass to her daughter Constance, and would be held in the meantime by Jocelyn of Courtenay, Count of Edessa, as regent. But when Jocelyn was killed in 1131, Alice rallied the counties of Edessa and Tripoli to her side in an effort to reassert her rule over Antioch against the claims of the new King of Jerusalem, Fulk of Anjou, whom she portrayed as a power-grabbing tyrant. Her revolt failed only after Fulk took his army north and defeated her allies on the field of battle.

Several years later, Alice conspired with the emperor John II Komnenos in an attempt to secure Constance's betrothal to his son and the future emperor, Manuel, but this inflamed the anti-Greek sentiments of some of her leading subjects, who feared that any marital alliance with Byzantium would spell the end of the independence of Antioch, the primacy of the Latin Church, and their own privileged positions. She next tried to arrange for her own marriage to Raymond of Poitiers, the younger son of William IX and one of the most powerful men in France.* Her trusted supporters appeared to favor the match, and the Latin patriarch of Antioch, Ralph of Dumfort, did everything he could to convince Alice it had support. But it was an elaborate sham. Raymond arrived, and while the countess stood waiting at the altar, Ralph was officiating over the count's wedding to Alice's daughter, Constance. This was a possibility Alice had probably not entertained, given that at six years of age, Constance was not even eligible for marriage by Church law. Betrayed and humiliated, the dowager countess, only twenty-six herself, retired to the seaside town of Latakia, where she died not long after.

Her legacy, however, would be a lasting one. Constance would be responsible for the arrival in the Holy Land of one of the most corrosive and dangerous personalities in the history of the Latin East: Reynaud de Châtillon, an opportunist par excellence, who more than almost any other single individual—and perhaps as much as even Salah al-Din—would contribute to the destruction of the Latin Kingdom of Jerusalem in 1187. As for Constance's two daughters, they would each unintentionally help provoke the destruction of the Byzantine Empire in 1204. Maria, who would reign as empress-consort to Manuel Komnenos, would stoke Latin-Greek tensions to the boiling point, while Philippa would take as her lover Andronikos Komnenos, the renegade prince and usurper who would become the unwitting nemesis to his own family's dynasty. He would put Maria and her son and heir, Alexios, to death, paving the way for the Fourth Crusade's sack of Constantinople.

These women, however, cannot be blamed for the disasters that awaited Byzantium and the Crusader states. No more or less than the

---

* He was the younger son of William IX, Duke of Aquitaine, who had fought the Muslims in Spain in the service of Alfonso VII of Castile and León. Raymond was the uncle of Eleanor of Aquitaine, the powerful duchess, queen of England, and mother of Richard the Lion-Hearted. Eleanor's first marriage was to Louis VII of France, whom she accompanied on the Second Crusade. The contemporary historian William of Tyre claims that Raymond seduced his niece when the Crusaders were staying in Antioch, prompting Louis to head south to Jerusalem and ultimately embark on the disastrous attack on Damascus.

men alongside and against whom they struggled, they were creatures of the tumultuous Near East of the twelfth century. And they were at a tremendous disadvantage: theirs was a man's world, and it was all but unprecedented for a woman to rule as queen in her own name, as Melisende did, let alone engineer a coup against her husband and king.* Though traditional gender roles were put to the test in the Crusader states, where it was not unheard of for women to don armor and ride into battle, the ascension of women into kingships and other high positions was inherently destabilizing. They were not recognized as being fully able to wield authority, and therefore their presence invited the disrupting intervention and competition of men. And yet Melisende, Hodierna, and Alice refused to be cowed. For the already fragile Latin principalities, that Baldwin II had three irrepressible and ambitious daughters and no son was a stroke of historically bad luck.

The Kingdom of Jerusalem was neither the pure, Christian land envisioned by the righteously brutal knights who conquered the city in 1099, nor the heavenly paradise conjured up by Peter the Hermit for the poor faithful who had naively set out on the People's Crusade in 1096. Far from lasting an eternity, the Kingdom of Jerusalem would endure no longer than the span of a single lifetime.†

---

* In northern Italy and southern France, women could inherit noble titles and even rule as countesses and duchesses—the most famous example being Duchess Eleanor of Aquitaine, Crusader and queen-consort of France and England. But women in this period ruled as queens only as regents in the name of minor sons (as did Alfonso VI of Castile's daughters Urraca, Queen of León, Castile, and Galicia, and the illegitimate Theresa, Countess and self-declared "Queen" of Portugal). In 1141 Matilda, the daughter of Henry I, inherited the English throne, but this provoked a civil war, and she was never crowned. Eventually her son came to the throne as Henry II—he would later become the husband of Eleanor of Aquitaine and father of Richard the Lion-Hearted.

† The Syrian diarist 'Usama ibn Munqidh was born in the year of the Council of Clermont and died the year after Salah al-Din reconquered Jerusalem.

10

Jerusalem Restored

It is one of the most vivid and dramatic scenes from the history of the Crusades. With the din and smoke of battle slowly fading, two figures— filthy, blood-spattered, and dazed—are brought into the luxurious interior of a royal campaign tent. They are prodded inside at sword and spear point, shuffling with the tired resignation of prisoners. Eyes bloodshot and glazed, lips parched and cracking, they stand before a trim, middle-aged man poised on a low stool, his hands resting lightly on his knees. He, too, wears armor, but his face is clean and his eyes are bright, a slight smile on his lips, a cup of iced julep in his hand. This is Yusuf ibn 'Ayyub: Salah al-Din, sultan of Egypt, lord of Syria, and now victor over the Kingdom of Jerusalem. Of the two before him, the younger man, in his late thirties, is Guy de Lusignan, King of Jerusalem, though now he hardly betrays the bearing of a king. The other is a large, strong man of about sixty, but fearsome and unbowed by the years, his eyes sparkling with defiance and hatred, even in defeat. He is Reynaud de Châtillon, lord of Kerak.

Taking a cup from a platter in front of him, the sultan holds it out to the king. Guy gulps thirstily, then, remembering courtesy, passes it to his companion, who quaffs the rest without hesitating. Salah al-Din turns to

Guy and speaks in Arabic. His interpreter says, "You are the one who has given him a drink. I have not given him any drink." Salah al-Din does not so much as glance at Reynaud.

After being shown to their own quarters, the two are summoned again. The king is ordered to wait in the entry chamber while Reynaud enters. He finds Salah al-Din relaxed, in the company of a few servants, having washed and changed out of his armor. The sultan speaks to him directly, as Reynaud would have likely understood his Arabic. "Here I am," Salah al-Din says, "having asked for victory through Muhammad, and God has given me victory over you." Would Reynaud now admit that Islam was the true faith? The old Crusader's glower is answer enough; an enraged Salah al-Din rises and, drawing his sword, cuts him deeply through neck and into the shoulder. Servants toss Reynaud's shuddering, spurting body out into the entranceway, where he is finished off by the sultan's guards at the feet of a panicking Guy, before his mangled corpse is dragged out. The king is summoned next to appear before the sultan; but Salah al-Din's rage has passed, and trying to calm his captive, he says, "It is not for princes to kill princes, but this man knew no limits, and so has suffered his fate." Salah al-Din had given Guy a drink, and in the custom of Arab hospitality that had made him a guest—he would not be killed.*

It was July 4, 1187, and on this hill overlooking the Sea of Galilee, it was clear to Guy de Lusignan as much as to Salah al-Din that the days of the Kingdom of Jerusalem were all but over. On that afternoon virtually the entire military force of the kingdom had been destroyed. Every available Latin man of fighting age had been mustered before the battle, and now, with few exceptions, all lay dead on the battlefield or were being led away as slaves. The Templars and Hospitallers who had survived were being rounded up and executed. Pyramid-shaped piles of severed Frankish heads and mounds of stripped corpses littered the hillside. Within three months, the Holy City would once more be under Muslim rule. Guy would never see Jerusalem again. Kept under guard in Damascus until the following year, he would be released upon swearing that he would return across the sea to the land of the Franks and never again raise arms against Islam. Once freed, he broke his pledge, fleeing west to Tyre, in a

---

* This account is based on the recollections of one of Salah al-Din's biographers, Baha' al-Din ibn Shaddad. Other accounts vary slightly, having Salah al-Din decapitate Reynaud or merely ordering his men to kill him.

vain effort to reconstitute his kingdom. But from this moment on "King of Jerusalem" would be little more than an empty title.

As for Reynaud de Châtillon—or "Arnat," as his Arab-speaking contemporaries pronounced his name (when they did not refer to him simply as "a devil")—his was a fate foretold. Salah al-Din had long ago sworn to kill him by his own hand, and his offer of clemency in exchange for conversion was no more than a gesture. But few Franks would miss the lord of Kerak, either. In a Crusading career that had spanned almost thirty-five years, Reynaud had earned as many Christian enemies as he had Muslim ones. Although his reputation has suffered from the hostility of the chroniclers of his age, and although he was unquestionably a more complex character than many have allowed, there is also no doubt that he epitomized the self-serving ambition of certain Latins who journeyed east, or that he bears a great deal of responsibility for the destruction of the Crusader kingdom in 1187.

BLIND AMBITION

Reynaud arrived in the Holy Land in 1147 as a member of the Second Crusade, having set out from northern France in search of fortune and glory. Historians are unsure of his origin. He seems to have been relatively highborn, but with few assets of his own, which may explain why he did not intend to return to Europe. After the Crusade's disastrous failed attack on Damascus, he entered the service of the young king, Baldwin III, then at war with his mother, Melisende. There is a reference in the sources to Reynaud's participation in the successful assault on Fatimid Ascalon in 1153, but few other details of his early years in the Levant survive. By this time, he seems to have been based in Antioch, then under the rule of Constance, the granddaughter of Baldwin II. Her husband, Raymond of Poitiers, had been killed at the Battle of 'Inab in 1149, when Nur al-Din, who had secured his hold on Syria, dealt a stinging defeat to the army of Antioch and its allies, the Assassins. But Raymond's death opened an opportunity for Reynaud, who managed to attract the affections of the widowed princess. She secretly married him in 1153, squandering what her advisers saw as a chance for a more useful marital alliance with a more prestigious lord from the West. A daughter and a son, Agnes and Baldwin, were born soon after.

What Reynaud lacked in lineage and dependents, he made up for with sheer bravado. As regent of Antioch (Raymond and Constance's son and heir, Bohemond III, was only a boy), Reynaud was an aggressive ruler, but so arrogant and ham-fisted that he caused more harm than good. His temper soon became legendary, and it did not take long for it to get him into trouble. From the outset, the elite of the principality had been against Reynaud, distrusting and fearing him, and so he looked for allies beyond its borders, notably the Knights Templar, and set out to punish those who had opposed him.

He first targeted Aimery of Limoges, Patriarch of Antioch, who had been a staunch supporter of Raymond of Poitiers. When Raymond arrived in the city in 1136 he had clashed with its patriarch, the ambitious Norman prelate Ralph of Dumfort, until after four years of bickering he deposed Ralph and appointed his own man, Aimery. A man of cunning and ambition, Aimery had been a lowly deacon prior to his elevation. His chief attributes seem to have been loyalty to his lord and their common pedigree; both had been born to the aristocracy of Aquitaine.* Aimery had served the principality and the patriarchate well, amassing a huge fortune for his church, and acting as an adviser and deputy for Raymond. When the prince was killed fighting at 'Inab, he rallied the population of Antioch, and raised the tribute from his own estates to pay Nur al-Din in exchange for not attacking the city. As guardian of the young Bohemond III, Aimery became the principality's effective ruler. He opposed Constance's marriage to Reynaud, as it would effectively cut him out of power. To Reynaud, the patriarch was a dangerous rival who had to be dealt with decisively.

Reynaud's second target was the emperor Manuel Komnenos, who in the years prior had been pressing Raymond of Poitiers to recognize Byzantine suzerainty over Antioch and to promise to appoint an Orthodox patriarch to the city's see—both of which were terms of the Peace of Devol that Bohemond of Taranto had been forced to sign in 1108, and neither of which Raymond had done. Reynaud's rise initially led to a thaw

---

* That said, Aimery was no bumpkin; as a young man he had journeyed to Toledo, where he had studied among the Christian clergy, Jews, and Muslims who were engaged in translating works of Islamic science and philosophy into Latin. He may have been drawn to Antioch, because this city, too, had become an important center for the translation of Arabic learning.

in relations with Byzantium, due to his and the empire's shared interest in weakening the Armenian principality of Cilicia, Antioch's neighbor to the north. Manuel proposed that Reynaud attack Cilicia, promising to help finance the expedition. The pretext for the invasion was T'oros II's seizure of a castle called Getim, which controlled one of the strategic passes through the Taurus Mountains. The castle had previously been in the possession of the Knights Templar, whom Raymond of Poitiers had invited to the region as a check against the Armenians and the Greeks, and whom Reynaud had now taken to supporting. The invasion, however, did not go as planned: T'oros put up a spirited resistance and repelled the Franks. The humiliated Reynaud placed the blame for the debacle on Manuel, and the emperor's refusal to hand over the subsidy he had guaranteed Reynaud in support of the Cilician campaign.

Reynaud and T'oros then found common cause. T'oros II, or "the Great," was a scion of the Roupenid family, another of the noble Armenian warrior clans that had broken away from the Byzantine Empire in the decade after Manzikert, and which had founded an independent kingdom based at Sis (modern Kozan) in the Taurus Mountains in 1080. T'oros had little love for the Byzantines, who in 1137 had occupied the kingdom of his father, Leo I, and imprisoned him and his family in Constantinople. Leo I had died in captivity, and T'oros's brother, Roupen, had been blinded. T'oros himself managed to escape in 1143, claimed the crown of Cilicia, and, with the aid of Antioch, remade his family's kingdom by taking on the imperial garrisons one town at a time. When Reynaud approached his former opponent and suggested that together they invade the Byzantine island of Cyprus, he found a willing confederate.

The large and semiarid island just fifty miles south of the Anatolian mainland and sixty-five miles west of the Levantine coast had been an important economic center in Antiquity but was largely neglected by Byzantium until the eleventh century—an isolated province that the empire had forcibly settled with people from across its lands (including a large population of Cilician Armenians). There were also Christians and Muslims who had come of their own volition. But in the mid-1100s, as trade in the Mediterranean increased, Cyprus acquired new value. By the 1140s the Genoese and Venetians had built bases there, and a sugar industry, which would see the island become prosperous in later centuries, was in its infancy.

When Reynaud announced that he would launch an invasion of

Cyprus, he also declared that he expected Aimery of Limoges to pay for it. Thus Reynaud would kill two birds with one stone: get his revenge against Emperor Manuel and strike at his enemy, the patriarch. The patriarchate was exceptionally well endowed, and Aimery was the richest man in Antioch. Reynaud's request was a means of showing him who held true power and to trim some of the fat from the prelate's estates. Aimery, horrified, had no intention of being trapped into committing his own resources—which is doubtless how he regarded the property of his see—to finance an assault on a Christian island belonging to the emperor. When he refused, Reynaud, indifferent to the dignities the patriarch might claim as the successor of Saint Peter, ordered Aimery to be seized, after which

> he stripped the man of his garments and first whipped his body with many lashes, and since summer was at its height, anointing his wounds with honey, he left him to be burnt by the sun. So wasps, bees, flies and other blood-drinking creatures settled on his entirely naked body and sucked his blood.

The battered and humiliated patriarch was left in a public square for all to see. A day later, he agreed to back the invasion. For good measure, Reynaud seized the properties of the patriarchate. Aimery, for his part, fled into exile in the Kingdom of Jerusalem. After this demonstration, few in Antioch would dare openly defy the prince-consort.

In 1155 or 1156 forces under the personal command of Reynaud and T'oros, among them a detachment of Knights Templar, landed on Cyprus's north shore, near the capital of Lefkosia (Nicosia). John Komnenos, a nephew of the emperor and the military commander (*doukas*) of the island, rode out to meet the invaders. At first, the battle seemed to be going in favor of the defenders, but John overextended his army and was defeated. Reynaud and T'oros ravaged the island. The monk Neophytus the Recluse, who witnessed the campaign, described the Franks as "barbarians, who [took] our fruit and our food," and "left our land and country deserted." By any standard, the pillaging exceeded the acceptable, if unwritten, rules of warfare, particularly warfare among Christians. The invaders rolled across the island, sacking churches, monasteries, and private homes, rounding up the cattle and the populace and herding them to the shore. To spread terror, they mutilated or killed those who resisted,

Reynaud de Châtillon tortures Patriarch Aimery of Limoges, from
William of Tyre's *History*, thirteenth century

cutting off the hands, noses, and ears of clergy and lay folk alike. After
three weeks of plundering, and as rumors arrived that a Byzantine fleet
was assembling, Reynaud and T'oros's men loaded their booty onto their
ships and weighed anchor. John Komnenos went with them as a prisoner,
as did other citizens of the island, all of whom would only be freed if the
populace raised their ransoms.

When the desperate petitions of his Cypriot subjects reached Manuel,
he vowed revenge. His own governors and his Armenian and Saljuq
proxies had been unable to defeat T'oros on the mainland, but in 1158
the emperor raised a new army and marched south to Cilicia. He moved
swiftly as T'oros's forces retreated before him, and took Tarsus, the Cilician capital. This had the desired effect. At a place called Mamistra,

about one hundred miles north of Antioch, T'oros and Reynaud submitted to the emperor. For T'oros the terms of surrender were not entirely disagreeable. He was spared arrest in exchange for swearing to honor Manuel as his lord. "Little Armenia," as Cilicia was called, would not be fully independent, but it would remain under T'oros's rule. At this time T'oros also settled Cilicia's long-festering conflict with the Templars. To seal the peace, his brother, Mleh, converted to Catholicism and joined the order.*

For Reynaud, the terms were harsher. Manuel was not an individual to cross lightly. The emperor was then the single most powerful individual in the Near East, having brought much of western Anatolia under imperial rule, and having married his niece, Theodora, to Baldwin III, thereby uniting the dynasties of Constantinople and Jerusalem. To save his position, and possibly his life, Reynaud was forced to grovel publicly for mercy. He arrived at Mamistra preceded by a crowd of barefoot and bareheaded monks, who begged Manuel to permit Reynaud to approach. With a great show of reluctance the emperor relented, and there on his dais, before the watching crowds and envoys from all the petty Muslim and Christian states of western Anatolia, the prince of Antioch walked forward, bareheaded and wearing the short-sleeved robe of a penitent, a noose tied around his neck, and holding his unsheathed sword by its blade—the last a symbol of absolute humiliation. Reynaud cast himself face down in the dirt in front of Manuel, rising only when the emperor bade him to do so. The Latin aristocracy was disgusted by Reynaud's debasement and by his agreement to hand over the citadel of Antioch to the emperor and to install a Greek Orthodox patriarch of Manuel's choosing. In the words of the contemporary statesman and chronicler William of Tyre, "the glory of the Latins was turned into shame."

On April 12, 1159, Manuel made his ceremonial entrance into Antioch as the liege lord of the principality, after Baldwin of Jerusalem had personally instructed the city's Latin elite to accept the emperor as

---

* As it happened, Mleh was neither a model Catholic nor a model Templar. In the 1170s he broke with the order, converted to Islam, and established an alliance with Nur al-Din, who was at the height of his power and threatening to destroy the Crusader states. Going to war against his former Templar brothers and Byzantium, Mleh seized the Kingdom of Cilicia and murdered his nephew, Roupen, who had succeeded T'oros as lord of Armenia. Mleh ruled as king until 1175, when he was murdered by members of his own household.

their new ruler. The king, despite his successes against the Saljuqs and the Fatimids, needed Manuel's protection, and when the emperor proclaimed himself the lord and protector of all Christians, Baldwin was in no position to object. But the people of Antioch were far from eager to accept Byzantine authority, and many began speaking of or actively plotting rebellion. Thus when Manuel rode into the city, he did so in force. Garbed in a shimmering, jeweled robe overlaying his heavy armor, he led a long procession flanked by his towering, battle-ax-wielding Scandinavian Varangian Guards. Baldwin followed humbly behind him, mounted but carrying no weapon. In a sign of their submission—and to serve as human shields in the event of an assassination attempt—Reynaud and the other leading noblemen of the city were ordered to accompany the

Empress Maria of Antioch, twelfth-century mosaic in Hagia Sophia, Constantinople

emperor's horse on foot, the prince holding the bridle and the others each with a hand resting on the side of his saddle.

Manuel stayed for eight days in Reynaud and Constance's palace, and to ensure his continuing influence in Antioch, threw his support behind the princess in her fight to maintain her control of the principality against the claims of her now grown son, Bohemond III. In 1161 Manuel would take the elder daughter of Constance and Raymond of Poitiers, the beautiful Maria of Antioch, as his wife, cementing his link with the city. So cowed was Reynaud by the emperor that the exiled Aimery of Limoges was able to return and recover his position as patriarch. By 1163 he would again serve as regent of Antioch, but it was not to last. That same year, with the support of Baldwin II and the people of the city, Bohemond III took power, and sent his mother, Constance, who had attempted to launch a countercoup, into exile. Aimery would soon suffer the same fate as his ally, when he was deposed by order of the emperor, who finally appointed a Greek Orthodox, Athanasius III, as patriarch. Retreating to his fortress of al-Qusayr on the southern frontier of Antioch, Aimery vainly excommunicated everyone who recognized the legitimacy of his Melkite nemesis. He was nothing if not a survivor: he would make another comeback in 1170, after Athanasius was killed during an earthquake, when the roof of the cathedral of Antioch collapsed on him as he was saying Mass.*

REYNAUD REBORN

By this time, Reynaud de Châtillon had long been out of the picture in Antioch. In July 1160 he had set out northeast toward Edessa on a mission to rustle cattle from local Christian peasants, and fell into the clutches of a local Saljuq amir. He was immediately turned over to the amir's kinsman and lord, Nur al-Din. The fact that they had once been allies did not stop

* Aimery's later career was no less interesting. In the 1180s he was exiled by Bohemond III, and fomented a rebellion of the local nobility and townsmen against him. In 1194, when Bohemond was captured by King Leo III of Cilicia and was forced to hand over Antioch as his ransom, Aimery organized commoners to resist and prevent the Armenians from taking over. Though we cannot be certain, it seems that Aimery of Limoges died in 1196, after fifty-six tumultuous years in total as patriarch—at least by his own reckoning—of Antioch.

Nur al-Din from imprisoning Reynaud in the fortress of Aleppo. He would remain there for sixteen years, outliving his captor. We cannot be sure what Reynaud experienced, whether he was kept in chains in the fortress's infamous dungeons, or in better accommodations. He may have been subjected to torture and forced labor, as were many prisoners during this period, or he may have been left to languish in isolation. Regardless, it would have been a terrible time for Reynaud, all the more so because no one of any consequence in the Latin kingdom was willing to come up with his ransom.

Ironically enough, the emperor Manuel would eventually rescue Reynaud, securing his release with a huge payment of silver. He was perhaps moved to do so by his wife Maria, Reynaud's stepdaughter. Or perhaps he saw it as his obligation, as Reynaud's liege lord. The result was that Reynaud became zealously pro-Byzantine out of his gratitude to Manuel, who had also welcomed his children to Constantinople after Constance's demise. Reynaud's daughter, Agnes, had wed one of the emperor's favorites, a young Hungarian prince named Béla. The sonless Manuel had been grooming Béla as a successor, and had given him the name "Alexios." But he abandoned the plan after Maria of Antioch gave him his own son. Béla would return home as king of his own land in 1172, so when Reynaud was released from the fortress at Aleppo, his daughter was reigning as Queen of Hungary thanks to the Byzantine emperor. Reynaud's son, Baldwin, had been given a commission as a commander in the imperial army, but in 1177 he was killed in action while leading a squadron of troops against the Saljuqs in northwestern Anatolia.

The trauma of his captivity and his son's death provoked a profound transformation in Reynaud. Whereas before he had been largely indifferent to Islam and Muslims, he was now motivated by a sincere hatred of them, and by a desire for revenge. If the Byzantines, Franks, Armenians, and Saljuqs had imagined he would emerge from nearly two decades of captivity aged and broken, they were mistaken. A man of uncommon willpower and passion, Reynaud, at age fifty, resumed his military career, which would last another decade. Few others would have had the physical and psychological endurance to spend hours in the saddle, day after day, in the desert heat; to wear into battle metal armor that could easily weigh 150 pounds; to swing, as Reynaud did, a three-pound longsword; and to grip a four-yard-long lance and charge headlong on horseback at enemies half his own age or younger, in a fight to the death.

Reynaud did not return to Antioch. Upon his release he was rewarded by the adolescent leper King of Jerusalem, Baldwin IV, with a marriage to Stephanie de Milly, a member of the old Frankish nobility who was descended from the knights of the First Crusade. Like so many other native noblewomen, Stephanie was at home on the frontiers of Christendom. Some twenty-five years Reynaud's junior, she had already buried two husbands, and was ruling on her own the vast Lordship of Oultrejourdain ("the Land Beyond the Jordan River"), which she had inherited from her mother, and the Lordship of Hebron, which had been passed down to her by her father. Oultrejourdain would be Reynaud's new power base. It was an extensive territory along the eastern banks of the Dead Sea, defended by the great fortresses of Montreal and Kerak, and controlling the route that connected Syria to Arabia and Egypt. But Reynaud would also become extremely influential in Jerusalem.

Reynaud quickly proved his worth to Baldwin, first by journeying to Constantinople, where he seems to have helped conclude a new treaty between the king and Manuel, and then in battle, in defense of the kingdom. In late 1177 an overconfident Salah al-Din had ventured into the kingdom at the head of a large army, and had started to raid and plunder the coastal plain west of Jerusalem. Reynaud rallied the nobility, liaised with the Templars, and surprised Salah al-Din's forces at a place called Mont Giscard. The battle was a rout. Many Muslims were killed, their baggage train was captured, and the sultan only narrowly escaped. Since the young Baldwin IV's health was clearly failing, forcing him to withdraw from active rule, he appointed his new champion, Reynaud de Châtillon, regent of the Kingdom of Jerusalem. In two short years, Reynaud had gone from forgotten prisoner in a Muslim dungeon to one of the most powerful men in the Levant.

He did not rest on his laurels, but rather prosecuted the war against Islam with an unrelenting fury, and with devastating consequences. Salah al-Din, having recovered from Mont Giscard, repaid Reynaud and the Franks in kind when he defeated them in the Golan in 1179. A truce was agreed to, the first in a series. But Reynaud launched raids into Salah al-Din's territory in violation of the treaties. The most provocative of these was his ambush in 1182 of a pilgrim caravan that was passing far to the south of Kerak on the way to the holy cities of Arabia. The spoils were rich, and the damage to Salah al-Din's prestige as protector of Islam was sullied. It was only a preview, however, of Reynaud's most daring and imaginative campaign. Later that year, he moved on Arabia itself, apparently with the intent of abducting the bones of the Prophet Muhammad.

Reynaud must have been planning the incursion for some time, given the elaborate preparations involved. He purchased probably five to ten ships, and had them sail to Ascalon, where they were disassembled and carried across the Negev Desert to the shore of the Gulf of 'Aqaba by caravan, with the aid of local Bedouin. There they were reassembled and launched—manned, one must conclude, by Arab crews who knew the waters and coastlines of the Red Sea, though with Reynaud and his knights in charge. Reynaud's first conquest was the port of Eilat at the north of the gulf. Next the Franks took the fortress on the Isle of Graye, at the gulf's southern end. Reynaud had cut Syria off from Egypt. For a month and a half his forces raided the shipping and coast of the Red Sea with impunity, while he stayed in Eilat. His ships sacked the port of 'Aydhab on the Egyptian coast, and did not make it to Jidda, Mecca's port, only because they were blown off course. Eventually Reynaud's navy reached Aden, the gateway to the Indian Ocean.

Salah al-Din must have been astonished by the Franks' audacity. They were spreading havoc in what had been to that point an Islamic sea and, as the corridor for the lucrative Indian Ocean trade, a region vital to the wealth of the Muslim world. The sultan hastily dispatched from Egypt the materials with which to assemble a fleet of his own. These were carried by caravan to Suez, where the ships were constructed and launched. After a number of skirmishes at sea, the Franks landed in Arabia and began to march toward Medina. They were intercepted a few miles from their target and, severely outmanned, they were defeated. Those who survived the battle were sent to Mecca, Cairo, and Alexandria, where they were publicly put to death. The pilgrim and diarist Ibn Jubayr was in Alexandria when the captives were paraded into the city on camelback, facing backward to demonstrate their ignominy. By this time Reynaud was back in the Oultrejourdain, plotting his next move.

Reynaud's adventures in the Red Sea achieved no lasting results, and passed all but unnoticed by Latin chroniclers. But for Salah al-Din, who was struggling to impose his authority on a far-flung imperium that included Egypt, Yemen, and Syria, they were a major blow to his standing, and evidence that the problem of Reynaud de Châtillon would have to be addressed.

The sultan responded by striking at Reynaud's headquarters at Kerak, an exceptionally large castle perched on a spur among the craggy hills about twenty miles east of the Dead Sea. Kerak had massive towers, thick walls, a broad stone-paved glacis, and a deep moat. Salah al-Din arrived in November 1183. Reynaud's troops met him outside the walls, but after a short skirmish retreated inside. Salah al-Din did not plan on allowing the fortifications to stand in the way of his revenge, and soon his mangonels and other artillery pieces began to pound the fortress. The siege happened to coincide with the marriage at Kerak of Reynaud's stepson (Stephanie's son by her second marriage), Humphrey of Toron, to Isabella, the eleven-year-old half sister of Baldwin V of Jerusalem. As the former ruler of Oultrejourdain, Stephanie had had previous dealings with Salah al-Din, and there existed a certain degree of respect between them. When she sent a message to inform the sultan of the wedding, he replied that the attack would have to continue, but that he would not bombard the section of the castle where the ceremony was taking place.

Meanwhile, back in Jerusalem Baldwin IV raised a relief force, which he headed up in person. By this time the king was twenty-two years old. As a boy he had been diagnosed with Hansen's disease, or leprosy, the debilitating bacterial infection that attacks the nerve endings, mucous membranes, and skin, causing disfigurement and blindness. In medieval Europe leprosy was seen not only as an illness, but as a mark of God's disfavor. Lepers were shunned, reduced to begging, and were sometimes accused and attacked, much as Jews were, for plotting to spread disease or poison the well water of good Christians. As a king Baldwin may have been above such opprobrium, but he was so weak at this point that he could barely mount a horse. Nevertheless, word of the imminent arrival of the Frankish army prompted Salah al-Din to break off the assault. But he was back again within the year, and with an even larger force, determined to dislodge, if not kill, Reynaud. The second siege began in August 1184 and lasted two months, and the fortress would likely have fallen had not the ever sicker Baldwin IV rallied once more to the rescue of de Châtillon. Losing his sight from leprosy and unable to ride, the king had to be carried on a litter.

The rivalry between Salah al-Din, the *mujahid*, and Reynaud, the Crusader, would soon become deeply personal. The straw that would break the proverbial camel's back—if Reynaud's Red Sea actions were not enough—came in 1186, the same year the sultan sealed a three-year truce with the Kingdom of Jerusalem that gave both sides a much-needed respite. Yet once again, in the season of the pilgrimage and in violation of the treaty, Reynaud swooped down from Kerak and pillaged a hajj caravan en route from Damascus to Mecca. Salah al-Din sent a petition to the new King of Jerusalem, Guy de Lusignan, in complaint. Reynaud was judged by the High Court of the kingdom to have violated the peace and was ordered to return the prisoners and plunder and to pay compensation to the sultan. He refused, and it was upon receiving this news that Salah al-Din swore he would one day personally kill Reynaud.

THE AGE OF THE *MUJAHIDIN*

Despite their mutual enmity, in some respects Salah al-Din and Reynaud de Châtillon were not that different from each other. Both were self-made men prepared to use religion as a means to further their personal ambitions. Salah al-Din's moral sense may have been somewhat more robust than Reynaud's, and he was certainly the subtler thinker of the two. History has also treated him much better, as it customarily does the victors. Whereas Reynaud would go down as a violent brute whose lack of scruples brought the Crusader enterprise to ruin, Salah al-Din became a hero to Muslims—both as a political figure and as a man of religious principle—and the epitome of chivalry and honor to medieval Latin Christians.

Because the warrior aristocracy of East and West shared many of the same values—bravery, loyalty, honesty, generosity—the respect accorded Salah al-Din by Latins was understandable. Nor was it unique. On the death of Nur al-Din, champion of *jihad* and scourge of the Franks, the archbishop and historian William of Tyre was moved to concede that although he had been a "mighty persecutor of the Christian name and faith," he had also been "a just prince, valiant and wise, and according to the traditions of his race, a religious man." But the Latin mania for Salah al-Din was far greater, and would reach its height in the centuries following his recapture of Jerusalem, when the sultan became a protagonist in popular romances and chivalric fables, notwithstanding the great injury most Christians believed he had done to God and their faith. Latin writers even spun tales of Salah al-Din's late-life conversion to Christianity and his supposed romantic encounters with Frankish noblewomen, and introduced fanciful speculations that his mother had been a Christian woman of aristocratic lineage.

In truth, Salah al-Din's origins are quite obscure, another characteristic he shared with Reynaud. The first of his ancestors to arrive on the historical stage were his father, Ayyub, and his uncle, Shirkuh. Members of a Kurdish family living in eastern Anatolia, both found success in the service of the Saljuqs: first 'Imad al-Din Zengi, and then his son, Nur al-Din, who rewarded them with lordships in Syria. When Nur al-Din intervened in the Egyptian civil war of the 1160s, it was Shirkuh whom the sultan sent at the head of his army. This expedition would be of far greater importance than Nur al-Din could have foreseen. Shirkuh eliminated the two rivals for the Fatimid wazirate, fended off the Franks, and took the title of *wazir* of the caliphate in January 1169. When he died two months later, his nephew, Yusuf, barely thirty years of age, succeeded him in that office. What the young commander lacked in experience he made up for with innate talent. Within three years his supremacy in Egypt was unchallenged, and he was confident enough to dissolve the Fatimid Caliphate, thereby accomplishing the goal of the original Saljuq *jihad*.

It soon became evident that Yusuf, who publicly deferred and submitted to Nur al-Din, had become wealthier and more powerful than his lord. In the mind of Nur al-Din, who had completed his father's mission of uniting Syria, Egypt was of secondary importance to the larger endeavor of defeating the Franks and taking control of the 'Abbasid Caliphate. Yet Salah al-Din understood that were he to unite Egypt with Syria, he would end up funding Nur al-Din's march to glory. As the aging Nur al-Din prepared for a push on Latin Jerusalem and for the succession of his realms to his children and kin, Salah al-Din quietly worked at cross-purposes. He did not want to see Jerusalem retaken or the kingdom weakened yet, nor for Nur al-Din to establish a territorial link between Syria and Egypt. The perpetuation of the Frankish occupation of Oultrejourdain, which separated the two lands, was key to Salah al-Din's ambitions.

In 1172, when Nur al-Din ordered Yusuf to attack the castle of Kerak—then under the control of Stephanie de Milly and her first husband, Humphrey III of Toron, with Reynaud still five years from his release from the fortress at Aleppo—and afterward to join him in a two-pronged assault on the Crusader kingdom, Salah al-Din decided that the mission should fail. But he could not show his true intentions to Nur al-Din. Thus, when the defenders of Kerak agreed to surrender in the face of his siege, Salah al-Din suddenly and inexplicably retreated, leaving the castle in Crusader hands and claiming to his lord that he had to return to Cairo to put down a Shi'a rebellion. Nur al-Din was furious. The following year, he ordered a second attack on Kerak. Salah al-Din again laid siege to the castle, but when his agents informed him that Nur al-Din would soon arrive with his own army, he called off the siege and again headed back to Egypt, excusing himself—to his incredulous commander—on the grounds that his father had fallen ill. To Nur al-Din, there was no doubt now of Salah al-Din's deceitfulness. The sultan sent auditors to review the Egyptian financial accounts, and began preparing for an invasion of Egypt, with the goal of deposing his insubordinate commander. But it was not to be. Passing through Damascus, Nur al-Din fell ill, and despite the best efforts of his physicians, he died on May 15, 1174, at age fifty-six.

Salah al-Din had been biding his time for such an opportunity. Nur al-Din's Syrian territories devolved to various members of the Zengi clan, who began to bicker and fight, while his eleven-year-old son and designated successor, Isma'il, was elevated to the throne in Damascus with the help of his father's loyal retainers. Before the year's end, however, Salah al-Din was in Damascus and had declared himself regent. In 1176 he married Nur al-Din's widow, and by 1181 the powerless Isma'il was dead.

In the last decades of his life, Nur al-Din had crafted a self-image as a pious warrior dedicated to the cause of holy war—no longer to be waged on the Fatimids, but on the Franks. He was famous for his rejection of sinful distractions, such as alcohol and music, and this endeared him to the religious class, but not necessarily to his warriors and commanders. And it was largely due to Nur al-Din that Jerusalem became a focus of Islamic consciousness, and that its recovery from the infidels came to be seen as a higher calling. Salah al-Din had undergone his own religious awakening in 1169. Having been criticized for his worldly ways, he very publicly reaffirmed his faith and determined—or so his propagandists told it—to live thereafter a life of strict piety. Salah al-Din's rebirth as a religious warrior marked the beginning of a process that would see him claim that he was the true spiritual and political heir of Nur al-Din.

Among Nur al-Din's kinsmen and dependents, Salah al-Din was not regarded as an heir in any sense, let alone a hero of Islam. To them, he was a disloyal usurper and an upstart who was not a Saljuq, and not even an Arab. For ten years, Salah al-Din would wage constant war against the various Muslim princes of Syria and Anatolia who held out against him. Aleppo, a center of fierce resistance, did not yield until as late as 1183, and only then after Salah al-Din had called on both the Nizaris and the Franks of Antioch for assistance. He failed to take Mosul, but in 1186 its ruler, a cousin of Nur al-Din, agreed to recognize Salah al-Din as his lord.

No less than the Frankish knights of Latin Europe, the Arab and Turkic warriors of the East were proud individualists who did not readily submit to anyone. And like the nobility of Christendom, at bottom their loyalty was first and foremost to themselves, and after that only to their family, their clan, and finally to their ruler (in that order). In their view, a sultan or king was someone they chose to follow, not someone entitled to command them, even though many, in fact, had received grants of land or tax rights from their sultan in exchange for military service. Like the Frankish knights, these warriors also fought for plunder, and were always conscious of the risks in supporting a long campaign or leaving their own lands unattended for any substantial period of time. The commanders they followed were those who they felt would bring them victory and wealth. But victory and the wealth that often came with it were not always welcomed by the commander himself, for once his troops had gotten their fill of plunder, they would abandon the campaign and return home.

Salah al-Din's evolving identity as a *mujahid*, or holy warrior, would hold his imperial project together. By declaring that he served God and Islam rather than his own ambitions, the sultan could claim a moral authority over the Saljuq warlords that he would not have otherwise been able to. He was no longer a parvenu Kurd, but a Muslim Everyman. Similarly to the way that Urban II had harnessed the violence of the Frankish aristocracy by legitimizing it under the banner of religion and under his authority, Salah al-Din presented the war against Crusaders as a religious struggle that took priority over all others, and as a conflict unlike any other the Muslim warrior elite had been engaged in. Salah al-Din saw that he could also use the same principle to rationalize warfare against those Muslim princes who resisted his call to *jihad* and the expansion of his own power.

Salah al-Din's emergence as a holy warrior and a model of piety and nobility was a brilliant public relations coup—one made possible by his force of personality, his shrewdness, and the support he received from family members and followers. His family, notably his brother al-'Adil, took over much of the day-to-day running of his domains, while his bril-

Twelfth-century portrait of Salah al-Din

liant secretary, al-Qadi al-Fadil, organized his chancery. They allowed the sultan to dedicate himself to his campaigns and to appear to rise above the banalities of kingship. At the same time, he patronized religious men, became a copious almsgiver, prayed five times daily, read Scripture, fasted in the holy month of Ramadan, and declared his intention of performing the hajj, though this he continuously postponed due to the demands of the *jihad*. Ostentatiously avoiding the luxuries of the world and sacrificing his own creature comforts, Salah al-Din came to be seen as a living martyr for the cause. His palace was a campaign tent, his crown a helmet, and his pulpit his steed. But for all his apparent simplicity, he also cultivated a reputation for higher learning, and was praised as an expert on Islam and the Traditions of the Prophet. With the possible exception of France's Saint Louis, no other figure in the Middle Ages represented the conjunction of king, warrior, and saint as effectively as Salah al-Din.*

* Louis IX (r. 1226–70) was a tireless Crusader and a fanatical Catholic. Early in his reign he stamped out the Cathar heresy in the southwest of France; at the Siege of Montségur in 1244, two hundred Cathar faithful were burned at the stake. His later Crusades

Al-Qadi al-Fadil, along with 'Imad al-Din al-Isfahani and Baha al-Din ibn Shaddad, two other *qadis* in Salah al-Din's service, wrote biographies that portrayed the sultan as the distillation of Islamic virtue and devotion. So thoroughly did they praise him that even today it is all but impossible for historians to pierce the idealized vision of Salah al-Din the *mujahid*, and understand Yusuf ibn Ayyub the man. And while Salah al-Din's religious reputation may have endeared him to the populace and the *'ulama'*, and helped to inspire his warriors to risk their lives in the name of Islam, this alone was not enough. On the battlefield, it was his comportment as a warrior and skill as a commander that won his subordinates' loyalty and his adversaries' respect.

Salah al-Din personally commanded his troops and rode at the head of his army in battle, leading charges and wading into the melee, sword in hand. No one doubted his bravery or his prowess. His generosity became proverbial, as all the wealth he gained in victory he gave to his followers or as alms. Largesse was the glue of both Latin and Islamic warrior societies, in which personal loyalty and character were paramount, and in which it was not wealth that was idolized but rather the capacity and willingness to share it. Salah al-Din would have understood, much as the Cid had, that with his generosity he was purchasing the loyalty of those who benefited from it. Even more important, it helped him become known, among both Muslims and Christians, as a man of honor. To the same end, he scrupulously kept his word, avoided losing his temper, and never acted impulsively. The trust that he inspired as a result enabled him not only to turn his Muslim rivals into confederates, but to forge the alliances and treaties with Christian princes upon which his success would depend.

Salah al-Din's progression from governor and warrior to *mujahid*, however, carried certain expectations, chiefly that he would wage war against the infidels. But this at first put him in a difficult position, given the political situation in the Near East. Until he had consolidated his rule over Syria, he could not act with confidence against the Franks. The

---

were less successful. The Seventh Crusade, launched against Egypt in 1249, resulted in a total victory for the Muslims and the capture of Louis and his army. The Eighth Crusade, which he launched against Tunis in 1270, was also a debacle; Louis came to a messy and unchivalric end, dying from the dysentery that swept through his camp. He was canonized in 1297.

Zengid princes, Nur al-Din's kinsmen and clients, would take advantage of any sign of weakness, and would not hesitate to align themselves with the Crusaders to preserve their independence. Meanwhile, until 1180, Manuel Komnenos remained the main power broker in the region, and he had sworn to protect the interests of the Kingdom of Jerusalem. And disorganized as it may have been, the Frankish kingdom still had considerable fight in it. Salah al-Din learned this in 1177 at Mont Giscard, and later when the Latins launched incursions into his lands. He had little choice but to make treaties and truces with the Kingdom of Jerusalem, the Principality of Antioch, and the leading Frankish nobles. Caught between his desire for power and the demands he placed upon himself as a self-fashioned religious warrior, al-Malik al-Nasir—"the King, Victorious by God"—as this brilliant and calculating general was also known, bided his time.

CRESCENT OVER CROSS

His moment would come in summer 1187. If the excesses of Reynaud de Châtillon served as catalyst for his conquest, or gave him additional satisfaction after his victory, their personal rivalry was a footnote. The history of the Kingdom of Jerusalem in the last decades of the twelfth century reads like the chronicle of a death foretold.

To a great extent the Crusader kingdom survived after the Second Crusade of 1149 because Nur al-Din and then Salah al-Din faced two major distractions: the resistance from fellow Muslims as they tried to unite Syria, and the cost of keeping their fickle warrior class focused. But whereas the Muslim sultans could not afford a war on two fronts, the Franks could scarcely afford a war on one. They relied on Manuel Komnenos, whose nearly four-decade-long reign constituted the last chapter of Byzantium's glory, to protect them. In the 1160s the emperor mediated an accord among himself, Nur al-Din, and Jerusalem, in which he promised not to attack Nur al-Din on the condition that the sultan not attack Jerusalem. This left each free to pursue his other enemies: Nur al-Din concentrated on fighting his Muslim challengers in Mesopotamia and Anatolia, Byzantium was able to strike back at the Latin powers in Italy and the Balkans, and Jerusalem could make a play for the failing Fatimid Caliphate.

The Latin campaign against Egypt was undertaken by Amalric I of Jerusalem, the brother and successor of Baldwin III, who had died childless in 1163, only two years after his indomitable mother, Melisende. Baldwin III's most important accomplishment had been the conquest in 1153 of the port of Ascalon, the Fatimid fleet's northern base, after which his kingdom's coast was safe from Egyptian attack, and he was able to force the caliphate to pay a regular tribute. Amalric invaded Egypt for the first time in 1163, after the Egyptians had refused to pay their dues, but he withdrew after the Fatimids breached the dikes of the rising Nile and flooded the area where his army was camped.

It was at this point that Nur al-Din sent Shirkuh and his nephew Yusuf to Egypt to put the caliphate in order and to reinforce the position of the new *wazir*, Shawar, and to prevent a Frankish takeover. Shawar, however, sensed that Shirkuh had larger goals, and so he made an alliance with Amalric that led to a second Latin incursion and the establishment of a Frankish protectorate over Egypt. Such a scenario would have been unthinkable fifty years earlier. Latin knights were stationed in Cairo guarding the palace of the caliph, while Amalric's army sparred with Shirkuh's forces. In 1167, with the support of the caliph, al-'Adid, the Franks surrounded Shirkuh and Salah al-Din in Alexandria, blockading the city with the help of the Pisan navy. But Shirkuh slipped away before the city could be taken. The following year, Pisan and Frankish forces raided the coast, the event that prompted Shawar to set fire to al-Fustat as a preemptive defensive measure, and that destroyed the *wazir*'s local support. Consequently, by 1169 the tide had turned against Amalric. Shawar had been killed, Shirkuh had seized the office of *wazir*, and the Egyptian people, both Christians and Muslims, had come to view the Franks as savage barbarians.

With the caliphate on the verge of disintegration and Nur al-Din closing in, Manuel and Amalric saw the necessity of launching a decisive attack on the Fatimids, as the survival of the Frankish kingdom depended on the disunity of Egypt and Muslim Syria. By this time relations between the empire and the kingdom were quite close. Amalric had wed a Byzantine princess, just as his brother had done, and other imperial daughters and nieces were being matched up with members of the native Frankish nobility and with lords in the West. Marriage would not solve the problem of Egypt, though, and Amalric and Manuel prepared for war: the Byzantines would outfit a massive fleet, and the Latins would make up the majority of the forces on land.

Both the Byzantines and the Latins reached the port of Damietta in October 1169. Shirkuh had since died and Salah al-Din had made himself *wazir* and master of Egypt. Al-'Adid, the caliph whom Salah al-Din would soon depose, opened up his treasury to the new *wazir*, enabling the latter to raise an army large enough to contain the Christian forces. Back in Syria, Nur al-Din began raiding deep into the largely undefended Kingdom of Jerusalem, hoping to draw Amalric's attention away from Egypt. As a result Amalric was forced to fall back after about two months, with little to show for his expensive campaign in Egypt and no plunder to share out. It would be the last such invasion by the Kingdom of Jerusalem. Less than a year later, in June 1170, a major earthquake would strike Syria and Palestine, leveling ancient fortresses and city walls that had stood for centuries. It may have been an omen: within two decades the dynasties of Jerusalem, the Komnenoi, and Nur al-Din would all have crumbled as well.

When Amalric I died in 1174 he had the distinction of being only the second King of Jerusalem to produce a male heir, but it soon became apparent that his son, Baldwin IV, was a leper. The fact that the boy would not live long or himself sire an heir set off a flurry of intrigue among the nobility of the kingdom and the foreigners who had married or insinuated their way into the royal court. Baldwin's sister, Sybilla, only a year older than him, became the dynasty's great hope. At sixteen she married the dashing knight William Longsword of Montserrat. He died a year later, but left her pregnant with a son and new heir to the kingdom, whom they would also christen "Baldwin."

Two factions vied to control Baldwin IV and Sybilla, and through them the Kingdom of Jerusalem. One, led by Raymond III of Tripoli, Baldwin's first regent, represented those among the native nobility who remained loyal to the dynasty, which they had conspired to keep weak and vulnerable. There is little doubt, too, that Raymond, the closest male blood relative to the crown, coveted the throne himself. The other faction was headed by Reynaud de Châtillon, Baldwin's second regent and the undeclared leader of the more recent arrivals among the noblemen from the Latin West. The conflict between the two factions erupted at precisely the time that Salah al-Din was conquering Syria. The Latin aristocracy needed to be united, but instead they were mired in an internal struggle that prevented them from perceiving the mortal danger their kingdom was in. As the 1180s wore on, the situation would only get worse.

On March 16, 1185, Baldwin IV died at age twenty-four, leaving his seven-year-old nephew, Baldwin V, as heir. Raymond III of Tripoli was appointed regent. But Baldwin V, a sickly child, died only eighteen months into his reign. This left two contenders for the throne: the half sisters Sybilla and Isabella, the latter the daughter of Amalric by his second wife, the Byzantine princess Maria Komnene. Again the court was divided between the natives and the newcomers, the former favoring Isabella and the latter Sybilla. Sybilla had the stronger claim, but she had taken as her second husband Guy de Lusignan, a French knight who had the support of de Châtillon's party and was loathed by the native nobility. Once again civil war threatened. It was averted only when a compromise was reached: the native nobility would recognize Sybilla as queen if she would annul her marriage with Guy, while Sybilla, for her part, once crowned, would be able to marry whomever she wished. But the compromise was a trick. As soon as she was on the throne Sybilla announced that her new choice of husband was none other than her recently separated Guy de Lusignan.

In 1186 Guy became king-consort of Jerusalem. Few envied him. Byzantium, which had been the guarantor of the kingdom for three decades, was collapsing. Salah al-Din, ruler of Egypt, was completing his conquest of Syria. Within the kingdom, Guy had the support of Reynaud, but they would soon clash. The native nobility continued to make it plain that they favored Isabella, and worked against the new king. The Templars and Hospitallers, who were in theory dedicated to preserving the kingdom irrespective of who was on the throne, were caught up in their political machinations and pursuing their own agendas.

The Military Orders' neutrality was something of a facade. The Templars were allies of de Châtillon, while the Hospitallers cautiously leaned toward Raymond III of Tripoli. Above all, though, their concerns were for their status in Europe, and the Holy Land was of secondary importance for them. Most seriously, the orders had gotten in financial trouble as a consequence of their codependent relationship with Henry II, who was King of England and lord of Scotland, Wales, and Ireland, as well as of most of what is now France. Henry had been diverting taxes and tithes that were due to the Church to the Templars and Hospitallers, reasoning that this money would be used to fund a new Crusade against the infidels, which would be, of course, a religious cause. But his planned Crusade had yet to materialize, and he began pressuring the orders to show concrete results for his investment. In other words, the Templars and the Hospitallers in the Near East were spoiling for a fight. Guy was cautious, as he had already been stung by Salah al-Din. But he was dogged by an episode in 1183 in which he had avoided confronting the sultan in battle. However reasonable from a tactical perspective his decision may have been on that occasion, his enemies and rivals accused him of cowardice, implying that he was not fit to be king. He could not afford to be seen as running away from Salah al-Din again.

The Latin kingdom was protected from attack by Salah al-Din thanks to the truce the two sides had negotiated. Thus Reynaud's attack on the hajj caravan in 1186 was a gift to the sultan. When Reynaud was found guilty by his own peers on the High Court of Jerusalem, and yet refused to render compensation for his illegal raid, Salah al-Din had a legal basis for reprisals against the Kingdom of Jerusalem. Sensing the danger, Raymond of Tripoli and Bohemond of Antioch made separate treaties with Salah al-Din, hoping to save their own territories, while the sultan began gathering his largest army yet, summoning warriors from across Syria, southern Anatolia, and the north of Mesopotamia. Unified and committed, their goals were to reclaim the Holy City, and to push the infidel *Ifranj* into the sea.

To ensure he could not be accused of breaking his truce—which would have been seen as dishonorable and might have made it harder for him to make treaties with Christians in the future—Salah al-Din set a trap. On April 30, 1187, the sultan's son al-Afdal asked Raymond III for permission to traverse Galilee, a region he ruled as lord of Tiberias, with a large reconnaissance force. By the terms of their treaty, Raymond could not say no. The Muslims crossed the region, maintaining discipline and formation, but they were spied by a detachment of ninety Templar knights and a number of Hospitallers, who could not abide such a provocation, and attacked. It was as foolhardy as it was brave—the Franks were massacred, with only three escaping alive. For al-Afdal, it was a notable victory: the Hospitallers' grand master was among the dead. For Salah al-Din, it was the justification he needed. He could now claim that Jerusalem had broken the treaty. The sultan had his war.

In the face of this undeniable danger, the nobility of the Kingdom of Jerusalem finally set their rivalries aside. Raymond of Tripoli and the native aristocracy reconciled with Guy de Lusignan, and the king called up all the knights and nobles of the land, as well as all the able-bodied Latin commoners who could bear arms. The fortresses and cities were emptied of troops, with only skeleton garrisons made up of the very old and very young left behind. The Templars and Hospitallers turned out in force, united in their determination to avenge their dead. Raymond of Tripoli counseled caution; Reynaud de Châtillon and the commanders of the Military Orders counseled aggression. Guy dared not show any sign of hesitation.

On July 1 Salah al-Din's army arrived at the Sea of Galilee, and in short order overran the town of Tiberias, while Eschiva, Raymond's wife, hunkered down in the castle with her knights, who held off the Muslim besiegers. By this point the Christian army was on the march. On July 2 it camped at Zippori, just north of Nazareth and west of Tiberias. His wife's situation and the principles of chivalry notwithstanding, Raymond begged the king not to attempt to aid Eschiva and fall into what he believed was another trap. Instead, he advised fighting Salah al-Din at Zippori, on ground of the Christians' choosing. But Raymond was shouted down by his opponents, and on July 3 the Frankish army advanced.

Crossing the waterless expanse between Zippori and the Sea of Galilee took the Franks the entire day. Weighed down by their armor and sweltering in the summer heat, the Frankish column moved at a turtle's pace. They were harassed by Muslim light cavalry, archers mounted on swift Arabian horses who showered volleys of arrows on the Franks from a distance, requiring the Franks to repeatedly stop and take defensive positions. Their casualties further burdened the knights and slowed their progress. At nightfall, Guy's forces pitched camp by the Horns of Hattin, an extinct volcano overlooking Tiberias and the Sea of Galilee. His thirsty troops, who had had no water since leaving Zippori, saw the glistening sea below and were driven to desperation. Making matters worse, Salah al-Din, camped on the shore, ordered his men to set fire to the brush on the hillside, driving hot smoke and embers up through the already parched Christian camp. Under the cover of night, his army, which outnumbered that of the kingdom by several times, surrounded the Franks.

When dawn broke on July 4, Salah al-Din's troops attacked with archers and cavalry through the hot and stinging smoke, as the fires continued to rage. Rallying a detachment of knights in the chaos, Raymond of Tripoli led a charge against the attackers, and then regrouped and charged again. But on his second pass the Muslims deliberately opened their lines, letting Raymond through, apparently out of respect for his bravery and sense of honor. Once he was through the enemy lines, to turn around would mean certain death. Since it was clear that the Franks would be decisively defeated, the count's knights would be needed to defend the kingdom. So Raymond and his men rode on. They would reach Tripoli, where he would eventually be united with Eschiva, to whom Salah al-Din would grant clemency and safe passage after she had surrendered the castle of Tiberias. Raymond's comrades at Hattin were not so fortunate. Many of the infantry panicked and headed for higher ground, while others broke ranks and rushed headlong downhill toward the inviting waters of the Sea of Galilee. Most were killed or captured on the way. Guy, his noblemen, and the knights of the orders fought valiantly, rallying around the king's standard and his tent as the waves of enemy troops overwhelmed them, each of the Franks fighting until he was dead or utterly exhausted.

For Salah al-Din, Hattin was a total victory. In a single day he had killed or captured almost the entire warrior class of the Kingdom of Jerusalem, including the king himself, and had seized the symbol and the battle standard of the Franks: the relic of the True Cross, upon which Christ himself was said to have been crucified, and which had been borne into battle by the bishop of Acre (another casualty).* As for the survivors, the Templars and Hospitallers were put to death en masse, decapitated by volunteers from among Salah al-Din's followers. Common soldiers and knights were enslaved, and important prisoners were kept either for ransom or to exchange in return for the surrender of the remaining Frankish cities and castles. Salah al-Din killed Reynaud himself, as he had vowed to do. The Kingdom of Jerusalem had been lost.

---

* The relic of the True Cross—Jesus's crucifix—had been venerated since it was fortuitously "discovered" by Constantine the Great's mother, Saint Helena, on a pilgrimage to the Holy Land in the 320s. In the centuries that followed, bits were broken off and distributed across Christendom as relics (where purported pieces can still be found today). The cross was briefly taken by the Sassanid Persians after they conquered Jerusalem in 614; it was restored to the Church of the Holy Sepulchre by the Byzantine emperor Heraclius in 630, where it resided through the Muslim occupation. The forces of the Crusader Kingdom of Jerusalem carried a fragment of the cross when they marched into battle against the Muslims, and it was this that was captured by Salah al-Din, never to be seen again.

Another victorious general might have worried that his warriors, now in possession of spoils beyond their imagining, would head home. But the men under the pious *mujahid* Salah al-Din felt themselves to be involved in a higher cause, and knew their mission would not be complete until the Holy City was returned to Islam. But instead of heading directly from Hattin to Jerusalem, Salah al-Din took a circuitous route, conquering or causing the surrender of the other fortresses and towns of the Latin kingdom. The humiliated Guy was brought along to negotiate with his subjects and to persuade them not to resist. To the vanquished, Salah al-Din consistently showed generosity and grace, allowing many of the surviving Latin noblemen to evacuate, even if they had resisted him. Guy, too, would eventually be released. The common folk, at least those in towns that fought the Muslim army, were not so lucky: they were sent off to the slave markets of Cairo and Damascus or distributed as booty among his men.

Meanwhile, Jerusalem attempted to ready itself for Salah al-Din's arrival. Balian of Ibelin, the senior Latin noble who remained at large, took up the city's defense after the departure of Queen Sybilla, whom Salah al-Din allowed to rejoin the captive Guy. But Balian's task was hopeless. Jerusalem was crowded with the elderly, women, and children; there were only two knights in the city. Nevertheless, when the Muslim army appeared, the city refused to surrender, but ten days later, on September 30, 1187, Salah al-Din's warriors breached the walls. Soon after, the sultan negotiated the end of Latin Jerusalem. As part of the agreement, thousands of Christians were able to redeem themselves from slavery by raising their own ransoms, through the support of Balian. Salah al-Din also freed several thousand as an act of chivalry and largesse. Muslim observers noted with disdain how the Latin patriarch of the city was not so generous, escaping with his cartloads of treasure after having paid only for his own freedom and that of his clergy. Although thousands of Latins were enslaved, in stark contrast to the fall of Jerusalem to the Franks in 1099, there was no massacre, and most refugees reached the coast and left the Near East without being harassed.

Salah al-Din had shown himself yet again to be a man of honor, but there were also practical reasons for his restraint. Taking on too many slaves at one time was not easy: they had to be fed and cared for, at least minimally, and the greater the supply of slaves in a region, the lower the demand for and value of each. By granting the Latins the privilege of ransoming themselves, Salah al-Din was able to turn difficult-to-care-for prisoners into easy-to-manage cash, while appearing to have performed an act of mercy. Beyond these immediate considerations, he understood that the Latin and Muslim worlds were too deeply intertwined to fully disengage, however complete his victory and however sincere his religious convictions. He hoped, for instance, that the Latin merchants of the coast would continue their commerce with Muslim Syria despite the defeat of the Frankish kingdom.

Many Christians responded positively to Salah al-Din's actions, non-Latins most of all. The native Christian clergy of Jerusalem expressed their gratitude for the sultan's defeat and banishment of the Latins; the Byzantine emperor, Isaac Angelos, successor to the now defunct Komnenos dynasty, sent his congratulations to Salah al-Din; and Bohemond III of Antioch pledged to recognize Salah al-Din as the legitimate ruler of the lands he now occupied. And these were many. By the end of 1188, when Salah al-Din demobilized what remained of his army, only Antioch, Tripoli, Tyre, Tortosa, and the Hospitaller castles of Marqab and Krak des Chevaliers remained under Latin rule. The starving garrison at Kerak, Reynaud's former base, had surrendered in late 1188. As for the title King of Jerusalem, it would survive through the Middle Ages, but as little more than a fiction.

THE END OF AN ERA?

The most significant Latin response to Salah al-Din's conquest of Jerusalem was the Third Crusade. In 1189 Richard the Lion-Hearted arrived in the Holy Land, where he famously locked horns with the sultan. Richard outfought the Muslims at Acre (where he executed three thousand unarmed Muslim prisoners) and at Arsuf, but recapturing Jerusalem was beyond his grasp—and his ambition. Instead, he attempted to resolve the "Jerusalem problem" in the other time-honored fashion of the medieval nobility: through a marriage alliance. He proposed to marry his sister, Joan (the widow of William II, the Arabophile king of Sicily), to Salah al-Din's brother, al-'Adil; but since al-'Adil was a Muslim, their union would not receive the recognition of the Church. The Crusading king settled for a treaty with the sultan that allowed Christian pilgrims and traders to visit the city.

This was hardly the stuff of glory, but Richard was more concerned with the plots and conspiracies that surrounded the succession of the title King of Jerusalem than anything else. This contest was little more than an extension of the political game he was playing in the European heartland against his rival and fellow Crusader, King Philip Augustus of France. In the end, the only major conquest Richard made in the region was Cyprus, which he took from the Byzantines and pillaged ruthlessly, before first selling it to the Templars and then granting it to his ally, the former king, Guy de Lusignan.* As for the surviving Crusader nobility, the capture of Guy and the fall of the Holy City only intensified the struggle for power in what remained of the kingdom, and an astonishing series of usurpations, assassinations (including one defenestration), betrayals, and incestuous liaisons ensued as the natives and newcomers continued to fight among themselves, with little or no thought of their supposed enemies, the Muslims.

By the time the Third Crusade had concluded, the recovery of the Holy Land had become an afterthought, or a rationalization for a process of expansion in which Jerusalem held a symbolic value at best. By the beginning of the thirteenth century, controlling Asian and African trade was the true goal of Latin efforts in the East, and the Italian trader states took on an ever greater role. In 1204 the Crusaders would conquer Christian Constantinople and destroy the Byzantine Empire, and thereafter the princes and republics of Latin Europe would turn their violent energies on Egypt and Tunis. These campaigns could be characterized as Crusades only because trade routes and termini they set out to conquer happened to be in Muslim hands. When Tyre, the last mainland possession of the Crusaders, fell to the Egyptian Mamluks in 1291, it may have marked the end of an era, if the era, in the most important senses, had not already ended some time before. As the fourteenth century dawned, though the rhetoric of holy war was still being used as pretext

---

* The depiction of Richard the Lion-Hearted as a successful and honorable Crusader and a patriotic English king is a fantasy dating from the nineteenth century. Richard considered himself French, and rarely visited England. He was an inveterate liar and bully. Returning from the Crusade to the Holy Land, he was captured by one of the many people he had double-crossed and handed over to the Holy Roman Emperor, Henry VI. Richard was freed only when his seventy-year-old mother, Eleanor of Aquitaine, personally interceded for him; and his ransom bankrupted the Kingdom of England.

or motivation, the Christian and Muslim powers of the Mediterranean were even more interdependent than they had been a century earlier.

But this fact is not inconsistent with the history of the Crusades from their outset. The Crusades were, indeed, a religious movement, and there can be no doubt that many who participated in them believed they were doing the Lord's work. Yet to understand the Crusades to the East and the Muslim response as only religious in nature, or to presume that a sense of higher calling defined the policies and ambitions of those who fought in these campaigns, is to ignore the overwhelming weight of evidence that does not square with this vision—evidence that religion and religious identity were at best two of many forces that shaped the history of the Near East and the aspirations of the Christians and Muslims who strived to dominate it.

As for Salah al-Din, his anti-Christian rhetoric had largely served its purpose by the time Richard departed from the Holy Land; when he was faced with the threat of the Third Crusade, he had called on Byzantium to join in a grand and permanent alliance against the Franks. Nor was he bothered by the continuing existence of the Principality of Antioch, once it had sworn him loyalty. Yusuf ibn Ayyub, known as Salah al-Din, "Righteousness of the Faith," and al-Malik al-Nasir, "the King, Victorious by God," and his clan had become the rulers of Egypt, Syria, Palestine, and Arabia, and he himself passed into legend during his own lifetime. And with good reason. He was, among many other things, a man who appeared to have lived by the ideals he professed: when he died on March 3, 1193, his funeral had to be paid for by charity. All his money had gone to alms and gifts. For all the lands he conquered and all the plunder he had taken, he owned no personal property, and his treasury contained only one gold coin and forty silver pieces. Salah al-Din's biographer Ibn Shaddad's recounting of the despair of the sultan's mourners serves as a fitting epitaph for his age:

> Then the years and their players have passed away,
> As though they all had been merely dreams.

Epilogue: The Decline and Fall of the Roman Empire

The fall of the Roman Empire, established by Augustus Caesar in 27 B.C.E., would be no less sudden or dramatic than that of the Kingdom of Jerusalem. It would be conquered less than two decades after the city of Jerusalem, not by Salah al-Din, or the Saljuqs who had overrun Anatolia in the 1070s and 1080s, but rather by the descendants of the Latin Christians who had pledged to liberate the empire from Turkish oppression when they embarked on the First Crusade. And, much as the intemperate ambition of Reynaud de Châtillon had undermined the already weak Frankish realms of the East, the crises leading up to the end of Byzantine Constantinople in 1204 resulted in part from the actions of one man: Andronikos Komnenos, a scion of the imperial family whose thirst for power, like Reynaud's, was untempered by any sense of loyalty or honor.

The Komnenoi rose as a leading military family in the tenth century, and during the upheavals of the eleventh they made their first play for the empire. Isaac Komnenos's coup was successful, but perhaps premature; he ruled only from 1057 to 1059. The dynasty would return to power in 1081 when Isaac's nephew, the general Alexios Komnenos, seized the throne in the aftermath of the Battle of Manzikert and the Saljuq occupation of Anatolia. His reign would be defined by near-constant warfare,

A Byzantine emperor surrounded by dignitaries of his court, from the eleventh-century *Madrid Skylitzes*

as the Saljuqs, Normans, and the pagan Pechenegs and Cumans from the north each attacked imperial lands. It was his empire the first Crusaders arrived to save in 1097. Alexios hung on, and managed to achieve political stability in the empire by appointing members of his extended family to its key offices. He also turned the Latins' expansionist drive to his own advantage, encouraging intermarriage with the leading nobles of the West, and granting trade privileges to the Italian merchants, notably the Venetians.

Alexios reigned for thirty-seven years, and produced a son who was no less politically astute and who would rule for nearly as long. John II, who came to power in 1118, expanded his father's empire, forcing the petty and disunited Christian and Muslim princes of Anatolia and Syria (including the Crusaders) to acknowledge the empire's overlordship. Yet his large family, though it allowed him to integrate the aristocracy of the West into the empire, also created tensions, as power and positions that had previously been reserved for blood relatives had to be shared with outsiders. The Latins at his court began to covet the wealth, power, and standing of the empire. Also troublesome were the generous trade treaties his father had granted Venice. John II attempted to renege on them, but the Italians raided the Byzantine coast until he had no choice but to restore their privileges.

In 1143 John II was succeeded by his son, Manuel, whose rule would represent the high point of Byzantine power in the age of the Crusades. During his reign the papacy was at war with the Holy Roman Empire, the Normans were in crisis, the Fatimids were in decline, the Saljuqs were divided—and his Roman Empire was ascendant. Manuel aspired to restore Constantinople and the empire as the ultimate religious and secular authority for all Christians, especially the Latin principalities of the Holy Land. In his thirty-three years as emperor, however, the destabilizing trends that appeared under his predecessors accelerated. The influence of Latins in the palace became more insidious, and members of the royal clan—those sent to more isolated provinces above all—began to shrug off the emperor's orders or plot among one another. The courtly and military culture of the empire changed. Western ideas of chivalry were introduced to Byzantium, and Manuel updated the army by outfitting his troops with long Western-style shields and having his cavalry trained to fight with long lances, so that they could meet Frankish knights as equals on the field of battle. At the same time, the large and expensive imperial navy, which had been the guarantor of Byzantine supremacy in the East, was allowed to decline as Manuel effectively outsourced its responsibilities to the fleets of Venice and Genoa.

The culmination of these trends can be seen in Manuel's choice of his second wife, Maria of Antioch, the daughter of Constance of Antioch and Raymond of Poitiers. The forty-three-year-old emperor was widowed in 1159, and married the seventeen-year-old Maria two years later. The match was mainly intended to help Manuel dominate Constance's Antioch, but Manuel also grew deeply attached to his beautiful new wife, who bore him a long-awaited son and heir, Alexios, in 1169. Thanks in part to Maria's influence, the Latin element in the palace only expanded, as did the role and privileges that the Venetians enjoyed in Constantinople. Manuel's family, the Orthodox clergy, and the common people of the capital resisted these changes, seeing the Latin ascendancy as a threat— and the empress as its cause.

When Manuel died in 1180, his son Alexios was only eleven, and Maria, who had for appearances' sake taken the vows of a nun, but who began a scandalously open affair with one of her deceased husband's nephews, became the regent and effective ruler of the empire. Tensions in the imperial court mounted. Maria's stepdaughter (by Manuel's first marriage) and her Latin husband, Renier of Montferrat, staged a revolt that found significant support among the populace, but Alexios and Maria arranged for a truce, and summoned Manuel's cousin, Andronikos, to Constantinople, hoping that he would be a source of order. He would be anything but.

At sixty years of age, Andronikos Komnenos was infamous for scandal and betrayal. His career as a soldier started dashingly when he was taken captive by the Saljuqs at age twenty-three. He was ransomed, and returned to court a year later. Manuel showered him with favor; the two were the same age and had been raised almost as brothers, and early in the emperor's reign they had fought side by side in a campaign against the Sultanate of Rum. But Andronikos (who was already married) started an open and public affair with one of his own nieces, Eudoxia, to the humiliation of her family. After her brothers attempted to kill Andronikos in 1152, Manuel sent him out of the capital, giving him a military command in Cilicia, where he was ordered to suppress the uprising of T'oros II. But instead of attacking the insurgents, "he devoted himself to indolence and sports in his tent," until the Armenian king overcame his fears and defeated the Byzantine force.

Manuel was so attached to Andronikos that he welcomed him back to the capital despite the defeat. The emperor next stationed him on the Hungarian frontier. Here, Andronikos, unaware that Manuel's agents were monitoring his correspondence, hatched a plot with King Géza II of Hungary and Manuel's rival, the Holy Roman Emperor, Frederick I, to overthrow his cousin. Manuel was still reluctant to punish Andronikos, but in 1155 he had him cast into prison. Three years later Andronikos escaped, and eventually threw himself on the emperor's mercy.* Charismatic and brave, he was forgiven. Manuel saw that he could be an asset, even if he could never be trusted. As the contemporary chronicler Niketas Choniates, who had no love of the upstart prince, wrote about Andronikos's imprisonment:

---

* Andronikos dug a tunnel out of the prison, concealing its entrance so well that when his wife was arrested and held as a hostage in the same cell, he was able to sneak back inside at will. His son, John, was conceived in the prison during one of his clandestine conjugal visits.

no less a cause was his constant outspokenness and the fact that he excelled most men in bodily strength; his perfect physique was worthy of empire, and his pride was not to be humbled. All these things generate suspicion and provocation deep in the hearts of rulers because of the fear that surrounds the throne. For these attributes as well as his cleverness in battle and the nobility of his birth . . . Andronikos was viewed with a jaundiced eye and was greatly distrusted.

When Andronikos employed Armenian soldiers in two unsuccessful attempts on the emperor's life, Manuel reluctantly cast his cousin into prison again, but out of mercy or affection did not blind him or cut off his nose, the customary punishment for would-be usurpers. Andronikos was confined for five years, until in 1164 he escaped. Sneaking out of the capital disguised as a slave, he was caught on the eastern frontier of the empire, more than six hundred miles to the east, but slipped away from his captors, eventually finding refuge in Galicia (modern western Ukraine). He worked his way back into his cousin's good graces by raising an army to assist in the campaign against the Kingdom of Hungary.

In 1166 he was rewarded by an appointment to Armenian Cilicia to serve as the emperor's representative; but once more, Andronikos, "the king of the dandies," neglected his duties and immersed himself in a life of luxury. More seriously, he so angered T'oros (by allegedly arranging the assassination of his brother) that the Armenian king had his troops massacre the local Greek garrisons. Andronikos was rather more successful in his sexual conquests. On a visit to Antioch, he encountered the seventeen-year-old Philippa, the sister of Manuel's wife, Maria, and Prince Bohemond III, and a young lady of extraordinary beauty. To the emperor's incredulity, Andronikos began an affair with his in-law, and when Manuel demanded that he return to the capital, Andronikos instead abandoned his disgraced young lover and headed south to Jerusalem, taking the treasuries of Cilicia and Cyprus with him.*

In the Holy City he impressed King Amalric, who accepted him into his service and appointed him lord of Beirut. But here, too, he continued in his lascivious ways, "like a horse in heat covering mare after mare beyond reason." On a visit to Acre, he fell in love with its ruler, his

---

* Philippa eventually recovered, and was married off to Humphrey II of Toron, a high-ranking member of the nobility of the Kingdom of Jerusalem.

kinswoman, Theodora Komnene, a niece of the emperor Manuel and the widowed queen of Baldwin III of Jerusalem. The twenty-one-year-old dowager soon moved to Beirut, where she and Andronikos lived brazenly in "an unlawful and unholy love." Manuel, who could no longer tolerate his cousin's outrageous behavior, sent a message to Baldwin IV, ordering him to arrest Andronikos, gouge his eyes, and return him to Constantinople. Theodora, however, got wind of the plans, and she and Andronikos fled east, the only direction in which they could not be pursued. They stayed for a time in Damascus at the court of Nur al-Din (who must have delighted in Manuel's humiliation) before traveling to Baghdad, and then to the Sultanate of Rum, whose ruler, Qilij Arslan II, had recently inflicted a major military defeat on Manuel. An outlaw and excommunicate among his own people and Church, Andronikos was given a castle at Ünye on the Black Sea coast by Qilij Arslan, and from there he raided Byzantine territory, carrying off prisoners and loot on behalf of his Saljuq lord.

After Manuel died in 1180, the dowager empress Maria took power, and the empire started its downward spiral. The aristocracy and the provincial bureaucracies, unrestrained by a strong emperor, began to institute oppressive policies, the frontiers were no longer secure, the imperial navy had been disbanded, and the distant provinces were breaking away. It was a perfect moment for Andronikos to return. Capitalizing on popular discontent with Maria, he arrived in the capital to a hero's welcome.

Andronikos lost no time in eliminating his rivals. He poisoned Manuel's daughter, Maria Komnene, and her husband, Renier, and had the empress Maria herself arrested and then strangled on charges of treason.* (Andronikos forced her son, Alexios, to sign the death warrant.)

---

* Renier de Montferrat was a younger brother of William Longsword, the husband of Queen Sybilla of Jerusalem and the father of Baldwin V. The Montferrat family was perhaps the most successful of the Latin noble clans who attempted to marry their way into power in the Eastern Mediterranean. Renier had been named a "Caesar" (a sort of deputy emperor) by Manuel, and might have come to power in Constantinople had he not been assassinated by Andronikos. Another brother, Conrad, organized the defense of Tyre after Salah al-Din's victory at Hattin, and refused to recognize Guy de Lusignan's claim to the throne. Conrad married Sybilla's half sister, Isabella, and on this basis claimed the throne of Jerusalem in 1192. But two days after his title had been ratified by the nobility of the kingdom, he was murdered by two Assassins (probably working on the orders of Richard the Lion-Hearted). A fourth brother, Boniface, was one of the leaders of the Fourth Crusade. After the conquest of Constantinople in 1204, he al-

Andronikos Komnenos seizes power, from Boccaccio's *On the Fates of Famous Men*, fourteenth century

Next, Andronikos had himself appointed co-emperor, and shortly after ordered Alexios deposed, and strangled like his mother. Within a year of his arrival, Andronikos was crowned in all pomp and ceremony at the great church of Hagia Sophia. He took Alexios's betrothed, the thirteen-year-old French princess Agnes (the daughter of Louis VII), as his wife.

Initially, Emperor Andronikos was greeted with enthusiasm by the populace, who saw the regime change as an opportunity to take out their frustration on the Latins in the capital. Thousands, mostly Venetians, were murdered with Andronikos's tacit complicity, a crime the people of Venice would neither forgive nor forget. He enacted popular and much-needed measures, reforming tax collecting practices and overhauling the

---

most succeeded in being elected emperor; after that failed, he staked out his own independent Kingdom of Thessalonika, in what is now northeastern Greece. It lasted until 1224, when it was conquered by the Despotate of Epirus, to the west.

corrupt imperial bureaucracy. Rebellious governors were brought to heel, and those who resisted were subjected to brutal reprisals.

But the aristocracy and imperial officials turned against Andronikos, whose capricious and cruel punishments of anyone who dared criticize him also caused the people of Constantinople to become disillusioned. In 1185 William II of Sicily launched an invasion of the empire in support of the claims of a nephew of Manuel. The invasion was a failure, but the Sicilians sacked Thessalonika, putting the lie to Andronikos's supposed invincibility and emboldening his enemies. In response, the emperor spiraled into violent paranoia, ordering the mass arrest and execution of those aristocrats he suspected had opposed him.

One of these individuals, a distant cousin named Isaac Angelos, who enjoyed broad support among the nobility, struck dead the official sent to arrest him and then took refuge in Hagia Sophia. As word of Isaac's act of resistance spread through Constantinople, throngs gathered outside the church, and Isaac was acclaimed emperor by the common people. Andronikos, shocked, tried to escape the city by boat, but was apprehended. Brought before the new emperor in shackles, he was beaten, his hair shaved and beard torn out in humiliation. His right hand, with which he had signed so many execution orders, was hacked off. The next morning he was turned over to the crowds, who tortured and abused him for several days. Finally, he was dragged to the Hippodrome, where he was hung upside down. Two Frankish knights were allowed to finish him off in revenge for the massacre of the Latins; the two competed, each taking turns to see who could run his sword deeper into the body of the once-emperor. His corpse was never buried, but left to rot in the open for all to see. On September 12, 1185, at the age of sixty-seven, Andronikos had met his end, and with him went the Komnenos dynasty of Constantinople.

But the rise of Isaac Angelos brought no respite to the empire. Still riven by intrigue, it now became the target of the Frankish nobility. As the Third Crusade was coming together, Isaac began to negotiate an alliance with Salah al-Din himself. When the Latins learned of this, it only reinforced their conviction that the Byzantines were disloyal and traitorous schismatics.

Meanwhile, Isaac Angelos was overthrown in 1195 by his own brother, who ruled as Alexios III. The new emperor had Isaac blinded and imprisoned together with his son and heir, also named Alexios. But

Thirteenth-century mosaic of Frankish soldiers of the Fourth
Crusade, Church of San Giovanni Evangelista, Ravenna

the young Alexios escaped, and in 1202, as Latin forces were gathering in
Venice to launch the Fourth Crusade, he appeared before them. He presented the Crusade's leaders, who were already hopelessly in debt to their
Venetian partners, with an offer: restore him and his father to their rightful place and he would reward them with riches and submit the Greek
Church to the authority of the papacy. The pope, Innocent III, the Venetians, and the Latin leadership eagerly accepted, and when the Crusader
fleet weighed anchor, it sailed not for the Holy Land or Egypt, but for
Constantinople. Only a few knew of the plan; the knights and soldiers of
the Crusade still believed they were going to liberate Jerusalem. They dis-
embarked at Constantinople, and after a brief siege the Latins reinstalled
the blind Isaac on the throne, alongside his son, now crowned as Alexios IV. Yet it became clear that the huge sums the young prince had
promised the Crusaders were beyond his means, and that the people
of the capital would never consent to pay the hated Latins. Their resistance turned to violence, and they expelled the Crusaders. After another
siege, the city fell on April 13, 1204, by which time Alexios IV had been
murdered by rebels within his palace, and the aged and addled Isaac
had dropped dead from shock.

The Latins and their Venetian allies swept through the city, looting
churches, palaces, and homes, and killing indiscriminately, as massive
fires raged through the city and destroyed whole neighborhoods. Thousands of saintly relics were stolen, to be distributed to churches across
the Latin West, while the fixtures and furnishings of important buildings were packed up, lock and stock, by the Venetians and shipped home,

where they decorate St. Mark's Square to the present day. The empire was partitioned between the Venetians and the Latins, who together appointed a Frankish nobleman, Count Baldwin IX of Flanders, to serve as the figurehead for the little that remained of the once mighty Roman Empire, and which now amounted only to the territory around Constantinople and most of what is now Greece.* But this new "Empire of Romania" would be a short-lived experiment. In 1261 the Latins would be defeated, and a Greek Byzantine Empire based at Constantinople would reappear and limp on, moribund, until its conquest by the Ottoman Turks in 1453. But this was no longer even a shadow of the sprawling empire founded by Augustus a quarter century before the birth of Christ, or the splenderous luxury of twelfth-century Komnenoi.

The twelve hundred years of the Roman Empire, which had seen wars with Persia, the onslaught of barbarians, and the aggression of Muslim Arabs and Turks, were brought to an end not by infidels but by fellow Christians. Its demise resulted from the same forces that had brought the Komnenoi, not to mention the Saljuqs and Fatimids, to power, and the Crusader states into being. Indeed, if there was one unqualified loser in the contests of the period, it was not the Franks or the Muslims, but Byzantium, the one political entity that did not come to rely on the rhetoric of religious conflict for its political legitimacy, and that had relatively little interest in the Holy Land. Just as the First Crusade was a by-product of aggression among Christians, the early Crusades came to a close with the conquest by Christians of the greatest Christian empire in history. Perhaps, as Alexios I Komnenos evidently suspected in 1096, when the Crusading Frankish armies were massing outside the walls of Constantinople, this had been the intention from the start.

---

* In 1204 the Venetian and Latin conquerors only managed to take control of the part of the empire around the capital, and four other successor states sprang up. Boniface of Montferrat, an unsuccessful candidate for the title of emperor, set up an independent Kingdom of Thessalonika to the west; Mikhael Doukas, a cousin of Isaac II, set up the Despotate of Epirus on the Adriatic coast; and Alexios Megas Komnenos (the grandson of Andronikos) established an Empire of Trebizond on the southeastern coast of the Black Sea. Theodoros Laskaris, a son-in-law of Alexios III, also claimed the imperial title; he founded an empire based at Nicaea, and went to war against the Latins. In 1261 Mikhael VIII Paleologos, co-emperor in Nicaea, conquered Constantinople and reestablished the Byzantine Empire.

Afterword: Holy War, a User's Manual

Christianity, Islam, and Judaism are each scriptural, monotheistic religions that profess to worship the same God, "the God of Abraham." Yet each presumes that it alone embodies the true message of God, and regards the others, on the level of doctrine, at best as mistaken and at worst as threats. Because of this, and because each enjoins believers not only to follow God's commands in their own lives, but to attempt to change the larger world according to these commands, each of the three religions calls on its adherents to convert members of the other faiths—or at least to oblige them to acknowledge the superiority of their own—and to prevent the conversion of their coreligionists. As a result, from a theological perspective the members of the Abrahamic religions saw themselves locked in an unceasing struggle against the rival faiths. This struggle took the form at times of debate, at other times of polemic, and in the worst times of violence. The stakes were high: not only did one's personal salvation depend on obeying God's will, but to fail to bring infidels into the fold, to allow them to persist in their error or to defy the divine law, constituted an offense to God and a neglect of one's duty to provide unbelievers an avenue to salvation. To contest, undermine, or attempt to destroy another Abrahamic faith could, therefore, be seen as an act of virtue. By the same token, contact with the infidel, whether on the level of state politics—that is, through treaties, alliances, or trade agreements—or on the personal level, was, in religious terms, dangerous and immoral.

Because nearly every inhabitant of the Mediterranean region—Latin Europe, Byzantium, Islamic North Africa, the Near East—was a member of one of the three Abrahamic faiths, they were all implicated in this struggle, at least in principle. The societies of the Mediterranean world were organized around religious identity, and religious authorities legislated and enforced laws. There were rules regarding the clothes one could wear, the food one could eat, when one could work, whom one could work for and do business with, and what kind of business one could engage in. Religion determined the festivals one celebrated, whom one could marry or have sex with, and what taxes and other obligations one bore. It was the source of one's community, and defined one's culture and social relations. Religious authorities, beyond their roles as ministers to their congregations and leaders within their communities, could also steer state policies, and subvert the authority and legitimacy of rulers who strayed from or defied God's will.

This is to say that religion in the Middle Ages was not synonymous merely with theology, or with belief. It was a powerful force that could shape one's entire life. Indeed, the overwhelming majority of people belonged to a particular religion for the simple reason that they were born into it. And leaving one's religion was no simple matter. Each of the three major religions defined apostasy (not to mention atheism) as a crime punishable by death; and, even in those cases where conversion was possible, the consequences were daunting. Conversion was seen as a form of betrayal, and typically carried a high cost: the loss of one's family and friends, right to inherit, cultural moorings, and economic partnerships. Converts, moreover, were eyed with suspicion by their new coreligionists.

What is often forgotten about the Middle Ages, and the era of Crusade and *jihad* above all, is that practice often diverges from principle. Because religion was largely a social, cultural, and political phenomenon, and because most people had little choice about their religious identity, many did not believe strongly in, know about, or even care about the finer theological details of their own faith. In the Mediterranean societies of the time, religion may have been as omnipresent as the air people breathed, but we tend not to spend much time thinking about air, unless it becomes polluted and harmful, at which point it becomes an urgent concern. Only when the religious liberties extended to infidels seemed to contaminate the integrity of the majority faith did people take notice. For the most part, though, in the day-to-day life of an ordinary person in the Middle Ages, religious consciousness tended to fade into the background. Even the rituals and rites that marked the seasons could take on an unconscious and rote quality.

Religion was only one aspect of one's identity, after all. Individuals were also defined by their gender, class, profession, tribal or family connections, physical appearance (such as skin color), philosophical orientation, and local, national, ethnic, and cultural affiliations—as well as the languages they spoke, the music they listened to, their commercial and political relationships, their friendships, and the diversions they enjoyed. Each individual belonged to a variety of formal and informal communities simultaneously, and the boundaries of these communities often crossed religious and ethnic lines. A Latin Christian who was a nobleman and a warrior would move in Christian circles, but also in circles that included Muslims and Jews, who may have been fellow soldiers, aristocrats, chess players, or poets. A Muslim might have more in common with Christians and Jews who worked in the same trade, or came from the same city, than with a foreign Muslim or one in a different profession. People in the Middle Ages were not the two-dimensional caricatures they have frequently been imagined to be. Rather, they were complex individuals living in diverse societies, who pursued numerous and ever shifting ambitions (material wealth, social prestige, religious salvation, sexual satisfaction, and so on). And no less than people today, they were able to rationalize and reconcile aspects of their lives that might appear to be contradictory or immoral.

Thus Isma'il ibn Naghrilla, a man who styled himself the Jewish Messiah, and who was hailed as the greatest rabbi of his time, could squeeze tax revenues from his coreligionists in the service of a Muslim king and spend drunken nights writing sensuous odes in Arabic to smooth-cheeked slave boys, without suffering an existential crisis. Crusaders and *mujahidin*—the Cid, Reynaud de Châtillon, Andronikos Komnenos, or the legions of anonymous Muslim soldiers who served under Christian and Jewish commanders—could ride alongside one another into battle against their own kind and share the intimate and visceral camaraderie of blood and steel, even as they staked their glory and their salvation on their piety and their service to God. A Christian king such as Roger II could present himself as an amir and sultan, and surround himself with crypto Muslim courtiers and commanders while dreaming of becoming king of Muslim "Africa." And a near-divine caliph like the Fatimid imam, al-Hafiz, could debase himself in public at the funeral of a disgraced, infidel prime minister.

The Romans in the centuries leading up to and following the birth of Jesus were the last group powerful enough to dominate the Mediterranean. Those who aspired to their achievement, whether Germanic "barbarians," Arabs, Greeks, Berbers, Franks, Normans, or Saljuqs, did not have the strength of numbers to transform the societies they conquered by force. Conquest was carried out as much by negotiation as by battle, and the threat of violence was employed as often as violence itself. Conquerors depended, instead, on the collaboration and consent of the peoples they came to rule. In Fatimid Egypt the administration remained largely in the hands of native Christians, while Jews figured prominently in key economic niches, notably the long-distance luxury trade. In Norman Sicily, Greek and Muslim functionaries were indispensable, while in Christian and Muslim Spain, Jews served as tax collectors and prime ministers. Across the region, from west to east, mercenaries and seekers of fortune—Arabs, Berbers, Turks, Franks, Normans, sub-Saharan Africans, and Armenians—sought employment with whoever would hire them. The Cid, Bahram Pahlavuni, Bohemond of Taranto, Reynaud de Châtillon, and Andronikos Komnenos were extraordinary only in terms of the notoriety they achieved. There were countless others like them, men who were prepared to do battle under the banners of infidel armies and betray those of their own faith for a greater share of plunder and glory, and women, like Constance of Antioch, Empress Maria, Melisende of Jerusalem, Sitt al-Mulk, and the calipha Rasad, who ruthlessly pursued their own agendas with no greater regard to higher ideals.

Astute rulers found that cultivating and protecting minority communities worked to their benefit in myriad other ways, too. They elevated infidels to powerful positions because they could be easily disposed of, and made ready scapegoats when it was necessary to implement unpopular policies. Often more important was that infidel communities provided a counterbalance to a ruler's coreligionists. The same sort of pragmatism fostered collaborative relations between kingdoms that should have been, according to the principles of their religions, deeply opposed. For the Crusader states in the East, alliances with nonbelievers became indispensable for their survival. Antioch persisted thanks only to its links with Aleppo, the Kingdom of Jerusalem's fate was tied to that of its ally Damascus, and the Templars and Hospitallers formed relationships with the Assassins.

The problems coexistence posed to theology were solved by the "majority" groups' (even though in many cases they were a numerical minority of the kingdom's subjects) granting of legal and religious legitimacy to subject communities. Hence in the Islamic world Jews and Christians were qualified formally as "People of the Book" and *dhimmis*, while in Christian lands Muslims and Jews were seen as "special" or "protected" subjects of the kings. The official attitude in both majority Muslim and majority Christian societies was that the religious minorities among them were wrong, but meant well—they were not evil, but merely mistaken. Neither Christian nor Islamic theology called for the forced conversion or the indiscriminate killing of nonbelievers. Rather, each saw every individual as a creature of God and therefore as possessing the capacity to be saved. And for this to happen, he or she needed the opportunity to come freely and willingly to the true faith.

Yet as integrated and cosmopolitan as these societies may have appeared, they were built on relationships of power in which the threat of violence was ever present. When members of different communities found themselves pitted against one another, whether for royal favor, political influence, or wealth, members of the majority could quickly turn against their minority neighbors, portraying them as hubristic, if not subversive and disloyal. These antagonisms were enthusiastically abetted by both pious ideologues and opportunists, who justified the repression and marginalization of unbelievers with Scripture and religious law. But even the most reactionary among the religious elites, whether monks, mullahs, or rabbis, frequently found themselves embroiled in dubious and ambiguous interfaith relationships in pursuit of their personal goals. In general, they were nearly as willing to bend the principles of their faith in order to protect their own position as anyone else.

What then of Crusade and *jihad*? They were, in most respects, outgrowths of the dominant forces shaping the medieval Mediterranean. With a crisis looming—economic collapse, political unrest, foreign invasion—or merely when enemy or rival kingdoms happened to identify with a different faith or denomination, the language of holy war was eagerly deployed.

These were violent times. Warfare, raiding, piracy, civil war, enslavement, and gruesome capital justice were part of people's daily lives. Generals, noblemen, and even kings were expected to risk life and limb in the heat of battle, leading the charge into enemy arrows and lances. For rulers, their deputies, and bureaucrats at home, the rewards of a successful war were immense, but the price of failure was usually no less dramatic. For commoners or officials, falling afoul of a capricious ruler could mean destitution or execution. One's entire community could easily be made to pay the price for a general's or an official's alleged disloyalty. A voyage by ship or land could end with enslavement and exile. Civil wars were common. An enemy siege would bring starvation and disease at best, and rape, enslavement, and massacre at worst. And when social, economic, or political tensions were perceived in religious terms—as in the case of the Jews of Granada after the death of Yusuf ibn Naghrilla or the Armenians in Egypt after Bahram Pahlavuni's reign—outbursts of repression or violence aimed at minority communities frequently ensued.

Such cataclysms were often sudden and catastrophic, but also rare. But even more rare were those formal military actions that can be truly described as "religious wars." Even the First Crusade and the initial Almoravid and Almohad incursions into al-Andalus had very worldly aims; as a rule, the various campaigns of conquest that took place across the Mediterranean in the eleventh and twelfth centuries were clearly prosaic in nature: their goals were territory, resources, and the expansion of trade. Religious difference provided a justification for a war, endowing it with greater meaning for its participants and bolstering their morale, but it was rarely, if ever, a *cause* of war. Eastern Christians, Latins, and Muslims were constantly in conflict with one other, and against their coreligionists. War was one way the ruling clans and cliques of the Middle Ages competed, and the wars that were fought between rival religious groups tended to be no more bloody than those between kingdoms of the same faith. Massacres, atrocities, looting, rape, and reprisals against civilians were commonplace. The Franks may have eaten their vanquished Muslim enemies at Ma'arat al-Nu'man, but there were earlier stories of their cannibalism of Christians as well as Muslims.

In fact—apart from the apparently single-minded focus on the capture of Jerusalem, a city of no great political or economic significance at the time—even the First Crusade, which appears so revolutionary in the European perspective, fits easily into the patterns of the medieval Mediterranean world. The Franks, for all their piety and rhetoric, were not so different from the Almoravids, the Normans, the Armenians, or the Saljuqs. Even before the Holy City had been taken and cleansed of its infidel inhabitants, the Crusaders were already starting to assimilate into the diverse East. They were allying with local Muslims, betraying fellow Christians, and grudgingly accepting infidels as subjects. And as unlikely as it may sound in view of the importance typically accorded to this moment, it is likely that even if Urban II had not made his speech at Clermont in 1095, the Crusades would have happened, given the forces that were transforming Latin Europe at the end of the eleventh century: the rising numbers of noblemen's sons in pursuit of fortune and glory; the arrival of delicacies from North Africa, the East, and beyond; and the emergence of the Italian trading republics, to name only a few. Latin and Byzantine Christendom had been on a collision course since the fifth century. The Crusades became the framework for this clash, and the threat of Islam, its pretext.

Nor did the Crusades cause a rupture between the Christian and Islamic worlds. On the contrary, the political interdependency that developed in the twelfth century only intensified in the aftermath of the fall of Jerusalem and Constantinople. Later wars fought among Franks, Italians, Byzantines, and Turks were a result of the engagement of Christendom with the *dar al-Islam*, and more specifically, of the Latin West's exposure to and thirst for the wealth and sophistication of the Greek and Islamic worlds. It may be true that over the five hundred years following the fall of Constantinople in 1204, Christian and Muslim kingdoms continued to battle against one another for territory, and to rely on the rhetoric of holy war, but warfare between Christian powers and between Muslim powers also intensified, and the language of religious difference and illegitimacy was increasingly used to justify conflicts within each of these faith communities.

The traditions of diplomacy and interreligious alliance that originated in the eleventh century would similarly intensify, as a result of the increasing economic interdependence of Christian and Muslim states. The peoples of the Mediterranean adopted elements of one another's style of dress, cuisine, art, and architecture more than ever before. They shared and borrowed ideas, technologies, and techniques, fueling a tremendous wave of innovation—agricultural, medical, navigational, mathematical, philosophical, theological, literary, and technological. Meanwhile, the collaborations and disputes among theologians, philosophers, and mystics of the three faiths transformed each, and laid the intellectual foundation for the European Renaissance, European Judaism, and Islamic modernity. Indeed, the ethnic and religious diversity of the Mediterranean in the era of Crusade and *jihad* was perhaps the factor that most directly prefigured the emergence of our modern globalized world, one in which the Europe of Latin Christendom, once an underdeveloped, barbarian fringe, would rise centuries later to uncontested dominance.

What can we learn from the history of the Crusaders and *mujahidin* who fought alongside unbelievers and against their own people? Of the kings and caliphs who staffed their administrations with heretics and infidels? And of the opportunists who cloaked their avarice and ambition in piety? Perhaps what they tell us is that for all its inherent chauvinism, righteousness, and moral certitude, we cannot blame religion for the violence of the past. The struggles and conflicts of the golden age of Crusade and *jihad*, the period from the mid-eleventh to the late twelfth centuries, were first and foremost struggles between individuals and between clans that did not act as representatives of theological principles, but rather pursued personal and earthly agendas. At times religious ideology may have provided a firm and convincing basis for their actions, a sense of higher purpose for their ambitions, or a moral justification for their violence, but it was neither a prerequisite nor a cause. This most violent of eras, if we look close enough, turns out to give us reason for hope. It shows, perhaps, that conflict among different peoples is not inevitable, as long as we are willing to make compromises as individuals and communities, and to regard one another as fundamentally well-intentioned, and as sharing the same basic goals.

Dynasty Trees

THE ZIRIDS OF GRANADA

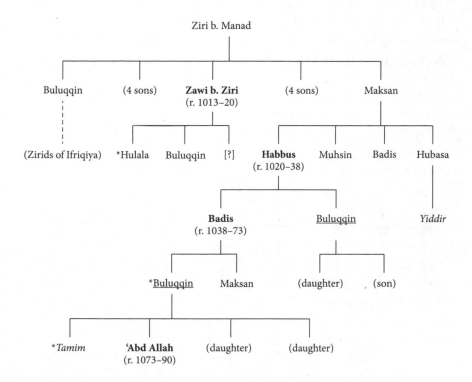

Names of Rulers of Granada appear in boldface.

Names of rebels are italicized.

<u>Underscored names are those of assassinated members of the dynasty.</u>

*Asterisks indicate heirs designate.

EASTERN CHRISTIAN RULERS IN THE AGE OF THE CRUSADES

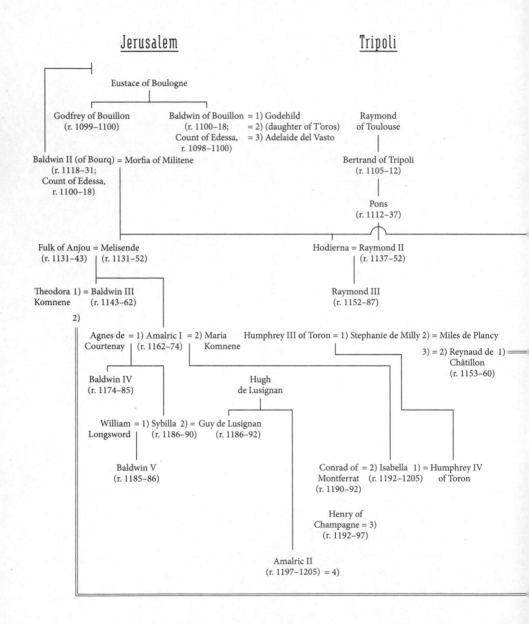

Jerusalem   Tripoli

Eustace of Boulogne

Godfrey of Bouillon
(r. 1099–1100)

Baldwin of Bouillon = 1) Godehild
(r. 1100–18;   = 2) (daughter of T'oros)
Count of Edessa,   = 3) Adelaide del Vasto
r. 1098–1100)

Raymond
of Toulouse

Baldwin II (of Bourq) = Morfia of Militene
(r. 1118–31;
Count of Edessa,
r. 1100–18)

Bertrand of Tripoli
(r. 1105–12)

Pons
(r. 1112–37)

Fulk of Anjou = Melisende
(r. 1131–43) | (r. 1131–52)

Hodierna = Raymond II
| (r. 1137–52)

Theodora 1) = Baldwin III
Komnene   (r. 1143–62)

   2)

Raymond III
(r. 1152–87)

Agnes de = 1) Amalric I = 2) Maria   Humphrey III of Toron = 1) Stephanie de Milly 2) = Miles de Plancy
Courtenay | (r. 1162–74) | Komnene

3) = 2) Reynaud de 1) =
Châtillon
(r. 1153–60)

Baldwin IV
(r. 1174–85)

Hugh
de Lusignan

William = 1) Sybilla 2) = Guy de Lusignan
Longsword | (r. 1186–90)   (r. 1186–92)

Baldwin V
(r. 1185–86)

Conrad of = 2) Isabella 1) = Humphrey IV
Montferrat   (r. 1192–1205)   of Toron
(r. 1190–92)

Henry of
Champagne = 3)
(r. 1192–97)

Amalric II
(r. 1197–1205) = 4)

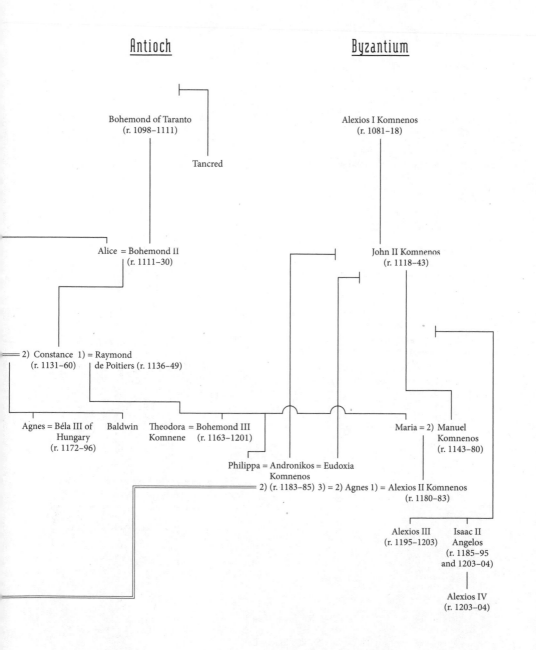

Antioch

Byzantium

Bohemond of Taranto
(r. 1098–1111)

Alexios I Komnenos
(r. 1081–18)

Tancred

Alice = Bohemond II
(r. 1111–30)

John II Komnenos
(r. 1118–43)

2) Constance 1) = Raymond
(r. 1131–60)   de Poitiers (r. 1136–49)

Agnes = Béla III of   Baldwin   Theodora = Bohemond III   Maria = 2) Manuel
Hungary   Komnene   (r. 1163–1201)   Komnenos
(r. 1172–96)   (r. 1143–80)

Philippa = Andronikos = Eudoxia
Komnenos
2) (r. 1183–85) 3) = 2) Agnes 1) = Alexios II Komnenos
(r. 1180–83)

Alexios III   Isaac II
(r. 1195–1203)   Angelos
                   (r. 1185–95
                   and 1203–04)

Alexios IV
(r. 1203–04)

FATIMID RULERS

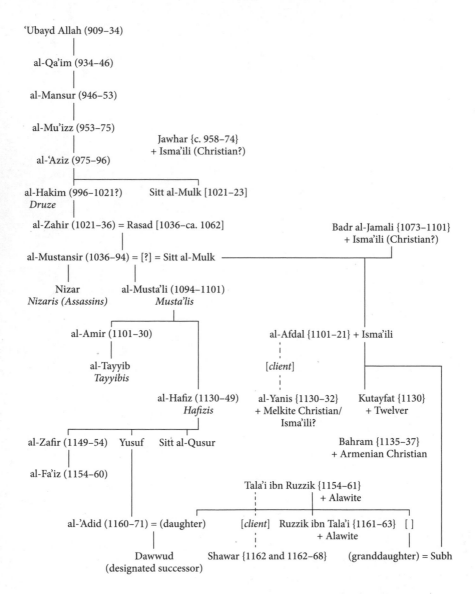

'Ubayd Allah (909–34)

al-Qa'im (934–46)

al-Mansur (946–53)

al-Mu'izz (953–75)

Jawhar {c. 958–74}
+ Isma'ili (Christian?)

al-'Aziz (975–96)

al-Hakim (996–1021?)   Sitt al-Mulk [1021–23]
Druze

al-Zahir (1021–36) = Rasad [1036–ca. 1062]

Badr al-Jamali {1073–1101}
+ Isma'ili (Christian?)

al-Mustansir (1036–94) = [?] = Sitt al-Mulk

Nizar   al-Musta'li (1094–1101)
Nizaris (Assassins)   *Musta'lis*

al-Amir (1101–30)   al-Afdal {1101–21} + Isma'ili

al-Tayyib   [*client*]
Tayyibis

al-Hafiz (1130–49)   al-Yanis {1130–32}   Kutayfat {1130}
Hafizis   + Melkite Christian/   + Twelver
Isma'ili?

Bahram {1135–37}
+ Armenian Christian

al-Zafir (1149–54)   Yusuf   Sitt al-Qusur

al-Fa'iz (1154–60)

Tala'i ibn Ruzzik {1154–61}
+ Alawite

al-'Adid (1160–71) = (daughter)   [*client*]   Ruzzik ibn Tala'i {1161–63}   [ ]
+ Alawite

Dawwud   Shawar {1162 and 1162–68}   (granddaughter) = Subh
(designated successor)

Imams are indicated by reign dates in parentheses (...),
ruling queens by dates in square brackets [...], and *wazirs* by
dates in braces {...}.

The names of dissident Isma'ili groups are italicized.

Glossary

'Abbadids An Arab-identifying Muslim dynasty that ruled over the *taifa* kingdom of Seville through most of the eleventh century.

'abid Black slaves from Central Africa (sing.: *'abd*).

al-Andalus Arabic term for the Iberian Peninsula (modern Spain and Portugal).

Alexandria Egyptian Mediterranean seaport on the western edge of the Nile Delta.

Allah "God" in Arabic, referring to the same God worshipped by Jews and Christians.

Almohads A religious-political-tribal movement dominated by Masmuda Berbers that originated in the Atlas Mountains in the early twelfth century and overthrew the Almoravid dynasty, establishing an empire that included the Maghrib, Ifriqiya, and what remained of al-Andalus (from the Arabic *al-Muwahhidun*, "Unitarians").

Almoravids A Berber movement originating among the Sanhaja tribes that coalesced along the southwestern edge of the Sahara Desert in the eleventh century, and which established an imperium that included Islamic Spain and much of the Maghrib and endured until the mid-twelfth century (from the Arabic name al-Murabitun, see p. 101).

al-Sham See *Bilad al-Sham*.

aman A truce or surrender agreement.

amir A Muslim "prince" or ruler whose authority was based on military or political power; a governor or military commander.

amiratus An admiral or military commander in Norman Sicily.

Anatolia The peninsula, also known as Asia Minor, bounded by the Black Sea, the Aegean Sea, and the Mediterranean, comprising most of modern Turkey.

Andalusi An inhabitant of al-Andalus, or a reference to the culture of al-Andalus.

Assassins See **Nizaris**.

Banu Hilal A Bedouin tribe that was settled in Upper Egypt by the Fatimids and was then dispatched to attack the rebellious Zirid dynasty of Ifriqiya.

Banu Ziri See **Zirids**.

Bilad al-Sham The area comprising modern Syria, Jordan, Israel, and Palestine (Arabic, "the Land on the Left").

Burgundy A region in the north-central part of modern France. It was particularly prosperous and dynamic in the eleventh and twelfth centuries as the point of origin of a dynamic warrior culture and the epicenter of the Cluniac monastic order.

caliph A successor of the Prophet Muhammad and the head of the Muslim community (from the Arabic *khalifa*).

camerarius A chamberlain, the official in charge of a royal household.

catholicos A patriarch in an Eastern Church.

Cluny A highly organized monastic order originating in Burgundy that became influential across Latin Christendom in the twelfth century, particularly in the transformation of the papacy and the institution of the Gregorian Reform.

Coptic Church The indigenous Christian Church in Egypt, considered heretical by the Catholic and Byzantine Churches.

da'i A missionary agent or propagandist employed by dissenting Islamic sects, Shi'a groups above all, and specifically the Fatimids.

dar al-Islam The area of the world under the rule of Islam (Arabic, "Abode of Islam").

de Hautevilles A family of Norman warriors who conquered southern Italy and Sicily and much of Ifriqiya in the eleventh and twelfth centuries, and who played a leading role in the Crusades.

dhimma The "pact of protection" extended by Muslim regimes to Christians, Jews, and other religious groups recognized as "People of the Book." The arrangement relegated these communities of *dhimmis* (protected peoples) to a secondary status, but recognized them as legitimate members of Islamic society.

dirham An Arabo-Islamic unit of currency derived from a Greek precedent.

diwan A chancery register or bureaucratic department in Islamic government; also, an anthology of literature, particularly poetry.

Druze A member of an offshoot of Isma'ili Islam that venerates the Fatimid caliph al-Hakim (pl.: Druze).

faqih An expert on *fiqh*, Islamic religious law and jurisprudence.

Fatimids An Isma'ili dynasty (909–1171), based first in Ifriqiya, then Egypt, that claimed the title of caliph.

fatwa In Islamic law, a nonbinding juridical decision issued in response to an actual or hypothetical situation.

fitna Disorder or unrest, antithetical to the order and stability of Islam.

Geniza A treasure trove of documents discovered at the Ben Ezra Synagogue in Cairo, revealing the history of the Jews of medieval Egypt and their relations across the Mediterranean and the Indian Ocean (Hebrew, "storage area").

Gregorian Reform A series of reforms of the Latin Church undertaken beginning in the eleventh century with the aim of institutionalizing the Church, establishing the primacy of the papacy, clarifying doctrine, and raising the moral and educational standards of the clergy.

hajib   An official who acted as a liaison between a caliph and his subjects, roughly equivalent to "chamberlain."

Ifranj   Franks, or, broadly, Latin Christians.

Ifriqiya   The Arabic name for the former Roman province of Africa, corresponding to modern Tunisia, eastern Algeria, and western Libya.

imam   The supreme spiritual leader of an Islamic community, particularly in Shi'a Islam; also used commonly to indicate an individual of religious authority, or any Muslim appointed to lead a prayer service.

Isma'ili   A branch of Shi'a Islam with a strong esoteric and messianic orientation.

jallaba   A loose-fitting robe or kaftan worn by men and women.

jihad   A striving toward moral good, which can take a range of forms, from individual improvement to the expansion of the Islamic world by force of arms.

Ka'aba   The formerly pagan shrine located in Mecca that is the focus of the obligatory hajj, or pilgrimage, in Islam.

Kalbids   A Muslim dynasty that ruled Sicily from the mid-tenth to the mid-eleventh centuries, first as governors for the Fatimids and then independently.

katib   A scribe (Arabic).

khalifa   See **caliph**.

Kharijites   A branch of Islam that originated in 657 at the Battle of Siffin (Arabic, "those who departed"). Kharijites emphasize the primacy of the Qur'an as a source for Islamic law, and believe that leadership within the *'umma* should be based on piety alone. A movement popular among nomads, its adherents regarded Sunni and Shi'a Muslims as unbelievers.

Komnenoi   The powerful and capable dynasty of Byzantine emperors who ruled from 1081 to 1185, halting the decline of the empire and becoming regional power brokers.

Kutama   A powerful Berber clan based in Ifriqiya that helped the Fatimids come to power.

Lombards   The native Latin Christians of the Italian Peninsula in the eleventh and twelfth centuries.

Madinat al-Zahara   The enormous palace complex established outside Córdoba by 'Abd al-Rahman III as the seat of the Umayyad Caliphate of al-Andalus.

Maghrib   A region of northwestern Africa that is now modern Morocco and western Algeria (Arabic, "the West").

Mahdi   "The Rightly Guided One"; a messianic figure, particularly important in Shi'a Islam.

malik   A military or secular ruler, as distinguished from a caliph (Arabic, "king").

Manichaeanism   A dualist religion derived from Zoroastrianism and influenced by Eastern faiths, which saw the universe as being in the grips of a battle between the forces of Good and Evil, of Spirit and Material. It influenced early Christianity, but was considered heretical.

mashrabiyya In Islamic architecture and decoration, a screen of crisscrossed lattice-work.

Medina "The City of the Prophet," formerly known as Yathrib; one of the holy cities of Islam.

Melkite A Byzantine Christian (later known as Greek Orthodox) (from the Arabic *malik*, referring to the Byzantine emperor).

mihrab The niche in a mosque that indicates the direction of prayer (i.e., toward Mecca).

Mozarab A Christian of al-Andalus who was culturally assimilated (from the Arabic *must'arab*, "wanna-be Arab").

mufti A legal expert in Islam who produced *fatwas*.

mujahid One who practices *jihad*, usually in the sense of "holy war" (pl.: *mujahidin*).

muqarnas A cuplike decorative element employed widely in Islamic architecture.

Nagid A leader of an exilic Jewish community (Hebrew, "prince," or "leader").

Nasi A title given to a leader of an exilic Jewish community (pl.: *Nasim*) (Hebrew, "prince" or "commander").

Nawruz The festival commemorating martyrs and saints that marks the Coptic New Year (September 11).

Nizaris An esoteric Muslim sect, an offshoot of the Isma'ili branch of Shi'ism, originating in early-eleventh-century Egypt. Its members, loyal to the memory of an assassinated Fatamid prince, Nizar, fled to northern Persia, from where agents were dispatched to assassinate the sect's opponents. They subsequently established a power base in Syria's Orontes Valley. Also called **Assassins**.

Normans Descendants of Norwegian Vikings who converted to Christianity and settled in northern France in the tenth century; many, including the de Hautevilles, served as mercenaries in Italy in the eleventh century.

parias Tribute or "protection money" paid by the *taifa* kings of al-Andalus to Christian princes.

patriarch The head of an Eastern Christian religious community, or the heir of an apostolic see (e.g., Alexandria, Antioch, Rome, and Jerusalem).

Paulicianism A heretical Christian sect that arose among the Armenians of eastern Anatolia, and drew on Gnosticism, Manichaeanism, and Islam.

protonobilissimos A high-ranking title in the Byzantine court, sometimes granted as an honor to foreigners.

qadi An Islamic judge.

qa'id A military commander (Arabic).

Qaraites A branch of Judaism whose adherents believed that the whole of Jewish law ccould be found in the Hebrew Scripture, and who rejected the authority of the Talmud.

Rabbinical Judaism The dominant branch of Judaism, which developed from the fourth to the sixth centuries as a consequence of the Diaspora and in response to the rise of Christianity. Central to Rabbinical Judaism is the elaboration of the Talmud, the body of interpretation of Jewish oral law and tradition. Two major schools of interpretation emerged: the Academy of Jerusalem (also known as the Palestinian Academy) and the Babylonian Academy.

Ramadan   The holy month in Islam, a time of communal fasting and observance.

ribat   A fortress usually set on the frontiers of the Islamic world, where pious Muslims would spend a period of time engaged in study, contemplation, and military *jihad*.

Rioja or **La Rioja**   A region of northern Spain that was on the frontier between Castile and Navarre.

Rum   A term used to refer to Greeks or Byzantines, and the Byzantine Empire (Arabic, "Roman").

sadaq   A bride-price paid by a husband or his family, or placed as a guarantee in the event of widowhood or divorce.

Sahel   The grasslands along the southern fringe of the Sahara Desert.

Saljuqs   Turkic nomads originating in Central Asia who converted to Islam in the tenth century and emigrated to 'Abbasid lands as mercenaries, eventually taking political control of the caliphate. (Alternatively spelled "Seljuks.")

Samaritans   A community of Jews who observed traditions distinct from those of Qaraites and Rabbinical Jews, and grounded in pre-Exile practices.

Sanhaja or **Sinhaja**   A Berber tribal confederation (not unlike a "nation") whose members lived throughout the Maghrib, Ifriqiya, and the Sahel.

Santiago de Compostela   A town and the seat of a bishop in northwestern Spain where the body of Saint James was said to be buried; the terminus of the Camino de Santiago, the most important medieval Christian pilgrimage route.

saqaliba   A slave or captive of Eastern European pagan or Latin Christian origin (Arabic, "slave" or "Slav").

Sharq al-Andalus   The northeast coastal region of al-Andalus; the area around Valencia.

sheikh   An "elder" whose wisdom and authority is respected (Arabic).

Shi'ism   The branch of Islam that holds that the descendants of 'Ali ibn Abi Talib, the cousin and son-in-law of the Prophet Muhammad, are the legitimate leaders of the *'umma*. Its adherents are the **Shi'a**.

sultan   A secular political authority in Islam, similar to an amir or *malik*.

Sunnism   The "orthodox" or majority Islamic community, which holds that Islamic law is grounded in the Qur'an as well as the *Sunna* (the sayings and practices of the Prophet and other important Muslims). Its adherents are the **Sunni**.

taifa **kingdoms**   The petty principalities that arose in al-Andalus after the collapse of the Umayyad Caliphate of Córdoba in the early eleventh century (from the Arabic *muluk al-tawa'if*, "sectarian kings").

Thaghr al-'Aqsa   "The Farthest Frontier," the province of al-Andalus in the northeast that had Zaragoza as its capital.

tiraz   A royal silk workshop, such as the ones established by the Fatimids and the Norman kings of Sicily (Arabic).

Twelvers   The majority branch of Shi'a Islam, whose members believe that the twelfth imam, Muhammad al-Mahdi, went into occultation (or hiding) in 941, and will eventually reemerge alongside Jesus to establish a peaceful and just world.

'ulama'   The community of learned Muslims, particularly experts in law, doctrine, and theology (plural of Arabic *'ilm*).

Umayyads An Arabic dynasty, related to Muhammad's family, who ruled as caliphs of Islam from their capital at Damascus from 661 to 750, and subsequently in al-Andalus, first as amirs (756 to 929) and then as caliphs (929 to 1031).

'ushr A tithe, an obligatory tax paid by Muslims according to Islamic law (Arabic, "tenth").

wazir A high-ranking official or government minister in an Islamic administration. A *wazir* could serve as the deputy for a king, prince, or caliph, and *wazirs* frequently wielded more real power than the sovereigns whom they formally served.

Zallaqa The site of the Almoravids' landmark victory over the army of Castile in October 1086; known as "Sagrajas" in Christian sources.

Zanata A Berber tribal confederation whose members lived throughout the Maghrib, Ifriqiya, and the Sahel.

Zirids A Sanhaja Berber clan from Ifriqiya; one branch ruled over the *taifa* kingdom of Granada (1019–90) and another over Ifriqiya (972–1148), first as governors of the Fatimids and later as independent kings.

Zoroastrianism A dualistic Persian religion originating in the sixth century B.C.E. that became the state religion of the Achaemenid Empire; it influenced Judaism, Christianity, and Islam, and was the forerunner of Manichaeanism. Zoroastrians were considered "People of the Book" by Muslims.

Sources, Background, and Further Reading

What follows is not an exhaustive bibliographical essay, but an overview of the most accessible primary sources and scholarly studies on the individuals, kingdoms, and cultures that appear in the book. There is much more that interested readers can discover on their own, either by following the scholarship or visiting these lands, and walking in the footsteps of the heroes, scoundrels, holy men, and hypocrites who populate these pages.

As a historian, I must confess to having pushed the limits of acceptable methodology by including hypothetical reconstructions of some of the more dramatic episodes in these narratives. I haven't done this with any intention to manipulate or mislead the reader; it is simply impossible to evoke the atmosphere of these events and the feeling of the time without taking judicious liberties. The moments where I have taken such liberties should be quite evident, and I hope they will have helped me accomplish another goal in writing this book, which is to bring this thousand-year-old period to life, and to share the excitement and fascination it has sparked in me.

INTRODUCTION: THE MEDITERRANEAN WORLD
A comprehensive and detailed review of the historiography of the premodern Mediterranean can be found in Part One, "'Frogs Round a Pond': Ideas of the Mediterranean," in Horden and Purcell's *The Corrupting Sea*, which remains itself the seminal work of what might be called "New Mediterranean Studies"—a rethinking of history by putting the Mediterranean in the middle rather than on the edge of the action. For all its originality and daring, it is a dense, technical work, and not one that nonscholars are likely

to find engaging. *The Corrupting Sea* itself is built on the foundations of the French historian Fernand Braudel's work, especially *The Mediterranean and the Mediterranean World in the Age of Philip II.* Other seminal works include Pirenne's *Mohammed and Charlemagne* and Goitein's *A Mediterranean Society.* Pirenne's thesis is gripping and provocative, but clearly outmoded, and should only be considered alongside critiques, such as Hodges and Whitehouse's *Mohammed, Charlemagne, and the Origins of Europe.* Shlomo Goitein's multivolume work used the documents found in the Cairo *Geniza* to reconstruct the networks of Jewish traders whose activities spanned the Mediterranean and the western Indian Ocean.

Most of the recent work contributing to this new, more sophisticated vision of the Mediterranean is scholarly and not particularly accessible. However, a number of overarching histories are both reliable and readable, including Bradford's *Mediterranean: Portrait of a Sea*, Norwich's *The Middle Sea*, and, most recently, Abulafia's *The Great Sea*, each of which presents the sea as protagonist in a narrative that begins in prehistory and comes up to the present. For a comparative analysis of politics and religious identity in the medieval Mediterranean, see Catlos's "'Accursed, Superior Men.'"

PART I: THE (JEWISH) MAN WHO WOULD BE KING

There are a number of contemporary accounts and documents relating to the careers of Isma'il and Yusuf ibn Naghrilla, some of which have been published in English. The most important Arabic source is the *Tibyan*, written by 'Abd Allah ibn Buluqqin, who reigned as the last Zirid king of Granada, and wrote an apologetic and memoir while living out his years as a prisoner of the Almoravids. The most accessible source for the history of the *taifa* kingdoms, including Granada, is the idiosyncratic historical digest compiled by the Moroccan historian al-Maqqari in the seventeenth century and published in partial English translation by Gayangos as *The History of the Mohammedan Dynasties.* The main Hebrew source is Ibn Daud's *Book of Tradition*, which traces the history of the Rabbinate from its origins to the early twelfth century. Like the *Tibyan*, it is marked by a strong "political" agenda.

The best English-language history of the Zirid regime is Handler's *The Zirids of Granada*, although Idris's *La Berbérie orientale sous les Zirides* and Golvin's *Le Magrib central à l'époque des Zirides* are more comprehensive. For an overall account of the *taifa* period, see Wasserstein's *The Rise and Fall of the Party-Kings* and Kennedy's *Muslim Spain and Portugal* for a broader political context. Norris's *The Berbers in Arabic Literature* and Brett and Fentress's *The Berbers* provide overviews of Berber history and culture.

Several books and articles have been produced in English on Isma'il's life and works, for example: Weinberger's *Jewish Prince in Moslem Spain*; Schirmann's "Samuel Hannagid, the Man, the Soldier, the Politician"; and chapter 3 of Roth's *Jews, Visigoths, and Muslims in Medieval Spain*, "Jews Under Umayyads and *Taifas*." Scheindlin's *Wine, Women, and Death* also contains a selection of poems, as does Peter Cole's *Selected Poems of Shmuel Hanagid.* *The Penguin Book of Hebrew Verse* is an excellent guide for understanding the literary context of Isma'il's compositions. For Yusuf, see also Bargebuhr, "The Alhambra Palace of the Eleventh Century." For Jews in Spain, Ashtor's *The Jews of Moslem Spain* is comprehensive, but dated and unreliable. Gerber's *The Jews of Spain* is better. The world of the courtier-poets is best accessed through the works of Brann, including *The Compunctious Poet* and *Power in the Portrayal*. His chapter on "Arabized Jews," Wasserstein's "Jewish Élites in al-Andalus," and Alfonso's *Islamic Culture Through Jewish Eyes* look at the Judeo-Arabic aristocracy as a whole. For Muslim perspectives on Isma'il, see Wasserstein's "Samuel Ibn Naghrila Ha-Nagid and Islamic Historiography in Al-Andalus" and García Gómez, "Polémica religiosa entre Ibn Hazm e Ibn Al-Nagrila."

For the Arabic poetic tradition and examples of contemporary works, see Menocal et al., *The Literature of Al-Andalus*; Abu-Haidar's *Hispano-Arabic Literature*; and García Gómez, *Cinco poetas musulmanes*. For *taifa*-era poetry in English, see Franzen's *Poems of Arab Andalusia* (translations of García Gómez's translations into Spanish), Gorton's *Andalus*, and Monroe's authoritative *Hispano-Arabic Poetry*.

As for physical evidence of the Banu Naghrilla and their city, virtually nothing remains. The present Alhambra Palace was built in the fourteenth century on the site of Isma'il and Yusuf's home. It is thought that the fountain in the "Patio of Lions," ringed by eroded statues of twelve lions, said to represent the Twelve Tribes, may have been part of the original building, and some of the fortifications are undoubtedly original. There is an eleventh-century bathhouse, where celebrations and parties would have been held, just below the Alhambra and across the Darro. The winding lanes of the Albaicín neighborhood certainly capture the ambience of historical al-Andalus.

PART II: A CHRISTIAN SULTAN IN THE AGE OF "THE RECONQUEST"

The study of the Cid and the literature he has inspired has prompted something of an industry in the academic and trade publishing worlds, although the quality and reliability of the work varies tremendously. Older scholarship and works by nonacademics should be treated with caution (especially those without notes or bibliography), given how our understanding of both the figure and his times have changed, and the considerable portion of his legend that has come to be regarded as fact.

There are many editions and translations of the *Poema* (or *Cantar*) *de mío Cid*; the dual-language editions of Michael, Hamilton, and Perry and of Smith are excellent and allow the English-reader to at least follow the poetry of the original. Smith's study *The Making of the Poema de mío Cid* looks at the genesis of the poem, while de Epalza's *Le Cid: personnage historique et littéraire* follows the figure of the Cid from his time to the present. Wright's *Early Ibero Romance* studies it in the context of contemporary Spanish literature. The *Historici Roderici* and other related texts are translated into English in Barton and Fletcher, *The World of El Cid*, as well as in Smith, Melville, and Ubaydli, *Christians and Moors in Spain*, which also contains excerpts from Arabic works. Al-Maqqari's chronicle and the *Tibyan* (see Part One above) contain material on the Cid, Alfonso, and the Almoravids, while many contemporary Arabic sources have been translated into French and Spanish, including Ibn 'Idhari's *Al-Bayan al-Mughrib* (by Huici Miranda). For the poetry of the *taifa* period, see Part One above.

For the historical Cid, the best work by far is Fletcher's *Quest for El Cid* (to which these chapters owe a tremendous debt). This should be read alongside Reilly, *The Kingdom of León-Castilla under King Alfonso VI*, and Smith, "Two Historians Reassess the Cid," as well as with Wasserstein's *The Rise and Fall of the Party-Kings* and Kennedy's *Muslim*

Spain and Portugal. For the Christian conquest of northeast Spain, see the first chapter of Catlos, *The Victors and the Vanquished*, and chapter 1 of Catlos, *Muslims of Medieval Latin Christendom* for the peninsula in general, as well as the first chapters of O'Callaghan, *Reconquest and Crusade in Medieval Spain*. The most comprehensive work on Islamic Valencia remains (despite its age) Huici Miranda's three-volume *Historia musulmana de Valencia* (the second volume covers the era of the Cid). For the *taifa* kingdom of Zaragoza, see Beech, *The Brief Eminence and Doomed Fall of Islamic Saragossa*; Turk, *El Reino de Zaragoza*; and *El Cid en el Valle de Jalón*. For the Almoravids, Messier, *The Almoravids and the Meanings of Jihad*, is superb, but lacks notes, and can be supplemented with Lagardère, *Les Almoravides jusqu'au règne de Yūsuf b. Tāšfīn*, and the aging Béraud-Villars, *Les Touareg au pays du Cid*.

For the controversy regarding Castro and Sánchez-Albornoz, see Castro's *The Spaniards* and Sánchez-Albornoz's *Spain, A Historical Enigma*, as well as Russell, "The Nessus-Shirt," Glick and Pi-Sunyer, "Acculturation as an Explanatory Concept," and Catlos, "Christian-Muslim-Jewish Relations, Medieval 'Spain,' and the Mediterranean." Cluny and the Burgundians in Spain are the subject of Barton, "El Cid, Cluny and the Medieval Spanish Reconquista"; Iogna-Prat provides an overview of the order in *Order and Exclusion*. The mission of the "monk of France" and al-Baji's reply is studied in Cutler, "Who Was the Monk of France?" and Dunlop, "A Christian Mission to Muslim Spain." For an overview of Christian approaches to Islam, see Tolan, *Saracens*. Hitchcock, *Mozarabs in Medieval and Early Modern Spain*, is an accessible survey of the Christians of al-Andalus, although Aillet's magisterial *Les Mozarabes* is much more precise and comprehensive. For Sisnando Davídez, see Menéndez Pidal and García Gómez, "El conde mozárabe." Barton's "Traitors of the Faith?," McCrank's "Norman Crusaders," and Clément's "Reverter et son fils" look at mercenaries and fortune seekers in Spain and the Maghrib.

For those on a personal quest for the historical Cid, much remains of the architecture and art of his time. The various Spanish regions where the Cid was active have marked touristic routes (typically designated as El Camino del Cid or La Ruta del Cid) that follow Rodrigo's peregrinations. Nothing substantial remains of the Cid's Valencia, but in Zaragoza the impressive Aljafería Palace of al-Muqtadir has been restored as the regional parliament. In Toledo, the former mosque, now the Church of Cristo de la Luz, and other contemporary monuments survive. The crumbling castle of Rueda still sits perched above the Jalón. The Monastery of San Pedro de Cardeña outside Burgos can be visited, while the Cid and Ximena rest in Burgos Cathedral (where the Cid's casket is also on display). Of the Cid's two swords, "Tizona," a blade forged in Córdoba and said to have been owned by Syr ibn Abi Bakr, can be seen in Burgos, while a sword reputed to be "Colada"—the weapon he won from Berenguer Ramon at Almenar in 1082—can be seen in the collection of the armories of the royal palace in Madrid.

PART III: KINGS OF SICILY, KINGS OF AFRICA

There is no shortage of recent scholarship in English on the court and culture of Norman Sicily. For the administration, the key works are Johns's *Arabic Administration in Norman Sicily: The Royal Dīwān*, and Takayama's *The Administration of the Norman*

Kingdom of Sicily—both academic books that dissect in great technical detail the complex workings of the kingdom and court. Chalandon's *Histoire de la domination normande en Italie et en Sicilie* is the most comprehensive general history, but is beginning to show its age; Matthew's *The Norman Kingdom of Sicily* is shorter but more accessible. For the Norman admiralty and navy, see Ménager's *Amiratus—Ἀμηρᾶς* and Stanton's *Norman Naval Operations in the Mediterranean*. On the cultural program of the de Hauteville rulers, Tronzo's *The Cultures of His Kingdom* has justifiably become a classic, while Mallette's *The Kingdom of Sicily, 1100–1250* provides an excellent survey of the Arabic literary heritage of the Christian kingdom. The Norman conquest is analyzed in Brown's *The Norman Conquest of Southern Italy and Sicily* and in Loud's *The Age of Robert Guiscard*. Roger II has been the subject of a substantial and readable biography, Houben's *Roger II of Sicily*. For the Islamic period there is the rather old and dated *A History of Islamic Sicily*, by Aziz, while Kreutz's *Before the Normans* is a more recent and broader study. For the post–de Hauteville era, the most accessible work is Abulafia's monumental biography, *Frederick II: A Medieval Emperor*.

The Muslim community of medieval Sicily is the subject of two books by Metcalfe: his eminently accessible *The Muslims of Medieval Italy* and the more technical *Muslims and Christians in Norman Sicily*. The post-Norman period of exile is the subject of Taylor's recent *Muslims in Medieval Italy*. The Palace Saracens are discussed by both Johns and Metcalfe, and Philip of Mahdia is the subject of articles by Birk and Catlos. The campaigns of Ifriqiya have not been the subject of a book-length study, but are analyzed in several articles by Brett (see Works Cited), and are seen (from the Islamic perspective) in Idris's *La Berbérie orientale sous les Zirides*. Takayama and Johns both review Norman-Fatimid relations.

There is also a relative abundance of primary sources in translation. Amari's *Biblioteca arabo-sicula* is a digest of Arabic historical sources relating to the kingdom (translated into Italian). English translations of the Arabic and Latin accounts of Philip of Mahdia have been translated by Johns and Houben (See Johns, *Arabic Administration*, 215–17; and Houben, *Roger II of Sicily*, 110–12). Translated chronicles include Falcandus's *The History of the Tyrants of Sicily*, Malaterra's *The Deeds of Count Roger of Calabria*, and Amatus of Montecassino's *The History of the Normans*; a number of others (including al-Idrisi's *Kitab Rujjar*) are excerpted in Loud's *Roger II and the Creation of the Kingdom of Sicily*. Peter of Eboli's later chronicle, famous for its lavish visual depictions of the Sicilian court, the *Liber ad honorem augusti sive de rebus Siculis*, should be consulted in its facsimile edition. Finally, the travel memoir of Ibn Jubayr has been translated by Broadhurst as *The Travels of Ibn Jubayr*, and Mallette's literary history includes a generous appendix of poetry, literature, and letters in translation.

For the visitor today, a surprising amount of the Sicily of Philip of Mahdia survives, particularly in Palermo. The highlight here is Roger's stunning Palace Chapel (*Capella palatina*) with its dazzling inlay and painted and paneled ceilings. Nearby is the Ziza, a hunting palace of Islamicate design built by William II (and praised, perhaps, by Ibn Jubayr). In the center of the city, the old Kalsa neighborhood evokes the winding and narrow lanes of pre-Norman Palermo, and at the center of the old town stands the Matorana, or Church of Santa Maria dell'Ammiraglio, founded by George of Antioch, and still containing the famous mosaic depiction of Roger II's coronation. In Tunisia, Mahdia, Sfax, and Sousse, as well as the capital, all have significant surviving monuments that date back to the age of Roger II and well before.

PART IV: INFIDEL RULERS OF A HERETICAL CALIPHATE

The Fatimid Caliphate has not been the subject of an overall study in recent years, and the older works are largely obsolete, although Wiet's *L'Égypte arabe* is still of value. That said, there are many excellent thematically oriented book- and article-length studies, including Brett, *The Rise of the Fatimids*; Daftary, *The Isma'ilis*; Halm, *The Empire of the Mahdi*; and Hamdani, *The Fatimids*. For the sources, see Walker, *Exploring an Islamic Empire*. For Fatimid doctrine as ideal and in practice, see Daftary, *Mediaeval Isma'ili History and Thought*; Bierman, *Writing Signs: The Fatimid Public Text*; and Van Reeth, "The Rise of Extremist Sects." For medieval Cairo and its people, elites, and ceremonies, see Staffa, *Conquest and Fusion*; and Sanders, *Ritual, Politics, and the City*. The Persian traveler Naser-e Khosraw's *Book of Travels* contains evocative firsthand descriptions. Lev has written extensively on the Fatimid Caliphate, particulary the administration and the military; see, for example, "The Fāṭimid Army" and *State and Society*. Bacharach's "African Military Slaves" is also important. For royal women, see Cortese and Calderini, *Women and the Fatimids*; Calderini's "Sayyida Rasad"; and Walker's "The Fatimid Caliph Al-'Azīz and His Daughter."

The institution of the wazirate and the role of Armenians in the caliphate have been the subject of a number of works. Al-Imad's *The Fatimid Vizierate* is excellent, and the works of Dadoyan (or Parsumean-Tatoyean) are indispensable, including *The Fatimid Armenians*, "The Phenomenon of the Fatimid Armenians," and *The Armenians in the Medieval Islamic World*, as is Canard, "Notes sur les Arméniens." For Badr al-Jamali, see Brett, "Badr al-Ǧamālī and the Fatimid Renascence"; den Heijer, "Le vizir fatimide Badr al-Ǧamālī"; and van Donzel, "Badr al-Jamali, the Copts in Egypt and the Muslims in Ethiopia." For Bahram Pahlavuni, see also Canard, "Un vizir chrétien" and "Une lettre du calife fâtimite." A near-contemporary source for the Armenians and the Copts is Abu Salih's fourteenth-century *The Churches and Monasteries of Egypt*. For Salah al-Din and the fall of the caliphate, see Lev, *Saladin in Egypt*.

The story of Ibn Dukhan is analyzed in Catlos, "To Catch a Spy." General studies of the Copts and the Christian communities of Egypt include Tagher, *Christians in Muslim Egypt*; Meinardus, *Two Thousand Years of Coptic Christianity*; and Swanson, *The Coptic Papacy*; as well as Brett's "Al-Karāza al-Marqusīya" and den Heijer's "Le patriarcat copte d'Alexandrie à l'époque fatimide." For their relation to government, see Samir, "The Role of Christians"; and Saleh, "Government Intervention." For conversion to Islam, see O'Sullivan, "Coptic Conversion and Islamization of Egypt"; and Lev, "Persecutions and Conversion to Islam." Coptic sources are reviewed in den Heijer, "Coptic Historiography in the Fatimid, Ayyubid and Early Mamluk Periods," whereas the substantial contemporary chronicle, by Sawirus ibn al-Mukaffa' (and his continuers), has been translated as *The History of the Patriarchs of the Egyptian Church*. Griffith's *The Church in the Shadow of the Mosque* presents an overview of Christian churches under Islam. For the Jews of Fatimid Egypt, see Goitein's *A Mediterranean Society* and *Let-*

ters of Medieval Jewish Traders, as well as Rustow's recent *Heresy and the Politics of Community*.

Cairo remains one of the world's great historical cities, and although the old Fatimid capital has been rebuilt and built over many times, abundant monuments remain from the era of the caliphate. Much of the ancient palace still stands, and Bayn al-Qasrayn is still the heart of Cairo—but is now clogged with narrow lanes and later construction. One quarter, the Darb Qirmiz, which dates back to the Fatimid period, has been restored, and a group of Fatimid-era houses survives in Fustat. Unfortunately, the monastery complex that included the Armenian Church of St. George, where Jawhar, Solomon of Nubia, and Bahram Pahlavuni were all buried, has long been destroyed—and its location is uncertain. The al-Azhar mosque and university that Jawhar founded remains one of the great centers of learning in the Islamic world, and his street plan of Cairo is still discernible. Several of Badr al-Jamali's constructions remain, notably three of his great fortified gates: the Bab al-Nasr, the Bab al-Futuh, and the Bab al-Zuwayla, as does his Masjid al-Juyush (Army Mosque) and a tomb or shrine complex that he commissioned but was not buried in. Ibn Ruzzik's mosque, the Masjid al-Salih Tala'i—built to hold the relic of the head of 'Ali's martyred son, Hussayn—also stands. There are many surviving monuments of the Coptic community, the most famous of which can be found in Old Cairo (Fustat and Babyon). St. Mercurius was the seat of the patriarchs in the Fatimid period, and the churches of the Virgin, St. Menas, and St. Barbara still have eleventh- and twelfth-century features. An important collection of historical artifacts is on display in the Coptic Museum. For details on Cairo's monuments, see Yeomans's *The Art and Architecture of Islamic Cairo*.

PART V: AMBITION, OPPORTUNISM, AND THE END OF AN ERA

Few subjects have garnered as much scholarly attention as the Crusades in the East. At the two poles of English-language scholarship stand the "classics": Runciman's realist *A History of the Crusades* and the apologetically flavored works of Riley-Smith (see Works Cited for a selection), together with those who have followed in their wake, such as Tyerman and Madden. The multivolume collaborative *A History of the Crusades*, edited by Setton, is, overall, more balanced. The French historian Richard's shorter but very comprehensive *The Crusades* is excellent—its readability suffering only as a consequence of the complexity of the material. The same can be said for the German historian Mayer's *The Crusades*. Kostick's *Social Structure* is an important revision of the composition and motivations of the First Crusade. For a history of the First Crusade from the perspective of the Islamic world, the novelist Maalouf's *The Crusades Through Arab Eyes* remains a vivid and engaging portrayal, although, as he acknowledges, it is not a scholarly history; Hillenbrand's richly illustrated *The Crusades: Islamic Perspectives* is also excellent. Examples of important specialized studies include Erdmann's *The Origin of the Idea of the Crusade*, Smail's *Crusading Warfare*, Penny Cole's *The Preaching of the Crusades*, and Kostick's *Siege of Jerusalem*, to name a few. For the politics of the Crusader principalities, see also Prawer, *The Latin Kingdom of Jerusalem*; and Bernard Hamilton, *The Leper King and His Heirs*. Nicolle's *Hattin 1187* dissects, in richly illustrated detail, the battle that brought down the Crusader kingdom.

For the history of the Saljuq Counter-Crusade, Eddé's careful and critical biography, *Saladin*, and Elisséeff's detailed *Nur ad-Din* (the latter in French), are the best. For the Nizaris, Lewis's *The Assassins* remains the standard work; but see also Smarandache's "The Franks and the Nizārī Ismāʿīlīs." For Byzantium, Ostrogorski's stiff and politically oriented *History of the Byzantine State* has weathered the decades as a reference book, but Herrin's *Byzantium* is broader and far more engaging. Studies specific to this period include Angold, *Church and Society in Byzantium Under the Comneni*; and Magdalino's *The Empire of Manuel I Komnenos*. For Byzantium's troubled relationship with Venice, see Nicol, *Byzantium and Venice*; for Greek–Crusader relations, see Lilie, *Byzantium and the Crusader States*. In *The Crusader States and Their Neighbours*, P. M. Holt provides a regional context for the politics of the Frankish East. MacEvitt's *The Crusades and the Christian World of the East* looks at the experience of Eastern Christians in the Crusader lands; for that of Muslims, see Catlos, *The Muslims of Medieval Latin Christendom*; and for that of Jews, Prawer, *The History of the Jews*.

Of the lesser personages of these chapters, Reynaud de Châtillon has been treated most thoroughly, although the single monograph study remains the old, French-language *Renaud de Châtillon*, by Schlumberger. A number of recent articles focus on his career, including Mallett, "A Trip Down the Red Sea"; Hamilton's "The Elephant of Christ"; Hillenbrand's "The Imprisonment of Reynald of Châtillon"; and Milwright's "Reynald of Châtillon." For Melisende, see Mayer, "Studies in the History of Queen Melisende." For the women of Antioch and their court, see Asbridge, "Alice of Antioch," and Hamilton's articles, including, for example, "Aimery of Limoges, Patriarch," "Aimery of Limoges, Latin Patriarch," and "The Templars." The career of Andronikos Komnenos is reviewed in the relevant chapter in Diehl's *Figures byzantines* (in French).

Two primary sources for Andronikos's reign are *The Deeds of John and Manuel Comnenus*, translated by Brand, and *O City of Byzantium*, translated by Magoulias, both written by contemporary authors deeply hostile to the emperor. The remarkable memoir of Alexios I's daughter, Anna, *The Alexiad*, is an important source for Byzantine views of the First Crusade. There are English translations of many of the Frankish sources for the East in the twelfth century, including these anthologies: Peters's *The First Crusade*; Edbury, *The Conquest of Jerusalem*; and William of Tyre's *A History of Deeds Done Beyond the Sea*, to name only three. Important Arabic-language sources in translation include Gibb's translation of *The Damascus Chronicle*; Richards's *The Chronicle of Ibn al-Athir*; and Baha al-Din ibn Shaddad's hagiographical biography, *The Rare and Excellent History of Saladin*, also translated by Richards. The traveler Ibn Jubayr was an eyewitness to Frankish-Muslim relations, which he describes in his *Travels*, but the most detailed and intimate picture is painted by ʿUsama ibn Munqidh in his *Book of Contemplation*, translated by Cobb, whose biography, *Usama ibn Munqidh*, is also excellent.

Little remains of the Frankish East or pre-1204 Constantinople, apart from the ruins of once massive castles, such as Marqab, Belvoir, and Safed. Reynaud's stronghold of Kerak is in reasonable shape, and both Krak des Chevaliers and Masyaf (the Assassin headquarters in Syria) have been lavishly restored. Their fate, however, is at risk, together with the rest of the extremely rich historical patrimony of Syria, including much that was built by or standing at the time of Nur al-Din and Salah al-Din—including the Aleppo citadel and the Umayyad Mosque in Damascus. Many of the Syrian sites have been destroyed or damaged or are under threat because of the current civil war. In Jerusalem the Dome of the Rock and al-Aqsa Mosque survive, as does the Tower of David, and the much-altered Church of the Holy Sepulchre. In Constantinople, much remains of the massive fourth-century walls that were breached by the Franks in 1204, and the sixth-century imperial church, Hagia Sophia, now a museum and girded by minarets, still impresses. Of the royal palace of the Komnenoi at Blacharnae in the northwest of the old city, only foundations remain. For a tantalizing hint of Byzantine glory, one can visit instead the smaller but much better-preserved Chora Church. Only a short walk from Hagia Sophia, one can also stroll through the scant remains of the Hippodrome, where Andronikos met his ignominious end.

Notes

INTRODUCTION: THE MEDITERRANEAN WORLD

3 *"... without Mohammed, Charlemagne"*: Gibbon, *The Decline and Fall of the Roman Empire*, 5:389.

1. AN ORNAMENT, TARNISHED

16 *When he was rudely silenced*: Tibi, *The Tibyān*, 75.

20 *The poet Ibn Zaydun would recall*: Franzen, *Poems of Arab Andalusia*, 34–35.

25 *Hrosvitha of Gandersheim had described it*: Menocal, *Ornament of the World*, 32.

29 *"If we kill one of them"*: Tibi, *The Tibyān*, 49.

33 *"There is no god but God"*: The Arabic is *La ilah ila Allah, wa-Muhammad rasul Allah*.

37 *"Warfare is our line of work"*: Adapted from Handler, *The Zirids of Granada*, 14.

38 *"The Jew [Isma'il] possessed"*: Tibi, *The Tibyān*, 56. "Buluqqin," a Berber name, is transliterated variably also as "Buluggin" and "Bulughgin," since the Arabic spelling sometimes uses the letter *qaf* and sometimes the letter *ghayn*.

41 *"achieved great good for Israel"*: Ibn Daud, *The Book of Tradition*, 74. "Israel" at this time did not refer to a kingdom, or even a place, but the larger community of Jews living throughout the Afro-Eurasian world.

41 *"the king raised him above"*: Schirmann, "Samuel Hannagid," 104.

42 *"O you who believe!"*: Qur'an, 5:15; taken from *The Holy Qur'an*, translated by Shakir, with "God" substituted for the word "Allah."

43 *"Soar, don't settle for earth"*: Peter Cole, *Selected Poems of Shmuel Hanagid*, 107.

2. THE RULES OF THE GAME

45 *As Isma'il put it in one of his poems*: Constable, *Medieval Iberia*, 97.

46 *As he recalled in a celebratory poem*: Ibid., 89.

46 *And his contention that the Almerians' plan was*: Ibid., 85.

47 *When Seville attacked Granada's ally*: Translated from Idris, "Les Zirides," 70.

47 *When, in 1041, Isma'il defeated al-Yiddir*: Adapted from Roth, *Jews, Visigoths, and Muslims*, 95.

47 *"Tell me, has the body of Ibn Abi Musa"*: Weinberger, *Jewish Prince in Moslem Spain*, 47.

47 *Of a battle against Seville he recalled*: Peter Cole, *Selected Poems of Shmuel Hanagid*, 45.

48 *And of his defeat of Yiddir*: Adapted from Weinberger, *Jewish Prince in Moslem Spain*, 5.

48 *For Isma'il war was transformed*: Peter Cole, *Selected Poems of Shmuel Hanagid*, 106.

48 *"The king's fickleness"*: Ibid., 99.

48 *In one poem Isma'il recalls passing*: Weinberger, *Jewish Prince in Moslem Spain*, 16.

49 *The* Nagid *was a fierce partisan*: Ibid., xlvii.

50 *With all the modesty of a king*: Ibid., 276.

50 *If Ibn Hazm is to be believed*: See Genesis 49:10.

52 *"In the morning dark"*: Franzen, *Poems of Arab Andalusia*, 55.

52 *"The eyes of the young lad"*: Weinberger, *Jewish Prince in Moslem Spain*, 108.

52 *"When he said: 'Bring me down honey'"*: Ibid., 119.

53 *Of Isma'il, the poet Ibn al-Fara wrote*: Roth, *Jews, Visigoths, and Muslims*, 94.

54 *"Seek his welfare and find hope"*: Schirmann, "Samuel Hannagid," 120.

54 *Another poet, al-Munfatil, identified*: Brann, *Power in the Portrayal*, 95.

54 *Isma'il knew this better than most*: Peter Cole, *Selected Poems of Shmuel Hanagid*, 90.

54 *"The foolish enemy's face tells all"*: Ibid., 110.

55 *"Go, tell all the Sanhaja"*: Constable, *Medieval Iberia*, 97.

56 *Once he established the incoherence*: Baron, *A Social and Religious History of the Jews*, 95.

56 *"A man who was filled with hatred"*: Bargebuhr, "The Alhambra Palace," 194.

57 *Ibn Hayyan, regarded as the greatest historian*: See Brann, *Power in the Portrayal*, 36.

58 *"in the age of Rabbi Hasdai the Nasi"*: Ibn Daud, *The Book of Tradition*, 102.

59 *"I'm sick with the service of kings"*: Peter Cole, *Selected Poems of Shmuel Hanagid*, 56.

59 *"I was taken with him when he went"*: Ibid., 191.

59 *"Of all the fine qualities which his father possessed"*: Ibn Daud, *The Book of Tradition*, 76.

62 *"All the resentment and hatred of the masses"*: Ashtor, *The Jews of Moslem Spain*, 3:188–89.

62 *"The Jew turned and fled for his life"*: Tibi, *The Tibyān*, 75.

63 *"The Berber princes became so jealous"*: Ibn Daud, *The Book of Tradition*, 76.

63 *"more than three thousand"*: Translated from Ibn 'Idhari, *Al-Bayan al Mughrib*, 3:275–76.

3. THE CID RIDES AGAIN

77 *"They give themselves grandiose names"*: See Meri, *Medieval Islamic Civilization*, 594.

77 *"Al-Andalus originally belonged to the Christians"*: Tibi, *The Tibyān*, 90.

81 *As the contemporary historian Ibn Bassam remarked*: "Treasury of the Delights of the People of the Island (al-Andalus)," in Menéndez Pidal and García Gómez, "El conde mozárabe," 31–32.

82 *The Castilian king whom Sisnando put his*: See Smith, Melville, and Ubaydli, *Christians and Moors in Spain*, 3:89, for sketches of Sisnando and Alfonso.

85 *In the vivid but unreliable imagination*: See Smith, Melville, and Ubaydli, *Christians and Moors in Spain*, 1:89.

86 *Every inch a king, Alfonso promptly kicked*: See O'Callaghan, *The History of Medieval Spain*, 203.

89 *Zaragoza, or* Saraqusta *in Arabic*: According to Muhammad al-Idrisi, the court geographer to Roger II of Sicily, who was writing in the 1060s, the city was called white because its walls and fortifications were painted in quicklime. He also noted its prodigious gardens and palaces, and that there were no snakes there, as any that entered the city would die. See Jaubert, *Géographie*, 2:34.

90 *Al-Muqtadir was the epitome of the successful* taifa *king*: See "Hudids" in *The Encyclopedia of Islam*, 2nd ed.

90 *Ahmad responded, "to his friend King Sancho"*: See Catlos, *The Victors and the Vanquished*, 75.

90 *When Norman adventurers besieged his town*: See chapter 5, "A Norman Conquest," pp. 140–41.

93 *"Now we have knowledge of your law"*: From Dunlop, "A Christian Mission," 263–64 and 272.

4. RODRIGO DÍAZ, *TAIFA* KING OF VALENCIA

98 *Ibn Tashufin is said to have been shocked*: Smith, Melville, and Ubaydli, *Christians and Moors in Spain*, 3:97.

99 *All the sources say that the battle raged*: For an overview of the various Muslim accounts of the battle, see Lagerdère, *Les Almoravides*, 116–21.

103 *It was said of Yusuf ibn Tashufin*: See "Yūsuf b. Tāshufīn" in *The Encyclopedia of Islam*, 2nd ed.

104 *When his advisers warned him*: See al-Maqqari, *The History*, 2:273.

107 *For his part, the Cid mocked*: See Barton and Fletcher, *The World of El Cid*, 133–36.

111 *In 1085 one in a series of Jewish* wazirs: See Roth, *Jews, Visigoths, and Muslims*, 87. In fact, Ibn Hasday eventually converted to Islam, ostensibly because he fell in love with a Muslim girl, but likely for professional reasons. His son Yusuf, however, did not, and remained a respected poet, philologist, and political operator in his own right.

114 *To the conquerors, the common people were accountable*: See, for example, the poetry in Wasserstein, *The Rise and Fall of the Party-Kings*, 281.

114 *As for Rodrigo, following a final estrangement*: Barton and Fletcher, *The World of El Cid*, 131.

114 *The Cid sacked Nájera and Calahorra*: "In the *Era* 1109 Ruy Diaz entered Logroño in the land of Navarre and in the land of Calahorra with a great host and set a great fire through all the land": see *España Sagrada*, 23:360.

117 *On his arrival a delegation of the city's leading citizens*: Menéndez Pidal, *Primera crónica general*, 1:588.

118 *In the words of the poet and historian Ibn Bassam*: Béraud-Villars, *Les Touareg*, 158.

119 *Now that he was secure as ruler of Valencia*: Montaner Frutos, *Guerra en Sarq Al'andalus*, 235.

120 *As Ibn Bassam put it, "this man"*: Fletcher, *The Quest for El Cid*, 185.

121 *As a Muslim chronicler wrote*: Ibn 'Idhari, *Al-Bayan al-Mugrib: Nuevos fragmentos*, 102.

122 *As one eulogy put it, "The prince had"*: Ibid., 113.

122 *In recalling the king's death, an anonymous Cluniac monk*: From Ubieto Arteta, *Crónicas anónimas*, 33.

5. A NORMAN CONQUEST

128 *According to the only contemporary Christian account*: Catlos, "Who Was Philip of Mahdia?," 100–101; Loud, *Roger II*, 266–68.

132 *One of their first military actions*: Malaterra, *The Deeds of Count Roger*, trans. Kenneth Baxter Wolf, 116.

133 *The last of Tancred's sons to rule Apulia*: Comnena, *The Alexiad of Anna Comnena*, 54.

134 *The Norman barons' respect for Robert*: Loud, *The Deeds of Robert Guiscard*, 7.

135 *In exchange for their aid, he formally invested Robert*: Loud, *The Age of Robert Guiscard*, 130.

140 *"they were unwilling to violate or relinquish"*: Malaterra, *The Deeds of Count Roger*, trans. Kenneth Baxter Wolf, 125.

142 *After visiting in the 970s, Ibn Hawqal*: Granara, "Ibn Hawqal in Sicily," 97.

142 *There was also a strong Shi'a element*: For Shi'a Islam, see chapter 7, "After the Messiah," p. 186.

143 *Eventually, under his successors, most notably*: See Mallette, *The Kingdom of Sicily*, 161–62.

145 *All the more remarkable is that*: Peters, *The First Crusade*, 24. This excerpt is from a letter from Urban II to the Christians of Flanders, dated December 1095. It predates by several years any accounts of his speech at Clermont, which are unreliable, as their authors were influenced by subsequent events, above all the outcome of the Crusade.

146 *"I console my soul, since I see my land"*: Mallette, *The Kingdom of Sicily*, 135.

148 *But for all the references to God and the Virgin*: Loud, *The Deeds of Robert Guiscard*, 34–36.

6. DON'T ASK, DON'T TELL

159 *The Andalusi traveler Ibn Jubayr*: Ibn Jubayr, *Travels*, 349.

161 *In 1185 Ibn Jubayr would liken*: Ibid., 348.

161 *When Ibn Jubayr visited Sicily*: Ibid., 350.

162 *This great chamber reflects an eclectic*: See Tronzo's magisterial study, *The Cultures of His Kingdom*.

163 *Legends in florid Kufic script bordered*: See the translation by Johns in ibid., 45.

168 *In his contemporary* Chronicon, *Archbishop Romuald*: Catlos, "Who Was Philip of Mahdia?," 101; Loud, *Roger II*, 266–68.

170 *As Romuald reported, Roger had personally raised*: Catlos, "Who Was Philip of Mahdia?," 101; Loud, *Roger II*, 266–68.

174 *As Ibn Shaddad, a Zirid prince*: See Johns, *Arabic Adminstration*, 284–85.

176 *Ibn Jubayr, who met William II in 1185*: Ibn Jubayr, *Travels*, 340.

176 *Seeing that the king had overheard*: Ibid., 341.

178 *So it may appear curious that Ibn al-Athir*: Adapted from Catlos, "Who Was Philip of Mahdia?," 102.

7. AFTER THE MESSIAH

185 *Passing under the arches of the gate*: Canard, "Notes sur les Arméniens," 98.

185 *According to the thirteenth-century chronicler*: Canard, "Un vizir," 111.

185 *A century and a half earlier, 'Ubayd Allah*: See Parsumean-Tatoyean, *The Armenians in the Medieval Islamic World*, 66–67.

191 *According to Jawhar, his caliph al-Mu'izz*: Staffa, *Conquest and Fusion*, 52.

193 *These were hastily hauled out*: Walker, "Social Elites at the Fatimid Court," 106.

193 *As he processed through the streets*: For a vivid description of old Cairo and an account of the ceremony marking the opening of the canal of the Nile, see Naser-e Khosraw, *Naser-e Khosraw's Book of Travels*, 38–62.

194 *The Fatimid world was so interconnected that*: See Udovitch, "Fatimid Cairo," 681. The letter reached Abraham's brother, but in Norman Palermo, not in Mahdia.

198 *Most people then and now believe he was killed*: See, for example, Lev, "Persecutions"; and Vatikiotis, "Al-Hakim bi-Amrillah."

202 *The Fatimids were powerless to regain*: See chapter 5, "A Norman Conquest," p. 136.

205 *He would be remembered as "a friend"*: Quoted in Parsumean-Tatoyean, *The Armenians in the Medieval Islamic World*, 127.

208 *Later, in a letter to Roger II of Sicily*: Canard, "Un vizir," 92.

208 *In 1135 Bahram was duly appointed*: Dadoyan, *The Fatimid Armenians*, 97.

208–209 *As long as he was not granted religious powers*: See Zachariah 9:9.

212 *Because of his Christian identity*: Dadoyan, *The Fatimid Armenians*, 94.

8. TRAITORS AND SPIES

213 *"Then he turned to al-Malik al-Salih"*: Catlos, "To Catch a Spy," 103 and 106. The Scripture cited is Qur'an 5:73.

219 *Later, in the early 1200s, for example*: Catlos, "To Catch a Spy," 112, n. 36.

222 *"Become Christian, for Christianity is the true religion!"*: Ibid., 105, n. 17.

222 *Al-'Aziz pardoned the poet*: See C. E. Bosworth, "The Protected Peoples," 22.

225 *A later French romance,* The Song of Antioch: See J. Rubenstein, "Cannibals and Crusaders," 549.

225 *In 1105, when the Damascene preacher al-Sulami*: See Christie and Gerish, "Parallel Preachings."
230 *The officials of the financial bureaucracy*: Catlos, "To Catch a Spy," 106, n. 19.
230 *The most sensational charge was that of spying*: Ibid., 103 and 106.
231 *The notion that God is an indivisible One*: For an introduction to early anti-Christian polemic, see Thomas, *Anti-Christian Polemic in Early Islam* and *Early Muslim Polemic Against Christianity*. For an early example from the 'Abbasid Caliphate, see Gottheil, "A Fetwa."
232 *Not surprisingly, the meeting between*: Catlos, "To Catch a Spy," 102, n. 11.
233 *In the folk traditions of Muslim Egypt*: Ibid., 106.
233 *The only contemporary allusion to the event*: For the poem, see ibid., 103–104, n. 15. 'Umara was a shameless panderer to those in power. He was a creature first of Tala'i ibn Ruzzik, and then of Ruzzik ibn Tala'i. When the latter was overthrown and executed by Shawar in 1163, he threw his syrupy support behind the new *wazir*. See Smoor, "'Umāra's Poetical Views."
237 *One of these luminaries, the sheikh*: Abu Salih, *The Churches and Monasteries of Egypt*, 107.
237 *The story of Ibn Dukhan struck a chord*: See, for example, Gottheil, "An Answer to the Dhimmis"; and Gril, "Un émeute." This tradition is reviewed in Catlos, "To Catch a Spy."

9. A HEAVENLY KINGDOM?

241 *"now that our men had possession"*: Adapted from Peters, *The First Crusade*, 259–60.
242 *"Now that the city was taken"*: Adapted from ibid.
244 *"For as most of you have been told"*: Ibid., 52–53.
244 *"[The Turks] destroy the altars"*: Ibid., 27.
248 *It appears that as an incentive to encourage*: See chapter 3, "The Cid Rides Again," p. 90, and chapter 5, "A Norman Conquest," p. 140.
250 *"In a place called Lorca, towards the east"*: Melczer, *The Pilgrims' Guide*, 77–78.
252 *"Let those who are accustomed to wage private wars"*: Adapted from Peters, *The First Crusade*, 53.
255 *T'oros was an Armenian Melkite*: For Vahram, see chapter 6, "Don't Ask, Don't Tell," p. 166.
259 *To them the Eastern Christians were*: See MacEvitt, *The Crusades and the Christian World of the East*.
261 *When the armies rallied, a Christian chronicler recalled*: Walter the Chancellor, *The Antiochene Wars*, 89.
262 *Ibn Jubayr, who visited Damascus*: Ibn Jubayr, *Travels*, 300.
263 *They were roundly regarded as uncouth*: See, for example, Usama ibn Munqidh, *The Book of Contemplation*, 153.
268 *Late in life, Fulcher of Chartres would wax*: Krey, *The First Crusade*, 280–81.
268 *One of those infidels was 'Usama ibn Munqidh*: For 'Usama's life and career, see Cobb, *Usama ibn Munqidh*.

269 *Some gave him shelter and protected him*: Usama ibn Munqidh, *The Book of Contemplation*, 145.

274 *Though traditional gender roles were put to the test*: See, for example, the observations of contemporary Muslim chroniclers in Hillenbrand, *The Crusades*, 348–49.

10. JERUSALEM RESTORED

276 *The king is summoned next to appear*: See Richards, *The History of Saladin*, 74–75.

280 *When he refused, Reynaud*: Brand, *The Deeds of John and Manuel Comnenus*, 139.

280 *The monk Neophytus the Recluse*: Galatariotou, *The Making of a Saint*, 188.

282 *In the words of the contemporary statesman*: See Hillenbrand, "The Imprisonment of Reynald de Châtillon," 81.

289 *On the death of Nur al-Din*: William of Tyre, *A History of the Deeds Done Beyond the Sea*, 2:394.

305 *"Then the years and their players have passed away"*: Richards, *The Rare and Excellent History*, 245.

EPILOGUE: THE DECLINE AND FALL OF THE ROMAN EMPIRE

310 *Manuel sent him out of the capital*: Brand, *The Deeds of John and Manuel Comnenus*, 98.

310 *Manuel was still reluctant to punish Andronikos*: Magoulias, *O City of Byzantium*, 60–61.

310 *As the contemporary chronicler Niketas Choniates*: Ibid., 59.

311 *In 1166 he was rewarded by an appointment*: Ibid., 79.

311 *But here, too, he continued in his lascivious ways*: Ibid., 80.

312 *The twenty-one-year-old dowager soon moved*: Brand, *The Deeds of John and Manuel Comnenus*, 188.

314 *But the aristocracy and imperial officials turned*: As Niketas Choniates recounted, "On one and the same day, one would often see the same man, both crowned and butchered, praised and cursed." See Magoulias, *O City of Byzantium*, 144.

314 *On September 12, 1185*: For the gruesome details of his death, see ibid., 191–94.

Works Cited

Abu-Haidar, Jareer. *Hispano-Arabic Literature and the Early Provençal Lyrics*. Richmond, UK: Curzon, 2001.

Abulafia, David. *Frederick II: A Medieval Emperor*. London: Allen Lane, 1988.

———. *The Great Sea: A Human History of the Mediterranean*. London: Allen Lane, 2011.

Abu Salih al-Armani Maqrizi, Ahmad ibn Ali. *The Churches and Monasteries of Egypt and Some Neighbouring Countries*. Translated by B.T.A. Evetts and A. J. Butler. Oxford: Clarendon Press, 1895.

Aillet, Cyrille. *Les Mozarabes: Christianisme, islamisation et arabisation en Péninsule Ibérique (IXe–XIIe siècle)*. Madrid: Casa de Velázquez, 2010.

Alfonso, Esperanza. *Islamic Culture Through Jewish Eyes: Al-Andalus from the Tenth to Twelfth Century*. London: Routledge, 2008.

al-Idrisi, Muhammad. *Géographie d'Édrisi traduite de l'arabe en français d'après deux manuscrits de la Bibliothèque du Roi et accompagnée de notes*. Edited and translated by P. A. Jaubert. 2 vols. Paris: L'imprimerie Royale, 1836.

Al-Imad, Leila S. *The Fatimid Vizierate, 969–1172*. Berlin: K. Schwarz, 1990.

al-Maqqari, Ahmad ibn Muhammad. *The History of the Mohammedan Dynasties in Spain*. Translated by Pascual de Gayangos. 2 vols. London: Oriental Translation Fund, 1840.

Amari, Michele, and Umberto Rizzitano. *Biblioteca arabo-sicula: Ossia raccolta di testi arabici che toccano la geografia, la storia, le biografie, e la bibliografia della Sicilia*. 2nd ed. Palermo: Accademia Nazionale di Scienze Lettere e Arti, 1987.

Amato of Montecasino. *The History of the Normans by Amatus of Montecasino*. Edited and translated by Prescott N. Dunbar and G. A. Loud. Woodbridge, UK: Boydell Press, 2004.

Angold, Michael. *Church and Society in Byzantium Under the Comneni, 1081–1261*. New York: Cambridge University Press, 1995.

Asbridge, Thomas S. "Alice of Antioch: A Case Study of Female Power in the Twelfth Century." In *The Experience of Crusading*, vol. 2, *Defining the Crusader Kingdom*, 29–47. Cambridge: Cambridge University Press, 2003.

Ashtor, Eliyahu. *The Jews of Moslem Spain*. 3 vols. Philadelphia: Jewish Publication Society of America, 1973.

Aziz, Ahmad. *A History of Islamic Sicily*. Edinburgh: Edinburgh University Press, 1962.

Bacharach, Jere L. "African Military Slaves in the Medieval Middle East: The Cases of Iraq (869–955) and Egypt (868–1171)." *International Journal of Middle East Studies* 13 (1981): 471–95.

Bargebuhr, Frederick P. "The Alhambra Palace of the Eleventh Century." *Journal of the Warburg and Courtauld Institutes* 19 (1956): 192–258.

Baron, Salo W. *A Social and Religious History of the Jews*. Vol. 3, *High Middle Ages, 500–1200: Heirs of Rome and Persia*. New York: Columbia University Press, 1957.

Barton, Simon. "El Cid, Cluny and the Medieval Spanish Reconquista." *English Historical Review* 126 (2011): 517–43.

———. "Traitors to the Faith? Christian Mercenaries in Al-Andalus and the Magreb, c. 1100–1300." In *Medieval Spain: Culture, Conflict and Coexistence*, edited by Roger Collins and Anthony Goodman, 23–45. New York: Palgrave Macmillan, 2002.

———, and Richard A. Fletcher. *The World of El Cid: Chronicles of the Spanish Reconquest. Selected Sources Translated and Annotated*. New York: Manchester University Press, 2000.

Beech, George T. *The Brief Eminence and Doomed Fall of Islamic Saragossa: A Great Center of Jewish and Arabic Learning in the Iberian Peninsula During the 11th Century*. Zaragoza: Instituto de Estudios Islámicos y del Oriente Próximo, 2008.

Béraud-Villars, Jean. *Les Touareg au pays du Cid: Les invasions almoravides en Espagne aux XIe et XIIe siècles*. Paris: Plon, 1946.

Bierman, Irene A. *Writing Signs: The Fatimid Public Text*. Berkeley: University of California Press, 1998.

Birk, Joshua. "From Borderlands to Borderlines: Narrating the Past of Twelfth-Century Sicily." In *Multicultural Europe and Cultural Exchange in the Middle Ages and Renaissance*, edited by James Peter Helfers, 9–31. Turnhout, Belgium: Brepols, 2005.

Bosworth, C. E. "The 'Protected Peoples' (Christians and Jews) in Medieval Egypt and Syria." *Bulletin of the John Rylands University Library of Manchester* 62 (1979): 11–36.

Bradford, Ernle. *Mediterranean: Portrait of a Sea*. London: Hodder and Stoughton, 1971.

Brand, Charles Macy. *The Deeds of John and Manuel Comnenus*. New York: Columbia University Press, 1976.

Brann, Ross. "The Arabized Jews." In *The Literature of Al-Andalus*, edited by María Rosa Menocal, Raymond P. Scheindlin, and Michael Anthony Sells, 435–54. Cambridge: Cambridge University Press, 2000.

———. *The Compunctious Poet: Cultural Ambiguity and Hebrew Poetry in Muslim Spain.* Baltimore: Johns Hopkins University Press, 1991.

———. *Power in the Portrayal: Representations of Jews and Muslims in Eleventh- and Twelfth-Century Islamic Spain. Jews, Christians, and Muslims from the Ancient to the Modern World.* Princeton, NJ: Princeton University Press, 2002.

Braudel, Fernand. *The Mediterranean and the Mediterranean World in the Age of Philip II.* Berkeley: University of California Press, 1995. First published 1949.

Brett, Michael. "Al-Karāza al-Marqusīya: The Coptic Church in the Fatimid Empire." In *Egypt and Syria in the Fatimid, Ayyubid and Mamluk Eras IV*, edited by Urbain Vermeulen and J. van Steenbergen, 33–60. Leuven, Belgium: Peeters, 2005.

———. "The Armies of Ifriqiya, 1052–1160." In *Guerre et paix dans l'histoire du Maghreb*, 107–25. VIe Congrès d'Histoire et de Civilisation du Maghreb. Tunis, Décembre 1993. Tunis: Cahiers de Tunisie, Université de Tunis, 1997.

———. "Badr al-Ğamālī and the Fatimid Renascence." In *Egypt and Syria in the Fatimid, Ayyubid and Mamluk Eras IV*, edited by Urbain Vermeulen and J. van Steenbergen, 61–78. Leuven, Belgium: Peeters, 2005.

———. "The City-State in Medieval Ifriqiya: The Case of Tripoli." *Cahiers de Tunisie* 34 (1986): 69–94.

———. "Muslim Justice Under Infidel Rule: The Normans in Ifriqiya, 517–555 A.H./ 1123–1160 A.D." *Cahiers de Tunisie* 43 (1995): 1–26.

———. *The Rise of the Fatimids: The World of the Mediterranean and the Middle East in the Tenth Century C.E.* Leiden, Netherlands: E. J. Brill, 2001.

———, and Elizabeth Fentress. *The Berbers.* Oxford: Blackwell, 1996.

Brown, Gordon S. *The Norman Conquest of Southern Italy and Sicily.* Jefferson, NC: McFarland, 2003.

Calderini, Simonetta. "Sayyida Rasad: A Royal Woman as 'Gateway to Power' During the Fatimid Era." In *Egypt and Syria in the Fatimid, Ayyubid and Mamluk Eras V*, edited by Urbain Vermeulen and Kristof d'Hulster, 27–36. Leuven, Belgium: Peeters, 2007.

Canard, Marius. "Notes sur les Arméniens à l'époque fâṭimite." *Annales de l'Institut d'Etudes Orientales de la Faculté des Lettres d'Alger* 13 (1955): 143–57.

———. "Une lettre du calife fâṭimite al-Ḥâfiẓ à Roger II de Sicile." In *Atti del Convegno Internazionale di Studi Ruggeriani*, 125–46. Palermo: Boccone del Povero, 1955.

———. "Un vizir chrétien à l'époque fatimite, l'arménien Bahram." *Annales de l'Institut d'Etudes Orientales de la Faculté des Lettres d'Alger* 12 (1954): 84–113.

Castro, Américo. *The Spaniards: An Introduction to Their History.* Berkeley: University of California Press, 1971.

Catlos, Brian A. "'Accursed, Superior Men': Political Power and Ethno-religious Minorities in the Medieval Mediterranean." *Comparative Studies in Society and History* 56 (2014).

———. "Christian-Muslim-Jewish Relations, Medieval 'Spain,' and the Mediterranean: An Historiographical Op-Ed." In *In and of the Mediterranean: Medieval and Early Modern Iberian Studies*, edited by Núria Silleras-Fernández and Michelle M. Hamilton, 1–16 (Minneapolis: University of Minnesota Press, 2014).

——. *Muslims of Medieval Latin Christendom, c. 1050–1614*. Cambridge: Cambridge University Press, 2014.

——. "To Catch a Spy: The Case of Zayn Al-Dîn and Ibn Dukhân." *Medieval Encounters* 2 (1996): 99–114.

——. *The Victors and the Vanquished. Christians and Muslims of Catalonia and Aragon, 1050–1300*. Cambridge: Cambridge University Press, 2004.

——. "Who Was Philip of Mahdia and Why Did He Have to Die? Confessional Identity and Political Power in the Twelfth-Century Mediterranean." *Mediterranean Chronicle* 1 (2010): 73–103.

Chalandon, Ferdinand. *Histoire de la domination normande en Italie et en Sicilie*. 2 vols. New York: B. Franklin, 1960.

Christie, Niall, and Deborah Gerish. "Parallel Preachings: Urban II and al-Sulamī." *Al-Masaq* 15 (2003): 139–48.

Clément, François. "Reverter et son fils, deux officiers catalans au service des sultans de Marrakech." *Medieval Encounters* 9 (2003): 79–106.

Cobb, Paul M. *Usama Ibn Munqidh: Warrior-Poet of the Age of Crusades*. Oxford: Oneworld, 2005.

Cole, Penny J. *The Preaching of the Crusades to the Holy Land, 1095–1270*. Cambridge, MA: Medieval Academy of America, 1991.

Cole, Peter. *Selected Poems of Shmuel Hanagid*. Princeton, NJ: Princeton University Press, 1996.

Comnena, Anna. *The Alexiad of Anna Comnena*. Edited and translated by Edgar Robert Ashton Sewter. Baltimore: Penguin Books, 1969.

Constable, O. Remie, ed. *Medieval Iberia: Readings From Christian, Muslim, and Jewish Sources*. Philadelphia: University of Pennsylvania Press, 1997.

Cortese, Delia, and Simonetta Calderini. *Women and the Fatimids in the World of Islam*. Edinburgh: Edinburgh University Press, 2006.

Cutler, Allan. "Who Was the Monk of France and When Did He Write?" *Al-Andalus* 28 (1963): 149–69.

Dadoyan, Seta B. *The Fatimid Armenians: Cultural and Political Interaction in the Near East*. Leiden, Netherlands: E. J. Brill, 1997.

——. "The Phenomenon of the Fatimid Armenians." *Mediterranean Encounters* 2 (1996): 193–214.

—— (as Seda Parsumean-Tatoyean). *The Armenians in the Medieval Islamic World: Paradigms of Interaction: Seventh to Fourteenth Centuries*. New Brunswick, NJ: Transaction Publishers, 2011.

Daftary, Farhad. *The Isma'ilis: Their History and Doctrines*. 2nd ed. Cambridge: Cambridge University Press, 2007.

——. *Mediaeval Isma'ili History and Thought*. New York: Cambridge University Press, 1996.

den Heijer, J. "Coptic Historiography in the Fatimid, Ayyubid and Early Mamluk Periods." *Medieval Encounters* 2 (1994): 67–98.

——. "Le patriarcat copte d'Alexandrie à l'époque fatimide." In *Alexandrie médie-*

vale 2, edited by Christian Décobert, 83–97. Cairo: Institut Français d'Archéologie Orientale, 2002.

———. "Le vizir fatimide Badr al-Ğamālī (466/1074–487/1094) et la nouvelle muraille du Caire: Quelques remarques préliminaires." In *Egypt and Syria in the Fatimid, Ayyubid and Mamluk Eras V*, edited by Urbain Vermeulen and Kristof d'Hulster, 91–108. Leuven, Belgium: Peeters, 2007.

Deyermond, A. D., Ian Richard Macpherson, and Keith Whinnom. *The Age of the Catholic Monarchs, 1474–1516: Literary Studies in Memory of Keith Whinnom*. Liverpool: Liverpool University Press, 1989.

Diehl, Charles. *Figures byzantines*. Paris: A. Colin, 1906.

Dunlop, D. M. "A Christian Mission to Muslim Spain in the Eleventh Century." *Al-Andalus* 17 (1952): 259–310.

Edbury, Peter W. *The Conquest of Jerusalem and the Third Crusade: Sources in Translation*. Aldershot, UK: Ashgate, 1998.

Eddé, Anne-Marie. *Saladin*. Cambridge, MA: Belknap Press of Harvard University Press, 2011.

El Cid en el Valle de Jalón: Simposio internacional. Ateca-Calatayud, October 7–10, 1989. Zaragoza: IPF, 1991.

Elisséeff, Nikita. *Nur ad-Din: Un grand prince musulman de Syrie au temps des croisades (511–569 A.H./1118–1174)*. Damascus: Institut Français de Damas, 1967.

Encyclopedia of Islam. 2nd ed. Leiden, Netherlands: E. J. Brill, 1955–2005.

Epalza, Miguel de, and So'ad Guellouz. *Le Cid: Personnage historique et littéraire: Anthologie de textes arabes, espagnols, françaises et latins avec traductions*. Paris: G.-P. Maisonneuve et Larose, 1983.

Erdmann, Carl. *The Origin of the Idea of Crusade*. Princeton, NJ: Princeton University Press, 1977.

España Sagrada. Theatro geographico-historico de la iglesia de España: Origen, divisiones y terminos de todas sus provincia: Antigüedad, traslaciones y estado antiguo y presente de sus sillas, en todos los dominios de España y Portugal. Edited by Enrique Flórez et al. 58 vols. Vol. 23: *Continuacion de la memorias de la Santa Iglesia de Tuy y coleccion de los chronicones pequeños publicados è ineditos, de la historia de España*. Madrid: Oficina de la viuda é hijo de Marin, 1799.

Falcando, Ugo, G. A. Loud, and Thomas E. J. Wiedemann. *The History of the Tyrants of Sicily by "Hugo Falcandus," 1154–69*. Manchester: Manchester University Press, 1998.

Fletcher, Richard A. *The Quest for El Cid*. New York: Knopf, 1990.

Franzen, Cola. *Poems of Arab Andalusia*. San Francisco: City Lights Books, 1989.

Galatariotou, Catia. *The Making of a Saint: The Life, Times, and Sanctification of Neophytos the Recluse*. Cambridge: Cambridge University Press, 1991.

García Gómez, Emilio. *Cinco poetas musulmanes: Biografías y estudios*. 2nd ed. Madrid: Espasa-Calpe, 1959.

———. "Polémica religiosa enre Ibn Hazm e Ibn al-Nagrila." *Al-Andalus* 4 (1936): 1–28.

Gerber, Jane S. *The Jews of Spain: A History of the Sephardic Experience*. New York: Free Press, 1992.

Gibb, H.A.R. *The Damascus Chronicle of the Crusades*. London: Luzac, 1932.

Gibbon, Edward. *The Decline and Fall of the Roman Empire*. 6 vols. London: Peter Fenelon Collier and Sons, 1901. First published 1772–98.

Glick, Thomas F., and Oriol Pi-Sunyer. "Acculturation as an Explanatory Concept in Spanish History." *Comparative Studies in Society and History* 11 (1969): 136–54.

Goitein, S. D. *Letters of Medieval Jewish Traders*. Princeton, NJ: Princeton University Press, 1974.

———. *A Mediterranean Society: The Jewish Communities of the Arab World as Portrayed in the Documents of the Cairo Geniza*. 4 vols. Berkeley: University of California Press, 1983.

Golvin, Lucien. *Le Magrib central a l'époque des Zirides. Recherches d'archéologie et d'histoire*. Paris: Arts et Métiers Graphiques, 1957.

Gorton, T. J. *Andalus: Moorish Songs of Love and Wine*. London: Eland, 2007.

Gottheil, Richard. "An Answer to the Dhimmis." *Journal of American Oriental Studies* 41 (1921): 383–457.

———. "A Fetwa on the Appointment of Dhimmis to Office." *Zeitschrift für Assyriologie und verwandte Gebiete* 26 (1912): 203–14.

Granara, William. "Ibn Hawqal in Sicily/ ابن حوقل في صقلية." *Alif: Journal of Comparative Poetics* (1983): 94–99.

Griffith, Sidney Harrison. *The Church in the Shadow of the Mosque: Christians and Muslims in the World of Islam*. Princeton, NJ: Princeton University Press, 2008.

Gril, Denis. "Un émeute anti-chrétienne à Qus au début du VIIIe/XIVe siècle." *Annales Islamologiques* 16 (1980): 241–74.

Halm, Heinz. *The Empire of the Mahdi: The Rise of the Fatimids*. Leiden, Netherlands: E. J. Brill, 1996.

Hamdani, Abbas. *The Fatimids*. Karachi: Pakistan Publishing House, 1962.

Hamilton, Bernard. "Aimery of Limoges, Latin Patriarch of Antioch (c. 1142–1196) and the Unity of the Churches." In *East and West in the Crusader States: Context, Contacts, Confrontations*, edited by Krijna Nelly Ciggaar, Herman G. B. Teule, and A. A. Brediusstichting, 1–12. Acta of the Congress Held at Hernen Castle in May 1997. Leuven, Belgium: Uitgeverij Peeters, 1999.

———. "Aimery of Limoges, Patriarch of Antioch, Ecumenist, Scholar and Patron of Hermits." In *The Joy of Learning and the Love of God: Studies in Honor of Jean Leclercq*, edited by Jean Leclercq and E. Rozanne Elder, 269–90. Kalamazoo, MI: Cistercian Publications, 1978.

———. "The Elephant of Christ: Reynald of Châtillon." *Studies in Church History* 15 (1978): 97–108.

———. *The Leper King and His Heirs: Baldwin IV and the Crusader Kingdom of Jerusalem*. Cambridge: Cambridge University Press, 2000.

———. "The Templars, the Syrian Assassins and King Amalric of Jerusalem." In *The Hospitallers, the Mediterranean and Europe: Festschrift for Anthony Luttrell*, edited by Karl Borchardt, Nikolas Jaspert, and Helen J. Nicholson, 13–24. Hampshire, UK/ Burlington, VT: Ashgate, 2007.

Handler, Andrew. *The Zirids of Granada*. Coral Gables, FL: University of Miami Press, 1974.

Herrin, Judith. *Byzantium: The Surprising Life of a Medieval Empire*. Princeton, NJ: Princeton University Press, 2007.

Hillenbrand, Carole. *The Crusades: Islamic Perspectives*. New York: Routledge, 2000.

———. "The Imprisonment of Reynald of Châtillon." In *Texts, Documents, and Artefacts: Islamic Studies in Honour of D. S. Richards*, edited by Chase F. Robinson, 79–102. Leiden, Netherlands: E. J. Brill.

Hitchcock, Richard. *Mozarabs in Medieval and Early Modern Spain: Identities and Influences*. Aldershot, UK: Ashgate, 2008.

Hodges, Richard, and David Whitehouse. *Mohammed, Charlemagne, and the Origins of Europe: Archaeology and the Pirenne Thesis*. London: Duckworth, 1983.

Holt, P. M. *The Age of the Crusades: The Near East From the Eleventh Century to 1517*. Harlow, UK/New York: Addison Wesley Longman, 1986.

———. *The Crusader States and Their Neighbours, 1098–1291*. Harlow, UK/New York: Addison Wesley Longman, 2004.

The Holy Qur'an. Translated by M. H. Shakir. Elmhurst, NY: Tahrike Tarsile Qur'an, 1983.

Horden, Peregrine, and Nicholas Purcell. *The Corrupting Sea: A Study of Mediterranean History*. Malden, MA: Blackwell, 2000.

Houben, Hubert. *Roger II of Sicily: A Ruler Between East and West*. Cambridge: Cambridge University Press, 2002.

Huici Miranda, Ambrosio. *Historia musulmana de Valencia y su región: Novedades y rectificaciones*. 3 vols. Valencia: Ayuntamiento de Valencia, 1969–70.

Huntington, Samuel P. *The Clash of Civilizations and the Remaking of World Order*. New York: Simon and Schuster, 1996.

Ibn al-Mukaffa', Sawirus. *History of the Patriarchs of the Egyptian Church*. Edited and translated by Yassa 'Abd al-Masih and Aziz Suryal Atiya. 2 vols. Cairo: Institut Français d'Archéologie Orientale, 1959.

Ibn Daud. *The Book of Tradition (Sefer Ha-Qabbalah)*. Edited and translated by Gerson D. Cohen. London: Routledge and Kegan Paul, 1969.

Ibn 'Idhari, Abu al-Abbas Ahmad. *Al-Bayan al-Mughrib*. Edited by Évariste Lévi-Provençal. 3 vols. Paris: P. Geuthner, 1930.

———. *Al-Bayan al-Mugrib: Nuevos fragmentos almorávides y almohades*. Translated by Ambrosio Huici Miranda. Valencia: Graficas Bautista, 1963.

Ibn Jubayr. *The Travels of Ibn Jubayr, Being the Chronicles of a Mediaeval Spanishmoor Concerning His Journey to the Egpyt of Saladin, the Holy Cities of Arabia, Baghdad the City of the Caliphs, the Latin Kingdom of Jerusalem, and the Norman Kingdom of Sicily*. Edited and translated by Muhammad ibn Ahmad and Ronald J. C. Broadhurst. London: J. Cape, 1952.

Ibn Khaldûn. *The Muqaddimah. An Introduction to History*. Translated by F. Rosenthal. 3 vols. London: Routledge and Kegan Paul, 1958.

Idris, Hady Roger. *La Berbérie orientale sous les Zirides, Xe–XIIe siècles*. Paris: Adrien-Maisonneuve, 1959.

——. "Les Zirides d'Espagne." *Al-Andalus* 29 (1964): 39–137.

Iogna-Prat, Dominique. *Order and Exclusion: Cluny and Christendom Face Heresy, Judaism, and Islam (1000–1150). Conjunctions of Religion and Power in the Medieval Past*. Ithaca, NY: Cornell University Press, 2002.

Johns, Jeremy. *Arabic Administration in Norman Sicily: The Royal Dīwān*. Cambridge: Cambridge University Press, 2002.

——. "Malik Ifriqiyah: The Norman Kingdom of Africa and the Fatimids." *Libyan Studies* 18 (1993): 89–101.

——. "The Norman Kings of Sicily and the Fatimid Caliphate." *Anglo-Norman Studies* 15 (1993): 133–59.

Kennedy, Hugh. *Muslim Spain and Portugal: A Political History of al-Andalus*. Harlow, UK/New York: Addison Wesley Longman, 1996.

Khosraw, Naser-e. *Naser-e Khosraw's Book of Travels (Safarnama)*. Translated by W. M. Thackston. Albany, NY: Bibliotheca Persica, 1986.

Kostick, Conor. *The Siege of Jerusalem: Crusade and Conquest in 1099*. London: Continuum, 2009.

——. *The Social Structure of the First Crusade*. Leiden, Netherlands: E. J. Brill, 2008.

Kreutz, Barbara M. *Before the Normans: Southern Italy in the Ninth and Tenth Centuries*. Philadelphia: University of Pennsylvania Press, 1991.

Krey, August C. *The First Crusade: The Accounts of Eye-witnesses and Participants*. Gloucester, UK: P. Smith, 1958.

Lagardère, Vincent. *Les Almoravides jusqu'au règne de Yūsuf b. Tāšfīn (1039–1106)*. Paris: Éditions l'Harmattan, 1989.

Lev, Yaakov. "The Fāṭimid Army, A.H. 358–427/968–1036 C.E.: Military and Social Aspects." *Asian and African Studies* 14 (1980): 165–92.

——. "Persecutions and Conversion to Islam in Eleventh-Century Egypt." *Asian and African Studies* 22 (1988): 73–91.

——. *Saladin in Egypt*. Leiden, Netherlands: E. J. Brill, 1999.

——. *State and Society in Fatimid Egypt*. Leiden, Netherlands: E. J. Brill, 1991.

Lewis, Bernard. *The Assassins: A Radical Sect in Islam*. London: Al Saqi, 1985.

——. *What Went Wrong? The Clash Between Islam and Modernity in the Middle East*. New York: Perennial, 2003.

Lilie, Ralph-Johannes. *Byzantium and the Crusader States, 1096–1204*. Oxford: Clarendon Press, 1993.

Loud, G. A. *The Age of Robert Guiscard: Southern Italy and the Norman Conquest*. Harlow, UK/New York: Addison Wesley Longman, 2000.

——. *Roger II and the Creation of the Kingdom of Sicily*. Manchester, UK: Manchester University Press, 2012.

Lourie, Elena. "Black Women Warriors in the Muslim Army Besieging Valencia and the Cid's Victory: A Problem of Interpretation." *Traditio* 55 (2000): 181–209.

Maalouf, Amin. *The Crusades Through Arab Eyes*. London: Al Saqi, 1984.

MacEvitt, Christopher Hatch. *The Crusades and the Christian World of the East: Rough Tolerance*. Philadelphia: University of Pennsylvania Press, 2008.

Madden, Thomas F. *The New Concise History of the Crusades*. Lanham, MD: Rowman and Littlefield, 2005.

Magdalino, Paul. *The Empire of Manuel I Komnenos, 1143–1180*. Cambridge: Cambridge University Press, 1993.

Magoulias, Harry J., ed. and trans. *O City of Byzantium: Annals of Niketas Choniates*. Detroit: Wayne State University Press, 1984.

Malaterra, Goffredo. *The Deeds of Count Roger of Calabria and Sicily and of His Brother Duke Robert Guiscard*. Translated by Kenneth Baxter Wolf. Ann Arbor: University of Michigan Press, 2005.

Mallett, Alex. "A Trip Down the Red Sea with Reynald of Châtillon." *Journal of the Royal Asiatic Society* 18 (2008): 141–53.

Mallette, Karla. *The Kingdom of Sicily, 1100–1250: A Literary History*. Pittsburgh: University of Pennsylvania Press, 2005.

Matthew, Donald. "The Chronicle of Romuald of Salerno." In *The Writing of History in the Middle Ages: Essays Presented to Richard William Southern*, edited by R. W. Southern, R.H.C. Davis, and J. M. Wallace-Hadrill. New York: Oxford University Press, 1981.

———. *The Norman Kingdom of Sicily*. Cambridge: Cambridge University Press, 1992.

Mayer, Hans Eberhart. *The Crusades*. London: Oxford University Press, 1972.

———. "Studies in the History of Queen Melisende of Jerusalem." *Dumbarton Oaks Papers* 26 (1972): 93–181.

———, and Lawrence F. McCrank. "Norman Crusaders in the Catalan Reconquest: Robert Burdet and the Principality of Tarragona, 1129–55." *Journal of Medieval History* 7 (1981): 67–82.

Meinardus, Otto Friedrich August. *Two Thousand Years of Coptic Christianity*. Cairo: American University in Cairo Press, 2002.

Melczer, William. *The Pilgrim's Guide to Santiago de Compostela*. New York: Italica Press, 1993.

Ménager, Léon Robert. *Amiratus—Ἀμηρᾶς: L'Émirat et les origines de l'amirauté, XIe–XIIIe siècles*. Paris: S.E.V.P.E.N., 1960.

Menéndez Pidal, Ramón, ed. *Primera crónica general de España*. 3rd ed. 2 vols. Madrid: Gredos, 1977.

———, and E. García Gómez. "El conde mozárabe Sisnando Davídez y la política de Alfonso VI con los taifas." *Al-Andalus* 22 (1947): 27–41.

Menocal, María Rosa. *The Ornament of the World: How Muslims, Jews, and Christians Created a Culture of Tolerance in Medieval Spain*. Boston: Little Brown, 2002.

———, Raymond P. Scheindlin, and Michael Anthony Sells. *The Literature of Al-Andalus*. New York: Cambridge University Press, 2000.

Meri, Josef W., and Jere L. Bacharach. *Medieval Islamic Civilization: An Encyclopedia*. New York: Routledge, 2006.

Messier, Ronald A. *The Almoravids and the Meanings of Jihad*. Santa Barbara, CA: Praeger, 2010.

Metcalfe, Alex. *Muslims and Christians in Norman Sicily: Arabic Speakers and the End of Islam*. New York: Routledge, 2003.

———. *The Muslims of Medieval Italy*. Edinburgh: Edinburgh University Press, 2009.

Michael, Ian, Rita Hamilton, and Janet Perry, eds. and trans. *The Poem of the Cid: A New Critical Edition of the Spanish Text*. Manchester: Manchester University Press, 1975.

Milwright, Marcus. "Reynald of Châtillon and the Red Sea Expedition, 1182–83." In *Noble Ideals and Bloody Realities: Warfare in the Middle Ages*, edited by N. Christie, 235–59. Leiden, Netherlands: E. J. Brill, 2006.

Monroe, James T. *Hispano-Arabic Poetry: A Student Anthology*. Piscataway, NJ: Gorgias Press, 2004. First published 1974 by University of California Press.

Montaner Frutos, Alberto, and A Boix Jovaní. *Guerra en Sarq Al'Andalus: Las batallas cidianas de Morella (1084) y Cuarte (1094)*. Zaragoza: Instituto de Estudios Islámicos de Oriente Próximo, 2005.

Nicol, Donald MacGillivray. *Byzantium and Venice: A Study in Diplomatic and Cultural Relations*. Cambridge: Cambridge University Press, 1992.

Nicolle, David. *Hattin 1187: Saladin's Greatest Victory*. London: Osprey, 1993.

Norris, Harry T. *The Berbers in Arabic Literature*. Harlow, UK/New York: Addison Wesley Longman, 1982.

Norwich, John Julius. *The Middle Sea: A History of the Mediterranean*. New York: Doubleday, 2006.

O'Callaghan, Joseph F. *History of Medieval Spain*. Ithaca, NY: Cornell University Press, 1975.

———. *Reconquest and Crusade in Medieval Spain*. Philadelphia: University of Pennsylvania Press, 2003.

Ostrogorski, Georgije. *History of the Byzantine State*. New Brunswick, NJ: Rutgers University Press, 1969.

O'Sullivan, Shaun. "Coptic Conversion and Islamization of Egypt." *Mamlūk Studies Review* 10 (2006): 65–79.

Owen, C. A. "Scandal in the Egyptian Treasury: A Portion of the Luma' Al-Kawānīn of 'Uthmān ibn Ibrāhīm Al-Nābulusī." *Journal of Near Eastern Studies* 14 (1955): 70–80.

Parsumean-Tatoyean, Seda. *The Armenians in the Medieval Islamic World: Paradigms of Interaction: Seventh to Fourteenth Centuries*. New Brunswick, NJ: Transaction Publishers, 2011.

The Penguin Book of Hebrew Verse. Edited by T. Carmi. New York: Penguin Books, 1981.

Pérès, Henri. *La Poésie andalouse en arabe classique au XIe siècle: Ses aspects généraux, ses thèmes principaux et sa valeur documentaire*. 2nd ed. Paris: Adrien-Maisonneuve, 1953.

Peters, Edward. *The First Crusade: The Chronicle of Fulcher of Chartres and Other Source Materials*. 2nd ed. Philadelphia: University of Pennsylvania Press, 1998.

Petrus [Peter of Eboli], Theo Kölzer, Marlis Stähli, and Gereon Becht-Jördens. *Liber ad honorem augusti sive de rebus siculis. Codex 120 II der Burgerbibliothek Bern: Eine Bilderchronik der Stauferzeit*. Sigmaringen, Germany: J. Thorbecke, 1994.

Pirenne, Henri. *Mohammed and Charlemagne*. London: G. Allen and Unwin, 1958. First published 1937.

Prawer, Joshua. *The History of the Jews in the Latin Kingdom of Jerusalem*. Oxford: Clarendon Press, 1988.

———. *The Latin Kingdom of Jerusalem: European Colonialism in the Middle Ages*. London: Weidenfeld and Nicolson, 1973.

Reilly, Bernard F. *The Kingdom of León-Castilla Under King Alfonso VI, 1065–1109*. Princeton, NJ: Princeton University Press, 1988.

Richard, Jean. *The Crusades, c. 1071–c. 1291*. Cambridge: Cambridge University Press, 1999.

Richards, D. S., ed. and trans. *The Chronicle of Ibn al-Athir for the Crusading Period From Al-Kamil fi-l-tarikh*. Aldershot, UK: Ashgate, 2006.

———. *The Rare and Excellent History of Saladin; or, Al-Nawadir al-Sultaniyya wa'l-Mahasin al-Yusufiyya*. Aldershot, UK: Ashgate, 2002.

Riley-Smith, Jonathan Simon Christopher. *The Crusades, Christianity, and Islam*. New York: Columbia University Press, 2008.

———. *The First Crusaders, 1095–1131*. Cambridge: Cambridge University Press, 1997.

———. *The Oxford History of the Crusades*. New York: Oxford University Press, 1999.

Roth, Norman. *Jews, Visigoths, and Muslims in Medieval Spain: Cooperation and Conflict*. Leiden, Netherlands: E. J. Brill, 1994.

Rubenstein, Jay. "Cannibals and Crusaders." *French Historical Studies* 31 (2008): 525–52.

Runciman, Steven. *A History of the Crusades*. 3 vols. Cambridge: Cambridge University Press, 1951–54.

Russell, P. E. "The Nessus-Shirt of Spanish History." *Bulletin of Hispanic Studies* 36 (1959): 219–25.

Rustow, Marina. *Heresy and the Politics of Community: The Jews of the Fatimid Caliphate*. Ithaca, NY: Cornell University Press, 2008.

Saleh, Marjlis. "Government Intervention in the Coptic Church in Egypt During the Fatimid Period." *Muslim World* 91 (2001): 381–98.

Samir, Samir Khalil. "The Role of Christians in the Fāṭimid Government Services of Egypt to the Reign of Al-Ḥāfiẓ." *Medieval Encounters* 2 (1996): 177–92.

Sánchez-Albornoz, Claudio. *Spain, A Historical Enigma*. Madrid: Fundación Universitaria Española, 1975.

Sanders, Paula. *Ritual, Politics, and the City in Fatimid Cairo*. Albany, NY: State University of New York Press, 1994.

Sato, Tsugitaka. *State and Rural Society in Medieval Islam: Sultans, Muqta's, and Fallahun*. Leiden, Netherlands: E. J. Brill, 1997.

Scheindlin, Raymond P. *Wine, Women, and Death: Medieval Hebrew Poems on the Good Life*. Philadelphia: Jewish Publication Society, 1986.

Schirmann, Jefim. "Samuel Hannagid, the Man, the Soldier, the Politician." *Jewish Social Studies* 13 (1951): 99–126.

Schlumberger, Gustave Léon. *Renaud de Châtillon, Prince d'Antioche, Seigneur de la terre d'Outre-Jourdain*. Paris: Plon, 1923.

Setton, Kenneth Meyer. *A History of the Crusades*. 2nd ed. 6 vols. Madison: University of Wisconsin Press, 1969.

Smail, R. C. *Crusading Warfare, 1097–1193*. 2nd ed. Cambridge: Cambridge University Press, 1995.

Smarandache, Bogdan. "The Franks and the Nizārī Ismāʿīlīs in the Early Crusade Period." *Al-Masaq* 24 (2012): 221–39.

Smith, Colin. *The Making of the Poema de Mío Cid*. Cambridge: Cambridge University Press, 1983.

———, ed. *Poema de mío Cid*. Madrid: Cátedra, 1976.

———. "Two Historians Reassess the Cid." *Anuario medieval* 2 (1990): 155–71.

———, Charles Melville, and Ahmad Ubaydli, eds. and trans. *Christians and Moors in Spain*. 3 vols. Warminster, UK: Aris and Phillips, 1988.

Smoor, Pieter. "'Umāra's Poetical Views of Shāwar, Ḍirghām, Shīrkūh and Ṣalāḥ al-Dīn as Viziers of the Fatimid Caliphs." In *Culture and Memory in Medieval Islam: Essays in Honour of Wilferd Madelung*, edited by Farhad Daftary and Josef W. Meri. 410–32. London: I. B. Tauris, 2003.

Staffa, Susan Jane. *Conquest and Fusion: The Social Evolution of Cairo, A.D. 642–1850*. Leiden, Netherlands: E. J. Brill, 1977.

Stanton, Charles D. *Norman Naval Operations in the Mediterranean*. Woodbridge, UK: Boydell Press, 2011.

Swanson, Mark N. *The Coptic Papacy in Islamic Egypt (641–1517)*. Cairo: American University in Cairo Press, 2010.

Tagher, Jacques. *Christians in Muslim Egypt: An Historical Study of the Relations Between Copts and Muslims From 640 to 1922*. Altenburg, Germany: Oros Verlag, 1998.

Takayama, Hiroshi. *The Administration of the Norman Kingdom of Sicily*. Leiden, Netherlands: E. J. Brill, 1993.

Taylor, Julie. *Muslims in Medieval Italy: The Colony at Lucera*. Lanham, MD: Lexington Books, 2003.

Thomas, David. *Anti-Christian Polemic in Early Islam: Abū 'Īsā al-Warrāq's "Against the Trinity."* Cambridge: Cambridge University Press, 1992.

———. *Early Muslim Polemic Against Christianity: Abū 'Īsā al-Warrāq's "Against the Incarnation."* Cambridge: Cambridge University Press, 2002.

Tibi, Amin T. *The Tibyān: Memoirs of 'Abd Allāh B. Buluggīn, Last Zīrid Amīr of Granada*. Leiden, Netherlands: E. J. Brill, 1986.

Tolan, John Victor. *Saracens: Islam in the Medieval European Imagination*. New York: Columbia University Press, 2002.

Tronzo, William. *The Cultures of His Kingdom: Roger II and the Cappella Palatina in Palermo*. Princeton, NJ: Princeton University Press, 1997.

Turk, Afif. *El reino de Zaragoza en el siglo XI de Cristo (V de la Hégira)*. Madrid: Instituto Egipcio de Estudios Islámicos en Madrid, 1978.

Tyerman, Christopher J. *God's War: A New History of the Crusades*. London: Allen Lane, 2006.

———. *The Invention of the Crusades*. Basingstoke, UK: Macmillan, 1998.

Ubieto Arteta, Antonio, ed. *Crónicas anónimas de Sahagún*. Zaragoza: Facsímil, 1987.

Udovitch, Abraham L. "Fatimid Cairo: Crossroads of World Trade—From Spain to India." In *L'Égypte fatimide: Son art et son histoire*, edited by M. Barrucand, 681–91. Paris: Université de Paris-Sorbonne, 2000.

Usama ibn Munqidh. *The Book of Contemplation: Islam and the Crusades*. Translated by Paul M. Cobb. New York: Penguin Books, 2008.

van Donzel, E. "Badr al-Jamali, the Copts in Egypt and the Muslims in Ethiopia." In

Studies in Honour of Clifford Edmund Bosworth, edited by Ian Richard Netton and C. E. Bosworth, 297–309. Leiden, Netherlands: E. J. Brill, 2000.

Van Reeth, J. "The Rise of Extremist Sects and the Dissolution of the Fatimid Empire in Egypt." *Islamic Culture* 31 (1957): 17–25.

Vatikiotis, P. J. "Al-Hakim bi-Amrillah: The God-King Idea Realised." *Islamic Culture* 29 (1955): 1–8.

Vermeulen, Urbain, and Kristof d'Hulster, eds. *Egypt and Syria in the Fatimid, Ayyubid and Mamluk Eras V: Proceedings of the 11th, 12th and 13th International Colloquium Organized at the Katholieke Universiteit Leuven in May 2001, 2002 and 2003*. Leuven, Belgium: Peeters, 2007.

Vermeulen, Urbain, and J. van Steenbergen, eds. *Egypt and Syria in the Fatimid, Ayyubid and Mamluk Eras IV: Proceedings of the 9th and 10th International Colloquium Organized at the Katholieke Universiteit Leuven in May 2000 and May 2001*. Leuven, Belgium: Peeters, 2005.

Walker, Paul Ernest. *Exploring an Islamic Empire: Fatimid History and Its Sources*. London: I. B. Tauris, 2002.

———. "The Fatimid Caliph Al-ʿAzīz and His Daughter Sitt Al-Mulk: A Case of Delayed but Eventual Succession to Rule by a Woman." *Journal of Persianate Studies* 4 (2011): 30–44.

———. "Social Elites at the Fatimid Court." In *Court Cultures in the Muslim World: Seventh to Nineteenth Centuries*, edited by Albrecht Fuess and Jan-Peter Hartung, 105–22. London/New York: Routledge, 2011.

Walter the Chancellor. *Walter the Chancellor's "The Antiochene Wars."* Translated by Thomas S. Asbridge and Susan Edgington. Aldershot, UK: Ashgate, 1999.

Wasserstein, David. "Jewish Élites in Al-Andalus." In *The Jews of Medieval Islam: Community, Society, and Identity*, edited by Daniel Frank, 101–10. Proceedings of an International Conference Held by the Institute of Jewish Studies, University College London, 1992. Leiden, Netherlands: E. J. Brill, 1995.

———. *The Rise and Fall of the Party-Kings: Politics and Society in Islamic Spain, 1002–1086*. Princeton, NJ: Princeton University Press, 1985.

———. "Samuel Ibn Naghrila Ha-Nagid and Islamic Historiography in Al-Andalus." *Al-Qantara* 14 (1993): 109–26.

Weinberger, Leon J., ed. and trans. *Jewish Prince in Moslem Spain: Selected Poems of Samuel Ibn Nagrela*. University: University of Alabama Press, 1973.

Wiet, Gaston. *L'Égypte musulmane de la conquête arabe à la conquête ottomane, 642–1517 de l'ère chrétienne, etc.* Paris: Plon, 1937.

William of Tyre. *A History of Deeds Done Beyond the Sea*. Translated by Emily Atwater Babcock and August C. Krey. 2 vols. New York: Columbia University Press, 1943.

Wright, Roger. *Early Ibero-Romance: Twenty-One Studies on Language and Texts from the Iberian Peninsula Between the Roman Empire and the Thirteenth Century*. Newark, NJ: Juan de la Cuesta, 1994.

Yeomans, Richard. *The Art and Architecture of Islamic Cairo*. Reading, UK: Garnet, 2006.

Acknowledgments

Many people deserve my thanks for helping to bring this book to press.

Among those who merit the most gratitude are my wife, Núria Silleras-Fernández, who offered advice, a critical eye, and support through yet another project; my kids, Alexandra and Raymond, who once more had to endure an overly busy and occasionally cranky father; my agent, Dan Green, for coaxing me to transform what had been for many years a vague idea into a viable proposal; Thomas LeBien, who generously commissioned the book; and Dan Gerstle, who as my editor gave me the time I needed to finish it and then whipped the manuscript into shape. I also thank Simon Barton (Exeter University) for checking over Part II; Joshua Birk (Smith College), who read and critiqued the chapters on Sicily; Yaacov Lev (Bar-Ilan University) for looking over the section on the Fatimids; Peter Cowe (UCLA) for reading the parts on the Armenians; and Anthony Kaldellis (Ohio State University) for reviewing the Epilogue. It goes without saying, any errors or omissions are my responsibility entirely.

Credit is due as well to the University of California Office of the President, which has for the last four years funded the Mediterranean Seminar, a scholarly project that I cofounded and have codirected since 2007 with my colleague and longtime collaborator, Sharon Kinoshita (University of California, Santa Cruz), as a UC multicampus research project. The many workshops, conferences, and institutes we have organized and directed have provided me with opportunities to learn much from both established and emerging scholars, whose knowledge and expertise span the Mediterranean and range from art history, musicology, and cultural and literary studies to political, economic, and intellectual history. I am grateful for being able to "test drive" the present book with the excellent and engaged students of my class, Humanities 3850, "The Mediterranean: Religion Before Modernity," in spring 2014. I should also thank the Department of Religious Studies at the University of Colorado Boulder, for generously providing support for obtaining the rights to the images reproduced in this book. Finally, let me mention María Rosa Menocal, a generous colleague and a brilliant scholar, now sorely missed, whose *Ornament of the World* is a model of popular scholarly writing, and Wadjih F. al-Hamwi ("Abi"), whose grace and friendship have been an ever-present source of reassurance and inspiration to me over the last quarter century. Thank you.

Index

Page numbers in *italics* refer to illustrations.

Abbadids, *taifa* kings of Seville, 38, 41, 42, 55, 63, 64, 74, 113, 15; end of, 113–14

'Abbas ibn Yahya, 234, 268

'Abbasids, caliphs, 32, 49, 104, 185, 189–91, 200, 203, 217, 225–28, 233

'Abd al-'Aziz, *taifa* king of Valencia, 31

'Abd Allah ibn Buluqqin, *taifa* king of Granada, 38, 43, 62–63, 77, 96, 104, 112, 113*n*

'Abd al-Malik, *hajib* of Córdoba, 24, 37

'Abd al-Rahman I, amir of Córdoba, 189

'Abd al-Rahman III, Caliph of Córdoba, 17 and *n*, 18–22, 26–28, 32, 46

Abrahamic religions, 317–18

Abu Bakr ibn 'Ammar, 47

Abu Bakr ibn 'Umar, Almoravid amir, 101

Abu Fadl ibn Hasdai ibn Shaprut, 91

Abu Ishaq, 57, 64

Abu 'l-Qasim Muhammad ibn 'Abbad, *taifa* king of Seville, 31, 46, 47

Acre, 262, 303, 311

Adelaide de Vasto, Countess of Sicily and Queen of Jerusalem, 148, 149–51, 270

adhab, 35

Africa, 5, 6, 7, 10, 11, 17, 18, 20, 26, 79, 99*n*, 129, 224; gold, 17, 35, 101; Roger II as "king," 164–68, 173–76; slaves, 171–72; Sudanese Blacks, 200–204. *See also* Ifriqiya; *specific countries*

Aghlabids, 190

Aghmat, 101

Agnes, Queen of Hungary, 285

agriculture, 36, 249, 324; Egypt, 193

Aimery of Limoges, Patriarch of Antioch, 278 and *n*, 280, *281*, 284 and *n*

al-'Adid, Fatimid caliph, 296, 297

al-'Adil Abu Bakr ibn Ayyub, 292, 303

al-Afdal ibn Badr al-Jamali, 205–207, 223, 267, 299
al-Amir, Fatimid caliph, 206
al-Andalus, 10, 15–66, 136, 142, 147, 189, 259, 320; Battle of Zallaqa, 71, 96–100, 104; Berbers, 10, 17–18, 21, 24–66, 80, 99, 103; Christian "reconquest" of, 10, 71, 78–123, 147–48; Christians, 10, 17 and n, 20, 21 and n, 22, 24, 28n, 38, 44, 56–57, 69–123; Cid and, 69–97, 105–23; civil war, 25, 27–28, 35; collapse of Caliphate, 25, 31, 34–36, 46, 50, 101, 111; Córdoba, 16–35; culture, 16–66, 69–123; decline of, 111–14, 120–23; economy, 16–17, 28, 31, 35, 36, 44, 79; Granada, 28–29, 31, 36–66; Islam-Christian relations, 69–123; Jewish-Muslim relations, 15–66, 110–11; Jews, 15–17, 21–66, 79, 80, 110–11, 119, 322; massacre of 1066, 61–65; Naghrilla dynasty, 35–66; politics, 16–66, 69–123; society, 16–66, 69–123; taifa period, 30–35, 36–66, 69–123; trade, 17, 18, 21, 36, 44, 51, 79; Umayyad, 17, 22, 24–25, 27, 30, 31, 32, 38, 42, 49, 50, 75, 89, 100, 102, 189; Zaragoza, 89–96, 105; Zirid, 27–66, 77
Alawites, 214, 233, 235
al-'Aziz, Fatimid caliph, 197, 198, 219–22
al-Baji, Abu 'l-Walid Sulayman, 93–94
Albarracín, 118
Alcudia, 115
Aledo, 74, 105–106
Aleppo, 226, 259, 260–62, 272, 285, 290, 292, 321
Alexander II, Pope, 248
Alexandria, 137, 153, 177, 183, 191, 193, 194, 202, 205, 215, 220, 229, 287; Church of, 194
Alexios Megas Komnenos, 316n
Alexios I Komnenos, Emperor, 150 and n, 253–54, 256, 261, 264, 271, 307–308, 316
Alexios III, Emperor, 314–15, 316n
Alexios IV, Emperor, 315

al-Fa'iz, Fatimid caliph, 213
al-Fallahi, Yusuf, 202
al-Faraj, 115–17
Alfonso I, King of Aragon, 122, 151n
Alfonso VI, King of Castile and Emperor of León, 73–80, 80, 81–82, 85–87, 94n, 95–97, 102–106, 109, 110, 112, 114, 115, 121, 122, 136, 152, 165; at Battle of Zallaqa, 96–100; conquest of Toledo, 79–82, 87, 88, 103; death of, 122
Algeria, 173n
al-Hafiz, Fatimid caliph, 171, 184–86, 206–12, 213, 219, 320
al-Hakam II, Caliph of Córdoba, 20–23
al-Hakim bi-'Amr Allah, Fatimid caliph, 192–93, 196–99, 200, 201, 218–22
Alhambra. See al-Hamra Palace, Granada
al-Hamra Palace, Granada, 15 and n, 16, 58, 64, 96, 337
Alice, Princess, 272–73, 274
al-Idrisi, Muhammad, 134, 135, 161; world map of, 161, 162
'Ali ibn Abi Talib, Caliph, 186–88
'Ali ibn Yusuf, Almoravid ruler, 109, 121
Aljafería Palace, Zaragoza, 90–91, 91, 92, 96
al-Mahdi, Fatimid caliph, 28
al-Ma'mun. See Yahya al-Ma'mun, King of Toledo
al-Mansur (Muhammad ibn Abi Amir), hajib of Córdoba, 22–25, 27, 29, 30, 31, 35, 37, 50, 83, 90
Almería, 16, 31, 45–46, 55, 61, 105, 112; Jews, 46, 63
Almohads, 111, 122, 153, 164, 174, 176–79, 229–30, 322
Almoravids, 62, 66, 70, 74, 75, 100–123, 152–53, 164, 259, 322, 323; conquest of Seville, 113–14; culture and society, 100–123; law, 102; return to Valencia, 121; Siege of Valencia and, 114–19
al-Mu'izz, Fatimid caliph, 29, 185–86, 190–91
Almuñecar, 47

al-Munfatil, 54

al-Muqtadir, *taifa* king of Zaragoza, 74, 90–94 and *n*, 122

al-Murtada, 28–29

al-Musta'in, *taifa* king of Zaragoza, 28, 74, 122

al-Musta'in II, *taifa* king of Zaragoza, 74, 95–96, 105, 106, 108

al-Musta'li, *taifa* king of Zaragoza, 206, 267

al-Mustansir, Fatimid caliph, 202–206

al-Mu'tadid, *taifa* king of Seville, 42, 47

al-Mu'taman, *taifa* king of Zaragoza, 94, 95, 111, 122

al-Mu'tamid, *taifa* king of Seville, 31, 60, 77, 78, 96–100, 104, 105, 112, 113 and *n*

al-Mutawakkil, *taifa* king of Badajoz, 80–81, 96, 114, 121

al-Muzaffar. *See* Badis ibn Habbus al-Muzaffar, *taifa* king of Granada

al-Nabulusi, Uthman ibn Ibrahim, 214–15, 232, 233, 237; *Kitab al-tajrid*, 237

al-Naya, 60, 61, 65

alphabets: Armenian, 165; Berber, 26

Alpuente, 46–47, 61

al-Qadi al-Fadil, 293, 294

al-Qadir, King of Toledo and King of Valencia, 74, 80–81, 88, 90, 93–94, 105, 106, 108, 111, 114–19

al-Qarawi, Ali ibn, 59–60

al-Safi, 237

al-Sulami, *A Treatise on Holy War*, 225

al-Turtusi, Abu Sa'd, 202

Álvar Fáñez Minaya, 109, 112, 113

al-Yanis, 207

al-Yazuri, 221

al-Zafir, Fatimid caliph, 234

al-Zahir, Fatimid caliph, 198–99, 200, 202

Amalfi, 131

Amalric I, King of Jerusalem, 296–98, 311–12

Anacletus II, Pope, 151–52 and *n*

Anatolia, 165, 166 and *n*, 204, 208, 225–26, 246, 252, 254, 265, 282, 299, 307

Andalusi (term), 18 and *n*

Andronikos Komnenos, Emperor, 11, 307, 310 and *n*, 311–13, *313*, 314, 319, 320

Anna Komnena, 133

'Annaba, 127, 173 and *n*, 174*n*, 177, 251

Anselm, Saint, Archbishop of Canterbury, 145

Antioch, 148, 166, 207, 209, 224–26, 255, 260–62, 270, 277–84 and *n*, 292, 303, 321; Crusades and, 224–25, *246*, 256, 260–62, 272, 273 and *n*, 277–84, 305; Principality of, 256; Siege of, 138, 145, *246*, 256, 260

apostasy, 147 and *n*, 157, 177, 178, 318

Apulia, 133, 134, 141, 151, 167, 174

Arabia, 6, 187, 286–87, 305

Arabic, 6, 7, 21, 26, 33, 36, 37, 51, 78, 92 and *n*, 137*n*, 154, 159–60, 194, 237; numbers, 160; poetry, 50–51; in Sicily, 159–60, 162 and *n*

Arabo-Judaic (term), 137 and *n*

Arabs, 22, 317–24; Andalusi, 15–66, 69–123; Arabic-Islamic renaissance in Sicily, 159–64. *See also specific countries and groups*

Aragon, 73, 74, 94, 95

Arians, 188*n*

Aristotle, 137

Arjona, Battle of, 47

Armenian Church, 165 and *n*, 183, 188*n*, 204 and *n*, 207–12, 216, 219, 255

Armenians, 11, 153, 165 and *n*, 166–68, 183–86 and *n*, 194, 203–12, 214, 233–36, 255 and *n*, 320, 322, 323; Crusades and, 255, 259, 265, 279; decline of, 233–36; Fatimid Caliphate and, 203–12, 233–36

Ascalon, 204, 210, 229, 258, 277, 296

Ashtor, Eliyahu, 62

Asia, 5, 6, 224. *See also specific countries*

'Assal clan, 237

Assassins. *See* Nizaris

astrology, 83, 93, *169*, 176, 191, 218

astronomy, 206*n*

Asturias, 83, 87
Atapuerca, Battle of, 76
Athanasius III, Pope, 284
Augustine, Saint, 32, 173n, 247
Augustus, Emperor, 89
Auvergne, 83
Avempace. See al-Baji, Abu 'l-Walid
    Sulayman
Awlad 'Assal. See 'Assal clan
Axum, 220
Ayyubids, 215, 237
Azariah, 63
Azaz, Battle of, 270

Babieca, 81, 120
Babylon, 191 and n, 194
Badajoz, 96–100, 114, 116, 121
Badis ibn Habbus al-Muzaffar, taifa king
    of Granada, 16, 41, 42, 44–50, 53, 54,
    55, 59–61, 65
Badr al-Jamali, 203–205 and n, 214, 220,
    223
Baghdad, 17, 18, 32, 34, 41, 58, 152, 185,
    189, 192, 203, 217, 225, 265
Bahrain, 188
Bahram Pahlavuni, 11, 166 and n, 167,
    184–85, 207–12, 213, 218, 231, 320, 322
Baldwin of Ibelin, 228
Baldwin I, King of Jerusalem, 150–51 and
    n, 208–10, 252, 255 and n, 257, 260,
    262, 269–70
Baldwin II, King of Jerusalem, 270–71,
    274, 277, 282–84
Baldwin III, King of Jerusalem, 234, 271,
    277, 282, 296, 312
Baldwin IV, King of Jerusalem, 272, 286,
    288, 297, 298, 312
Baldwin V, King of Jerusalem, 288, 297,
    298, 312n
Baldwin IX, Count of Flanders, 316
Balian of Ibelin, 302
Banu (term), 27 and n
Banu Djahwar, 31

Banu Hilal, 136, 202
Banu Hud, taifa kings of Zaragoza, 90, 122
Banu Kalb. See Kalbids
Banu Qudama, 228
Banu Sulayman, 202
Banu Sumadih, taifa kings of Almería, 31
Banu 'Umayya, 186. See also Umayyads
Banu Ziri. See Zirids
baraka, 89n
Barbastro, 140, 248
Barcelona, 24, 74, 89n, 106–107, 115
Barjawan, 197 and n
Basil II, Emperor, 130, 169, 192–93
Bayan al-Mughrib, 119
Bedouins, 175–76, 187, 200, 202, 235
Benedict X, Pope, 135
Berbers, 10, 17, 18 and n, 21, 24, 25–31, 80,
    99, 101, 103, 111, 119, 142, 152–53, 164,
    189, 192, 200, 320; Granada, 27–66;
    Kutama, 190, 199, 200 and n;
    terminology, 26 and n. See also
    Almoravids
Berenguer Ramon II "the Fratricide,"
    Count of Barcelona, 94 and n, 95, 105,
    106–108, 110, 120, 121n
Bermudo III, King of León, 76
Bernard de Sedirac, Archbishop of
    Toledo, 85–86
Bertrand, Count of Toulouse, Count of
    Tripoli, 259
Bethlehem, 258
Bilad al-Sudan (land of the Blacks), 99
    and n
Blacks, 200–204; eunuchs, 201–202;
    slaves, 99, 171–72, 196, 201–202;
    soldiers, 99, 200–203; Sudanese,
    200–204; women, 202–203
Boccaccio, On the Fates of Famous Men,
    313
Bohemond of Taranto, Prince of Antioch,
    148, 252, 256–57, 260–61, 278, 320
Bohemond II, Prince of Antioch, 272, 299
Bohemond III, Prince of Antioch, 278,
    284 and n, 303

Bône. *See* 'Annaba
Boniface of Montferrat, 316*n*
Bouillons, 252–53
Buluqqin, 38, 41, 48, 59–60, 63
Burdet, Robert, 111
Burgos, 86
Burgundians, 82–87, 252–53, 257
Byzantium, 5, 7, 10, 12, 18, 19, 129–37,
    142, 148–55, 156, 165 and *n*, 170–71,
    190, 193, 198, 204, 212, 219, 225–26,
    243, 250–56, *308*, 323; architecture,
    157 and *n*, 158, *158*, 159, 162–63, 168;
    collapse of, 273, 298, 304, 307–16;
    Crusades and, 253–56, 261–65, 271–84,
    297, 305, 307–16 and *n*; eunuchs,
    169–70, 171; Komnenoi, 11, 150, 253–56,
    278–84, 297, 303, 307–16; Sicily and,
    129–55, 156–68; society and culture,
    129–55, 156–71

Cabrera, Castle of, 61
Caesaraugusta, 89
Cairo, 17, 34, 104, 137*n*, 152, 153, 156,
    183, 186, 191–212, 287, 296, 302;
    al-Azhar, 192; culture and society,
    192–212, 213–38
Calabria, 134, 144, 149, 150, 151, 167
caliph (term), 11 and *n*
caliphate, 16; collapse of, 25, 31, 34–36,
    46, 50, 101, 111; Córdoba, 16–35, 75,
    76, 189; end of Fatimid, 177, 233–36;
    Fatimid, 19, 27, 100, 133, 136, 148–49,
    152–56, 165–67, 174, 177, 183–212,
    213–38, 296; Umayyad, 17, 22, 24–25,
    27, 30–32, 38, 49, 50, 75, 89, 100, 102,
    189, 192, 217; in the West, 16–22
cannibalism, 117, 257, 322
Capua, Siege of, 145
Carmona, 47
Carthage, 26
Castile, 17*n*, 73–80, 87, 94, 95, 97, 102,
    106, 114, 115, 121, 122
castration, 128, 169–70, 171 and *n*, 178

Castro, Américo, 71, 72 and *n*
Cathar, 293*n*
Catholic Church, 7–12, 157, 249. *See also*
    Christianity; Latin Church; Orthodox
    Church; papacy
celibacy, 265
ceramics, Egyptian, *220*
Chalcedon, Council of, 194, 216
Charlemagne, Holy Roman Emperor, 84,
    89, 131*n*, 250*n*
Charles the Simple, King of Western
    Francia, 130
China, 6, 193
chivalry, 79, 108, 265, 268, 289, 300, 302
Christianity, 3–5, 6, 7–12, 56–57, 69–123,
    127–55, 165, 188 and *n*, 317–24;
    Andalusi culture and society, 69–123;
    calendar, 127*n*; chivalry, 79, 108; Cid
    and, 69–97, 105–23; concubines, 17 and
    n; corruption, 85, 131; Crusades, 11, 75,
    85, 121, 129, 135, 138, 145, 150, 151*n*,
    166, 233–30, 231, 241–74, 275–316;
    Dark Ages, 84–85; East-West Schism,
    132, 253; Fatimid Egypt and, 183–212,
    213–38, 296; festivals, 221; Frankish,
    82–87, 223–30, 241–74, 275–305;
    Gregorian Reform, 85, 131–32, 243,
    248; -Islam relations, in Egypt,
    183–212, 213–38; -Islam relations, in
    Jerusalem, 241–74, 275–305; -Islam
    relations, in Sicily, 127–55, 156–79;
    -Islam relations, in Spain, 69–123;
    -Jewish relations, in Europe, 38;
    -Jewish relations, in Spain, 79;
    marriage, 39, 40 and *n*; missionaries'
    misunderstanding of Islamic society,
    93–94; Mozarab, 78–79, 82, 83, 86; in
    Muslim Egypt, 215–23; Norman
    conquest of Sicily, 127–55, 156–79;
    persecution of, 221–22; pilgrimage,
    84, 246–47, 249–50, 266; polemic
    tradition, 55–57; power and, 108, 109;
    "reconquest" of Spain, 10, 71, 78–123,
    147–48; relics, 249–50, 301 and *n*;

Christianity (*cont.*)
Rome and, 32, 49, 86, 93, 131 and *n*,
157, 247, 253; sacrament, 85; in Sicily,
127–55, 156–79; in Spain, 10, 17 and *n*,
20, 21 and *n*, 22, 24, 28*n*, 38, 44, 56–57,
69–123; warfare and, 79–123, 132,
241–74; women, 17*n*, 40 and *n*, 161–62,
195, 219. *See also* Crusades; Latin
Church; Orthodox Church; papacy;
specific denominations
Christodoulos, 150, 151, 158, 159, 166,
167, 175
Chronicles of the Kings of León, 80
Cid, 10, 11, 69–97, 138*n*, 148, 165, 294,
319, 320; at Battle of Zallaqa, 96–100;
death of, 120–21; in exile, 72, 74, 87,
107; honor and, 72, 118 and *n*; as
inspiration for Crusades, 123; legend
of, 71–75, 120–23; rogue actions,
105–108; as ruler of Valencia, 74–75, 81,
107–108, 114–20; Siege of Valencia,
114–19; signature of, *119*; in Zaragoza,
89 and *n*, 90–96, 105, 114
Cilicia, 279, 281, 282 and *n*, 310, 311
circumcision, 244, 250 and *n*
Civitate, Battle of, 133
Clermont, Council of, 243–45, 248, 252,
258, 268, 323
Cluniac Order, 84–87, 93, 101, 131, 248
Cluny, 84, 123. *See also* Cluniac Order
Codex Calixtinus, 249–50
coins, 164, 217; Egyptian, 217; Islamic, *53*;
Maravedis, 102; of Roger II, 164
Companions of the Prophet, 89 and *n*
comparative religion, 51
concubines, 17*n*, 40, 51, 141, 171, 195;
Black, 202
Conrad of Montferrat, King of Jerusalem,
312*n*
Constance, Queen of Castile and León,
82, 85
Constance, Princess of Antioch, 272–73,
277, 278, 284, 309, 320
Constance, Queen of Sicily, 177

Constantine I (the Great), Emperor, 32,
131*n*, 165, 253, 301*n*
Constantine VII, Emperor, 20, 21*n*
Constantine VIII, Emperor, 130–31
Constantine IX, Emperor, 132*n*
Constantinople, 6, 17, 20, 131–32, 136,
137 and *n*, 148, 166, 167, 212, 216, 226,
245, 253–54, 263, 273, 282, 286, 304,
316 and *n*, 323; Hagia Sophia (church),
283, 313, 314; Komnenoi, 11, 150,
253–56, 278–84, 297, 303, 307–16; sack
of, 264, 273, 315
convivencia (term), 71
Coptic Church, 153, 183, 185, 188*n*,
194–95, 197, 205, 208, 212, 214, 216–20,
220, 221–22, 230, 233, 236–37
Córdoba, 16–35, 36, 47, 51, 63, 64, 83, 84,
87, 89, 91, 113, 137 and *n*, 147 and *n*,
190; caliphate, 16–35, 75, 76, 189;
collapse of caliphate, 25, 31, 34–36, 46,
50, 101, 111; Madinat al-Zahara, 18, 19,
19, 20–21, 25, 50, 192; politics, 16–35;
society and culture, 16–35, 50; *taifa*
period, 30–35
Counter-Crusade, 226–29, 233
Covadonga, Battle of, 87
Cristo de la Luz (church), Toledo, 81
Crusades, 4, 5, 7–12, 129, 150, 157 and *n*,
208, 210, 223–30, 231, 236, 241–74,
275–305, 307–16, 318, 320, 321, 323,
324; birth of, 244; Byzantium and,
253–56, 261–65, 271–84, 297, 305,
307–16 and *n*; call to, 223; Cid as
inspiration for, 123; conquest of
Jerusalem, 223–30, 241–74; Eighth,
294*n*; First, 11, 75, 85, 121, 129, 135,
138, 145, 150, 151*n*, 166, 223–30, 231,
241–74, 307, 316, 322, 323; four
principalities, 255–60; Fourth, 264,
273, 312*n*, 315, *315*; Frankish, 214,
223–30, 231, 241–74, 275–316; gender
roles and, 269–74; Jerusalem restored
to Muslim rule, 275–305; *jihad* against,
226–29, 233; Military Orders, 265–69,

276, 298–301; plundering, 257–58; Second, 129, 139, 269, 273*n*, 277; Seventh, 294*n*; terminology, 246, 247 and *n*; Third, 303–305, 314; trade and, 249–51, 262–64, 308–309; women and, 269–74. *See also specific Crusader states*

culture, 6, 7, 8, 10, 317–24; Almoravid, 100–123; Andalusi, 16–66, 69–123; Armenian, 165–67; Byzantine, 129–55, 156–71; Cairo, 192–212, 213–38; Christian, 69–123; Crusades, 241–74, 275–305; Fatimid, 153–54, 163–64, 183–212, 213–38; Granada, 35–66; Islamic, 16–66, 78, 90–94, 153–54, 159–64, 188–90; Sicilian, 127–55, 156–79

Cyprus, 272, 279–81, 311

Damascus, 32, 203, 226–28, 260, 261, 262, 269, 273*n*, 277, 291, 302, 321
dar al-Harb, 224
dar al-Islam, 6, 26, 34, 94, 103, 170, 224, 250, 323
Dark Ages, 84–85
Daroca, 108
de Hauteville dynasty, 130–35, 147, 148, 160, 177–78, 252, 255–57, 260–61
Demotic, 194
Denia, 90, 94, 105, 106, 108, 114, 115
Deuteronomy, 32, 33
Devil, 83, 85
Devol, Peace of, 261, 278
Dhi'l-Nun dynasty, 80, 81
dhimmis, 21, 22, 42, 51, 184, 194, 210, 217–18, 235, 236, 321
disease, 139, 256, 288, 322
Donatists, 188*n*
Dorylaeum, Battle of, 254–55
Doukas dynasty, 136
dowries, 40*n*
dress, 25, 127, 318, 323; Andalusi, 25, 51; Arabo-Judaic, 137*n*; Islamic, 25, 51, 78, 137*n*, 161–63, 197, 217; Kutama, 200*n*

Druze, 198, 199
Durazzo (Durrës), 148
dynasty trees, 325–27
dysentery, 139

economy, 5, 7, 9, 321; Andalusi, 16–17, 28, 31, 35, 36, 44, 79; Egyptian, 193, 217; Sicilian, 137, 141, 144, 149, 177
Edessa, 151*n*, 165, 204, 207, 226, 227, 255, 257, 260, 270, 284; County of, 129, 255
Egypt, 8, 9, 10, 27, 89, 147, 152–54, 159, 190 and *n*, 255, 263, 264, 275, 287, 290–91, 304, 305, 322; Coptic Church, 153, 185, 188*n*, 194–95, 197, 205, 208, 212, 214, 216, 217, 219–20, *220*, 221–22, 230, 233, 236–37; Crusades and, 296–97, 304; Fatimid, 10–11, 27, 133, 148–49, 152–56, 165–67, 174, 177, 183–212, 213–38, 296, 320; Islam-Christian relations, 183–212, 213–38; Jews in, 186, 194–98, 202, 215, 217, 218, 222; politics, 183–212, 213–38; slaves, 192, 195–96, 302; society and culture, 183–212, 213–38; trade, 193–94, 200, 209, 217; warfare, 200–201, *201*, 202–206, 296; women, 195, 198, 202, 219, 234–35
Eighth Crusade, 294*n*
Eilat, 287
El Cid (film), 71–72, 120
Eleanor, Duchess of Aquitaine, Queen of France, and Queen of England, 273*n*, 274*n*, 304*n*
Elvira, 28 and *n*
Elvira, Queen of Castile and León, 152
England, 4, 130, 298, 304*n*
ephebophilism, 53 and *n*
Eschiva, 300, 301
Ethiopia, 184, 193, 194, 204, 219–20
Ethiopian Church, 188*n*, 220
eunuchs, 128, 169–70, 171 and *n*, 172, 178, 192, 195, 197 and *n*, 200; Black, 201–202

Europe, 4, 5, 6, 12; Dark Ages, 84–85; Northern Christian, 82–87; pagan, 26, 76, 93, 130, 170. *See also specific countries*
excommunication, 248
exilarch (term), 41

family, 27 and *n*, 39–40; Christian, 39; Islamic, 17 and *n*, 39–40; Oriental model, 39–40; primogeniture, 39, 82
faqihs, 34
fart, of Roger I. *See* flatulence
Fath al-Ma'mun, 112–13
Fatima Zuhra, 186, 187, 189
Fatimids, 10–11, 19, 27, 100, 133, 134*n*, 142, 160, 163–67, 169, 171–72, 183–212, 213–38, 254, 258, 267, 290, 309, 316, 320; -Christian relations, 183–212, 213–38, 296; court scene, *197*; Crusades and, 260–65, 270–71; culture and society, 152–54, 163–64, 183–212, 213–38; decline of, 206, 233–36; Egypt, 10–11, 27, 133, 148–49, 152–56, 165–67, 174, 177, 183–212, 213–38, 296, 320; end of caliphate, 177, 233–36; eunuchs, 171, 195; ideology of messianic revolution, 196–99; warfare, 200–201, *201*, 202–206, 296
Fernando I, King of León, 75, 76, 78, 79
Fernando II, King of León, 111
Fez, 101
"The Field of Blood," Battle of, 261
First Crusade, 11, 75, 85, 121, 129, 135, 138, 145, 150, 151*n*, 166, 223–30, 231, 241–74, 307, 316, 322, 323; terminology, 246, 247 and *n*
fitna, 25, 27, 35
flatulence, 149 and *n*
folk traditions, 6, 15, 221, 233
food, 51, 139, 164, 263, 318, 323; Egypt, 193; Islamic, 51, 160, 161; shortages, 139, 202, 256, 322
foreskin. *See* Holy Foreskins

Fourth Crusade, 264, 273, 312*n*, 315, *315*
France, 4, 6, 10, 82–87, 130, 227, 241, 245, 273 and *n*, 293 and *n*; Norman conquest of Sicily, 127–55. *See also* Crusades; Franks
Franco, Francisco, 71, 72 and *n*
Franks, 82–87, 111, 210, 212, 223–30, 235–36, 320, 322, 323; Crusades, 214, 223–30, 231, 241–74, 275–316; -Islam relations, in Jerusalem, 241–74, 275–305; in Jerusalem, 223–30, 241–74, 275–305; *jihad* against, 226–29, 233; society, 82–87, 259–60, 269–74; women, 269–74
Frederick Barbarossa, Holy Roman Emperor, 174
Frederick I, Holy Roman Emperor, 310
Frederick II, King of Sicily and Holy Roman Emperor, 157*n*, 178
Fulcher of Chartres, 244, 257, 268
Fulk, Count of Anjou and King of Jerusalem, 270 and *n*, 271, 272
Fustat, 190–92, 193, 221

Galicia, 73, 77, 78, 311
Gaon, Rabbi Saadia, *Book of the Articles of Faith and Doctrines of Dogma*, 36
García, King of Navarre, 76, 77
gender roles, 6, 318, 319; in Crusader states, 269–74. *See also* men; women
Genesis, Book of, 50
Genoa, 111, 114, 131, 177, 251, 263, 279, 309
George, Saint, 148, 221
George of Antioch, 158, 159, 166, 167, 171, 172, 175
Geraldo Sem Pavor, 111
Gerbert of Aurillac (Pope Sylvester II), 83
Germany, 4, 177
Ghalib al-Nasiri, 23 and *n*
Ghana, 101
Gibbon, Edward, *The Decline and Fall of the Roman Empire*, 3, 4

Godfrey of Bouillon, ruler of Jerusalem, 150, 252, 258, 269

Golan, 262, 286

gold, 17, 35, 44, 99n, 100–102, 109, 115, 164, 220, 251, 266; African, 17, 35, 101; coins, 102

Gormaz, 105

Gospels, 33, 51, 93

Granada, 10, 15–16, 25, 28–29, 31, 36–66, 74, 77, 88, 105, 113, 146, 322; al-Hamra Palace, 15 and n, 16, 58, 64, 96, 337; Jews, 36–66; massacre of 1066, 61–65; politics, 35–66; society and culture, 35–66; taifa period, 36–66; Zirid, 28–66

Graus, Battle of, 76, 90

Greece and Greeks, 3–4, 6, 7, 12, 26, 35, 144, 160, 165 and n, 169, 170, 217, 313n

Greek Orthodox Church, 8, 129, 136, 157–60, 165 and n, 167, 185, 188n, 209, 215–16, 253, 316; in Sicily, 129, 136, 157–60, 168. See also Melkites

Gregorian calendar, 127n

Gregorian Reform, 85, 131–32, 243, 248

Gregory VII, Pope, 131, 132, 248–49

Grigor, Armenian Patriarch of Egypt, 208, 210–11

Grigor Martyrophile, Armenian Patriarch, 204 and n, 207–208

Guadix, 65

Guiscard, Robert, Duke of Apulia, 133–42, 252

Guy de Lusignan, King of Jerusalem, 275–77, 289, 298–302, 304, 312n

Habbus ibn Maksan, King of Granada, 29, 37–42, 45

Hagia Sophia (church), Constantinople, 283, 313, 314

hajib (office), 21, 30, 90

Hanbali school, 142n, 227–28, 231–33

Hanifa school, 142n

Hanok, Rabbi, 35

harems, 23, 171

Harun al-Rashid, Caliph, 189

Hasan ibn 'Ali, 187

Hasan ibn 'Ali, King of Ifriqiya, 167, 168

Hasdai ibn Shaprut, 21 and n, 35, 41, 91, 206n

Hassan al-Sabbah, 205, 206, 267

Hastings, Battle of, 130

Hattin, Battle of, 272, 300–302

Hebrew, 32, 36, 92, 153 and n, 162, 194

Hebrew Old Testament, 209, 215, 221

Hebrew Scripture, 32, 33, 49, 50, 56, 209, 215

Henry II, King of England, 274n, 298–99

Henry IV, Holy Roman Emperor, 144, 248–49

Henry VI, Holy Roman Emperor and King of Sicily, 177–78, 304n

Henry the Pious, Holy Roman Emperor, 133

Heraclius, Emperor, 301n

Hezekial, Exilarch, 58, 63

Hisham, Caliph of Córdoba, 23, 24, 27, 30, 32

Hisham al-Dawla, taifa king of al-Sahla (Albarracín), 105

Hispania, 6, 83, 87, 111

Historia Roderici, 72, 76, 86, 107, 114

Hodierna, Countess of Tripoli, 271–72, 274

Holy Foreskins, 250 and n

Holy Roman Empire, 131 and n, 133, 136, 151, 177, 309

Holy Sepulchre (church), Jerusalem, 198, 218, 301n

homosexuality, 23, 51, 52, 53 and n, 151n

honor, 6, 72, 109, 233, 289, 302; Cid and, 72, 118 and n

Hospitallers, 177, 265–69, 276, 298–301, 303, 321

Hrosvitha of Gandersheim, 25

Hugh, Count of Jaffa, 271 and n

Hughes de Payens, 266

Hugh the Great, Abbot of Cluny, 93
Humphrey de Hauteville, 133
Humphrey II of Toron, 311*n*
Humphrey III of Toron, 288, 290
Hungary, 245, 285, 310, 311
Hussayn ibn 'Ali, 187, 189

Iberian Peninsula, 10, 17, 72, 73, 108,
    138–39, 248
Ibn 'Abbad ("Benavert"), 144
Ibn 'Abbas, 45–46
Ibn al-'Arif, 37, 40, 41
Ibn al-Athir, 127, 149, 178
Ibn al-Fara, 53–54
Ibn al-Hawwas, Ali, 134, 135
Ibn 'Alqama, 117
Ibn al-Thumna, Muhammad, 134, 135
Ibn Anas, Malik, 142*n*
Ibn Bassam, 81–82, 120
Ibn Daud, 36, 37, 41, 58, 59, 63; *Book of
    Tradition*, 36
Ibn Dukhan, 11, 214–15, 230–38
Ibn Gabirol, Solomon, 92; *The Fountain
    of Life*, 92 and *n*
Ibn Hafsun, 147 and *n*
Ibn Hamdis, 146–47
Ibn Hanbal, Ahmad, 142*n*, 227–28
Ibn Hawqal, 137, 142
Ibn Hayyan, 57
Ibn Hazm, Abu Muhammad 'Ali ibn
    Ahmad, 11, 49, 50–51, 56–57, 64, 93;
    The Dove's Necklace, 51; poetry by,
    50–51
Ibn 'Idhari, 41
Ibn Jahhaf, 115–19
Ibn Jubayr, 159, 161, 171, 173, 176, 262,
    287
Ibn Khaldun, 199 and *n*
Ibn Muyassar, 185
Ibn Sa'id, 90
Ibn Shaddad, 305
Ibn Sumadih, *taifa* king of Almería, 16,
    61, 64, 65

Ibn Tashufin. *See* Yusuf ibn Tashufin,
    Almoravid ruler
Ibn Yasin, 'Abd Allah, 100–101
Ibn Zaydun, 20
Ifriqiya, 27, 29, 100, 101, 133 and *n*, 136,
    137, 147–51, 159, 161, 164–68, 175, 177,
    185, 190, 193, 194, 199, 202, 209, 229;
    Norman presence in, 164–68, 173–79
Il-Ghazi, 261
Imperial Church, 165*n*
India, 6, 18, 194
Innocent II, Pope, 152 and *n*
Innocent III, Pope, 157*n*, 315
intermarriage, 188, 195 and *n*, 196, 219
Investiture Controversy, 131
Iran, 189
Iraq, 32, 189, 226
Isaac Angelos, Emperor, 303, 307, 314, 315
Isaac ben Baruk, 63
Islam, 3–12, 56–57, 317–24; calendar, 127
    and *n*; -Christian relations, in Egypt,
    183–212, 213–38; -Christian relations,
    in Jerusalem, 241–74, 275–305;
    -Christian relations, in Sicily, 127–55,
    156–79; -Christian relations, in Spain,
    69–123; culture, 16–66, 78, 90–94,
    153–54, 159–64, 188–90; diversity of,
    188; division between secular and
    religious spheres, 32–35; dress, 25, 51,
    78, 137*n*, 161–63, 197, 217; elite, 50–57,
    78, 120, 109, 111, 160–61; family, 17 and
    n, 39–40; Fatimid, 10–11, 148–56,
    165–67, 183–212, 213–38, 296; food,
    51, 160, 161; Jerusalem restored to,
    275–305; Jewish relations, in Spain,
    15–66, 110–11; *jihad*, 32, 66, 109, 203,
    204, 210, 223–30, 247 and *n*, 289–95;
    318, 321, 324; law, 21*n*, 32–35, 51, 102
    and *n*, 114, 142*n*, 147, 170, 219, 237;
    marriage, 23, 39, 40 and *n*; *mujahidin*,
    289–95; poetry, 20, 35, 146, 147, 161;
    polemic tradition, 55–57; politics,
    16–66; "reconquest" of Spain and, 10,
    71, 78–123, 147–48; ritual, 33; in Sicily,

127–55, 156–79; slaves and, 170–73, 195; society, 16–66, 78, 79, 89 and *n*, 90–94, 102–3, 109–11, 142, 159–64, 188, 260; Spain, 10, 15–66, 69–123; Sunni-Shi'a divide, 186–89; taxes and, 103, 118; warfare, 16–66, 74–123, 247 and *n*, 291–95; women, 22–23, *39*, 40 and *n*, 51, 101, 118 and *n*, 128, 195. *See also* caliphate; Muslims; Shi'ism; *specific countries and sects*; Sunnism

Islamic Spain. *See* al-Andalus

Isma'il ibn Naghrilla, 10, 11, 25, 35–59, 64, 78, 91, 103, 110, 146, 319; at Alpuente, 46–47; *Ben Tehellim*, 47; death of, 57–59; as *Nagid*, 41, 49, 59; poetry by, 43, 45–56, 58–59, 61; as *wazir*, 37–43

Isma'ilism, 166*n*, 190–96, 199, 203, 206, 221, 267

Italy, 4, 10, 127–55, 248; city-states, 111, 130, 131, 251, 262–64, 304, 308–9, 313, 315–16; Norman conquest of Sicily, 127–55, 156–79; trade, 262–64, 308–309

ivory, 99*n*

Jaen, 65

Ja'far al-Sadiq, 189, 190

James, Saint, 83–84, 87, 89, 148

Jawhar al-Siqilli, 185–86 and *n*, 190–91, 192, 197, 200, 212

Jérôme de Périgord, Bishop of Valencia, 120

Jerusalem, 41, 75, 121 and *n*, 150, 152, 198, 208–10, 212, 225, 226, 236, 241–74, 321, 322–23; Crusades, 121, 129, 138, 150, 223–30, 231, 241–74, 275–305; decline of Kingdom of, 265, 275–305; end of Latin rule, 302–303; Frankish conquest of, 223–30, 241–74; Holy Sepulchre (church), 198, 218, 301*n*; Islam-Christian relations in, 241–74, 275–305; Jews in, 49, 258; restoration to Muslim rule, 275–305; Siege of, 257–58

Jesus Christ, 189, 215–16; circumcision, 250 and *n*; Crucifixion, 215, 245, 250, 301; relic of the True Cross, 301 and *n*

jihad, 4, 5, 7, 32, 66, 109, 147*n*, 174, 203, 204, 210, 223–30, 247 and *n*, 289–95, 318, 321, 324; anti-Frankish, 226–29, 233; Salah al-Din and, 291–95; terminology, 247 and *n*

Jocelyn of Courtenay, 270, 272

John Komnenos, 280, 281

John II Komnenos, Emperor, 157, 271–73, 308–309

Judaism, 4–11, 15–16, 32, 35, 56–57, 137*n*, 146, 169, 188, 245, 247, 250*n*, 317–24; Andalusi, 15–17, 21–66, 79, 80, 110–11, 119, 322; Arabo-Judaic, 137 and *n*; Babylonian captivity, 32; calendar, 127*n*; in Christian Europe, 38; -Christian relations, in Spain, 79; in Egypt, 186, 194–98, 202, 215, 217, 218, 222; exiles, 32; Granada, 36–66; in Jerusalem, 49, 258; massacre of 1066, 61–65; military policy, 32; -Muslim relations, in Spain, 15–66, 110–11; Naghrilla dynasty, 35–66; oral tradition, 49; poetry, 45–49; polemic tradition, 55–57; prejudice against, 55–57, 61–65, 288; Rabbinical, 35–36, 49, 56, 194; Roman destruction of Second Temple, 49; sexuality, 56; Sicily, 42, 162 and *n*; society, 32, 35–66, 79; Spain, 15–17, 21–66, 79, 80, 110–11, 119, 322; trade, 153 and *n*; warfare, 247; women, 195; Zaragoza, 91–92, 110–11

Justinian, Emperor, 170, 216

just warfare, 32, 247 and *n*

Ka'aba, 188

Kalbids, 134 and *n*, 136–38, 161, 202

Kerak, 275, 286, 287–89, 290–91, 303

Kharijites, 32*n*, 142, 187, 190

Khazars, 21*n*

Kitab Rujjar, 161

knights, 79, 110, 139, 210; Crusades, 241–74, 275–305; Military Orders, 265–69, 276, 298–301; Norman, 127–55. *See also specific orders*

Knights of St. John. *See* Hospitallers

Komnenoi, 11, 150, 253–56, 278–84, 297, 303, 307–16

Kurds, 200, 227, 235, 290, 292

Kutama, Banu, 190, 199, 200 and *n*

languages, 6, 7, 18, 26, 36, 37, 70, 92 and *n*, 153, 154, 194, 319; Berber, 26; in Egypt, 194, 217; Judeo-Arabic, 162 and *n*; in Sicily, 159–60, 162 and *n*. *See also specific languages*

Latin, 5, 6, 8, 11, 12, 36, 83, 92 and *n*, 108, 123, 131 and *n*; liturgy, 86

Latin Church, 7–12, 108, 131, 146, 157, 165 and *n*, 188*n*, 253, 273, 317–24; architecture, 157 and *n*, 158, *158,* 159, 162–63, 168; Crusades, 223–30, 241–74, 275–316; Gregorian Reform, 85, 131–32, 243, 248; Norman conquest of Sicily, 127–55. *See also* Christianity

law, 8–9, 318; Almoravid, 102; Islamic, 21*n*, 32–35, 51, 102 and *n*, 114, 142*n*, 147, 170, 219, 237; Maliki, 102 and *n*

Lebanon, 225

León, 17*n*, 19, 24, 73–80, 87, 97, 111, 222

Leo III, King of Cilicia, 284*n*

Leo IX, Pope, 131, 133

leprosy, 288

Libya, 177

Lisbon, 114; Siege of, 139

literacy, 34, 157

Logroño, 114

Lombards, 131, 133 and *n*, 136, 148, 176, 177

London, 4, 137*n*

Lothar III, Emperor, 152

Louis VII, King of France, 227, 273*n*, 313

Louis IX, Saint, King of France, 293 and *n*, 294*n*

Lucera, 178

Madinat al-Zahara, Córdoba, 18, 19, *19,* 20–21, 25, 50, 192

Madinat al-Zawi, 174*n*. *See also* 'Annaba

Madrid Skylitzes, 308

Maghrib, 26, 29, 101, 104, 137, 193, 194, 229

Magyars, 84

Mahdia, 149, 166–68, 171, 177, 178, 185, 194, 199

Maio of Bari, 176

Maksan, 48, 60

Málaga, 36, 37, 38, 65, 112

Maliki law, 142*n*

Maliki school, 142*n*

Malik Shah, 226

Mamluks, 215, 237, 304

Maniakes, George, 132 and *n*

Manichaeanism, 166*n*

Mann, Anthony, 71, 72, 120

Manuel I Komnenos, Emperor, 174, 273, 278–84, 285, 295, 296, 309–14

Manzikert, Battle of, 166, 225, 243, 255, 307

maps, 161; of Mediterranean world, *ix–xi;* "world," 161, *162*

Marash, 165

Margaret, Queen of Navarre, 178

Maria Komnene, Princess, 298, 312

Maria of Antioch, Empress, *283,* 284, 285, 309, 310, 312, 320

Mark, Saint, 215

Marrakesh, 101–102, 122

marriage, 23, 39–40, 318; Andalusi, 23, 39–40; Christian, 39, 40 and *n*; intermarriage, 188, 195 and *n*, 196, 219; Islamic, 23, 39, 40 and *n*

Martel, Charles, 3

Martyrophile. *See* Grigor Martyrophile, Armenian Patriarch

mathematics, 160

Mazdali ibn Tilankan, 70

Mecca, 33, 159, 190, 233, 247, 287

Medina, 172, 190, 247, 287

Melisende, Queen of Jerusalem, 270–72, 274, 277, 296, 320

Melkites, 167 and *n*, 183, 194, 208, 216, 217, 219, 230, 255, 256. *See also* Greek Orthodox Church

men, 6, 23, 53–54; eunuchs, 128, 169–70, 171 and *n*, 172, 178, 192, 195, 197 and *n*, 200; harems, 23; homosexuality, 23, 51–53 and *n*, 55, 151*n*; poets, 45–56

Merida, 35, 41

Mesopotamia, 299

Messina, 135, 157

Michael Cerularius, Patriarch of Constantinople, 131–32

Mikhael Doukas, Despot of Epirus, 316*n*

Mikhael VIII Paleologos, Emperor, 316*n*

Military Orders, 265–69, 276, 298–301

Mishnah Torah, 41

Mleh, 282 and *n*

monotheism, 317

Mont Giscard, 286, 295

Morocco, 17, 99, 101, 102, 105, 174, 179

mortal sin, 249

mosaics, 158, *158*, 159, 163, *283*, *315*

Moses ibn Ezra, 63

Mosul, 226, 292

Mozarabs, 17, 65, 78–80, 82, 83, 86, 92, 117, 137*n*

muftis, 34

Muhammad, Prophet, 3, 11*n*, 31–33, 56, 89*n*, 185, 186–87, 231, 287

Muhammad al-Mahdi, 189

Muhammad ibn Abi Amir. *See* al-Mansur (Muhammad ibn Abi Amir), *hajib* of Córdoba

mujahidin, 289–95, 319, 324

Mundhir al-Hajib, King of Denia and Lleida, 94, 95, 105–107

music, *39*, 160, 319; Islamic, *39*, 51, 217

Muslims, 3–12, 56–57, 317–24; Andalusi, 10, 15–16, 69–123; -Christian relations, in Jerusalem, 241–74, 275–305; -Christian relations, in Sicily, 127–55, 156–79; -Christian relations, in Spain, 69–123; crypto-, 172; Fatimid, 10–11, 148–56, 165–67, 183–212, 213–38, 296; Jerusalem restored to, 275–305; -Jewish relations, in Spain, 15–66, 110–11; *mujahidin*, 289–95; ritual, 33; in Sicily, 127–55, 156–79; Spain, 10, 15–66, 69–123; Sunni-Shi'a divide, 186–89. *See also* caliphate; Islam; Shi'ism; *specific countries*; Sunnism

Nablus, 228

Nag Hammadi, 215

Naghrilla dynasty, 10, 11, 16, 25, 35–66, 91. *See also* Isma'il ibn Naghrilla; Yusuf ibn Naghrilla

Nasi (plural, Nasim), 21, 58, 122, 195

Navarre, 17*n*, 73, 75–80, 94 and *n*

Nawruz, 221

Nazareth, 258

Nestorians, 188*n*

New Testament, 221, 247, 258

Nicaea, 166, 254, 316*n*

Nicene Creed, 253

Nicholas II, Pope, 135

Nicodemus, Bishop of Palermo, 146

Nile River, 193, 200, 202, 221

Nizar, 205–206, 267

Nizaris, 206, 266–68, 277, 292, 321

nomadism, 100

Normandy, 130

Normans, 111, 130–35, 160, 209, 308, 309, 320, 323; conquest and rule of Sicily, 127–55, 156–79; Crusades, 248, 252, 255–57, 261–62; terminology, 130

Norsemen, 84, 130

North Africa, 6, 10, 17, 19, 24, 26–29, 41, 66, 74, 101, 102, 109, 127, 130, 142, 149, 159, 171–79, 190; Arabic-Islamic cultural renaissance under Roger II, 159–64

Nubia, 193, 194, 204, 205, 219, 220

numeracy, 157, 160
Nur al-Din, Sultan of Aleppo and
    Damascus, 129, 226–29, 234–36, 268,
    272, 277, 278, 282n, 284–85, 289–91,
    295–97, 312

Old Testament, 209, 215, 221
opus mixtum, 157 and n
Order of Cluny. See Cluniac Order
Ordóñez, García, 73, 88
Ordóñez clan, 73, 88, 109, 114
Ordoño IV, King of León, 20–21
Orthodox Church, 8, 129, 136, 157–60,
    165 and n, 167, 185, 188n, 209, 215–16,
    253, 255, 316
Ottoman Turks, 316
Oultrejourdain, 286, 290. See also
    Transjordan

paganism, 26, 75, 93, 100, 130, 170, 308
Pahlavuni clan, 204, 207–208, 210
Palace Saracens, 175–79
Palermo, 127, 130, 134, 136–42, 143, 146,
    149, 150, 154, 161, 163, 167, 172, 176, 178;
    Santa Maria dell'Ammiraglio (church),
    158, 158, 159, 168; Siege of, 138–42
Palestine, 6, 190, 194, 203, 223, 225, 228,
    266, 297, 305
Pamplona, 24, 75–76, 89
papacy, 83–87, 93, 109, 131 and n, 136,
    146, 151–52 and n, 156, 157; Crusades
    and, 223, 243–52, 258, 268; Gregorian
    Reform, 85, 131–32, 243, 248; warfare
    and, 132, 243–74, 309
parasol, 153–54
parias, 76, 79, 90, 102, 105–106, 114, 122
Paschal, Pope, 151
Paul, Saint, 253
Paulicianism, 166n, 188n
peasantry, 34, 132, 157, 245, 259
Pelagius, 87
penance, 247

"People of the Book," 194, 195 and n, 321
Persia, 6, 12, 19, 35, 165 and n, 187, 189,
    216, 224, 316
Peter, Saint, 253, 256, 280
Peter of Eboli, 143; Liber ad honorem
    augusti sive de rebus siculis, 143, 154,
    169
Peter the Caid, 178–79
Peter the Hermit, 245–46, 257, 274
Peter the Venerable, Abbot of Cluny, 123
Philip Augustus, King of France, 304
Philip of Mahdia, 11, 127–29, 135, 168–75,
    178; trial and execution of, 171–75
Philip I, King of France, 243
Philippa, 311 and n
Phoenicians, 26
pilgrimage, 33, 83, 84, 159, 246–47, 249–50,
    263, 266, 303; commerce and, 250
Pirenne, Henri, 3, 4, 12
Pisa, 111, 114, 131, 177, 251, 263, 296
Plantagenet dynasty, 271n
poetry, 20, 45–56, 70, 146, 160; anti-
    Muslim, 55–57; Arabic, 50–51; on the
    Cid, 70–73; Islamic, 20, 35, 146, 147,
    161; by Isma'il ibn Naghrilla, 43,
    45–56, 58–59, 61; Jewish, 45–59;
    polemical, 55–57
pogroms, 4; Granada massacre of 1066,
    61–65
polemical literature, 55–57
politics, 5, 8, 9, 54, 109, 317–24; Andalusi,
    16–66, 69–123; Christian, 69–123;
    Córdoba, 16–35; Egypt, 183–212,
    213–38; Fatimid, 183–212, 213–38;
    Frankish Crusades, 241–74, 275–305;
    Granada, 35–66; Islamic, 16–66; power
    and, 108–11; Sicilian, 127–55, 156–79;
    taifa period, 30–35, 36–66, 69–123
polygamy, 40
polytheism, 121, 231
Portugal, 111, 122
power, 108–11; Christianity and, 108, 109;
    warfare and, 109–11
pre-prayer washing, 33, 207

primogeniture, 39, 82
Protestantism, 32
protonobilissimus (term), 150 and *n*
Proyençals, 252, 257
Ptolemy II, King of Egypt, 215
Pyrenees, 83, 89, 140

qadi, 18
Qaraites, 49, 194
Qarmatians, 188
Qayrawan, 29, 101
Qilij Arslan, Sultan of Rum, 254–55
Qilij Arslan II, Sultan of Rum, 312
Qur'an, 3, 23, 33, 42, 51, 55, 103, 118, 142, 187, 210, 218, 227; Latin translation of, 123, 153
Quraysh, 186
Qus, 209, 211, 214, 215, 234, 235

Rabbinical Judaism, 35–36, 49, 56, 194
Ralph of Dumfort, Patriarch of Antioch, 273, 278
Ramadan, 33, 127 and *n*, 293
Ramiro, King of Aragon, 76, 90
Ramiro Sánchez, King of Aragon, 120
Ramon Berenguer III, Count of Barcelona, 120, 12
Rasad, 202, 203, 320
Raymond of Aguillers, 241–42; *History of the Franks Who Captured Jerusalem*, 242
Raymond of Poitiers, Prince of Antioch, 273 and *n*, 277, 278, 279, 284, 309
Raymond of Provence, 266
Raymond II, Count of Tripoli, 271–72
Raymond III, Count of Tripoli, 272, 297–301
Raymond IV, Count of Toulouse, 252, 257, 259, 260
Reccemund, 21
Reconquista, 10, 71, 78–123, 147–48; roots of, 80–88

Red Sea, 287–88
relic of the True Cross, 301 and *n*
religion. *See* Christianity; Islam; Judaism; *specific religions, denominations, and sects*
Renaissance, 4, 324
Renier of Montferrat, 310, 312 and *n*
Reynaud de Châtillon, 11, 273, 275–81, *281*, 282–89, 295–301, 307, 319, 320; Salah al-Din and, 275–77, 286–90
Richard I the Lion-Hearted, King of England, 151*n*, 271*n*, 273*n*, 274*n*, 303–304 and *n*, 305, 312*n*
Ridwan ibn al-Walakshi, 210–11, 213, 222, 229
Ridwan of Aleppo, 261
Rioja, the, 72, 88, 114
Robert Guiscard de Hauteville. *See* Guiscard, Robert, Duke of Apulia
Robert of Ketton, 123
Robert of Rheims, 244
Rodrigo Díaz de Vivar. *See* Cid
Roger of Salerno, Regent of Antioch, 261
Roger I, Count of Sicily, 134–50, 169
Roger II, King of Sicily, 10, 11, 127–29, 135, 136, 143, 148, 149–55, 156–76, 208–12, 229, 270, 271*n*, 320; Arabo-Islamic renaissance and, 159–64; church depictions of, *158*, *163*; conquest of Ifriqiya, 164–68, 173–76; death of, 176; as "King of Africa," 164–68, 173–76; Philip of Mahdia and, 171–75
Roman Empire, 3, 4, 6, 20, 32, 33, 49, 83, 137*n*, 165 and *n*, 169, 170, 186*n*, 187, 216, 247, 316, 320; Christianity and, 32, 49, 86, 93, 131 and *n*, 157, 247, 253; decline and fall of, 216, 307–16; destruction of Second Temple, 49; walls, 138
Romanus IV Diogenes, Emperor, 225
Romuald, Archbishop of Salerno, *Chronicon*, 128–29, 170, 172, 173
Roncesvalles, Battle of, 89
Rueda, 95
Rylands Beatus, 243

Sabbath, 15, 62, 63

Sagrajas, Battle of. *See* Zallaqa, Battle of

Sahara, 17, 98–104, 171; trade, 102, 200

Salafists, 227

Salah al-Din, Sultan of Egypt and Syria, 11, 177, 186, 236–38, 262, 264, 267, 272, 273, 275–77, 286–305, 314; identity as *mujahid*, 292–95; *jihad* and, 291–95; origins of, 289–91; portrait of, *293*; recapture of Jerusalem, 275–77; Reynaud de Châtillon and, 275–77, 286–90

Salamiyya, 190

Saljuqs, 151*n*, 166*n*, 200–205, 223–29, 235–36, 243–44, 246, 254–55, 258–62, 265, 270, 284, 285, 290, 292, 307–309, 316, 320, 323

salt, 7, 17, 100

Samaritans, 49, 194

Samuel ibn Naghrilla. *See* Isma'il ibn Naghrilla

Sánchez-Albornoz, Claudio, 71, 72 and *n*

Sancho Ramírez, King of Aragon, 94 and *n*, 95, 96, 106, 114

Sancho the Great, King of Navarre, 75, 76

Sancho II, King of Castile, 73, 76, 77

Sancho IV, King of Navarre, 90, 94*n*

San Giovanni Evangelista (church), Ravenna, *315*

Sanhaja, 26–29, 38–39, 45, 48, 55, 59–61, 65, 66, 98–101, 111–12, 115, 122

Sanjul ('Abd al-Rahman), *hajib* of Córdoba, 24–25, 28, 30, 35, 64

Santa Maria dell'Ammiraglio (church), Palermo, 158, *158*, 159, 168

Santiago de Compostela, 24, 84, 249–50

Sassanid Persians, 216, 301*n*

Sayf al-Dawla, 111, 122

Sayyida, 113, 122, 152

Schism, East-West, of 1054, 132, 253

science, 7, 17, 35, 123, 146, 160, 218, 324

Sea of Galilee, 299–301

Second Crusade, 129, 139, 269, 273*n*, 277

Septuagint, 215

Seventh Crusade, 294*n*

Seville, 31, 36, 42, 45–47, 54, 55, 57, 63, 65, 73, 76–78, 83, 112–14; Almoravid conquest of, 113–14

Sfax, 167, 168

Shafi'i school, 142*n*

Sharq al-Andalus, 105, 107–108, 115, 120

Shawar, 235–36, 296

sheikh (term), 237 and *n*

Shi'ism, 8, 11, 19, 32, 142, 152, 172, 183, 184, 186–90, 196, 203, 206, 211; -Sunni divide, 186–89

Shirkuh, 290, 296, 297

Sicily, 10, 127–79, 190, 193, 199, 202, 209, 210, 219, 252, 320; Arabo-Islamic renaissance, 159–64; architecture, 157 and *n*, 158, *158*, 159, 162–63, 168; beginning of Norman period, 135–41; culture and society, 127–79; decline of Muslim, 175–78; Greek Orthodox Church, 129, 136, 157–60, 168; Islam-Christian relations, 127–55, 156–79; Jews, 142, 162 and *n*; language, 159–60, 162 and *n*; multicultural Palermo, 136–42, *143*; Muslim conquest of, 130, 134; Norman conquest and rule of, 127–55, 156–79; scribes, 153, 154, *154*; Siege of, 138–42; slaves, 141–43, 160, 161, 169–73; trade, 137, 144, 148, 153, 159, 164, 177; Zirids in, 136, 140, 143–44, 151, 164

siege warfare, 114–17, 138–42

Siffin, Battle of, 187, 210

silk, 28, 31, 137, 161, 193, 251

Silk Road, 263

silver, 102, 266

Sinan, Rashid al-Din, 267

Sis, 279

Sisnando Davídez, 78, 81–82, 85

Sitt al-Mulk (daughter of al-'Aziz), 198, 219, 320

Sitt al-Mulk (sister of Badr al-Jamali), 205 and *n*

Sitt al-Qusur, 234, 235

slaves, 7, 16, 30, 100, 129, 137, 141, 170–75, 302, 322; African, 171–72; Andalusi, 16, 17 and *n*, 18, 23 and *n*, 24, 30, 46, 51–52, 60; Black, 99, 171–72, 196, 201–202; in Egypt, 192, 195–96, 302; eunuchs, 128, 169–70, 171 and *n*, 172, 178, 192, 195, 197 and *n*, 200; in Islamic life, 170–73, 195; Latin, 302–303; in Sicily, 141–43, 160, 161, 169–73; soldiers, 99, 200–203; trade, 170–71; uprisings, 24; women, 141, 170, 171, 192, 195, 202

society, 5–8, 317–24; Almoravid, 100–123; Andalusi, 16–66, 69–123; Armenian, 165–67; Byzantine, 129–55, 156–71; Cairo, 192–212, 213–38; Christian, 34, 39–40, 56–57, 69–123; Crusades, 241–74, 275–305; division between secular and religious spheres, 32–35; elite Islam, 50–57, 109; eunuchs, 128, 169–70, 171 and *n*, 172, 178, 192, 195, 197 and *n*, 200; Fatimid, 152–54, 183, 212, 213–38; Frankish, 82–87, 259–60, 269–74; Granada, 35–66; intermarriage, 188, 195 and *n*, 196, 219; Islamic, 16–66, 78, 79, 89 and *n*, 90–94, 102–103, 109–11, 142, 159–64, 188, 260; Jewish, 32, 35–66, 79; Military Orders, 265–69, 276, 298; Sicilian, 127–55, 156–79; *taifa* period, 30–35, 36–66, 69–123; Umayyad, 17, 22, 24–25, 27, 30–32, 50, 75, 89

soldiers of fortune, 111

Solomon, King of Nubia, 205, 220

Song of Antioch, The, 225

Song of My Cid, 70–72, 107

Song of Roland, The, 89

Song of the Master of the Field, The, 72

Sousse, 167, 168

Spain, 4, 8, 9, 10, 15–66, 146, 147, 148, 170, 177, 217, 248, 320; Christian, 10, 17 and *n*, 20, 21 and *n*, 22, 24, 28*n*, 38, 44, 56–57, 69–123; Christian "reconquest" of, 10, 71, 78–123, 147–48; Cid and,

69–97, 105–23; civil war, 25, 27–28, 35; Córdoba, 16–35; creation of modern notion of, 75–76; Granada, 28–29, 36–66; Islam-Christian relations, 69–123; Islamic, 10, 15–66, 69–123; Jewish-Christian relations, 79; Jewish-Muslim relations, 15–66, 110–11; Judaism, 15–17, 21–66, 79, 80, 110–11, 119, 322; *taifa* period, 30–35, 36–66, 69–123; Umayyad, 17, 22, 24–25, 27, 30–32, 38, 42, 49, 50, 75, 89, 100, 102; Zaragoza, 89–96, 105

spices, 36, 99*n*, 251, 262

Stephanie de Milly, 286, 288, 290

Story of Bayad and Riyad, The, 39

Straits of Gibraltar, 26, 102

Subh, 22, 23 and *n*

Sudanese Blacks, 200–204

Sulayman ibn Hud al-Musta'in b'illah, *taifa* king of Zaragoza, 90

Sunnism, 8, 19, 32, 100, 102 and *n*, 142 and *n*, 183, 186–91, 196, 203, 205, 211, 212, 228–30, 236, 267; -Shia divide, 186–89

Sybilla, Queen of Jerusalem, 297–98, 302, 312*n*

Sylvester II, Pope, 83

Syracuse, 133, 144, 146

Syria, 6, 32, 165, 166, 190, 193, 203, 204, 207, 211, 216, 223–30, 265–67, 275, 287, 290, 294, 297, 303, 305

Syriac Church, 188*n*, 194, 216

Syr ibn Abi Bakr, 114, 116

taifa kingdoms, 30–35, 36–66; Christian relations with, 69–123; Cid and, 69–97, 105–23; end of, 111–12, 120–23; Zaragoza, 89–96, 105. *See also specific kingdoms*

Talai ibn Ruzzik, 214, 228, 232–36

Talmud, 41, 56

Tamarón, Battle of, 76

Tamim ibn al-Mu'izz, King of Ifriqiya, 151, 167

Tamim ibn Buluqqin, 60, 112

Tamim ibn Yusuf ibn Tashufin, 122

Tancred de Hauteville (father of Robert Guiscard and Roger I), 130, 132, 133

Tancred de Hauteville (nephew of Bohemond of Taranto), 252, 255, 257–61

taqiya, 172

Tarragona, 111

Tarsus, 165, 255, 260, 281

taxes, 33, 46, 118, 122, 262, 298, 318, 320; Andalusi, 33, 35, 37, 38, 59, 63, 76, 102–103; Egyptian, 193, 203, 204, 216, 217–18; Islam and, 103, 118

technology, 7, 160, 323, 324

Templars, 265–69, 276–80, 282 and *n*, 286, 298–301, 304, 321

Tévar, 107–108

textiles, 17, 18, 28, 31, 36, 137, 161, 193, 262

Thaghr, 89

Theodora Komnene, Queen of Jerusalem, 312

Theodoros Laskaris, Emperor of Nicaea, 316*n*

Theodosius, Emperor, 169

Theresa, "Queen" of Portugal, 81, 122, 274*n*

Thessalonika, 313*n*, 316*n*

Third Crusade, 303–305, 314

Tiberias, 258, 300, 301

timber, 7, 17, 263

Tiridates III, King of Armenia, 165

Titus, Emperor, 41

Toledo, 73, 74, 76, 77, 79–82, 85, 88, 114, 123; Christian conquest of, 79–82, 87, 88, 103, 104

Torah, 41, 51, 56

T'oros of Edessa, 151 and *n*, 255 and *n*, 269

T'oros II, King of Lesser Armenia, 279–82, 310, 311

Tortosa, 90, 94, 107, 303

trade, 6, 7, 17, 79, 99*n*, 100, 102, 137, 153 and *n*, 164, 171, 200, 224, 249–51, 262–64, 279, 287, 308–309, 319, 320, 322; Andalusi, 17, 18, 31, 36, 44, 51, 79; Crusades and, 249–51, 262–64, 308–309; Egypt, 193–94, 200, 209, 217; Indian Ocean, 287; Italian, 262–64, 308–309; Jewish, 153 and *n*; Saharan, 102, 200; Sicilian, 137, 144, 148, 153, 159, 164, 177; Silk Road, 263; slave, 170–71

Transjordan, 265. *See also* Oultrejourdain

Trinity, 215, 231, 253

Tripoli, 167, 168, 226, 259, 260, 301, 303; Principality of, 259

Tunisia, 17, 19, 27, 100, 127, 151, 152, 164, 175, 177, 304

"turn and flee" tactic, 119

Twelvers, 189, 206–207

Tyre, 223, 258, 276, 303, 304

'Ubayd Allah, Fatimid caliph, 185, 190

Uclés, Battle of, 122

'ulama', 33–34, 102, 103, 112

'Umara of Yemen, 233, 236

Umayyads, 17, 22, 24–25, 27, 30–32, 38, 42, 49, 50, 75, 89, 100, 102, 147 and *n*, 186–89, 190, 192, 210, 217

Urban II, Pope, 85, 86, 93, 129, 145, 151, 166, 292; Crusades and, 223, 243–48, 251, 252, 258, 268, 323

Urgell Beatus, 110

Urraca (sister of Alfonso VI), 77

Urraca, Queen of Castile and León, 82, 122, 274*n*

'Usama ibn Munqidh, 268–69, 274*n*

'Uthman, Caliph, 33

Valencia, 10, 31, 69–70, 74–76, 81, 90, 105, 106, 108, 114–23, 138*n*; Cid as ruler of, 74–75, 81, 107–108, 114–20; Siege of, 114–19

Vasak Pahlavuni, Governor of Antioch, 166, 207

Vasak Pahlavuni, Governor of Qus, 209, 211

veil, 101 and *n*, 128, 162

Venice, 131, 177, 251, 263, 264, 279, 309, 313, 315–16 and *n*

Vikings, 130, 132*n*

Virgin Mary, 81, 87, 89

Visigoths, 17, 71, 80, 83, 87, 89

Voluntary Martyrs of Córdoba, 21*n*

walled cities, 138–40

Walter "the Have-Not," 245

warfare, 4–5, 94–95, 109–10, *110*, 111, 322; Andalusi, 16–66, 74–123; Black soldiers, 99, 200–203; Christianity and, 79–123, 132, 241–44; cruelty, 109; Crusades, 214, 223–30, 241–74, 275–316; Fatimid Egypt, 200–201, *201*, 202–206, 296; Granada, 36–66; Islamic, 16–66, 74–123, 247 and *n*, 291–95; Jerusalem restored to Muslim rule, 275–305; Jewish, 247; *jihad*, 4, 5, 7, 32, 66, 109, 147*n*, 174, 203, 204, 210, 223–30, 247 and *n*, 289–95, 318, 321, 324; just, 32, 247 and *n*; logistics, 94–95; massacre of 1066, 61–65; Norman, in Sicily, 127–55; papacy and, 132, 243–74, 309; power and, 109–11; respect and, 110; siege, 114–17, 138–42; "turn and flee" tactic, 119; walled cities, 138–40; Zallaqa, 74, 96–100, 104. *See also specific countries, wars, and battles*

Wasil of Guadix, 65

whisk, 163 and *n*

White Monastery, 211

William de Hauteville, Duke of Apulia 133

William of Tyre, Archbishop of Tyre, 273*n*, 282, 289; *History, 281*

William I, King of Sicily, 161, 176, 178

William II, King of Sicily, 162, *169*, 171, 176–78, 303, 314

William IX, Duke of Aquitaine, 273 and *n*

William the Conqueror, Count of Normandy and King of England, 130

wine, 82, 198

wine party, 52

women, 6, 22–23, 320; Andalusi, 22–23, *39*; Black, 202–203; Christian, 17*n*, 40 and *n*, 161–62, 195, 219; concubines, 17*n*, 40, 51, 141, 171, 195, 202; in Crusader states, 269–74; in Egypt, 195, 198, 202, 219, 234–35; Fatimid, 195, 198, 202, 219, 234–35; harems, 171; Islamic, 22–23, *39*, 40 and *n*, 51, 101, 118 and *n*, 128, 195; Jewish, 195; as "queens," 82, 122, 270–74 and *n*; Sicilian, 161–62; slaves, 141, 170, 171, 192, 195, 202; veil, 101 and *n*, 128, 162

Ximena, 69–70, 74, 88, 120, 121

Yahya al-Ma'mun, King of Toledo, 77, 80

Yahya ibn Ibrahim, 100, 101

Yahya ibn Tamim, King of Ifriqiya, 167

Yaqub ibn Killis, 195, 222

Yemen, 287

Yiddir, 41, 42, 47–48

Yusuf ibn Ayyub. *See* Salah al-Din, Sultan of Egypt and Syria

Yusuf ibn Naghrilla, 10, 15*n*, 16, 25, 48, 55, 57–66, 77, 91, 92, 175, 322; fall of, 64–66; massacre of 1066 and, 61–65; as *Nagid*, 59

Yusuf ibn Tashufin, Almoravid ruler, 98–104, 105, 109, 112, 113 and *n*, 115, 118, 119; death of, 121–22

Zallaqa, Battle of, 74, 96–100, 104

Zamora, 73, 77

Zanaga, 70

Zanata, 26–29, 60, 65, 101

Zaragoza, 10, 31, 63, 74, 76, 81, 89–96, 105, 108, 110, 112, 114, 118, 122; Aljafería Palace, 90–91, *91*, *92*, 96; Almoravid rule, 122; Christian, 122–23; Cid in, 89 and *n*, 90–96, 105, 114; end of, 122–23; Jews, 91–92, 110–11

Zawi ibn Ziri, 25–31, 35, 37, 39–41, 133*n*, 174*n*

Zawila, 168

Zayn al-Din, 213–15, 228–35, 237; case against Ibn Dukhan, 230–33

Zengi, 'Imad al-Din, Sultan of Aleppo, 226

Zippori, 300

Zirids, 27–29, 31, 38, 77, 101, 112, 133 and *n*, 149, 156, 160, 167, 172, 202, 209; decline and fall of, 66, 112; rule of al-Andalus, 27–66; in Sicily, 136, 140, 143–44, 151, 164

Zone of Truce, 224

Zoroastrianism, 146, 165*n*, 216

Zuhayr, 46–47, 55